DATE DUE

GAYLORD			PRINTED IN U.S.A.

Corporate Entrepreneurship

How do large corporations encourage their senior managers to become more entrepreneurial? This is a key question which is seldom addressed in mainstream entrepreneurship studies. Vijay Sathe has written a pioneering book based on hundreds of hours of interviews with senior managers to help understand why some organizations and some top managers are better than others in fostering entrepreneurship leading to successful new business growth. *Corporate Entrepreneurship* explores the real world of top managers in a systematic and comprehensive way, examining business realities, the management culture, the corporate philosophy, the organizational politics, the personalities and the personal priorities of the people at the top. The book offers both a theory of corporate entrepreneurship and practical advice on how to manage it better. An original and valuable contribution to the literature on strategic management, this is a book that will appeal to graduate students, researchers and reflective practitioners.

VIJAY SATHE is Professor of Management in the Peter F. Drucker Graduate School of Management at Claremont Graduate University, California. He is the author of *Controller Involvement in Management* (1982), *Culture and Related Corporate Realities* (1985) and co-author of *Organization* (1992).

Corporate Entrepreneurship

Top Managers and New Business Creation

Vijay Sathe

Foreword by Peter F. Drucker

CAMBRIDGE
UNIVERSITY PRESS

PUBLISHED BY THE PRESS SYNDICATE OF THE UNIVERSITY OF CAMBRIDGE
The Pitt Building, Trumpington Street, Cambridge CB2 1RP, United Kingdom

CAMBRIDGE UNIVERSITY PRESS
The Edinburgh Building, Cambridge, CB2 2RU, UK
40 West 20th Street, New York, NY 10011–4211, USA
477 Williamstown Road, Port Melbourne, VIC 3207, Australia
Ruiz de Alarcón 13, 28014 Madrid, Spain
Dock House, The Waterfront, Cape Town 8001, South Africa

http://www.cambridge.org

First published 2003

Printed in the United Kingdom at the University Press, Cambridge

Typeface Plantin 10/12 pt.   *System* LaTeX 2_ε [TB]

A catalogue record for this book is available from the British Library

ISBN 0 521 82499 0 hardback

To over one hundred top managers – corporate executives, division general managers, and division top management team members – who gave so generously of their precious time for this project.

Contents

Figures

Tables

Hypotheses for the theory of corporate entrepreneurship: how the factors in each chapter influence new business creation

Foreword

Everybody knows that large enterprises do not innovate and do not create new businesses. And everybody also knows that the overwhelming majority of new businesses created in those two highly entrepreneurial decades, the 1980s and the 1990s, were built by individual entrepreneurs, starting on their own. AND EVERYBODY IS WRONG.

The great majority of new businesses during the last decades of the twentieth century (but equally in the decades before them, that is since World War II) were created and built by existing enterprises, and in large part by big or at least fair-sized ones. And when it comes to successful new businesses, the proportion initiated and built by existing enterprises is even larger. The casualty rate is, of course, high for all new businesses. But it is vastly lower for those started, developed and nurtured by existing enterprises and, in fact, within an existing business.

However, new business creation within the existing business, commonly called corporate entrepreneurship, requires *leadership from the top*. The successful "intrapreneur" who creates a new business at the bottom – and without senior-management support, if not without its knowledge – is largely pure fiction. Successful corporate entrepreneurship requires strong, active, determined leadership on the part of the company's CEO, on the part of its senior managers, on the part of the chief operating executives such as the division general manager in the large decentralized company. For successful new business creation faces very different challenges from those faced in running an established business with established products and established markets. It requires different policies, different measurements, different controls. Above all, it requires different human relationships within the senior-management group.

There is an abundance of books on that "folk hero," the lone entrepreneur who starts out in a woodshed, on the back burner in the kitchen, in the garage. But Vijay Sathe's book is, to the best of my knowledge, the first study of new business creation within the existing enterprise – that is on the American economy's central entrepreneurial challenge and its central opportunity.

New business creation must be considered the most important task of the senior executive in the existing enterprise, especially the larger one. Without it the enterprise is unlikely to survive, let alone do well, in a period of rapid transition such as the one we live in and are likely to live in for the foreseeable future. But it is also crucial for the economic and social stability of every developed country, and especially of the United States. Without it all developed countries face serious economic and social dislocation. Without it too, the existing leading economies are most likely to be overtaken by new competitors – the countries in which executives are not preoccupied with maintaining a glorious past and with defending yesterday. This book shows how to found tomorrow on today – above all, how to use the managerial knowledge and experience of the existing enterprise to invent and build the new businesses that will keep the enterprise young, growing, and successful.

Corporate Entrepreneurship is full of interesting people and interesting stories. But it is not a "popular" book of "miracle workers" and "originals." It is a book of ordinary executives doing the right thing but also making plenty of mistakes, fighting over risky and difficult decisions – and, above all, working very, very hard. It is based on more than twenty years of in-depth research and on Vijay Sathe's even longer career as a top-flight consultant to major businesses all over the world. The book shows what to do and what not to do; what the opportunities are and what the pitfalls are. It is a book both to enjoy and to study – but above all to apply its lessons to one's own enterprise.

Claremont, California   PETER F. DRUCKER
May 2002

Preface

This book examines how top managers – corporate executives, division general managers and the division's top management team members – influence new business creation in a corporate division. It is written for the aspiring manager, the practitioner, and the scholar.

The book takes the reader into the real world of top managers to explore a relatively uncharted territory in a systematic and comprehensive way. The business realities, the management culture, the corporate philosophy, the organizational politics, the personalities, and the personal priorities of the people at the top are vividly portrayed in these pages. It is not so much that the devil is in the details; it is that the details are the message, which is delivered herein by the top managers in their own unvarnished words.

To whet the reader's appetite, consider two well-known companies in this study – 3M and Xerox. The former is commonly viewed as a paragon of entrepreneurial virtue; the latter as a bumbling icon that fumbled the future. However, as the detailed descriptions in this book reveal, both caricatures miss the mark by a mile and conceal what is really important to understand – the human dynamics and influences that led ordinary top managers to achieve extraordinary results at 3M, and sensible top people to produce less than satisfactory outcomes at Xerox. How and why this happened – and the lessons for top managers striving to promote new business creation – is the subject of the book.

Although the press has derided Xerox management for their failures, they did many things well that others could learn from. Specifically, they perceived the opportunities in the emerging office automation market-place ahead of many others, and they developed remarkable technologies and products to pursue them, including Ethernet, the graphical user interface and the mouse, to name just three. These are industry standards today in the market for personal and office computing that they helped to create.

The top managers at 3M had a much better new business creation track record, but they made mistakes that they themselves and others could learn from. This book is not a good guy, bad guy story in which the top managers with the more successful new business creation track records did everything better than their less successful counterparts. The real world is far more complex and fascinating, and these pages try to bring this out.

To the best of my knowledge, this is the first systematic and comprehensive behavioral study of the influence of corporate top managers on new business creation. It began with my initial findings about the importance of management culture, which took me on a long intellectual journey. This journey included the development of a course and a book on corporate culture, which led to work on how to change culture in order to execute the desired strategy, and which in turn led to an interest in how strategy is conceived and developed. I now have come full circle with this book because new business creation is, of course, one of the pillars of strategy.

Some of the findings on the influence of management culture, covered in Part II, appear in my articles on corporate entrepreneurship included in the bibliography. All other material is presented for the first time.

Since the book is for scholars as well as for aspiring managers and practitioners, it is written in a straightforward manner in order to make it easily accessible to all these readers. A list of abbreviations is included. The endnotes are for scholars and others interested in the relevant literature.

I began this work while I was a faculty member at the Harvard Business School, where the Division of Research provided generous time and travel support for three years of intensive fieldwork. A number of faculty members and other colleagues offered comments and helpful criticism during the genesis of this project. I cannot possibly hope to acknowledge all of them individually, but I must mention the support and encouragement I received from Mike Beer, Jack Gabarro, John Kotter, Paul Lawrence, Jay Lorsch, Dick Rosenbloom, Howard Stevenson, Dick Vancil and Karl Vesper.

My colleagues within the Peter F. Drucker Graduate School of Management at Claremont Graduate University supported my intellectual pursuits – first into leadership for corporate transformation and then into business and corporate strategy. The University's sabbatical policy offered the opportunity to work on this book.

Two anonymous reviewers of an early draft provided thoughtful and constructive criticism that helped me to rethink, rework, and radically revise the book. Jill Nemiro read that draft and my interview notes and offered valuable input. Maria Savina transcribed about forty hours of tape recordings of the interviews and provided research assistance on the notes and the bibliography. Elizabeth Rowe transcribed the remaining twenty-five hours of recorded interviews. Jay Winderman provided excellent editorial assistance on the final draft. Deepak Shimkhada prepared many of the figures on PowerPoint and offered responsive administrative support.

Declan Quinn read the manuscript in detail and provided voluminous and valuable comments. Phil Barnett, Mike Csikszentmihalyi, Dick Ellsworth, Nigel Freedman, Bill Hicks, Pam Sveinson, Hatim Tyabji, and Klaus Volkholz also provided helpful feedback.

Chris Harrison, the book's commissioning editor at Cambridge University Press, provided thoughtful support throughout, and his encouragement helped me to reduce the book's length. Three anonymous readers commissioned by Cambridge provided excellent advice that I have tried to incorporate.

As the notes attest, this book is linked to the work of many others. Without repeating all the names here, I would like to thank them and acknowledge those whose contributions are cited most frequently in the notes: Zenas Block, Robert Burgelman, Clayton Christensen, Deborah Dougherty, Ian MacMillan, Scott Shane, James Utterback, Andrew Van de Ven, and S. Venkataraman. Their contributions, and those of the others cited in the notes, provide the intellectual foundation for the grounded theory of corporate entrepreneurship developed in this book.

Peter Drucker has been an inspiring and gracious colleague at Claremont. It is hard to find anyone in management who has not benefited from Peter's writings; those who are lucky enough to be around him are also the beneficiaries of his personal warmth and generosity. I am deeply grateful to him for his friendship and wisdom over the years, for providing comments on this book, and for contributing the Foreword.

My wife Shanu provided constant encouragement and buffered me from the many distractions that can derail such an undertaking. She read the manuscript at a critical juncture, and her insight did more for the book than she realizes. Our daughter, Sheila, and son, Jay, supported me with good humor and saved me from the deep end on many happy occasions! To all three of them I say, "Thanks for family time."

Over one hundred top managers – corporate executives, division general managers, and division top management team members – gave generously of their precious time for this project. I gratefully dedicate this book to them.

Claremont, California
October 2002

Abbreviations

AR	appropriations request (for capital expenditure)
BU	business unit
CAC	Corporate Advisory Council (the top twenty Monsanto executives)
CAD	computer-aided design
CB	Citizens' Band radio
CEO	chief executive officer
CFO	chief financial officer
CIM	continuous injection molding
Com	computer output microfilm
COO	chief operating officer
D&P	Detergents & Phosphates (a division of Monsanto Industrial Chemicals)
DGM	division general manager
DGM 1	division general manager when the study began
DGM 2	successor of DGM 1 during conduct of study
EMC	Executive Management Committee (the top five Monsanto executives)
EVP	executive vice president
FCC	Federal Communications Commission (a US government agency)
FDA	Food & Drug Administration (a US government agency)
GVP	group vice president
HR	human resources
MAT	marketing, administration, and technical expenses
MP&R	Monsanto Plastics & Resins group
NIH	not invented here
NPD	new product development
NPG	New Products Group
OPD	Office Products Division
OPET	oriented PET plastic bottle for hot-fill applications
PDA	personal digital assistant

PET	polyethylene terephthalate plastic bottle
PRC	Product Review Committee
R&D	research & development
RD&E	research, development & engineering
RF	radio frequency
ROC	return on capital
SBU	strategic business unit
TMT	top management team
UMC	unit manufacturing cost
VC	venture capitalist

1   Introduction

The age of entrepreneurship

After years of downsizing and restructuring, top managers are once again thinking about growth. But growth does not come as naturally or as automatically as it once did. Revitalization of industry and the creation of new jobs must increasingly depend on the development of new products and new markets to satisfy unrecognized and unmet public and personal needs. Such creation of economic value by perceiving and pursuing new business opportunities is what practitioners and scholars have in mind when they speak about the need for entrepreneurship.[1]

Much has been written about independent entrepreneurship, which refers to an individual or a group of individuals striking out on their own to start a new business. Stories of entrepreneurs who have created new industries and new wealth, such as Steve Jobs at Apple Computer and Bill Gates at Microsoft, as well as pioneers of the new economy such as Jeff Bezos of Amazon.com and Meg Whitman of eBay, are now part of the American folklore. The academic community has made great strides in both teaching and writing about this subject.[2] Independent entrepreneurship has created substantial job growth in the United States, and is the envy of other nations trying to emulate it. It is also evident that independent entrepreneurship is not well suited to the pursuit of opportunities requiring large capital investments and long time horizons because venture capitalists are typically impatient and prefer small bets.[3]

Corporate entrepreneurship, which refers to the efforts of corporations to generate new business, has, until recently, received far less attention.[4] Indeed, to those who view large firms as bureaucratic and inhospitable to creativity and innovation, the term "corporate entrepreneurship" is an oxymoron.[5] The 1950s and 1960s image of the corporate executive in the conservative gray flannel suit was replaced in the 1980s and 1990s by their caricature as overly compensated short-term thinkers who are unwilling to innovate and take risks. And in the post-Enron era, the word "corporate" followed by the word "entrepreneurship" conjures up dark images of greedy corporate executives who find creative and innovative ways, whether legal or not, to line their pockets with millions of dollars at the expense of shareholders, employees, and the public at large.

There is enough evidence to justify these stereotypes. Corporate greed and fraud made possible by flawed incentive systems, lax auditing, and failure of corporate governance will have to be set right before the word "corporate" regains much respect.[6] But scholars are in agreement with practitioners that large firms can be entrepreneurial in the positive sense of creating real economic value for everyone's benefit through the development of new products and new markets. And there is also agreement that corporations will need to become more entrepreneurial in the face of intensifying global competition and accelerating technological change.[7]

Corporate entrepreneurship is in the national interest not only because large firms account for much of the nation's economic output and jobs, but also because corporate and independent entrepreneurship complement and compete with one another. Having both enhances a nation's competitiveness. A case in point is the competition between bricks-and-mortar retailers such as Barnes & Noble and Internet pioneers such as Amazon.com. At first, the bricks-and-mortar players were written off as dead; now it looks as though the web ventures they have launched will give the upstarts a run for their money.[8] The point is that corporate entrepreneurship by bricks-and-mortar players and independent entrepreneurship by Internet pioneers are competing head-to-head, as well as collaborating with each other in the form of strategic alliances and joint ventures. Consumers and the economy are the beneficiaries.

Strategy and entrepreneurship[9]

Strategy provides a good starting point for the examination of corporate entrepreneurship. With a clear strategic intent, the core competence of the corporation can be effectively leveraged to create new businesses.[10] Well-known examples are Honda's forays into a range of new businesses based on its competence in high-performance engines, and Sharp's entry into a slew of new markets with products such as flat screens for televisions and computer monitors, personal digital assistants, and other viewing applications utilizing its core competence in liquid crystal displays. As these examples indicate, strategy drives entrepreneurship.

The story of Honda's entry into the US motorcycle market is a classic illustration of how entrepreneurship can also drive strategy. Faced with limited financing, major quality problems, weak dealer relationships, and negligible consumer brand awareness, it was the entrepreneurship displayed by Honda's US management team that led the company to a new strategy for success in the US market.[11]

Unfortunately, these insights about strategy and entrepreneurship do not automatically lead to successful new business creation. This is because the proper organizational context must be created[12] and the right process installed, monitored, and *influenced* appropriately for new business creation to flourish.[13] The work is the responsibility of top management, and is sometimes flawed in its basic conception or botched in execution. This book shows how and why this occurs and how top managers can do better.

Purpose of the book

Top managers of large firms are unable to promote successful entrepreneurship because the task is innately difficult.[14] Consider the findings of this study on what happened at Xerox. Corporate executives took a number of actions that seemed sensible enough. They appointed a proven entrepreneur, Greg Gibbons,[15] as division general manager (DGM) to spearhead the company's bold moves into the emerging office automation market. Recognizing that the corporate bureaucracy might stifle the entrepreneurial spirit, they gave Gibbons plenty of resources and a free hand to run the strategically vital Office Products Division (OPD) as he saw fit, with little or no corporate interference. And they granted Gibbons and his top management team big financial incentives, similar to those given to independent "Silicon Valley" entrepreneurs, to encourage the necessary risk-taking.

Gibbons, for his part, provided charismatic leadership that seemed appropriate too. He hand-picked his top management team, rallied the troops with a compelling vision of creating and dominating the Office of the Future, developed an innovative strategy for the "war" with IBM, and launched several exciting new products that could be interconnected into an office automation system targeted at Fortune 500 accounts with a new marketing and sales approach. After an encouraging start during Gibbons' first eighteen months, the division came in $100 million below the profit plan for Gibbons' second full year as DGM, and $150 million below plan for his third year – Gibbons left Xerox in the third quarter, with losses piling up.

What went wrong? First, the corporate executives, the DGM and his top management team took actions that seemed sensible but did not work – and in some cases actually backfired. Second, actions that needed to be taken were overlooked or under-emphasized. The underlying reason for both these errors, of commission and omission, is *not* that these were bad top managers; their critics might have suffered the same fate or worse.

Top managers fail in new business creation because it requires a *different* set of philosophies, attitudes, methods, and skills than those learned in running an existing business. And it does not help that top managers, as well as MBAs and executive students for that matter, are inadequately educated and trained for this important task. This book offers both a theory of corporate entrepreneurship based on the real-world experience of top managers and practical advice on how to manage it better.

The major lessons

Top managers with successful new business creation track records do several things *differently* than the others – not because they are geniuses, but because they have played this game long enough to know what is necessary to achieve success. There are six major lessons to be learned from their experience; these themes are developed more fully throughout the book.

First, corporate entrepreneurship is inherently unpredictable and risky and traditional controls are ineffective for managing the technical, product, and market uncertainties of new business. In fact, such controls can be worse than ineffective because they can bring new business creation to a screeching halt. This is why some top managers view control as the enemy of corporate entrepreneurship. They are wrong. When it is conceived properly and used skillfully, control is an essential companion of entrepreneurship. The successful players expect high failure rates and volatile results with new business, and they make allowance for this in how they control it.

Second, corporate entrepreneurship has some similarities to independent entrepreneurship, but there are fundamental differences as well. For example, except under a very restrictive set of conditions to be described later, successful managers do *not* use the "Silicon Valley" model of independent entrepreneurship that offers big financial rewards for success, because of its toxic side-effects. They use alternative approaches for motivating entrepreneurial behavior that work much better within the corporate context.

Third, it is inherently difficult for top managers to successfully create new business because they are also responsible for the health and growth of existing business.[16] In independent entrepreneurship, by contrast, new business creation gets the founder's undivided attention. Corporate attempts to overcome this challenge by separating existing and new business create other problems. Such dilemmas must be properly managed.

Fourth, successful top managers promote new business creation with the "small-is-beautiful" corporate philosophy, which is focused on many small opportunities. Those who pursue the "bigger-is-better" philosophy, focused on a few large opportunities, tend to stifle new business creation in the division. It is difficult to successfully pursue both corporate philosophies *simultaneously*, but, with appropriate skill and discipline, it can be done.

Fifth, successful top managers know that new business creation must be pursued *consistently*, because it takes a long time to achieve results. Consistency also affords the opportunity to learn from failure and develop new organizational competencies that open new vistas of opportunity and improve the performance of the *existing* business!

Finally, new business creation must be seen as a *process* that needs to be managed.[17] For some people, the word 'process' conjures up images of bureaucracy – checklists, procedures, and signoffs that slow things down and hamper creativity, flexibility, and innovation. As the quality revolution made clear, the management process to improve quality can degenerate into a bureaucratic exercise. But when thoughtfully applied as a management discipline, such a process can also lead to substantial improvements in cost and quality. A disciplined approach for new business creation makes it more fruitful, more predictable, and less risky.

Viewed constructively, the new business creation process consists of a number of stages: idea generation, concept development, market feasibility testing, business development, production scale-up, product standardization, and business termination.[18] The actual number of stages and their focus will differ by company and industry, but three overarching entrepreneurial tasks must be properly managed if new business creation is to be successful: (1) the perception and definition of new business opportunities; (2) the motivation and commitment of people, and the availability of sufficient resources, to pursue these opportunities; and (3) the control of new business initiatives and the learning of the new capabilities required to exploit these opportunities successfully.[19]

Definition of new business

Referring to Figure 1.1, everyone would agree that an entirely new product for an entirely new market constitutes new business. Honda's entry into the automobile market from its base of business in motorcycles is a case in point.[20]

Most managers would also view *either* entry into an entirely new market *or* the introduction of an entirely new product as new business.[21] Well-known examples are the recent entry of Western companies into the new China and India markets with existing products or product extensions, and 3M's innovation of Post-it notes for its existing consumer franchise in adhesive tape. The logic for calling such business *new* is that entry into entirely new markets requires much new learning about logistics,

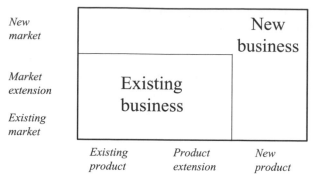

Figure 1.1. What is new business?

distribution channels, advertising, and so on; and the development of an entirely new product requires similar new learning about design, development, and manufacturing.[22]

Three distinctions are worth noting. First, a new business might be entirely consistent with the current strategy, or it might result from autonomous strategic behavior that falls outside the current concept of strategy.[23] An example of the latter is Intel's move into microprocessors from its base of business in memories.[24] Second, a new business might be new to the world, as in the case of the Newton, a hand-held PDA (personal digital assistant) introduced by Apple Computer, or new to the company only, as in the case of PDAs introduced subsequently by Motorola and Sharp.[25] Third, a new business might (or might not) cannibalize existing business. For instance, Sharp's Zaurus, a new product born of the marriage of the electronic organizer and the PDA, cannibalized Sharp's sales of electronic organizers, whereas Sharp's entry into notebook computers did not eat into its existing business. In this book, business created by a new product and/or a new market is defined as new business whether or not it falls within the current concept of strategy, whether or not it cannibalizes existing sales,[26] and even if it is only new to the company, not new to the world, because all these cases require significant new learning for the company.[27]

Definition of top managers

A large diversified company has managers at the corporate headquarters and in the divisions. The top managers are the corporate executives, the division general manager, and other members of the division's top management team (Figure 1.2).

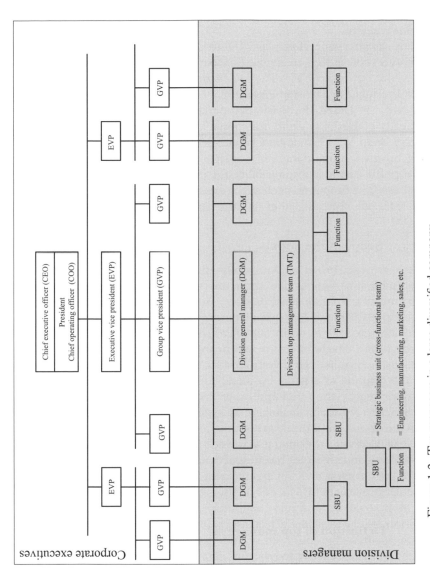

Figure 1.2. Top managers in a large diversified company.

The figure shows an organizational chart. The boxes and labels include:

Corporate executives:
- Chief executive officer (CEO) / President / Chief operating officer (COO)
- Executive vice president (EVP)
- Group vice president (GVP)
- EVP
- GVP

Division managers:
- Division general manager (DGM)
- Division top management team (TMT)
- SBU = Strategic business unit (cross-functional team)
- Function = Engineering, manufacturing, marketing, sales, etc.

The corporate executives are the chief executive officer (CEO), the president and/or chief operating officer (COO), the executive vice presidents (EVPs) responsible for major business sectors, and the group vice presidents (GVPs) responsible for a group of business divisions within a business sector.

The division general manager (DGM) is the leader of a business division and reports to a corporate executive, typically to a GVP or sometimes directly to an EVP. The DGM might have the title of Corporate Vice President or Division President.

Led by the DGM, the division's top management team (TMT) consists of heads of business units, functions, or both in the case of a matrix organization. TMT members might be called division vice presidents. The business units, commonly called strategic business units (SBUs), have profit and loss responsibility for product-market segments of the business. The functions, such as engineering, manufacturing, marketing, and sales, are typically either revenue centers or cost centers.

Scope of the book

There are two broad and relatively distinct arenas for corporate entrepreneurship. One is the spectrum of entrepreneurial activity carried out at corporate headquarters, including corporate mergers and acquisitions;[28] major strategic alliances,[29] corporate joint ventures,[30] and licensing agreements; utilization of corporate venture capital;[31] corporate research and development; new venture development;[32] and corporate spin-ins, spin-outs, and divestitures.[33] All these represent new business (or the disposal of existing business) for the corporation. They are typically driven by the CEO and other corporate executives, with the involvement of division managers as appropriate. These entrepreneurial activities are beyond the scope of this book.[34]

We will examine the other major arena for corporate entrepreneurship – the existing and emerging business divisions, which are the bread and butter of the corporation.[35] In an emerging division, the bulk of business is new. Examples are IBM's PC division for the personal computer market in the 1980s, and Apple Computer's Personal Interactive Electronics division for the personal digital assistant market in the 1990s. In an existing business division, both reactive moves in response to competitive pressures and proactive moves stimulate new business creation.[36]

Focus of the book

New business creation in a division of the corporation is a process driven by many forces, including the business environment, the management culture, and the top managers responsible for the division. This book examines all these influences and their combined effect[37] in one major division of each of four large corporations: (1) Signal Communications Division of AMP (AMP Sigcom), (2) Micrographics Division of 3M (3M Micrographics), (3) Fabricated Products Division of Monsanto (Monsanto Fab Products), and (4) Office Products Division of Xerox (Xerox OPD).

The top managers – the corporate executives, the DGM, and the division TMT members – responsible for AMP Sigcom and 3M Micrographics were in general better at influencing new business creation than were their counterparts at Monsanto Fab Products and Xerox OPD. They encouraged their divisions to perceive and define more and better new business opportunities and they generated better motivation and commitment among their people to pursue these opportunities. They also controlled the initiatives better and promoted the learning necessary to exploit these opportunities successfully.

The corporate executives and division managers responsible for AMP Sigcom and 3M Micrographics were on the whole more effective because they had consistently emphasized new business creation over a long time. They did many things well but were by no means perfect; they made mistakes that they and others could learn from. And although their counterparts at Monsanto Fab Products and Xerox OPD had a less successful record of new business creation, they also did many things well that others could learn from. The book brings out this real world of top managers – complex, subtle, and fascinating.

The influence of top managers

The book presents a theory of how various factors drive corporate entrepreneurship and make it more successful or less successful. Specifically, the theory explains how top managers influence new business creation in a corporate division, for better or for worse. It is a "grounded theory" because it was derived from the ground up using systematic induction – by constantly comparing and contrasting the more and less successful cases of new business creation in this study.[38] The data for this analysis were obtained from documents, personal observations, and repeated and extended interviews with over one hundred top managers in the four companies studied over a three-year period. Additional details concerning the methodology are at the end of the appendix to this chapter.

Top managers *directly* influence new business creation in a corporate division by their actions and behavior. They also do so *indirectly* if they change the business environment by re-chartering the division to compete

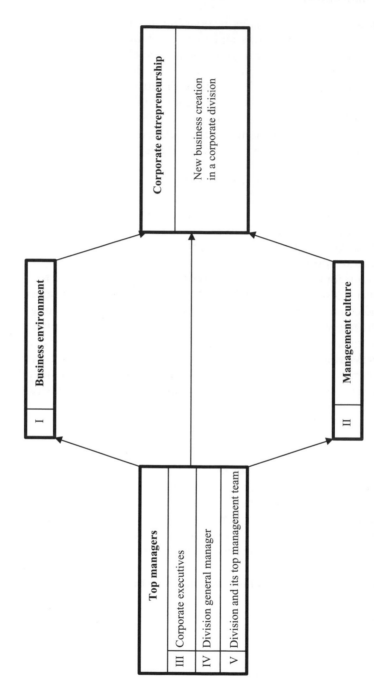

Figure 1.3. The direct and indirect influence of top managers.

in a different business arena, or if they change the management culture (Figure 1.3). Such indirect influence by any one generation of top managers is limited, because a division is seldom re-chartered, and changes in the management culture can take years to accomplish. But these two major factors – the business environment and the management culture – exert an important influence on new business creation, and they are examined in Parts I and II of the book respectively. The direct influences of top managers – the corporate executives, the division general manager (DGM) and the division's TMT – are examined in Parts III, IV, and V respectively.

The combined effect of all five major influences on new business creation is explored in Part VI. This last part of the book also highlights ten critical new business creation issues that cut across the five major influences, and provides guidance for top managers on how to manage them for better results.

A summary overview of this theory of corporate entrepreneurship – which is developed along with the supporting data and rationale throughout the book – is in the Appendix at the end of this chapter. The specific hypotheses of this theory are listed in Tables 3.1–18.1 which appear at the beginning of chapters 3–18. These tables summarize how various factors influence new business creation and convey the main points of each chapter at a glance.

Limitations

The book is based on interviews that I conducted, documents that I collected, and observations that I made over a three-year period in the early 1980s. All the managers' quotations in this book are taken from the interviews that I conducted during that time period.

The painful restructuring of the late 1980s, the corporate revitalization of the early 1990s, and the dawn of the Internet and the new economy in the mid-1990s have made corporations more efficient and agile. But the human drama at the top management levels described in this book has not changed much.[39] Top management clients and executives in the classroom continue to find the framework and the theory of the book to be both valid and useful. This claim needs to be tested with additional research.

Over one hundred corporate executives and division managers in a variety of positions were interviewed to provide as rich and as balanced a study as possible. However, I was not able to interview CEO John MacNeil at 3M and two top Xerox corporate executives, CEO Bill Nash and president Larry Wind. Their perspectives as represented by others – and by themselves in print and in other media – are included whenever possible.

Terminology: initiatives, champions, and sponsors

A new product initiative, a new market initiative, or a new product-market initiative, will be called a "new business initiative." A joint venture between a corporate division and another company, or a new business initiative that has a dedicated venture organization within the division, will be called a "new venture." All of these new business creation activities will be referred to as "new initiatives" or "new programs" or "new projects," or more simply as "initiatives" or "programs" or "projects."

The people who are most passionately and directly involved in driving an initiative are the "champions."[40] In a corporate division, these are typically operational level people (commonly in the technical or marketing areas), but they also can be higher-level managers, including the DGM or other members of the division TMT.[41] The principal champion is the one whose involvement is viewed as the most crucial in the transformation from concept to commercial business.[42]

The "sponsors" are those who believe sufficiently in the initiative to lend their support to it in the form of money, talent, and other tangible resources, as well as intangible resources such as their names and reputations to give it credibility. For initiatives within a corporate division, the sponsors are typically the DGM and one or more of his[43] TMT members, and can also include corporate executives. The sponsors support the champions just as venture capitalists support independent entrepreneurs.

Introduction to the participants

A brief introduction to the companies, the businesses, the initiatives, and some of the top managers is now presented. The reader will get a much better feel for all of these in the chapters that follow, as the people involved describe their perceptions, beliefs, agendas, and actions *in their own words*.

The companies

AMP, 3M, Monsanto, and Xerox were manufacturing companies whose primary customers were other companies.[44] AMP had revenue of $1.5 billion, and the other companies each had revenues of $6–8 billion.[45]

AMP manufactured electrical and electronic connectors. The company emphasized staying close to the customer, and designed its connectors into the customer's products. 3M produced specialty chemicals, pressure-sensitive materials, healthcare products, electronic products (including some connectors that competed with AMP's products), and imaging products, including copiers and micrographics products and supplies. Monsanto manufactured agricultural chemicals, industrial chemicals, specialty chemicals, resins, rubber, plastics, and fabricated products. Xerox produced copiers and duplicators based on plain paper technology, and it competed with 3M copiers for certain applications.

The business divisions

AMP's Signal Communications Division (AMP Sigcom) served numerous markets, such as aerospace, military, medical testing instruments, consumer electronics, computers, and telecommunications, with applications for high complexity, RF (radio frequency) analog, digital and optical signals which were transmitted through a variety of cables – coaxial, shielded, ribbon, and optical. The division was a design and assembly house, with all cable purchased from the outside.

3M's Micrographics Products Division (3M Micrographics) made microfilm machines, systems, and supplies for recording, archiving, and retrieving text and graphical information for the professional market. The division produced both products (machines and systems) and supplies (proprietary dry silver paper, film, and other coated supplies).

Monsanto's Fabricated Products Division (Monsanto Fab Products) made blownware products, such as plastic bottles for mineral water, colas, and other "cold-fill" applications; plastic film for commercial and agricultural storage and for consumer use in applications such as diapers; Fomecor products for commercial packaging and insulation; rolled goods and doormats for industrial and commercial applications; and Astroturf – an artificial surface for use in applications such as football stadiums.

Xerox's Office Products Division (Xerox OPD) pursued new business opportunities created by the emerging electronic information technologies. The division made word processors, facsimile machines, and electric typewriters, and introduced several new products and systems for the nascent office automation market.

Three of the four divisions in this study generated $200–300 million in revenue; the fourth, AMP Sigcom, had $20 million in revenue. Three of the four divisions were located at corporate headquarters; the fourth, Xerox OPD, was located a thousand miles away. AMP Sigcom did not have its own marketing and sales function, although it had product managers responsible for product marketing. It relied instead on a centralized marketing and sales organization that served all AMP divisions. 3M Micrographics had for many years relied on the centralized sales organization of the Business Products Group of which it was a part, but the sales function was decentralized back to the division just before this study began. Monsanto Fab Products and Xerox OPD had their own market-ing and sales functions, but OPD had relied on the Xerox copier sales force prior to this study.

The division general managers (DGMs)

The manager heading up each division when the study began will be re-ferred to as the "first-generation" division general manager, or "DGM 1." Their names were Mike Walker, Buddy March, Dan Stewart, and Greg Gibbons. All of them moved on one to two years into the study. Gibbons left the company; the other three were promoted. Each of their successors will be referred to as the "second-generation" division general manager, or "DGM 2" – Clay Smith, Ray Thorngate, Ian McVay, and Steve Carter.

AMP's DGM 1: Mike Walker   Mike Walker helped AMP Sigcom to define markets more broadly. He emphasized new business creation to tap new markets with both product extensions and new prod-ucts. He accomplished this not only by upgrading the human resources in his division through careful personnel selection and development, but also by getting the whole organization to think and act differently. Walker was personally focused on new business creation; he delegated the man-agement of the existing business to the product managers. He traveled extensively to visit customers and was personally involved in championing some initiatives and in sponsoring most others.

AMP's DGM 2: Clayton (Clay) Smith   When Mike Walker was promoted to group director (equivalent to group vice president, GVP, in other companies), his head of new products, called the development manager, succeeded him and continued to report to him. As DGM, Clay Smith supported the many new initiatives launched during Walker's tenure as DGM, and started several new ones while Walker was still the group director. When, toward the end of this study, Walker was promoted again, to a crucial overseas assignment – it was widely believed that he was being groomed to become CEO – Walker's successor as group direc-tor, Jon Grover, signaled a new emphasis for the Sigcom division. Grover emphasized product quality and customer service to enhance the prof-itability of existing products, and DGM Clay Smith shifted his emphasis accordingly.

3M's DGM 1: Buddy March   Beginning as a machinist, design engineer, and inventor, Buddy March was the head of a business for ten years before it was acquired by 3M and merged with an internal program to create the 3M Micrographics division, with March as DGM. March was a founder of the Micrographics Industry Association and was widely viewed as the industry godfather. Within 3M, March was seen as a flamboyant risk-taker, having stuck his neck out for many new initiatives, including two that his boss had opposed. These two initiatives and one other eventually became big winners in the marketplace. March remained DGM for eighteen years before he was promoted to GVP. The division grew tenfold during this period and spawned the highly successful Imaging Products division. The original 35mm lines, targeted primarily at the engineering design market, were split off as a semi-autonomous unit, the Engineering Products department. It also grew to become a division.

3M's DGM 2: Ray Thorngate   The Engineering Products division, and the rest of the original Micrographics division, continued to report to Buddy March after he was promoted to GVP. Only the Engineering Products division was tracked in this study. Ray Thorngate, the long-time technical director of 3M Micrographics, agreed to become DGM of Engineering Products at the insistence of March and his boss, Ed Baker. Thorngate would have preferred to move up but remain within the technical function during his last two years prior to retirement.

The business of Engineering Products grew faster and was more profitable after it became a separate unit. Nevertheless, Thorngate felt frustrated by the many challenges he faced as DGM. The industry was moving toward system integration, requiring investments in new competencies, at the same time as the corporation was demanding a greater profit contribution from the division.

Monsanto's DGM 1: Dan Stewart   Rising through sales and marketing, Dan Stewart was seen as a "people person" and a talented strategic thinker. When he took over as DGM of Monsanto Fab Products, he found an organization that was demoralized in the wake of his predecessor's "hatchet era." Some product lines had been sold, and headcount had been reduced. Stewart sought to mobilize the division by empowering the people to grow the existing businesses and generate new businesses via entrepreneurship.

Over the next three and a half years, the division's morale and the performance of some of its businesses improved, and two of the new initiatives sponsored by Stewart (Spray Guard and OPET bottle) began to show promise. By then, Stewart had acquired the reputation of a "corporate entrepreneur" and was given responsibility for two corporate ventures (Prism Separator and Radiation Dynamics, Inc.) and one other unit

(Enviro-Chem) during the last eighteen months of his five-year tenure as DGM. Only Fab Products, for which Stewart was still responsible as its DGM, was tracked in this study.

The three new units under Stewart were eventually combined with Fab Products to create the Engineered Products division. Stewart was named DGM of this new division and reported directly to an executive vice president (EVP) rather than to a managing director (equivalent to a GVP). It seems confusing, but Stewart remained DGM of Fab Products, which was still called a division although it was now a part of the Engineered Products division. This reorganization occurred just four months before Stewart was promoted to managing director of Monsanto Agricultural Products, the company's "crown jewel."

Monsanto's DGM 2: Ian McVay   Ian McVay was previously DGM of Detergents & Phosphates (D&P, part of Monsanto Industrial Chemicals). The confusing organizational designations were continued when McVay replaced Stewart as the DGM of both Fab Products and Engineered Products.

McVay had a successful track record both in new business creation and in asset management, and he advocated what he called a "balanced strategy" that emphasized both. He decided to reorganize Fab Products by separating what he viewed as the growth opportunities, including the initiatives he inherited from Stewart, from what he perceived as more mature businesses that he felt needed tighter asset management in terms of cost control and efficiency improvement.

As this study ended, Fab Products got a new head – a business director rather than a DGM – who reported to McVay, who continued as DGM of Engineered Products.

Xerox's DGM 1: Greg Gibbons   Starting as a research engineer, Greg Gibbons became the charismatic leader of Shugart, a successful start-up company that was later acquired by Xerox. Given his reputation as a proven entrepreneur, corporate executives appointed Gibbons as the DGM of Xerox OPD because they believed that this strategically vital emerging new business required a strong entrepreneurial thrust. Gibbons' star rose quickly within Xerox as OPD cut the projected annual loss during his first six months (July through December) as DGM. He turned in a small profit for the last quarter of his first full calendar year (January through December) as DGM – the first profitable quarter for OPD after six consecutive years of losses totaling $200 million.

However, Gibbons' star began to fall in his second full year as DGM when OPD began to miss its monthly sales and profit targets by wide margins. And his credibility plummeted when the division's new initiatives piled up huge losses that sank OPD $100 million below the profit plan for his second full year as DGM. Gibbons left Xerox to start a new company in October of his third full year as DGM, as the division continued to perform poorly, finishing $150 million below the profit plan for that year. Gibbons was succeeded by one of his subordinates, Steve Carter.

Xerox's DGM 2: Steve Carter   OPD was restructured after Gibbons left. The two big money-losing initiatives – Ethernet and Star, the professional workstation – were transferred out of OPD. As DGM, Steve Carter was responsible only for word processors, fax machines, and the one successful initiative of the Gibbons era that he had headed up, the Xerox Memorywriter "intelligent" typewriter (code-named Saber) which competed directly with the entrenched market leader, the IBM Selectric typewriter. The pendulum had swung from tight corporate control of OPD prior to Gibbons, to less stringent control during Gibbons' tenure, to tight control once again under Steve Carter.

The initiatives

The new business initiatives at AMP Sigcom focused on different market applications of existing and new products. Three initiatives were successful (Ribbon Coaxial Cable, or Ribbon Coax for short, and its connector – which together were called Cable Assembly; Commercial RF Connector; and Coaxial Cable Tapping Device, or Coaxial Tap for short, to connect or "tap" a shielded cable to a signal source). Two initiatives were not yet successful but were being pursued when the study ended (SMA F-Connector for military applications, and the Fiber Optics venture). Three initiatives were failures (Transmission Cable, Semi-Rigid Cable Assembly, and Tulip Plug – the first two were advanced cable designs and the third was a low-cost connector for consumer sales through outlets such as Radio Shack).

The initiatives at 3M Micrographics were part of a strategy of providing the market with a full line of products, systems, supplies, and services for recording, archiving and retrieving text and graphic information using microfilm. Most of these initiatives were new products, rather than new markets, given the strategy of leveraging 3M Micrographics' formidable distribution system. The success of three new initiatives (Dry Silver Paper for printing copies from microfilm, Imaging Products for special applications such as printing satellite images, and Tanaka Printer for high-quality printing from microfilm) greatly exceeded expectations. One other new initiative was a success (the 16mm family of File Management products for office applications), one was not successful but was being pursued (the 105mm family of microfiche products), and one was a financial disaster (Com, for Computer output microfilm – including an acquisition, Beta Com – a hybrid product based on a marriage of traditional microfilm and newer computer technology[46]). Several external programs, including joint ventures and licensing agreements, were also pursued at 3M Micrographics. None involved major commitments, but all either failed or did not achieve the desired results – with the notable exception of the Tanaka Printer, which was licensed and co-developed with a Japanese company.

The initiatives at Monsanto Fab Products sought to leverage the company's proprietary Cycle Safe and high-speed continuous injection molding (CIM) technologies into new markets. None of these initiatives was successful. One (RCA Disk Caddy, a plastic storage "jewel case" for the RCA videodisk) was de-committed, and the jury was still out on three others when the study ended (OPET plastic bottle for hot-fill applications such as juices and beer – a successor to the established PET plastic bottle for cold-fill applications such as soft drinks, Spray Guard mud flaps for truck tires, and Drainage Mat for systems designed to drain water off roads and highways).

The initiatives at Xerox OPD were part of a strategy of providing the market with a line of products that could be upgraded and interconnected into an office automation system targeted primarily at professionals. Of the four initiatives, one (Memorywriter typewriter) was successful, and the jury was still out on two others when the study ended (Ethernet, the pioneering local area network product, and the Xerox 820 personal computer). A fourth initiative was a financial disaster (the Star professional computer workstation – the successor to Xerox's pioneering computer named ALTO, for Xerox's Palo Alto Research Center – featuring the first commercial implementation of a graphical user interface and mouse).

The questions to be answered

Given the experiences of these companies and managers, the reader must now wonder whether the observed differences in new business creation were caused by differences in the business environments of these divisions, by differences in the cultures of these companies, or by other factors. How did the top managers influence new business creation in a division? What could they have done differently to achieve greater success?

We begin to answer these questions in Chapter 2 by exploring the importance of a consistent emphasis and approach for new business creation. Figure 1.4 provides a summary of the names and positions of the

Company	AMP	3M	Monsanto	Xerox
First generation (during tenure of DGM 1)				
CEO		John MacNeil		Bill Nash
President	Jim McGuire		Jim Reilly	Larry Wind
EVP		Ed Baker		
GVP			Hal Courtney	Jerry Tyson
VP Planning	Ted Rigby		Alf Hummel	
Division	Sigcom	Micrographics	Fab Products	OPD
DGM 1	Mike Walker	Buddy March	Dan Stewart	Greg Gibbons
TMT 1:				
Technology	Clay Smith	Ray Thorngate	Peter Dell	
Marketing		John Hypes		
Finance		Wim Williams		Rick Smale
Product manager	Jim Fitch			
Production engineering	Arjay Mason			
Commercial development			Joe Hurley	
SBU manager		Ralph West		Stu Little
Second generation (during tenure of DGM 2)				
EVP		Alex Hubble	Ed Costello	
GVP	Mike Walker (later: Jon Grover)	Buddy March		Jerry Tyson
Division	Sigcom	Engineering Products	Engineered Products	OPD
DGM 2	Clay Smith	Ray Thorngate	Ian McVay	Steve Carter
TMT 2:				
Technology	Jim Fitch	Tom Sonnenfeld	Peter Dell	
Product manager	Arjay Mason			
Commercial development			Joe Hurley	

Figure 1.4. Names and positions of the key players.

key players in this book. It is a convenient reference for keeping track of the cast of characters as the drama unfolds in Chapter 2 and beyond.

APPENDIX: A THEORY OF CORPORATE ENTREPRENEURSHIP

While our recognition of the importance of corporate entrepreneurship and our understanding of how to foster it continues to grow, there is precious little systematic evidence on how new business creation is influenced by *top managers*.[47] This stems in part from the difficulty of gaining research access to study these managers. This book adds to the limited literature on the subject by providing an in-depth look at how these managers influence new business creation in a corporate division.[48]

A conceptual framework showing the direct and indirect influence of top managers on new business creation was introduced earlier (Figure 1.3). The major factors of the theory of corporate entrepreneurship developed in this book and their influence on new business creation are indicated in the summary sections (for Parts I–VI) that follow. The specific hypotheses of the theory of corporate entrepreneurship are listed in Tables 3.1–18.1.

Part I: The business environment

The business environment has two parts, external and internal. First, consider the influence of the external business environment, which includes customers, competitors, and other industry and competitive forces, as well as the legal, regulatory, technological, and economic environment.

Customer pressures spur new business creation. But pressures from existing customers also make it difficult to pursue disruptive technologies that lead to new markets. And pressures encountered in co-developing a product with the customer, in competing with the customer, and in dealing with intimidation by the customer dampen new business creation. The threat of substitute products and services, and industry rivalry, spur new business creation.

Concerns about product liability dampen new business creation whereas strong patents encourage it. Government regulations facilitate new business creation by encouraging innovation or hinder it with bureaucratic procedures and delays. Sometimes they do both!

The absence of industry standards makes it difficult to introduce new products if customers hesitate to make purchases in anticipation of such standards. Successful industry players create industry standards or adapt quickly to emerging standards. Those who anticipate technology trends find new business opportunities in markets that others view as "mature." Those who ignore these trends end up as somebody else's lunch.

Adverse economic conditions inhibit new business creation by biasing the thinking and actions of top managers toward survival and near-term results. External advisors such as management consultants either facilitate or hinder new business creation depending on their assessments and agendas.

Next, consider the influence of the internal business environment, which refers to the condition of the division's existing business (whether it is growing, maturing, or declining), the relative amount and stage of development of the division's new initiatives, the availability of resources, and other internal factors such as the fear that new products might cannibalize existing business, or the bias toward product innovation versus process innovation.

When the existing business is growing, there is a tendency to neglect new business creation. However, when the existing business matures, top managers want new business creation "on demand" in order to rekindle growth. Unfortunately, new business cannot be created "on demand." This is one advantage of independent entrepreneurship – there is no existing business to worry about!

Introduction of new products, despite the fear of cannibalization of the existing business, helps in two ways. First, it pre-empts or counteracts similar moves by competitors. Second, it provides access to new customers, some of whom end up buying *existing* products because of their availability! New business creation is hindered if sufficient resources are not available for it, or if several new initiatives have been introduced to the market recently – because then the focus shifts to improving their performance to ensure their success. Both product innovation and process innovation spur new business creation.

Part II: The management culture

Management culture is defined as the beliefs that the corporate executives *and* the division managers share in common.

Contrary to popular opinion, financial incentives are not needed to promote corporate entrepreneurship if the right management culture prevails. Big financial incentives such as those offered to "Silicon Valley" entrepreneurs generate perceptions of inequity and resentment within the corporate setting, and are counter-productive except under a very restrictive set of conditions.

People are motivated to undertake new initiatives without the use of financial incentives, and despite the high probability of failure, if they believe there is no personal risk in doing so. What economists call the "moral hazard" in this approach – if people feel protected against personal risk, what is to prevent them from becoming sloppy? – is avoided with the right management culture.

Cultural taboos concerning opportunities not to be pursued constrain new business creation, whereas a shared belief in the right to pursue one's business convictions promotes it. New business creation is encouraged if the management culture permits rule-bending and limits the definition of irresponsible behavior to violations of personal integrity and business ethics. It is inhibited if rule-bending is not allowed and irresponsible behavior is defined more broadly to include violations of the prevailing business beliefs and practices.

The management cultures of companies with successful track records of new business creation help to control this activity, without stifling it, by emphasizing conviction-testing and by limiting aggregate investment. The corporate executives test the business convictions of the division managers, but do not make decisions for them. Corporate executives contain the financial risk inherent in new business creation by limiting the aggregate financial investment in the division, not by making decisions about the division's initiatives (thus controlling the financial exposure without micromanaging the specific initiatives).

Quarterly financial results that do not meet the expectations of financial analysts adversely affect the company's stock price, so corporate executives in all companies ask certain divisions for additional profit and cash contributions each quarter to offset anticipated shortfalls in other divisions. Division managers accept these calls for "quarterly giving" as a fact of corporate life and cut their budgets and delay their programs to comply. However, managers with less successful new business creation track records share the belief that the required budget cuts and program delays will *inevitably* hurt this activity. They invest little time and effort in deciding where to cut and delay programs, and how to communicate these decisions to the affected personnel.

Experience leads managers with more successful new business creation track records to the shared belief that too much money can diffuse a new program's focus, and that a delayed initiative sometimes can benefit from future technology or market developments. Accordingly, they believe in investing the time and effort necessary to carefully review all programs before deciding where to cut and delay. And they communicate the rationale for their actions to everyone involved. The management cultures in these companies view failure in new business creation as normal, and focus on learning from failure rather than on finding fault or apportioning blame. This helps to generate new knowledge as well as second-generation initiatives.

Part III: The corporate executives

Corporate executives influence new business creation by their corporate philosophy – either "bigger-is-better," focused on a few big opportunities, or "small-is-beautiful," focused on many smaller opportunities. It is difficult to pursue both philosophies *simultaneously* because of the fundamental differences in the scale of thinking, the duration of time, and the amount of resources needed to exploit bigger versus smaller opportunities.

Corporate executives using the bigger-is-better philosophy focus on the pursuit of big, attractive opportunities that are beyond the ambition or capability of a division. Because they view themselves as the only real entrepreneurs for the corporation, they also make the decisions about new business initiatives in the division. This dampens new business creation in the division. Another drawback to this philosophy is that the pursuit of one big opportunity (e.g. a $100 million opportunity) is more risky than the pursuit of several smaller opportunities (e.g. ten $10 million opportunities).

Corporate executives pursuing the small-is-beautiful philosophy set high performance expectations for the division – both for short-term results *and* for long-term growth – and give the DGM a great deal of autonomy, with no specific marching orders on how to deliver outstanding performance. The DGM cannot achieve short-term results by simply cutting back on investments, such as for research and development, because this will restrict long-term growth. The DGM must balance short-term and long-term considerations, which leads to a consistent emphasis on new business creation. These corporate executives challenge the thinking of the DGM rather than telling him what to do. Because the *division* is viewed as the corporation's primary center for entrepreneurship, these corporate executives are betting on the DGM's business convictions and judgments, rather than on their own judgments and convictions.

Although it is difficult to pursue the bigger-is-better and the small-is-beautiful corporate philosophies *simultaneously*, it can be done. Corporate executives need to be the corporate entrepreneurs for the bigger opportunities while allowing the DGMs to do the same for smaller opportunities, by not squeezing them dry of the autonomy and resources needed for entrepreneurship.

Strange though it seems, divisions with better track records of successful new business creation are *not* better than others at achieving the projected sales and profits for a specific new business initiative. All divisions miss their sales and profit forecasts for a new initiative by wide margins, commonly in excess of 100 percent of the plan for a new initiative's first year in the market. This is partly due to the tendency to make overly optimistic projections in order to gain acceptance of a new initiative. It is also due to the high levels of technical and market uncertainty that a new initiative must endure. Unrealistic corporate expectations that new initiatives will perform within the tolerances normally expected for existing business – for example, deviations within 5 or 10 percent of budgeted sales and profits – derail new business creation.

Corporate perceptions of opportunities in the division are colored by personal experience. Corporate executives previously "burned" by an opportunity, or those unfamiliar with its product, market, or technology, tend to perceive it as unattractive. A scarcity of management talent within the corporation, and the desire to develop seasoned managers quickly, results in moving DGMs around so rapidly that they have insufficient time to learn the business, make a contribution, and grow professionally. New business creation also suffers.

The DGM's boss (typically a GVP) has the difficult task of guiding and coaching the DGM without being perceived as interfering. This is particularly difficult if the DGM is engaged in new business creation because the inherent uncertainties make it impossible to be sure who is correct or what the right thing to do is. Guidance and coaching is ineffective if the DGM's boss has insufficient knowledge of the division's business, or inadequate time or interest to attend to the needs of the division and its DGM. Also ineffective is micromanagement of the DGM, or leaving the DGM alone, or giving him specific instructions rather than guidance.

DGMs do not like to be challenged by the corporate or division controllers. However, support and challenge is effective if the controller is perceived as having a good understanding of the business, if assistance in running the business is provided, and if information is requested and challenge is offered without presenting these as edicts. Controllers are ineffective if they are viewed as only interested in securing information for reporting and control purposes.

Part IV: The division general manager

The DGM's personal assets – personality, experience, and leverage with the corporate executives – influence new business creation. DGMs who are extroverted, intuitive, oriented to thinking (versus feeling), assertively self-confident, and have a low need for security, tend to facilitate new business creation. A DGM with prior new business creation experience is more likely to pursue new initiatives; someone who has successfully undertaken new initiatives that were opposed by either skeptics or higher-ups is more likely to pursue unpopular or counter-cultural new initiatives. A DGM who has greater leverage with the corporate executives is better able to bear the personal risks of new business creation. Leverage is greater if powerful corporate executives support the DGM, if he has credibility with corporate executives because of his track record, and if he is accepted in the management culture.

The DGM is motivated to undertake new business creation for three main reasons: business, organizational, and personal. A DGM who has a wider network of external contacts with customers, suppliers, competitors, and relevant others tends to undertake new business creation for business reasons. Such a DGM also is more likely to sponsor or champion new initiatives because wider external connections give the DGM greater insight into which initiatives are particularly important for serving the needs of customers, or for fighting competitors, and whether these programs require his support. Organizational reasons are that the boss expects it, or that the corporation values it, or that organizational layoffs can be avoided by growing the division out of its troubles via new business creation. Personal reasons are a quest for industry or public recognition, and the need to prove something to oneself or others.

Bold business visions and brilliant new business strategies are destined to fail without proper execution. Execution is effective when the DGM cultivates the support of his boss and higher-ups, and uses his political power to build corporate support and neutralize or overcome opposition to his new business creation strategy and initiatives. Those who do not play this game well – or worse, those who are cynical about "corporate politics" – are ineffective in implementing their new business creation strategies and initiatives.

Proper execution also requires the DGM to use three major levers to change the division's mindset and behavior for new business creation: by getting people to buy into the vision and strategy of new business creation; by educating, training, coaching, and mentoring them for the task; and by appropriately motivating and supporting them. Other human resource management tasks must be performed well for new business creation to be successful. These include assessment of people, their repositioning or removal if they are not right for the job or for the company, and the appointment of people with the right skills and attitudes.

Part V: The division and its top management team

New business creation requires the generation and exploration of new business opportunities, their proper specification, and a commitment to pursue them despite technical and market uncertainties. The division and its TMT must make investments to discover a new market, bid for new business before they know how to make the new product, and make delivery commitments to their customers without any certainty that these can be met. External programs reduce some of these risks by providing complementary resources and capabilities, but they carry other risks and have their limitations.

It pays to generate and explore a large number of new business opportunities in order find the most attractive ones to specify, commit to, and pursue. Contrary to popular belief, a disciplined system for doing this – consisting of project phases, milestones, reviews, and technical audits – yields better results. Of course, it is not the system *per se* but how it is used that makes a difference. People must be educated and trained to use it consistently and effectively.

Entrepreneurship is the pursuit of a new opportunity because of a deep personal conviction about its attractiveness, and a determination to pursue it against all odds. "Fake entrepreneurship" is the pursuit of a new opportunity without any zeal or real commitment. People go through the motions and use the right words because it is expected of them, or because *others* feel the new opportunity is worth pursuing. Top managers fail to detect fake entrepreneurship when they focus on form rather than on substance. They are likely to be fooled if they assume entrepreneurship has been unleashed when a new opportunity is identified, a program team is created, a "champion" is designated, and appropriate incentives are offered. They may learn later, if ever, that they had no real champions, except perhaps themselves.

Fake entrepreneurship can be avoided by recognizing that the corporation might not have a gene pool of innovators and by assuming there is lip service rather than real commitment to entrepreneurship. Real commitment is revealed when a qualified individual *wants* to take on the assignment because of the *challenge*, not because he is told to do it, or because of special incentives or other forms of extrinsic motivation.

A division can hide its new initiatives in the early stages by bootlegging them to avoid premature visibility, but not when they become serious enough to require prototype development, and certainly not when they are ready for production scale-up. Sooner or later, all divisions need to develop corporate visibility and support for new initiatives by managing corporate perceptions, selling influential executives, and cultivating the corporate godfathers. And this must be done without raising corporate expectations for results so high that they cannot be met.

New business creation requires new ways of designing, developing, manufacturing, marketing, and/or selling a product or a service. This creates disruption in the proven ways of running the business and dilemmas that must be managed.

Divisions with a relatively large base of existing business can absorb the greater volatility of new business and still deliver the forecasted divisional results. Others can also achieve such predictable performance by factoring the volatility of new business into the forecast of the division's overall results, by retaining slack in the budget for unforeseen expenditures that new initiatives invariably require, by having several smaller new initiatives rather than betting on a single big one, by diversifying new initiatives over time and across industries, and by selectively delaying new initiatives and cutting expenses to achieve the division's forecasted results.

Matrix organizations, based on shared responsibility and accountability, and functional or "silo" organizations, focused on functional specialization, inhibit new business creation. The "business unit (BU)" organization, with cross-functional resources dedicated to this task and clear accountability for results, is a better alternative. Nevertheless, because every organization has its limitations, frequent reorganizations in search of the "ideal" organization cause confusion and create disruption that hamper new business creation.

Successful new business creation requires the personnel in the division to have the necessary competence in technology, product development, marketing, sales, and other functions. Cross-functional competence and cross-BU collaboration is equally important.

Conflict is healthy if it arises from internal competition that spurs innovation. Conflict is dysfunctional if it is caused by a lack of collaboration across organizational "silos" – departments, functions, divisions, and other organizational entities. Among the usual suspects are geographical separation, an excessive emphasis on functional efficiency, unclear task responsibilities, and missing or ineffective mechanisms for cross-silo communication and collaboration. Unhealthy cross-silo conflict is overcome with better communication across silos using cross-silo teams and strong leadership.

All division TMTs have some degree of unresolved conflict concerning new business creation, at times submerged beneath the surface. TMTs are not always aware of this conflict, and might be unwilling or unable to address it constructively. New business creation suffers if conflicts remain unresolved or if the TMT does not compensate for the DGM's weaknesses.

Part VI: Putting it all together

The first five parts of the book examine each of the major influences on new business creation, one by one. This last part first considers how these influences interact to drive new business creation. Ten critical new business creation issues that cut across the book's first five parts are then examined, and recommendations for top managers on how to manage them for better results are provided.

Methodology

Each of the corporate divisions studied – AMP Sigcom, 3M Micrographics, Monsanto Fab Products and Xerox OPD – was visited four times, three to four days at a time, over a three-year period. Data collection involved the study of documents (including business plans and performance), observation (including attendance at management meetings), and repeated and extended interviews with the responsible corporate executives, the DGM, the division TMT members, and other division personnel. About 300 hours of interviews and observations were conducted at these four companies, totaling nearly sixty days in the field over a period of three years.

Interviews were recorded manually – over 2,000 handwritten pages – until the participants felt comfortable enough to permit the interviews to be tape-recorded. The resulting sixty-five hours of audio tapes were transcribed and yielded over 2,000 double-spaced typed pages. These qualitative data[49] were then analyzed using the constant comparative method.

2 Why a consistent emphasis and approach for new business creation is beneficial but difficult to achieve

Some indicators of the emphasis on new business creation

Three indicators reveal the extent of emphasis on new business creation: money invested, time invested, and size of the new business creation pipeline.

The amount of money invested in new programs and/or in research and development activities is one useful indicator of the emphasis on new business creation. This can be measured by expenditures on new products as a percentage of sales and R&D spending as a percentage of sales, relative to the industry. The amount of time that a top manager spends on new business creation activities is another indicator of his emphasis on it, as DGM Dan Stewart of Monsanto Fab Products pointed out:

How much time did I spend in commercial development reviewing these programs, visiting potential customers and all the rest? In my internal public orations, what percentage of my time did I spend talking about ongoing business and how much time did I spend talking about the new products?

The size of the new business creation pipeline is another important indicator, as DGM Ian McVay of Monsanto Engineered Products explained:

The index that I use is the number of active programs within NPG [New Products Group], and the number of ideas awaiting first review and submission. We've got about thirty-five new ideas awaiting first submission and we've got about a dozen active programs within NPG. That's an index I keep in the back of my mind.

Why a consistent emphasis is beneficial[1]

Consistency provides sufficient time to succeed

Xerox corporate executives attributed their poor track record of new business creation to lack of a consistent emphasis, which gave new initiatives insufficient time to succeed. Manfred Hoffmann, VP of strategic planning for the Xerox Information Products Group, put the problem in historical perspective:

Altogether over the last eight years, I can count seven major failures in Xerox's attempts to diversify out of our heritage position in the copier business and into information products and systems based on electronics technologies. Our experience with new business creation validates Ralph Biggadike's work based on the PIMS[2] data. He discovered one very important ingredient – consistency and commitment of top management are critical. It took on average seven years for a new venture to be successful.[3] Is top management willing to sweat it out? The quickest way to lose money and destroy the venture is to change in mid-course – in year three, the current profit is not so good, so the thing is immediately yanked. That's how many ventures end.

The top managers at AMP knew it would take several years for a new product to become successful in the marketplace and they stayed the course, as DGM Clay Smith of AMP Sigcom pointed out:

It takes a year to formulate the idea and postulate what needs to be done and it's going to take a year to tool something up. Also, until you get a year of sales under your belt it's at least another two years, maybe three. So it is five years from the time we begin working on a product idea until we really see a good, cumulative cash flow in a positive direction. It takes that long. And I don't think we're any different from others.

It takes less time today to develop a new product because of concurrent engineering, twenty-four-hour development using virtual teams that transfer work around the world each day, and fast and efficient prototyping.[4] Nevertheless, it still takes years, not months, for most new products to succeed in the marketplace, and a consistent emphasis on new business creation gives these products time to succeed.

Consistency facilitates second-generation initiatives and the development of new competencies

A consistent emphasis and approach creates momentum for new business creation.[5] Once such momentum is achieved, second-generation initiatives which incorporate the learning from the failed first attempts become possible. A long-term commitment to new business creation also helps to develop the competencies of the people involved, which reinforces and sustains this activity. Both of these benefits were derived at AMP Sigcom from the failed Transmission Cable initiative, as DGM Mike Walker explained:

Well, I made a bad decision in getting Transmission Cable consolidated into the division because it hasn't turned out to be successful. At the time the market was there, but our technical capability and product wasn't quite there. And it's taken an awful lot of our resources to try to doggedly go after the dog-gone thing and it hasn't proven out. And so in retrospect, looking back at all the investment we have put into it, it was a bad decision. But under that climate, I'd make that decision again. The risk was worth it, because it did teach us some other things that led us into other directions which are going to be very valuable for us. We perfected the wire rolling technology and learned more about the dynamics of retaining wires and grooves and all that, which principles are being used in other product lines.

Why a consistent emphasis is difficult to achieve

Frequent management transitions create disruptions

A new DGM may change the division's emphasis or approach for new business creation for many reasons, including personal preference, change in the competitive landscape, or new organizational realities. Frequent management transitions can lead to frequent changes in the emphasis or approach for new business creation, which result in confusion and loss of momentum for new initiatives.[6]

For example, Xerox OPD had five DGMs over ten years. During this time, the division's functions were split up into geographically separated entities, then re-combined, and then reorganized into SBUs. An Office of the President was created and dismantled, and Xerox OPD went from a cost center to a profit center and back again to a cost center. The division went from a strong emphasis and plenty of resources for new business creation to some retrenchment to extremely aggressive emphasis to a big retrenchment.

In sharp contrast, 3M Micrographics had operated with a consistent, strong thrust on new business creation for over two decades. One DGM – Buddy March – had been at the helm for eighteen years, followed by another DGM – Ray Thorngate – who had been the division's technical director for many years. The division had not only consistently emphasized new business creation but also had done so with no change in the organization and management approach used.

New business creation is not ingrained in the management culture

The importance of management culture is revealed by comparing what happened at AMP Sigcom and Monsanto Fab Products. Both divisions had three DGMs over nine years. In both, the predecessor of the first-generation DGM was a turnaround artist sent by corporate executives to salvage a troubled division. However, because new business creation was ingrained in the management culture at AMP, but not at Monsanto, AMP Sigcom maintained a greater consistency of emphasis on new business creation, and on the organization and management approach for achieving it, than did Monsanto Fab Products. Let us examine the experience of Monsanto first.

Inconsistent emphasis at corporate headquarters   Monsanto corporate executives had been inconsistent in their emphasis on new business creation over the years. Larry Ashridge, head of Corporate New Venture Development at Monsanto, noted the importance of consistent emphasis at the top:

I don't know of any system that can make innovation happen. You got to have the right environment. We have tried to take a very simplistic attitude: "We are going to be an innovative company." That's dangerous. We are not a particularly innovative company. We have come up with very little that is really new. 3M is an innovative company. It's part of their culture. It's the whole damn company. It has been done by consistent emphasis at the top.

Alf Hummel, Monsanto VP of corporate planning, believed that the commercial development function had been treated as a second-class citizen within the company, and this had hurt new business creation. But that was beginning to change. Joe Hurley, commercial development director of Monsanto Fab Products, described how the company had begun to place more emphasis on commercial development:

I think one of the things that has occurred over the last three years is that Alf Hummel is trying to get new business development recognized as really a critical area for Monsanto. And I've been on the task force that he organized the last three years; about seven or eight of us on it. And what we're trying to develop is improved credibility, improved communications, and improved status if you will of the commercial development people.

Inconsistent emphasis in the division   DGM Dan Stewart's predecessor at Monsanto Fab Products, Vic Thomas, pruned unprofitable lines but paid limited attention to new business creation. Thomas recalled the early history of the division and some of his actions as DGM:

Just before I became DGM, Fab Products got a bunch of consumer businesses that had been developed by NED [New Enterprise Division]. My boss, Al Bartley, told me to clean up that crap. I sold four of the ten businesses in two years. Jim Reilly was my next boss. He said, "Now what are you doing about running the businesses that you *should* be in?" Joe Hurley was making impassioned pleas for commercial development, so I said, "OK, here is the order of priority. One, get out of the dogs. Two, run what you have got better. And three, fund something new."

Joe Hurley, commercial development director of Monsanto Fab Products, felt DGM Vic Thomas was not really interested in funding anything new:

We had a very extensive market analysis done to determine what we should do with the Film business. And we came up with four opportunities. I thought two out of the four had real potential. One was for the sterilization of hospital supplies using ethylene oxide as a sterilizer. Johnson & Johnson was very interested in that. Well, that film is now in the marketplace. It can be done and they're using the same concept that we had – the film would present a very jagged, funny course so that the ethylene oxide gas molecules would be able to go in but the bacteria would not be able to go in because of the pathway that the bacteria had to follow. But Vic Thomas was not interested. He was focused on trying to sell the Film business and other businesses.

When DGM Vic Thomas' hatchet era ended, a new era emphasizing growth began under DGM Dan Stewart. Stewart reorganized the division into business units with dedicated cross-functional resources for each of the existing businesses to stimulate their growth. He also created a commercial development department under Joe Hurley reporting directly to him to pursue new business opportunities aggressively, including the Spray Guard and RCA Disk Caddy initiatives that Hurley had been bootlegging under Thomas. Stewart also championed the OPET bottle initiative and supported the Drainage Mat program. Ian McVay, the next DGM of Fab Products, compared his two predecessors:

Dan Stewart is a growth manager. Dan is a great cheerleader. Dan is a guy who likes to get a common cause, grow the business, make the business more profitable. Get everybody to rally around him and do this thing together – with a lot of social participation with his employees. He loves to develop a spirit of camaraderie among his employees. I think that Dan was more interested initially in sales, and then eventually profits. He skewed himself more toward growth. Vic Thomas [Stewart's predecessor] on the other hand is a tough cookie, and very hard on subordinates. Good businessman, good instincts, but takes what he gots [sic] and hones it down. Not ill-disposed toward research but tends to, in times of trouble, prune back. I really put myself more in the middle of those two guys.

When McVay took over as DGM of Fab Products, he called for balanced growth and asset management. Within three months, he reorganized the division by consolidating all the existing businesses into one big business unit, to be managed for operational efficiency and cost reduction. All new business initiatives were consolidated under commercial development director Joe Hurley, and they were to be evaluated and managed for growth.

Several months went by as his managers tried to figure out what McVay really wanted. He was learning the business and trying to figure out what *his* boss (EVP Ed Costello) really wanted. Nine months after McVay took over, it was finally decided that RCA Disk Caddy would be scrapped but Spray Guard, OPET bottle and Drainage Mat would be pursued. Ian McVay reflected on his time as DGM toward the end of this study:

The few things that Ed [Costello, McVay's boss] wanted me to do, I think have been done in the year that I have been here. And also in the long-range plan, I think we've proved that there are significant growth opportunities in this business and a potentially very profitable business here. We haven't achieved that yet. I hope that the corporation continues with this division and gives succeeding managers the same flexibility that I think that I've enjoyed under Ed Costello. Again, though, I have to wonder in the back of my mind how long I'm going to be around here.

As this study ended, Jim Barr was appointed business director (rather than DGM) of Monsanto Fab Products, reporting to McVay who continued as DGM of Monsanto Engineered Products. Fab Product managers were busy once again trying to figure out, as one of them said, "What is the new game?"

Business oscillations[7] It is clear that Monsanto Fab Products underwent fairly sharp changes in emphasis and approach to new business creation under three DGMs in nine years. President Jim Reilly of Monsanto described these changes as the normal ebb and flow of a business. Others have described them as "oscillations" – from an emphasis on new business creation with loose controls to an emphasis on efficiency, cost reduction, and asset management with tight controls, and back again to an emphasis on new business creation with loose controls.

All four divisions in this study exhibited this ebb and flow, or oscillation, over the years. However, the amplitude of oscillation was much smaller at AMP Sigcom and 3M Micrographics because the importance of a consistent emphasis and approach for new business creation was ingrained in their management cultures, and also because their top managers better controlled new business creation. Let us examine the experience of AMP Sigcom to illustrate this.

How a consistent emphasis is achieved[8]

Consistent emphasis at corporate headquarters

Corporate executives at AMP had consistently emphasized new business creation in their divisions for as long as anyone could remember, as DGM Mike Walker of AMP Sigcom pointed out:

AMP has always had built into its fabric a top management attention and concern for new product generation. It's almost been an axiom – when we have a lot of new products going, we're going to be healthy, but if we don't, we got to watch out, even if we are still growing... Our corporate growth is layered. One product line on top of another and that's what gives you the dollar volume. We classify each new product area with what its vintage is. So we know what the new products of the decade of the sixties contributed. What the decade of the seventies contributed. What the decade of the eighties has to contribute to achieve our growth. And we can pretty well tell you what part of the business life cycle each one of these families is in. Sometimes we find these families will spawn another spurt of growth. One of our major ones right now is in its fourth spurt of growth. Where something new was done, some new innovation occurred which rejuvenated people's attention to that product line. And it just went through the roof, so it's all a brand new cycle again. We're making an art now of how to rejuvenate old products and get them on another growth spurt.

Consistent emphasis in the division

DGM Chet Timmer of AMP Coax (as AMP Sigcom was then called) faced a turnaround situation very similar to that of Vic Thomas at Monsanto Fab Products, but he responded differently. Even as he pruned unprofitable lines and got the financial house in order, Timmer kept an eye on new business creation and successfully launched one big winner, the CB (Citizens' Band) radio connector initiative. Timmer had not been asked to do so; he did it because he believed in new business creation and knew it would be rewarded with recognition and advancement. Timmer recalled the situation in the division when he took over:

[President] Jim McGuire, who was then the group director [GVP], gave me the assignment – salvage the division! There were several distinct phases I went through in pulling that division out. We clarified the mission. We defined products and markets we would serve. We committed to growth, to developing new products, and reinvesting in our future. A fundamental philosophy of AMP is that the DGM is basically an entrepreneur and can recognize an opportunity. We did recognize CB as an exploding opportunity. We came out with a better solution and changed the game in our favor. We changed the design so we could manufacture by less expensive methods – forms of mechanization that were cheaper to use and install. We captured, in a very short time, 90 percent of the market. The division went from 32 percent gross margins to 42 percent gross margins while doubling sales in four years.

Chet Timmer's successor as DGM, Mike Walker, said the importance of new products was ingrained in the minds of AMP managers:

I think Chet [Timmer] will say that he planted new product seeds, and I believe he did. Ribbon Coax is one. Although Ben Schollenmeyer is the guy who invented it. He was the early pioneer. Now Chet Timmer also you have to say started the

CB product area. And a lot of new products that spawned out in the CB era. So he did a good job in that area. He was the first guy that started the Tulip plug. And got that going. So I can't say the seeds were not there because, as I say, every manager at AMP really is ingrained to the idea that you've got to pay attention to the new product area.

Mike Walker accelerated the new product development thrust as DGM, and his successor, Clay Smith, continued to emphasize new business creation, with Walker as his group director (GVP). Arjay Mason, who was a product manager under both Walker and Smith, compared the two DGMs:

When Mike Walker took over as DGM, he perceived what was required in order to effectively step on the gas. He did beef up the development department. He actually *got* more people working in development. But he also got the whole organization, including AMP marketing and the field sales force, thinking differently. Thinking that you're interested in new business. Mike also campaigned to broaden the charter of the division, renamed it AMP Sigcom, and got all the Transmission Cable activity in the company consolidated into this division. He also got Fiber Optics moved over here, since it could obsolete coaxial cable. And he supported my initiative to assemble and license Ribbon Coax cable. Without that we couldn't have grown that business. He recognized that Cable Assemblies and Commercial RF, being labor-intensive, would have lower gross margins. But he was emphasizing growth over cherry-picking products for high margin. He believed maybe you could improve margin by *process* innovation in manufacturing, by riding down the experience curve...I guess my perception of Clay [Smith, the current DGM] at this point is pretty much that he just wants to keep the new product engine running at the speed that it was handed to him at. I have seen him take a little bit of action in stopping some things which had been started and had a long enough period by now, so that it was apparent that we would probably be chasing good money after bad if we continued with some of these things. But, under Mike Walker most of those things had just been launched and it probably would have been premature to stop them.

When Walker was promoted a second time, his successor as group director (GVP), Jon Grover, decided to emphasize manufacturing efficiency, product quality, and customer service for existing products. DGM Clay Smith reordered his priorities accordingly but the emphasis on new business creation was retained rather than curtailed. As Smith said after he began reporting to Grover,

I don't mean to convey that we are going to slow down the new product effort. I think we would maintain the same emphasis that we had on it but not accelerate that emphasis. That's really what we are talking about. And so working with the same size development staff, we'd look for productivity improvements out of that staff, but by and large we wouldn't put more manpower into development.

Thus, despite the need to salvage the division (Timmer era), and later on a GVP who was not emphasizing new business creation (Grover),

AMP Sigcom managed to retain a relatively consistent emphasis and approach for new business creation under three DGMs over nine years. There was some ebb and flow – new business creation was higher under Walker than under either his predecessor or successor – but the amplitude of the oscillation was smaller than at Monsanto Fab Products or Xerox OPD. This occurred not only because new business creation was ingrained in the AMP management culture but also because the responsible top managers influenced new business creation appropriately, as subsequent chapters reveal.

Summary

Top managers place more or less emphasis on new business creation, and this can be measured by indicators such as the percentage of available resources – including their own time – that is invested in this activity, and the size of the new business creation pipeline.

A consistent emphasis and approach for new business creation yields three major benefits. First, it gives new initiatives the length of time normally needed – years, not months – to have a chance to succeed. Second, even if new initiatives fail, consistency offers the possibility of second-generation initiatives based on learning from the failures. Third, consistency fosters the development of new organizational competencies that can open new vistas of opportunity and improve the performance of the existing business.

Unfortunately, it is difficult to achieve and maintain a consistent emphasis and approach for new business creation. One common problem is frequent management transitions that create disruptions. Another common problem is business oscillations. When the existing business is doing well, new business creation is neglected. When the existing business matures or is in trouble, attention is focused on saving it or, if new business creation is sought, the necessary time and money are not available.

Despite these difficulties, AMP Sigcom and 3M Micrographics were able to maintain a relatively consistent emphasis and approach for new business creation over the years because of their management cultures and the actions of their top managers.

Part I

The business environment

Both the external business environment and the internal business environment influence new business creation (Figure I.1).

The external business environment includes customers, competitors, suppliers, and other industry and competitive forces, as well as the legal, regulatory, technological, and economic environment (Chapter 3).

The internal business environment refers to the condition of the division's existing business (whether it is growing, maturing, or declining), the relative amount and stage of development of the division's new initiatives, the availability of resources, and other internal factors such as the fear that new products might cannibalize existing business or the bias toward product innovation versus process innovation (Chapter 4).

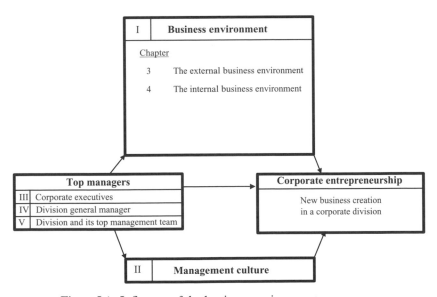

Figure I.1. Influence of the business environment.

3   The external business environment

Several factors in the external business environment influence new business creation (Table 3.1).

Industry and competitive forces[1]

Customer pressures can facilitate or hinder new business creation[2]

Demanding customers spur new business creation[3]   DGM Mike Walker's "let's get into a lot of trouble" philosophy prodded his AMP Sigcom division to work with the most demanding customers on the most challenging new products and applications. Once AMP Sigcom had acquired a reputation as an innovative supplier in the marketplace, demanding customers sought the division out and continued to energize its new business creation pipeline. This occurred even after Walker was promoted and the new group director (GVP) Jon Grover began emphasizing product quality and customer service instead.

3M had an explicit policy of working with lead users – those deemed to be the most advanced and sophisticated in their requirements – and the Micrographics division relied on them to energize new business creation.[4] For example, personnel from key customers were included on the division's new business creation teams.

Customers who are slow or not innovative hamper new business creation   Customers can dampen new business creation if they are slow to adopt new technology, as DGM Mike Walker of AMP Sigcom found: "We are slow on fiber optics because our customers have been slow – they are not using fiber in lieu of electrical as fast as I had hoped." Peter Dell, technical director of Monsanto Fab Products, mentioned a similar problem: "At Monsanto we always want to deal with the big customers. But they are not always the most innovative. Maybe we should also deal with smaller companies who are more innovative."[5]

Table 3.1. *How the external business environment influences new business creation*

Hypothesis	Factor	Influence on new business creation
Industry and competitive forces		
3.1	Customer pressures	+/−
3.2	Supplier's innovation and production capability	+/−
3.3	Threat of substitutes	+
3.4	Industry rivalry	+
Other external forces		
3.5	Concerns about product liability	−
3.6	Strong patents	+
3.7	Government regulations	+/−
3.8	Industry standards	+
3.9	New technology	+
3.10	Adverse economic conditions	−
3.11	External advisors	+/−

Co-development can constrain new business creation   The Coaxial Tap initiative at AMP Sigcom illustrates how a customer with whom a new product is being co-developed can lock the supplier into a customized design, making the creation of a new product for a broader market difficult. Clay Smith was the development manager when the program was started, and he described what happened:

The first models Ed Barrington [the project manager] made for NEK Electronics[6] [an important lead customer] had a printed circuit board enclosure that was about 3 inches by 5 inches. NEK wanted a much larger board, about 9 inches by 5 inches, because of the protocol and the system software and so forth that were needed. In all sincerity, though, it was a moving target. As fast as we would begin to solve a problem, they had changed the design of what they wanted. The thing got too complicated and there were too many ingredients in there that we customized to one customer [NEK].

Common concerns with co-development are that the customer/co-developer will pass on the know-how to other suppliers or one's competitors, or use it to estimate cost and squeeze the price. Joe Hurley, commercial development director of Monsanto Fab Products, explained how these concerns created great difficulties for the RCA Disk Caddy program:

Well, there was a key turning point early in that program. We had this three-way development program with RCA [the customer], PT [the external development consultants], and ourselves. The goal was to answer the question, "Can we make a flat ridge part for the RCA Disk Caddy?" We demonstrated we could do it effectively on a very small machine, which was paid by RCA and Monsanto, mostly by RCA. After that point in time, and in hindsight maybe it was the wrong way to go, we made a very key decision that, hey, we didn't want RCA in this joint development program anymore. And we went up there and told them that we would do the work ourselves. Which upset them greatly... We did that for two main reasons. One is we felt that even though we had the patent, the experience and knowledge of the technology was more valuable. So we didn't want RCA to continue down that path because then they would have as much expertise in that area as we did and would then start putting these garage shop operators in business down the street [to compete with us], and install a machine and let them make parts. And then we'd be dead with our larger overheads... Number two, we did not want RCA to know the process well enough to be able to estimate our costs. Because if they did then they're going to hammer us on price, which is the classical thing. We do exactly the same thing to our suppliers. And those were the two things that really had us concerned... In hindsight that may have been a mistake because if RCA had funded this program like they wanted to, along with us, they may have accepted things from a product standpoint that they would not accept from us since we had basically screwed them. Because our relationship deteriorated greatly after that. So that's a real dilemma. And that was the key turning point.

Customers can become competitors and constrain new business creation
If a new initiative competes with a customer's product, existing business with the customer may be held hostage, as DGM Mike Walker of AMP Sigcom pointed out:

Some of our customers are the harness-makers that actually buy our connectors and add cable to them and then sell them to an end user. In some of my new operations, I also make these cable assemblies, or harnesses as we call them. And of course, that's a constant by-play [with these customers] of, "Well, are you going to be a harness-maker or am I going to be a harness-maker?" And, we've had to be very careful, very deliberate in our actions on that kind of an area.

There is always the possibility that the customer may choose to bring the development or manufacture of a purchased product in-house, especially if it is a leading-edge product. For example, AMP Sigcom was concerned that two early customers, NEK Electronics and Hewlett-Packard, would eventually make their own fiber optics connectors. The opposite can also happen. A company making a competing product in-house may become a customer. Mike Walker gave one example:

Our field people didn't think IBM would ever buy a connector like that [for transmission cable] from us. So they never asked IBM, because they were making their own. I saw the presentation our manufacturing engineer made on how they had to make that damn thing and that was the most complex process and I said, "They [IBM] can't be making money on that damn thing. They can hide it but they aren't making money on it." So when we demonstrated our connector to IBM almost five years later, those guys jumped right on it.

Intimidation by a customer can hurt new business creation   Mike Walker also gave an example of how intimidation by a customer hurt the Cable Assembly initiative:

I've got to say that the project managers that NEK [a key customer] assigned were terrible, just terrible. Aggressive, screaming, and all that. *Not* very smart. The phone calls were going between their people directly to mine [on Cable Assemblies]. Creating changes and all that. It had never been cleared through their purchasing. We kept logs of that. We kept everything. Thank God. Because I smelled this guy was really bad. His project had cost overruns so he was trying to hold us back [on payments] to cover his fanny. The other thing that happened to us which was really bad was that he was feeding design data from AMP directly into our competition. And we absolutely resented that. So we got a patent suit that's going to go on. So it's a serious situation. NEK is a big customer. But I finally told everybody, "I'm sorry, we're just going to stick to our guns. What we think is reasonable we will do. And they can scream up to our Chairman of the Board and our Chairman of the Board can tell me how I can do it – which he won't, he's very practical too – then we're going to do it the way we think it has to be done. And they can pull all the threats and all that crap they want."

The chicken or egg game hinders new business creation   Potential customers are generally unwilling to place a firm order for one's new business if it is not new to the industry, because they already have other suppliers. Instead, they generally expect one's organization to make the investments necessary to demonstrate the new product. AMP product manager Arjay Mason described this experience with the Level 4 connector (part of the Transmission Cable program) that was being developed as a better mousetrap for an existing application:

Sometimes you get to a chicken and an egg situation. The customer says, "The business is yours, all you have to do is start shipping product to us." And we say, "We won't make the commitment until we get an order from you." When you're in a situation like that where they already have several suppliers, they have no reason to make a major commitment to you.

Supplier's innovation and production capability can facilitate or hinder new business creation

Innovative suppliers facilitate new business creation; poor quality or delivery from suppliers hurts new programs. The production engineering manager at AMP Sigcom was concerned that the SMA F-Connector initiative, which was anticipating big orders from the Air Force, might fail if the supplier could not keep up: "Only one vendor makes the needed stainless steel parts. If we get the business and the vendor cannot supply us with the quantities needed, we are in trouble."

Threat of substitution energizes new business creation

The threat of indirect competition from substitutes can lead an organization to acquire these products, services, or technologies, or to develop alternatives, which can facilitate new business creation. For example, it was anticipated that fiber optics would some day replace coaxial cable for some applications at AMP Sigcom. Thus, although the division was still behind in this technology, it had secured the Fiber Optics venture to deal with this threat of substitution on the horizon.

Industry rivalry spurs new business creation

Direct competition also spurs new business creation because this is a way to differentiate one's competitive position *vis-à-vis* industry rivals and create customer value.[7] Manufacturing manager Dick Nottley commented on how industry rivalry encouraged new business creation at AMP Sigcom:

If we didn't develop new products, we wouldn't stay stable, we'd go down. Undoubtedly. Because competition would be so ferocious they'd eat us alive if we didn't come up with something new. And the changes are more than just your product extension. They're usually massive changes. The marketplace says, "We have to get higher density cable assemblies. If you don't do it, somebody else will, okay?" The industry is forcing us into that.

Other external forces[8]

Concerns about product liability dampen new business creation[9]

DGM Mike Walker of AMP Sigcom explained how concerns about product liability were hurting the Fiber Optics venture:

What if someone looks into the end of the optical cable and damages his or her retina? The law says if someone *could have* misused a product, prevent it! We are working on a safety device that could add 25 dollars to a product price of 25 cents! So that's unsettled.

DGM Dan Stewart pointed out that Monsanto Fab Products had seriously explored the idea of using Doormat material on artificial "no-snow" ski slopes, but had abandoned it in part because of concerns about product liability:

The Japanese have been very successful with artificial ski slopes without snow. You know our "wet willies" that are sort of 100 feet long and they pour water on top and the kids go down them? The Japanese artificial ski slopes without snow are a little bit like "wet willies." They are for beginners, generally speaking. The concept was these little 100-yard long ski slopes that give people the sense of skiing. And they have 85 percent to 95 percent "feel of snow," however they count it. You use Doormat material and you don't crush the blades. And you put little polystyrene beads in there to give you the friction. You could have five or six of these things in Houston and Dallas and southern places where they don't ski and get people interested in skiing . . . I'm the eternal optimist, but it looks to me like a McDonald's franchise. You could put together a package and you wouldn't need much land, and if you could find hilly spaces it would even be cheaper because you wouldn't have to build the big superstructure. Hell, if you go to Head Ski or one of those companies and say, "First of all we are going to use a lot of skis and number two we're going to increase the number of skiers in this country from 2 percent to 4 percent. That means your business is going to double." That was the concept . . . But the corporate lawyers came in and they really gave us hell on that. At first I didn't understand the liability question and they said, "Well, on natural snow, who are you going to sue? You sue the owner of the resort, and they do that. But this is man-made and what testing have you done to show people that this is okay? You better run lots and lots of tests to prove it's safe." In the end the lawyers wore me down on that one. I guess I wasn't getting much enthusiasm from anybody to tell me this was a good market and the lawyers convinced me that the liability was well beyond anything we could ever make on it.

Commercial development director Joe Hurley added this: "The Japanese use the same Doormat material. They do have ski slopes over there, but they don't worry about product liability. They don't have the same type of legal structure and 'sue 'em' culture that we do over here."

Strong patents help new business creation

The perception that a patent is not strong enough to withstand a challenge in court hinders new business creation. One way to fight patent infringement is to try to get the case heard by a court with a history of rulings favorable to one's position. Another way is to license the patent to competitors who are expected to remain far behind on the learning curve. After considering the court's rulings and the judge's leanings, DGM Mike Walker of AMP Sigcom decided to use licensing to prevent competitors from infringing on AMP's patents for the Cable Assembly initiative. He said,

The courts have not been doing a very good job in the last few years of supporting the patent law and they bring in outside issues. They're debating in a court whether it's monopolistic or not, although that is not a patent law issue. So you have to weigh whether the patent is strong enough to fight against the judge's proclivities, and it's an art just picking what district you're going fight it in. And we know what the judges' proclivities are, we know their complete track record. That is the longest period of negotiation with somebody infringing as to what court you're going to try it in and what district, okay? I mean, seriously, that's the practical side of the thing . . . We finessed the issue with a licensing agreement that gave our competitors the right to manufacture a product similar to ours for a very small royalty fee, but at the same time acknowledging our ownership of that patent. So I have strengthened my position *vis-à-vis* other infringers because I have got six or seven competitors now who will acknowledge my patent. So what's a judge going to do now? So nobody is infringing. The irony is that nobody is producing either. What the competitors were after was the cable patent and I make a system, connectors and the whole thing, and the only way they can make use of it is to make the cable assembly, and they don't have it. They can't make it. So the competitors who licensed the patent from us signed onto a dream – because they were thinking about this market transition that didn't occur, from cable assembly into its component parts.

Government regulations can facilitate or hinder new business creation

Government regulations and their resultant bureaucratic procedures can hinder new business creation. DGM Mike Walker of AMP Sigcom explained how this delayed the Selective Signaling System that he had championed earlier in his career:

And the problem in anything like that in the public domain is that you've got to get through all the Public Utility Commissions, you've got to get experimental tariffs, you've got to get experimental operations going, demonstrate the fact that a market does want that, demonstrate that you've got enough subscribers to make it financially viable, demonstrate that it's a reliable system, so we did that. It took me a period of two and half years to go through all the field-trial testing and everything else.

But government regulations can also facilitate new business creation by encouraging the development of new technologies, products, and solutions. Joe Hurley, commercial development director of Monsanto Fab Products, described how a US Department of Transportation study and federal legislation provided the impetus for the Spray Guard initiative:

We had a very low-level effort on Spray Guard for a period of time. And the trigger point came when the Department of Transportation decided to run a $2 million field test on highway splash and spray caused by trucks [Spray Guard prevented the dirt from splashing and spraying the windshield of a following vehicle]. If that had not happened, we probably would have dropped it eventually. But that gave us the encouragement to go ahead . . . We kept in touch with the Congressmen who were pushing for legislation. We knew Senator Danson of Tennessee was a safety nut. He was head of the Commerce Committee where the big truck legislation bill was. We also enlisted Senator Emerson's support. Ed Costello [executive vice president of Monsanto] knows him personally; they grew up together. We were dealing with a staff aide to Senator Danson who called us one day and said, "Can you help to draft the language for this? We need it in three days" . . . Now it's the law. Starting two years from now, all new equipment must have splash and spray protection. Five years from now, all equipment on the interstate system must have such protection. It's a $75 million market. We want half of it.

At times the same government regulation both facilitates *and* hinders new business creation! For example, the FCC (Federal Communications Commission) rulings on allowable cross-talk and noise emission restrictions called for better signal protection, which made the engineering design and development of the Coaxial Tap much more challenging, as AMP Sigcom product manager Chad Blair explained:

Because of the FCC rulings, the insulation on the coaxial cable was beefed up so the cable now had four layers – foil, braid, foil, braid – and this made it more difficult for the tap to penetrate the cable. So the tap had to be beefed up and at one point became so large that some of us dubbed it "the battleship."

But the FCC regulations also made the Ribbon Coax initiative more attractive in the marketplace, because it had better shielding for reducing cross-talk. These regulations also helped the Fiber Optics initiative, because fiber optic cable had zero noise emission.

Industry standards help new business creation

Lack of an industry standard creates customer hesitation   It is difficult to introduce new products in an emerging market if there is customer hesitation. Buyers are wary of committing to products that they fear might be incompatible with an industry standard that might eventually emerge. This was one of the reasons why Xerox OPD took so much longer to sell its new products, as DGM Greg Gibbons discovered:

From the time you call on an account till the time you get that guy to buy your product, the selling cycle is absolutely two years. During that time IBM has made product announcements; Wang [the number two player in the market] has made product announcements; and other competitors have come to the marketplace with a whole array of new products – which just slows down the customer's decision-making process.

Lack of an industry standard makes it difficult to build volume. Product manager Arjay Mason explained how this hurt the Transmission Cable program at AMP Sigcom:

We had a neat crimp idea, but it was a custom business and there was not an industry technical standard, such as forty positions, ninety-five on cable and four corners ground. It seemed like everybody was doing a few assemblies here and a few hundred over there. With the solder system that Berg and Chavin [two key competitors] used, they were able to accommodate these changes that occur in ground patterns and cables without too much difficulty because it's just a matter of positioning the wire and then soldering it fast. When you're dealing with molded plastic housings that do that programming for you [AMP's new product innovation], that meant that every time somebody changed ground pattern we couldn't supply because we would have had to make a completely new mold.

It helps to create an industry standard or quickly adopt an emerging standard It pays to influence the development of an industry standard in one's favor, or to swiftly adopt an emerging standard. DGM Ray Thorngate of 3M Engineering Products had learned this lesson:

The Micrographics Association has moved much more into office automation, and so we helped create an industry subgroup interested in engineering automation. But we have had mixed feelings about that experience and have chosen to work instead, now, with a cross-section of key customers. We have learned that you either have to get in there and adapt to the way the technical standards seem to be evolving in the industry, or you get in there and try to influence the setting of standards so that they conform better to what you are about.

New technology spurs new business creation

It is difficult to foresee the impact of new technology The champions of the Star professional workstation at Xerox OPD – DGM Greg Gibbons and VP Stu Little – were convinced the new electronic information technology they were bringing to the office automation marketplace would render Xerox's huge investments and position in the copier business – based on chemical technology – obsolete.[10] As Gibbons noted,

If there's any company that should dominate office automation, it should be Xerox. And it comes out of pure need. Xerox grew to $8 billion in the copier business by making a copy of a document, duplicating it, and distributing it. Well, what's gonna happen now because of office automation? Those documents are gonna be generated electronically; they're gonna be communicated electronically; and they are going to be stored electronically and printed as needed. You're not gonna have, ten years from now, people walking into duplicating centers with hundred-page documents and making a hundred copies and putting it in the mail system. We can't afford to do it that way . . . The real big problem is gonna be to convince the corporation to switch horses; to get out of the copier business very, very fast – in a two, three year kind of time frame – and switch all those resources to selling office automation. If they do it a little at a time, they won't make it.

Xerox corporate executives saw things differently. There was no disagreement about the critical importance of the office automation market for Xerox. But these corporate executives did not believe the copier business had to be abandoned to succeed in office automation. They saw the real challenge as succeeding in office automation while fighting off the Japanese competitive attack on the copier business.[11] As Xerox CEO Nash told employees on videotape,

The real question that people should ask about Xerox, both inside the company and outside the company, is "How do we fit in?" Do we have the imagination, the wit, the aggressive spirit, the willingness to take risks, so that we will get for

Xerox over the next decade or so, a reasonable slice, however defined, of the information system business? We went into PCs, for example, not because word processing alone was an attractive business; it is. But word processing was an essential ingredient for the broader information system we call the "Office of the Future." There's no such specific office of the future; it was the concept of the future ... I've been very steadfast over the last few years to say that we must get ourselves in competitive shape with new products at the right manufacturing costs, the right development costs, in the copier business – because that's gonna pay the shot, so to speak, for what happens in certain other areas of information systems. And I think the outside world sees that we have a very much stronger competitive position in copying – a very large, still growing business – than we had a few years ago.

Thus, while Xerox corporate executives viewed the new electronic information technology as an opportunity to enter a new market (office automation), DGM Gibbons and VP Little saw it as disruptive[12] technology that would eventually cannibalize the corporation's copier sales.

Ignore technology trends at your own peril[13]   Since the impact of new technology is difficult to foresee, managers need to monitor technology trends carefully.[14] DGM Buddy March of 3M Micrographics spoke about the hazard of not paying attention to these trends:

In Copying Products [a sister division], we sat there with our heads in the sand and stuck to coated paper copying for so long because we felt that we could never make a plain paper copy engine at anywhere near as low the cost we could make a coated paper engine. But the trend was there. And the Japanese were bringing costs down ... We've had pretty good new product performance in Micrographics, but we have made the same mistakes. We felt that dry silver imaging and some of the things that we were doing – the lowest cost features – plain paper couldn't match. Well, the price now from those plain paper copy inventions has come down more than we thought initially.[15] So we look at trends much more carefully today.

Technology trends offer new business opportunities in "mature" markets   Technology trends offer opportunities for new business creation in markets that some people might view as "mature," as DGM Mike Walker of AMP Sigcom explained:

One can argue that the automotive market is mature, with stable sales and limited growth potential. But it has gone through some very significant technological trends that favor our corporation. And had we not recognized those, we would not be the factor we are in that industry. What happened? They went from electromechanical type of technology to electromechanical-electronic type technology. So we followed that trend and we innovated and increased our market position. There is another wave of technological change going on right now and that is to go to more robotic, automated production of vehicles. And so we are working on a major strategy now to build harnesses that can be robotically installed in the car body.[16]

Technology trends offer the opportunity to move from existing to new markets   Mike Walker gave another example from the experience of AMP Sigcom to indicate how technology trends offer the opportunity to move from what he called "measured" (existing) markets to what he termed "created" (new) markets:

The technology trend was that instead of RF equipment being put together with hard wired concepts, they had made a significant transition into total printed circuit wiring. So by knowing that technological trend, we tooled for it so our new product would be aesthetically pleasing to the customer but at the same time would give us a low-cost manufacturing process that was totally different than the traditional ways of manufacturing the product. That is, we went away from machined parts to cast parts. So there is where you take a measured market, look at a technology trend, and develop a created market concept off of that base.

Adverse economic conditions hurt new business creation[17]

DGM Dan Stewart of Monsanto Fab Products described how adverse economic conditions hurt the Prism Separator venture. He pointed out that the negative influence of the economic environment – in this case the low price of oil – was so huge that better internal management could not overcome it. The real leverage point for the business was external, Stewart said.

People believed the price of oil was going up to $40 a barrel, and that wasn't a bad assumption eighteen months ago or maybe twelve months ago. We sold $11 million worth of Prism Separators in the first year, and we were talking about that being a $100 million business. And then boom, all of a sudden oil prices fell and oil companies who were spending money like crazy stopped spending money. Because oil recovery using the Prism Separator is not economically attractive when oil prices are low.

Dan Stewart also described how an adverse economic environment hurt the Spray Guard initiative at Monsanto Fab Products:

We were trying to sell a premium product into an industry that was just coming under tremendous economic stress. It was a combination of the economy and deregulation. Of the ten top trucking companies, five or six were merging or filing for bankruptcy as we went to market. It was absolutely the wrong time to introduce something like this . . . Let's say you're making lots of money and I come in and say, "Hey, this will make it safer for other drivers on the highways, and much easier on their nerves, and it will cost you only $100 a truck." If you're in fat city, you say, "Yeah, OK. I will try it on five trucks." But if you have got a hundred trucks idle in the parking lot, and you are not making the payroll, and we say to you, "What meets the law in your truck today we will throw away, and add these Spray Guards for another $100 because they are so much better." That's a tough sell.

Dan Stewart's boss, GVP Hal Courtney, indicated how a bad economic climate hurt attempts to grow Monsanto Fab Products via new business creation:

We moved into an adverse economic climate and our horizon became short term – we had to do that for survival – so we were having difficulty implementing the concept of growth via the pursuit of new opportunities. We did not come up with any growth items during this time period of about two years.

External advisors can facilitate or hinder new business creation

External advisors such as management consultants facilitate or hinder new business creation depending on what their assessments and agendas are. For example, Dan Stewart was not very enthusiastic about the contribution of Premier Associates, the firm that Monsanto had retained to assist the divisions:

Monsanto has spent $5–10 million each year for three to four years now on Premier Associates. Their first piece of advice was, "What you need are growth opportunities; you have plenty of cash." Six months later it was reversed. Their approach is to minimize risk-taking.

On the other hand, Dan Stewart felt that another management consulting firm had made a worthwhile contribution to Monsanto: "Did I give you their report? I think it had some pretty good insights. One of their conclusions was that if the top guy doesn't live it (new business creation), forget about it. All the procedures and all the processes aren't really going to make any difference."

Summary

Customer pressures for better products and services facilitate new business creation. But customer pressures can also dampen new business creation. For example, a customer with whom a product is being co-developed can lock the organization into a customized design, making the creation of a new product for a broader market difficult. Or a customer/co-developer may pass on the know-how to one's competitors or use the knowledge to estimate cost and squeeze the price or make the product in-house. If the new initiative competes with a customer's product, one's existing business with the customer may be held hostage. A customer may even hurt new business creation by intimidating one's organization.

Other industry and competitive forces also influence new business creation. Suppliers that do not deliver parts or subassemblies with the necessary quality or speed hinder new business creation. The threat of substitute products and industry rivalry promote it.

Concerns about product liability dampen new business creation. Strong patents encourage it, whereas a concern that the courts will not uphold one's patents inhibits it. Government regulations either facilitate new business creation by encouraging innovation or hinder it with bureaucratic procedures and delays – sometimes they do both!

Industry standards help to build sales volume and create a mass market. The absence of standards makes it difficult to introduce new products if customers hesitate to make purchases in anticipation of such standards. An implication for top managers is that it is important to influence the creation of favorable industry standards or quickly adopt emerging standards.

New technology spurs innovation, but it is difficult to foresee its effects. As technology changes more rapidly, the risk of missing a technology trend increases. Those who ignore these trends end up as somebody else's lunch. However, those who anticipate and attend to technology trends find new business opportunities in markets that others view as "mature," and move from "measured" markets to "created" markets.

Adverse economic conditions hurt new business creation by biasing the thinking and actions of top managers toward survival and near-term results. External advisors such as management consultants facilitate or hinder new business creation, depending on their assessments and agendas.

4 The internal business environment

Several factors in the internal business environment influence new business creation (Table 4.1).

The influence of the existing business

Existing business as a drag and a distraction that hurts new business creation[1]

The demands of the existing business can take management's attention away from new business creation. As DGM Dan Stewart of Monsanto Fab Products said: "Well, certainly for the first year and a half, the ongoing business was a tremendous drag and took a lot of time. But once it was in good shape, it freed up time to get into new products." Stu Little, VP&GM of the Systems SBU of Xerox OPD, explained why Xerox's existing copier business was a drag on OPD's ability to compete in the office automation race:

I think one of the things that was very, very difficult for Xerox – always had been – was that the copier business was one with tremendously long product cycles, and tremendously high demands for end-user customer support, but very big profit margins. And you had a lot of time to make changes, and you could afford to be very logistics conscious in terms of what you did. That was the way it was determined that we would run the Xerox Corporation for quite a little while. And that wasn't a bad way to run it then, when it was an oligarchy. But you can't use that kind of scheme in the fast-paced, highly competitive office automation business. And yet, the industry culture didn't allow Xerox to change very easily. These things have natural roots and it's not hard to understand why that industry culture pre-existed. And it's also not hard to understand why it was terrible baggage in the office automation business.[2]

Rick Smale, CFO and Chief of Staff of Xerox OPD, added that difficulties were created by appointing people who were used to running one kind of business to run new businesses which had very different requirements: "I think we made two fundamental errors. First, we went into

Table 4.1. *How the internal business environment influences new business creation*

Hypothesis	Factor	Influence on new business creation
Influence of the existing business		
4.1	Existing business is a drag and a distraction	−
4.2	Existing business is growing	−
4.3	Existing business is maturing or threatened	+
Influence of other factors		
4.4	Introduction of new products despite the fear that they might cannibalize existing business	+
4.5	Several new initiatives are already in the market	−
4.6	Insufficient resources	−
4.7	Product innovation	+
4.8	Process innovation	+

these businesses with the mindset that we were going to be the market leaders. And second, we sent copier people to run these businesses or we had copier people calling the shots."

New business creation is hindered when the existing business is growing

When the existing business is growing, there is a tendency to focus on it and neglect or under-emphasize new business creation.[3] At AMP Sigcom under DGM Mike Walker's predecessor, Chet Timmer, one blockbuster new initiative – the CB radio connector – produced juicy gross margins and spectacular growth and accounted for half the division's revenue and more than half of the division's profit. As a result, Timmer paid less attention to new business creation. He was credited with the early feeding and care of only two other new initiatives – Ribbon Coax, which struggled along until Walker re-positioned it successfully as Cable Assemblies after he became DGM, and Tulip Plug, which failed.

New business creation is sought when the existing business is maturing or threatened

When the existing business is maturing or declining, new business creation is sought as a remedy.[4] Joe Hurley, commercial development director of Monsanto Fab Products under both DGM Stewart and his successor McVay, put it this way: "Both Stewart and McVay had to emphasize new business applications because most of the existing businesses they had were mature. There was no other place to get growth."

Managing a dilemma: focus on today while attending to tomorrow

Focused attention is needed for managing the existing business while attending to new business creation.[5] DGM Buddy March of 3M Micrographics had over the years diverted almost the entire internal development effort away from the original 35mm business in Engineering Products and into File Management products (16mm and 105mm microfiche) for office applications in a variety of industries and government agencies.[6] He had thus created, from ground zero, $120 million in new business. The division had maintained its heritage position in the 35mm market with external programs such as the Tanaka Printer, but the rate of growth of the 35mm product line had begun to slow down. In order to reverse this trend, a separate department was created for 3M Engineering Products. The aim was to maintain 3M's position in this business and grow it at a faster rate by giving it focused attention. It worked.

The influence of other factors in the internal business environment

Introduction of new products despite the fear of cannibalization helps new business creation

There is an understandable concern that introducing new products, or second-generation products, might cannibalize the sales of existing products.[7] However, it is unwise to delay new product introductions for fear of cannibalizing the existing business, as DGM Mike Walker of AMP Sigcom warned:[8]

We do that here at AMP sometimes. We sit there and say, "Well, gee, I don't dare release that product because it might hurt this other product." My counter-reaction is – "Do you want competitors to do it or do you want to do it?" They say, "Well, I don't want competitors to do it. Why do you think they'll do it?" To that I say, "If there's a market need out there and you don't fulfill it you'll create a vacuum and somebody will fill it. It's as simple as that." So whenever you're developing strategy you always have to think about that. If you can see a need that can be fulfilled, and you try to make a strategic decision and balance one product's health against another, you're headed down a long, wrong road because you are thinking that you can control what your marketplace is going to choose by what you do. And that's not true. Your marketplace is going to pick whatever it needs and is available. And if it's not available they're going to sit there and try to convince more and more people to try to make it available until they find somebody that does. And the first person that does is going to have a commanding lead in that marketplace if they execute it properly. And then you're going to be on the outside trying to buy your way in.

New products can increase sales of existing products   Rather than cannibalizing the existing business, new products can sometimes have the opposite effect. This is what happened at AMP Sigcom with the Commercial RF initiative, which was targeted at price points well below the Standard RF line. Some managers were concerned that the Standard RF customers would switch to the lower-priced Commercial RF line. This did not happen. Instead, the Commercial RF line helped AMP Sigcom to penetrate new accounts that had been unwilling to buy the high-priced Standard RF Connector. And, although this was never anticipated, some of these new accounts purchased the high-priced Standard RF connectors because of availability! AMP Sigcom's product manager described what happened:

The fact that the sales people are showing a new product, even if it's not available, sometimes will lead to the customer saying, "If we can't have that [Commercial RF, because it is in high demand and backed up] let's have this [higher-priced Standard RF]." It gives the customer an option and it's more in the salesman's bag. And a lot of times new products get you in the door. And it lights a fire in somebody and then they see some of your other products, existing ones, and then you sell those.

New business creation is dampened if several new products have been recently launched

If several new products have been recently introduced to the market, the emphasis typically is on growing this new business rather than on launching additional new initiatives. Clay Smith oversaw the launch of several new business initiatives when he was the development manager of AMP Sigcom. After he succeeded Mike Walker as DGM, he observed:

We've got a tremendous amount of new things going on right now which need to be refined and cleaned up, so to speak, and to get them free from manufacturing problems, number one, and number two, we do need to improve the overall profitability. We're making great strides in that area, and that's to focus on manufacturing costs and mechanization and process improvements and cost reduction areas. We've drawn money out of the corporate till to invest in new programs and new plants and new equipment, and now it's time to – in my own impression, no one's really pressing me for that – begin to pay back some of that and reward the corporation through higher gross margins.

Smith's development manager, Jim Fitch, agreed that this was appropriate because several new products had been recently introduced to the market:

> With all this scurrying around with new products and everything, when they hit production we couldn't ship them. Now it's time to clean them up and get them to work. And some of these new products, by the way, took off like a rocket. So you have instantaneous backlog and past-due problems. So what Smith is doing is needed.

Insufficient resources hinder new business creation[9]

Entrepreneurship is not resource-driven; resources follow attractive opportunities rather than the other way around.[10] Nevertheless, opportunities remain dreams without sufficient resources to pursue them.[11] DGM Mike Walker of AMP Sigcom had taken over a division in reasonable financial shape; otherwise he could not have launched into new business creation as quickly as he did, he said.

> Fortunately, operationally the division was healthy, so that did not have to be my first area of concern. If not, it would have been much more protracted and more difficult to kick-start new business. Because then the first thing that I would have had to pay attention to is getting the operating side in control. And then slowly modulating a new product effort to get it in there. But because the division was healthy [financially and operationally], I could concentrate on getting a new product effort in there and take advantage of my financial health to help fund it.

Both product innovation and process innovation spur new business creation[12]

The importance of product innovation is obvious. It creates new products for existing or new markets. The importance of process innovation is commonly under-emphasized. For example, 3M was a master of product innovation but not of process innovation.[13] DGM Buddy March called it 3M's Achilles' heel and said the company was trying to improve in this area:

> Realize that for years and years and even today, we won't show anybody our factories. I think we got over-impressed with the idea that we knew all there is [to know] about manufacturing and we're going to show somebody something. Today, I don't think we show them our factories because we're ashamed of the things they'd see in there, in many cases. [Laughter] Don't get me wrong – some of our factories are just outstanding. They're very modern and way more advanced. But we've got a great number of factories in this company that look like they come out of the sixties . . . The manufacturing process today is by far our biggest

Achilles' heel. We used to own 95 percent of the videotape business. All of a sudden, the Japanese[14] and a few others came in and made a better tape at substantially lower costs; they drove the price down and eroded our market shares pretty badly. We just kept lowering our selling prices to fight for market share and lost our shirt! We have a big, big program here now to improve our process to get the costs down in manufacturing... When you get into that game of process innovation, the importance of patents and so on seems to change, because it's not patent-driven so much as experience-driven. There has been a lot of discussion of that in 3M. For the first time, we may have to bring in more experienced people from other firms. And there's all the approval from management to do that, if that's what it takes. We've got consultants working in this area.

Technical director Tom Sonnenfeld of 3M Engineering Products added this:

There is a disturbing trend in 3M. Factory costs are becoming a greater and greater percentage of sales. It's the most important determinant of what the division's profit is. Lab costs in 3M divisions run from $1\frac{1}{2}$ percent of sales to 8 percent, with an average of $4\frac{1}{2}$ percent. My division is at the high end. So I can squeeze lab costs, but there's no comparison with what you can get out of manufacturing costs.

Process innovation can do much more than improve quality and drive manufacturing costs down to improve the profitability of new products. It can help to open new markets with new applications as costs and prices are reduced. This potential for new business creation from process innovation remains under-exploited.[15]

Summary

The existing business can become a drag and a distraction that hampers new business creation. Further, when the existing business is growing, there is a tendency to neglect new business creation. However, when the existing business starts maturing, or is under threat, new business creation is sought as a remedy.

Introduction of new products, despite the fear that this will cannibalize the existing business, helps in two ways. It pre-empts or answers similar moves by competitors, and it provides access to new customers, some of whom might end up buying existing products because of their availability!

If several new initiatives have been recently introduced to the market, or if sufficient resources are not available, new business creation is dampened. Both product innovation and process innovation spur new business creation.

Part II

The management culture

This part of the book examines the ways in which management culture influences new business creation (Figure II.1).[1,2]

There are many definitions of culture;[3] most people are familiar with the one adopted here – a set of beliefs shared by members of a community. The typical corporation has a number of corporate cultures and subcultures; for example, the beliefs shared by members of a functional discipline within the corporation, such as the engineering culture within AMP, or the beliefs shared by employees in a division of the company, such as the subculture of AMP Sigcom employees.[4] The corporate culture examined in Part II of this book is the set of beliefs that the corporate

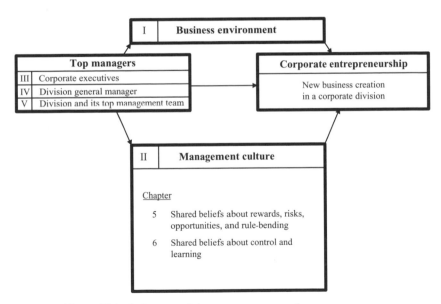

Figure II.1. Influence of the management culture.

executives *and* the managers in the division studied shared in common, i.e. the *management* culture.[5]

The importance of a consistent emphasis on new business creation was highlighted in Chapter 2. With such an emphasis over many years, AMP and 3M had developed management cultures that supported this activity.[6] Without such a history, Monsanto and Xerox had not developed management cultures that supported new business creation.

The shared beliefs are presented sequentially in the next two chapters, but they are in fact interrelated and this will become clear as these chapters unfold. In Chapter 5, the influence of the shared beliefs concerning rewards for new business creation, personal risks from mistakes and failures, opportunity taboos, rule-bending, and irresponsible behavior are examined. The shared beliefs concerning the control of new initiatives and the importance of learning from failure are the subject of Chapter 6, which closes with a discussion of how the management culture changes.

For brevity, the book uses the term "management culture" and refers to the shared beliefs of the "managers." However, it should be remembered that, for each company, these are the beliefs that the managers in the particular division studied *and* the corporate executives at headquarters shared in common.

5   Shared beliefs about rewards, risks, opportunities, and rule-bending

This chapter examines how shared beliefs about rewards, risks, opportunities, and rule-bending influence new business creation (Table 5.1).

Big financial incentives hurt new business creation[1]

Many people believe that corporate entrepreneurs must be rewarded in the same way as "Silicon Valley" independent entrepreneurs, with big financial incentives to offset the big personal risks of failure.[2] This is a flawed assumption, even for independent entrepreneurs, because some of them don't have much to lose, and for others the *opportunity costs* are quite low because there is not much else they can do or want to do.[3] *If* their perceived risk or opportunity cost is low, big financial incentives are not needed to motivate independent entrepreneurs.[4]

In any case, the belief that independent entrepreneurship and corporate entrepreneurship require similar incentives is flawed – because there are significant differences between the two.[5] The independent entrepreneur may seek rewards – such as the pride of starting one's own business and leaving it to posterity – that the corporation cannot hope to match. Also, as founder/owner, the independent entrepreneur's right to reap big financial gains in return for creating the company's wealth and its jobs is generally acknowledged by others. The corporate entrepreneur does not have the same right in the eyes of his or her associates because the corporate entrepreneur relies on resources that he neither paid for nor helped to create in the way that the independent entrepreneur did. It is not clear what the corporate entrepreneur's contribution really is because *inter*dependence is a fact of corporate life.[6]

Big financial incentives for corporate entrepreneurs create perceptions of inequity and resentment that harm new business creation. Consider the experience of Xerox OPD. In lieu of stock options normally available to Xerox managers, a short-term bonus plan was adopted for the top 300 OPD managers. It was tied to the achievement of the annual profit plan and paid as a percentage of the manager's base salary – up to 40 percent of

Table 5.1. *How shared beliefs about rewards, risks, opportunities, and rule-bending influence new business creation*

Hypothesis	Factor	Influence on new business creation
Shared beliefs of the management culture		
5.1	Big financial incentives are necessary to motivate people to undertake new initiatives	–
5.2	Financial incentives are not necessary to motivate people to undertake new initiatives if the perception of personal risk is minimized	+
5.3	Opportunity taboos	–
5.4	The right to pursue one's business convictions	+
5.5	Rule-bending is permitted	+
5.6	Irresponsible behavior is defined narrowly as violations of personal integrity or business ethics, not broadly to include violations of the prevailing business beliefs and practices	+

base salary for the division's TMT, up to 25 percent for people reporting to the division TMT, and up to 15 percent for the people reporting to them.

The long-term bonus, offered only to the top thirty OPD managers, increased based on cumulative profit in excess of plan, and had no cap. Thus, if the division delivered a planned cumulative net profit of $180 million over the next four years, each participant would receive 100 percent of his salary as bonus. If the plan was bettered by 10 percent, then an additional 100 percent bonus would accrue; if by 20 percent, then an additional 200 percent bonus; and so on. Thus, if management could deliver $360 million in cumulative net profit over the next four years (100 percent in excess of plan), the vice presidents would each receive about $1,500,000 in bonus (1,000 percent of salary of about $150,000). Bonuses for the other top thirty managers would average about a million dollars each. As Peter Coors, director of compensation for Xerox OPD, said, "The management compensation plans were part of the deal to get [DGM] Greg Gibbons to come here. We really want some millionaires to come out of OPD!"

This incentive program created perceptions of inequity within the company.[7] Others in Xerox OPD, including the 270 managers immediately below the top thirty – who were not on these big long-term incentives but were on the short-term bonus plan that paid up to 40 percent of base salary – saw the program as unfair. One of them echoed the general feeling when he said, "The top thirty are going to make out like bandits!" These perceptions of inequity hurt employee morale and collaboration within the division. The people in other company divisions also resented being excluded. This hurt inter-division collaboration which was needed to sell Xerox OPD's new products, particularly the Memorywriter typewriter.

Where big financial incentives work

Big financial incentives can be used without dysfunctional consequences if two conditions are met: (1) the people who are given these incentives are clearly separated from, and not dependent on, the rest of the organization; and (2) the success or failure of the people who are given these incentives is perceived as solely dependent on their own efforts and contributions, without help from the rest of the organization.[8] Both conditions were met for the "Chicago Seven" at Xerox OPD. These seven people had been assigned to a skunk-works project in Chicago with the aim of developing a dramatically cost-reduced key component for the Memorywriter typewriter, and were offered big financial incentives, as DGM Greg Gibbons said:

> Steve Kendall and the rest of the Chicago Seven are on steep incentives. Xerox pays their salary and they're on a very, very strong financial incentive. They stand to make a lot of money on this project if (a) we ship a lot of units, and (b) they meet the target of a $350 unit manufacturing cost [UMC]. For example, the way I wrote it, at a UMC of 600 bucks, Steve Kendall will make $200,000. But at 350 bucks UMC, he will make $4 million. He's well motivated to get the costs down.

There was resentment within Xerox OPD toward this group; calling them the "Chicago Seven" was a disparaging allusion to the Chicago Black Panther radicals of the 1960s. However, the adverse impact was limited for two main reasons. First, the Chicago Seven were geographically separated and were not dependent on Xerox OPD or other Xerox groups. Second, there was no doubt in anyone's mind that the success or failure of the critical component the Chicago Seven were developing was solely dependent on their efforts and contributions.

Non-financial rewards can *motivate new business creation*

Managers in AMP and 3M shared the belief that new business creation would be rewarded with recognition, enhanced status, and the opportunity to engage in such activity on a bigger scale. These rewards, along with the intrinsic motivation to pursue new business creation, drove managers in these companies to engage in this activity. Money was neither offered nor seen as a primary motivator.[9] As DGM Mike Walker said of AMP's approach,

Outsiders ask us, "What incentives do you give to foster innovation and productivity?" and the answer is little handouts and recognition, no money. We don't pay for suggestions, we don't pay for cost improvements. They say, "Well, gee, doesn't that dry it out?" And the answer is, "No, it's not a problem at all." We don't pay for patents, and I've argued both sides of the fence, but the older I've gotten, the more mature I've gotten, the more I realize the wisdom of not doing that. Because when you start paying sums for those things, you motivate people to do extraordinary things that may be funny as all hell. And they emphasize the wrong things. Now I have people that have the kinds of personalities that can sell a patent attorney anything to get a patent done, and if they were going to get rewarded for it, that patent attorney would be busier than anything and the patent may have no bearing on whether our corporation wants to do something with it or not. I have other inventors that can't even speak, they're very introverted, but they're very creative and you have to really dig to understand what they've accomplished for you, and their management supervision has to tell the patent department, "Hey you'd better talk to that guy, he's got a nice, hot little deal out there", and get it done . . . Most improvement projects I've seen, there's no one person that really did it – it's a team effort. How do you figure out who gets rewarded? And did you get left with a nice harmonious situation or did you get some animosity from people who said, "I should have had part of that but I didn't get it"? And we don't have that problem. People are motivated to keep the company healthy and I'd stack us up against any company that has an incentive program in terms of money, because money really doesn't do the job for you – in fact, it can do you a lot more harm.

The managers in 3M also did not believe that financial incentives were necessary to promote new business creation, as DGM Buddy March observed:

Our people contributed, I think, quite extensively – tremendous ideas coming in from the sales people and the marketing people and so forth. Even manufacturing people sent in new product ideas. There was no financial incentive for that. The Micrographics division was like a great big family and they all wanted the family to succeed. They all got thrills out of seeing new product announcements. Seeing us high on the list in some of the standings within the company. And there's tremendous accolades for the contributors; in fact, we have a recognition program, the "Golden Step Award," that just motivates the hell out of those laboratories. Because thousands of people are there from all across 3M when they get these awards. The program leader and the team get that award. These are new products that sell two million dollars a year and make a profit.

Reducing the perception of personal risk enhances new business creation[10]

People are motivated to undertake new initiatives without the use of financial incentives, and despite the high probability of failure, if they believe there is no personal risk in doing so.[11]

Job security does not necessarily create a shared belief that there is no personal risk in new business creation[12]

Monsanto was not a hire-and-fire company. Managers who did not succeed were shelved, not fired. Nevertheless, Monsanto managers shared the belief that there was considerable personal risk in pursuing new initiatives. They believed there was job security as long as one did not make mistakes. According to one manager in Monsanto: "Sure there is job security – but don't screw up!" Jason Singleton, the financial controller for Fab Products, said this: "My boss feels very strongly that the attitude in Monsanto is, 'You better succeed' – which does not promote entrepreneurship." Technical director Peter Dell of Monsanto Fab Products put it this way: "For me personally, there is a career risk if the OPET initiative doesn't succeed. I could be shelved into a staff job if OPET fails."

Managers in AMP and 3M shared the belief that there is no personal risk in new business creation

Managers in AMP and 3M believed they would lose the time they had invested in a new program if it failed, but they would not lose their pay, status, or job as a result. For example, even the disastrous Com initiative at 3M Micrographics did not hurt program manager Mat MacGregor; he was moved to another position. DGM Buddy March said that MacGregor's move did not cost him any political chips, and he added this: "We can't destroy program managers who fail. The MacGregor appointment was my mistake. I put him in the wrong spot. He is doing much better in his current position." Ralph West had worked on the Com program earlier and he agreed with Buddy March:

Bill Lieberman and I worked on Com in the early days. We lost time, and there was the opportunity cost, so we were somewhat hurt by it. But Bill is today a marketing director and I am a DGM, so it didn't really hurt us in the long run. I view Mat's current position as neutral – not a great leap forward, but not bad either.[13]

Technical director Ray Thorngate of 3M Micrographics said that failure was a common occurrence on the way to the top at 3M:

One of my observations at 3M is that a lot of new initiatives fail, but it really wasn't the fault of the guy in charge that the thing didn't work out. The probability of success being what it is, not everything works. That fellow, usually, bounces back and ends up getting more offers within the company than he would have gotten before he ever took that job. There are a lot of people in top positions at 3M that had some losers before they moved into a winner.

George Sweitzer, AMP's corporate VP of technology, explained the importance of what he referred to as a "mistake-tolerant" environment:[14] "We are the industry leader and highly profitable, but we are not as smart as you would think. We make a lot of mistakes. But we try to remember them and learn from them."[15] Ted Rigby, the AMP corporate planner, put it this way:

At ITT, where our founder previously worked, the attitude was, "When you goof, we fire you." Our setup is totally different. Our system fosters the creative person. An especially creative mind can get away with almost anything here. We can write a book on the creative, weird nuts we have put up with. Some of them really way out. The technically creative person cannot have freedom if the alternative to succeeding is failure.[16]

Group director (GVP) Mike Walker gave an example of AMP's "mistake-tolerant" environment:

Larry (one of the DGMs reporting to me) elected to align with a vendor on a brand new method of manufacturing a key product of which we had the dominant market share. It was a bad decision, and I was very upset after I learned of it because we violated two principles. One, you never teach technology that only you have. If you are going to a vendor, go with capacity in a well-known field. And two, you never give 100 percent of your capacity to a vendor – that exposes market intelligence as to what the true size is. So that was a really bad decision. I'm glad he made a decision, but I'm sorry that was the one, because it hurt us very badly. Two years later that vendor became a competitor . . . Is there a time to punish a bad decision? I don't think so. The way our decisions are arrived at, there are a lot of other people that contribute to it, including myself. And there are means of pulling out of those decisions before they happen . . . Very rarely do you replace people because they made a mistake.

How the shared beliefs at AMP and 3M avoided the "moral hazard"[17]

People may become sloppy and irresponsible if their mistakes and failures are tolerated. This is what economists call the "moral hazard." But it can be avoided if the management culture limits sloppy behavior and handles job failure appropriately.[18]

Limiting sloppy behavior   The management cultures at AMP and 3M limited sloppy behavior because of the shared belief in screening extremely tightly for talented, committed individuals who were seeking a long-term career with the company. People were carefully developed and promoted, creating a cadre of experienced managers who knew they would be in their jobs long enough to face the consequences of their actions.

These companies also shared the belief in high performance, which stretched their managers. This made sloppy behavior less likely, and made it more apparent to others when it occurred. Further, the managers in these companies believed they had been treated fairly by the company, and were predisposed to reciprocate. Thus, most managers in AMP and 3M were not motivated to become sloppy just because they had been protected against failure. Quite the opposite, as group director (GVP) Mike Walker explained:

AMP is basically not a punitive type company. Everybody's part of the fabric and if somebody falls off the fabric the rest of them try to join in and help. If the fabric is right, and they have a high level of loyalty to the entity, as I feel most AMP people do, then they're going to feel a lot worse about it than you could ever make them feel by punishment. And that's been the case every place I've seen in AMP. They feel much worse about it themselves than I could ever achieve by punishing them. In fact, I'd make it easier for them if I punished them. Because now you gave them an out. And then they get mad at the company. But this way they feel very badly about it... I remember some of the bad new products that were canceled on me and some of the bad decisions I made. I used to keep an account of how much money I'd lost for AMP. And one time I hit a peak of about $2.6 million, and I really felt a responsibility to gain that money back. And I did. But that is the difference. Now if they penalized me for the damage, then to hell with them, you know. They did not back me and I am not going to back them. So I don't think a punitive environment is a very healthy one. I'm not saying that people don't survive that way. I see people surviving in all sorts of different environments.

The same sentiments were commonly heard at 3M, as GVP Buddy March said:

We don't believe in talking about bad decisions and bad luck. We just call it a mistake. It goes back to McKnight [the legendary CEO who built the company into a powerhouse] and his philosophy – that if we're gonna grow, we're gonna take in people that are not ready for management, and we're going to have to be patient with their mistakes. That's part of the environment of 3M that I like so much – that you *can* make a mistake at 3M, and it's not the end of the world. You feel worse about it than anybody else around. Now, if you continually make mistakes, it's another story and we finally move the guy. We won't fire the person. In fact, making a mistake is not grounds for being fired.

Handling job failure appropriately   What about people who are clearly not doing well in their jobs, what most companies would consider failure on the job? Both AMP and 3M had the same shared beliefs about job failure – it was viewed as a problem of inappropriate job placement. According to AMP's Mike Walker, "If a person is not performing up to our expectations after he has had sufficient opportunity, then we erred by putting him in that job. We try to find him a job where he can contribute." DGM Clay Smith of AMP Sigcom explained how poor performers were re-positioned:

We have a thing called BUEs. Better Used Elsewhere. [Laughter.] They can be relatively new people who just weren't placed properly. They can also be people who have been around many years and their attitudes or values have changed or the job has outgrown them. Or they've been promoted beyond their capability.

DGM Buddy March said that senior managers at 3M who performed poorly were re-positioned: "If an individual has reached this level, there are usually several things he can do extremely well. We will find such an opportunity for the individual." In general, the question commonly asked in AMP and 3M in connection with someone's failure on the job was, "How can we make it possible for this person to contribute with dignity?" To answer this question constructively and proactively, both AMP and 3M spent a great deal of time in counseling sessions for their people. As Mike Walker of AMP said,

I think what separates our company from a lot of corporations is that we do spend a lot of time with people, in trying to develop them and develop their perceptions of themselves and develop our own perceptions of them – to be fair, and honest, and open, and sincere about it. It takes time. A lot of managers don't like to take that kind of time. But look what you get out of it. You can take this young man here [an example of a poor performer] and say, all right, he is a poor performing product engineer and you could fire him. But out of this we developed a darn good pricing guy, and now a good product manager. He's moving up a track that is very important.

The benefits of the AMP and 3M approach

The management cultures at AMP and 3M allowed a person to be as entrepreneurial as the situation[19] and his drive permitted. There was no perception of inequity – "Why is so and so allowed to try and fail but not me?" – because anyone who was willing to risk the loss of his own time to pursue a new business opportunity, despite the low probability of success, was free to do so.

The necessary conditions for the AMP and 3M approach to work

The AMP and 3M method of motivating entrepreneurial behavior will not work in a company that believes in promoting ambitious fast trackers, because it requires that people remain in their jobs long enough for their initiatives to bear fruit. Nor will this approach work with managers who believe in large financial incentives, such as Gibbons at Xerox, because it offers something different – status and advancement in the corporation for successful risk-taking, with no penalties for mistakes and failures.

Opportunity taboos constrain new business creation

Opportunity taboos, the shared beliefs concerning opportunities that are not to be pursued, constrain new business creation.[20] For instance, the management culture at AMP did not favor fixed-price government contracts because a prior generation of managers had been badly burned by cost overruns on such contracts.

Taboos concerning particular initiatives also constrain new business creation. For example, the PET and the OPET technologies were frowned upon at Monsanto because the company had lost millions of dollars on Cycle Safe, a related technology. As technical director Peter Dell of Monsanto Fab Products said,

Now that we are finally going into OPET, someone could ask, "Why is Monsanto not in PET *already*? They have the technology and the distribution." But after Cycle Safe – we lost $200 million on it – no one had the stomach for it. So we missed out on PET, the greatest success story in food packaging. And we are going to be late on OPET because it has taken a long time to get everyone on board.

Opportunities that are considered taboo are generally not pursued, nor even perceived. And those who do perceive and pursue such opportunities are met with more or less organizational resistance, depending on the following shared belief.

The right to pursue one's business convictions promotes new business creation

New business creation is facilitated if people believe they have the right to pursue their business convictions. Monsanto managers did not have this shared belief. They were driven instead by what they believed their superiors wanted, as DGM Dan Stewart lamented:

One of the guys in my organization said, "I think D Building [where the corporate executives are located] will buy that." And I said, "What difference does that make? Tell me if it is the right thing to do. And not that D Building will buy it or this will satisfy them. If they want to edict us to do it their way, fine, but at least let's go to them with what we believe is right." More times than you can imagine at Monsanto, it's anticipating what does Steele [CEO] want? What does Reilly [president] want? And that restricts people's thought processes.

Since the shared beliefs among Monsanto managers did not offer them the right to pursue their business convictions, initiatives that were unconventional or unpopular with senior management were either not pursued or encountered organizational resistance. A good example is the Spray Guard initiative. Several managers had been interested in the concept but none had been willing to champion it, for two main reasons. First, the projected revenue was well below the minimum threshold of $50 million that the corporation had set for new businesses. Second, both the product and the market were alien to the company.

When DGM Stewart championed this initiative and tried to use his credibility and influence to push it along, he encountered mostly apathy or discouragement from others. When he finally got to present it to the Corporate Policy Committee – consisting of the senior executives of Monsanto – Stewart said he was greeted with "smirks" (obnoxious smiles) around the table, and unrelenting questions in a tone that he felt was hostile – "Are you telling us this is a *Monsanto* product?" "You can't be *serious* about this!" "This is silly, we don't know anything about selling to the trucking industry." "We don't make this kind of product, period."

In sharp contrast, managers in AMP and 3M shared the belief that one had the right, indeed the obligation, to pursue one's business convictions. If these convictions were at odds with the views of higher-ups, or contrary to the management culture, one had the right to challenge these views and, if necessary, to deviate from them. A typical comment at AMP was, "I feel I can do anything here as long as it is legal, ethical, and profitable." AMP Sigcom product manager Arjay Mason commented on the Tulip Plug initiative:

After AMP had failed several times with this product, our corporate top management had said, "We don't want to see this product again!" And yet [DGM] Walker silently resurrected this product. Tandy was the customer and we were trying to innovate on applied cost.

Among 3M managers, the shared belief concerning the right to pursue one's business convictions went further, to include insubordination under certain conditions. In the words of one of their senior executives,

We do not *encourage* insubordination; that would breed lawlessness. But experience indicates we are not all-knowing and all-wise, so we *tolerate* insubordination provided it is within reasonable bounds and results indicate it was justified. Several of our top managers have built their careers on successful initiatives that their superiors had at one time asked them to drop!

New business creation is facilitated by permitting rule-bending and limiting proscribed behavior

Corporate entrepreneurship and new business creation are encouraged if the management culture permits rule-bending and limits what is considered irresponsible behavior to violations of personal integrity and business ethics. New business creation is inhibited if rule-bending is not permitted and irresponsible behavior is defined more broadly to include violations of prevailing business beliefs and practices.[21]

New business creation is inhibited if rule-bending is not permitted

The management culture of Monsanto gave people less freedom to pursue new business initiatives because rule-bending was not permitted. People felt there was excessive bureaucracy in the company. As one manager said, "You are okay here as long as you play by all the rules."[22] Another manager said, "This is like a government bureaucracy. Stay in line and you'll be fine."

DGM Ian McVay of Engineered Products had a different point of view. He described how Monsanto had evolved from a country club atmosphere to a company that had a degree of bureaucracy that he felt was appropriate to its size and complexity. He also believed that skillful managers in any company learn to work around the rules:

I can remember, before [CEO] Richard Steele came here, we did not have a good senior management. We were accused, and I think with considerable justification, of being a country club company . . . They didn't have any systems. They didn't worry about strategic plans. They went through the motions and they always had something to say when *Fortune* magazine came out and interviewed them so they didn't look like klutzes. We were not a very sophisticated company. And [CEO] Steele changed all that . . . My own experience is that we now certainly seem to have our share of written rules. Are they a pain in the ass? Yes. Are they excessive? Probably not. In running a company like Monsanto you have to have certain standards and I think that the bureaucracy is probably about appropriate to the make-up and size of our company. Does it get in the way? Yes. Does it get in the way to the extent that it has to be worked around? Yes. And to me that's one of the marks of an effective manager – a guy who somehow works roughly within the rule but expedites through all the bureaucracy and all the bullshit and gets the job done.

Dan Stewart and many others agreed with Ian McVay that Monsanto's country club heritage needed the imposition of systems and procedures to instill discipline. They also agreed that an effective manager gets things done despite the bureaucracy. But the consensus opinion was that the pendulum had swung from no discipline to an excessive reliance on formal rules, procedures, and systems that hurt risk-taking and entrepreneurship. Stewart, who was widely regarded as a corporate entrepreneur not awed by authority or formal rules, put it this way: "In Monsanto there is a culture of telling the boss what he wants to hear. And a culture of rules and procedures and systems."

Cultural conformity: an emphasis on style versus substance at Monsanto   There was a conspicuous lack of diversity in the physical stature and appearance – such as height, weight, baldness, beard, and mustache – of the top managers I met at Monsanto at the time of the study in the early 1980s. DGM Dan Stewart commented on this at the time:

I think it has to do with style versus substance. We worry about what a guy looks like compared to our perception of what a DGM should look like, and forget about what he is doing. I am thinking about the CAC [Corporate Advisory Council]. I don't think we have a beard or a mustache on the CAC. Maybe some could lose some weight, but we don't have any heavy or fat people on the CAC.

Stewart's successor, Ian McVay, also lamented the management culture's emphasis on conformity in style rather than on substance in those days:[23]

I wanted to appoint a business director for Fab Products so I could run it more at arm's length and attend more to the RDI and the Prism Separator ventures. I thought my former marketing director from D&P was the best candidate, but he looks a little different – short and bald – from how it was felt a GM should look. But he is a damn smart businessman. My boss didn't want him. He suggested I consider a list that he gave me. I screened that list and recommended my [former] marketing director again. My boss resisted again. Then HR [Human Resources] got involved and asked me to consider Art Malone [former marketing director for Astroturf when Stewart was DGM] – but there was a concern that he looks young for his age, and also a concern about whether his former peers will accept him as a boss. We ended up with Jim Barr as business director of Fab Products.

Ian McVay also said that he got some ribbing from the Monsanto corporate executives on his personal grooming and excess weight:

Our senior managers are intelligent. They're generally outgoing and articulate. They'll react to this, but they're very attractive people. I don't mean they're all movie stars, but you don't see senior managers who are bald or fat. I have a serious, probable weight problem and every once in a while some senior manager will say something like, "Oh, I see that it's getting a little tight, don't you think?" It's a little subtle. Or, "Gee, how can you hear what we're saying with all that hair over your ears?" You get the message. Very subtle but it does come through. The senior managers here are neat and clean and I think that's part of the image. They are broad-gauged and able to conduct themselves with poise and polish in just about any situation.

Permitting rule-bending facilitates new business creation

The management cultures of AMP and 3M permitted rule-bending, giving their managers greater freedom to pursue their new business convictions.[24] Several managers at AMP said this: "It is permitted, even expected, that you will bend some rules." DGM Clay Smith of AMP Sigcom elaborated:

We don't have rigid rules. There are no real formal rules except a code of conduct that we sign. There is an ongoing business responsibility to develop an environment that our people enjoy and are productive in and cause our organization to grow. The informal rules on financial performance, such as 15 percent real growth, 40 percent gross margin, etc. are not rigid; they are adapted to the situation.

Development manager Jim Fitch added this:

You can do anything in AMP, as long as you do it first and then tell them [higher-ups]! They rarely come down with big edicts. Grass-roots mentality prevails. Very few policies. If you thoroughly offend the elders, they will ignore you. That is their way of punishing you! It's a very friendly company; but competitive as hell. The attitude at corporate is: "We have the money. Come and get it!"

Ted Rigby, the AMP corporate planner, recalled this incident:

When I was a DGM, one of my promising young salesmen said to me, "We are giving poor delivery to the customer. I have done everything the system permits me to do." I told him, "Use every honorable means to see that an important customer's order is met. You are not measured by whether you follow rules." It works because people know when to break the rules... We don't believe we are all-wise. We don't have many published policies, but one irrevocable policy is common sense. We only disapprove a lack of common sense.

Here is an example of rule-bending at AMP. DGM Mike Walker skirted group-level capital approval procedures for acquiring personal computers by assembling parts requisitioned separately (each part fell below the $2,000 limit beyond which group-level approval was required). Walker did this *after* all managers had received instructions from the corporate data processing people *not* to purchase personal computers, because the corporate systems and procedures department was trying to develop a policy on their purchase and use. The group controller was surprised when he found out what Walker had done, but Walker showed him the impressive productivity gains that had been achieved with these computers. Based on this evidence, Walker persuaded both the group controller and the corporate systems and procedures department to authorize additional personal computer purchases not only for his division, but for other divisions as well. Walker described his thinking on this subject:

> You don't have to have, in a large company, a lot of debilitating impositions on the entrepreneur. Many *do* have that because, like the systems and procedures group coming out with a directive, in some corporations that carries such power that the people don't dare move because someone is going to say you broke rule number 1-5-8-2. And that becomes a mark on your record. And there are a lot of top management people and management people like myself in AMP that have never read the company's systems and procedures from cover to cover. Now, I know where they are, there's a whole shelf of the damn things. But, the company doesn't force you to take an overt crash course in learning every little element of systems and procedures. How do I know the company's systems and procedures? When I go afoul of them. In some cases, I go afoul of them because they should be gone afoul of. That has given us a lot more freedom to do it the way it ought to be done ... And I think that's one of the things that has kind of kept me at AMP. Every time I think maybe the systems are taking too long, people like myself test them and we finally will modify them, we break them, and we try something different. We approach our culture very pragmatically, and we discuss it, and we don't feel inhibited by the fact there is a *written* system, and we rewrite systems a lot. And we ignore 'em a lot. In order to do what is right for the conditions we are faced with.

3M managers also shared the belief that most rules were bendable. DGM Ralph West of 3M Imaging Products put it this way:

> There aren't many rules at 3M; some rules become clear as you function. We have to be very careful about antitrust, and we are pretty religious about EEO [equal employment opportunity] and pollution control, etc. But other than those, the only rules – really traditions – revolve around those for financial performance [20 percent pre-tax profit, 10 percent real growth]. Most of the other rules – work procedures, time to come in the morning, vacations, hiring freeze, etc. – I don't have any qualms about not observing, if your ends can justify the means.

According to Jim Peters, group director for human resources at 3M, "What we say is, 'Follow the concept, not the rule.' Do what we are after – figure out the concept and do it! We can do anything here as long as it makes sense." Managers at 3M learned the "no exception" rules. All other rules could be bent, depending on what the circumstances warranted.[25] Several 3M managers echoed the following sentiment: "Insubordination is tolerated here if results indicate it was justified." Clay Renault, manufacturing manager of 3M Micrographics, provided some examples of acceptable rule-bending:

I have seen thirty or more "no more hiring" mandates come down from corporate top management over the years, but never one that came out later saying, "It's over; it's okay to hire now!" So after a while you begin to test the system; people slowly begin to stretch the rule to see if they can get away with it ... It is possible to go around the boss, if necessary. For example, if I really felt cornered on the Heat Film program, I could go directly to my boss's boss [Baker, the EVP] and say, "We need to review Heat Film." It has to be done in a very positive manner, but it can be done. And Baker would say to my boss [DGM Buddy March], "Buddy, I have this feeling ... Let's review that program."

DGM Ray Thorngate of 3M Engineering Products described how he circumvented the rules at 3M:

Instead of trying to change the rules, you have to rig what I call the "plausible exception" – "this is a different situation, and wasn't contemplated when that policy was made, when that rule was drawn up. And here are the reasons why it is different. And this is why it's important and this is what we should do about it."

New business creation is enabled by defining irresponsible behavior narrowly

Where does entrepreneurship end and irresponsible behavior begin? The management cultures of AMP and 3M limited the definition of irresponsible behavior to violations of personal integrity or business ethics. One AMP manager put it this way: "You will not be fired here except if you lie, cheat, or are dishonest." At 3M it was commonly said, "You will not be punished here except for dishonesty or immoral behavior." These managers were free to pursue new opportunities based on their business convictions and judgments, without fear of this being seen as irresponsible conduct.

DGM Buddy March's insubordination on the Dry Silver program and on the Tanaka Printer were not seen as irresponsible behavior within 3M, because personal integrity and business ethics were not in question. But such insubordination was generally seen as irresponsible and far more personally risky in Monsanto – two DGMs had been fired in recent memory for proceeding on the basis of their business convictions and against their boss's instructions.

Examples of irresponsible behavior that received punishment at AMP and 3M   AMP had very few cases of managerial misconduct. One DGM had been fired in recent memory, and that was for accepting kickbacks from a supplier. As far back as anyone could recall, two 3M managers had been fired for theft, and one for playing games with an expense account. One VP was fired for taking his girlfriend on the company plane to a remote hotel; a top executive found this out when he ran into them at the hotel!

Several 3M managers confirmed the following unbelievable story of unbecoming public conduct by a sales manager. Greatly admired for his rah-rah spirit, this manager had been reprimanded for becoming unruly after he had had one drink too many. Once while traveling on company business, he knocked down hotel-room doors at night to see if he could find people in bed making love! He was dismissed immediately. DGM Buddy March said, "You get fired for such things in 3M, and for lying or cheating, not because you are making losses on a program or your business is in trouble."

Summary

A shared belief that big financial incentives are necessary to motivate people to undertake new initiatives hurts new business creation because big incentives generate perceptions of inequity and feelings of resentment within the corporate setting, and are counter-productive except under a very restrictive set of conditions.

This is a key difference between independent entrepreneurship and corporate entrepreneurship. As founder/owner, the independent entrepreneur's right to reap substantial financial gains in return for creating the company's wealth and its jobs is generally acknowledged by others. The corporate entrepreneur who is offered big financial incentives is generally resented by his associates, because the corporate entrepreneur relies on resources that he neither paid for nor helped to create in the way that the independent entrepreneur did. Furthermore, it is not always clear what the corporate entrepreneur's contribution really is because interdependence is a fact of corporate life.

People are motivated to undertake new initiatives without the use of financial incentives, and despite the high probability of failure, if they believe there is no personal risk in doing so. What economists call the "moral hazard" – if people are protected against personal risk, they will become sloppy – is avoided with the right management culture.

Cultural taboos concerning opportunities that are not to be pursued constrain new business creation; a shared belief in the right to pursue one's business convictions promotes it. Corporate entrepreneurship and new business creation are also encouraged if the management culture permits rule-bending, and limits what is considered irresponsible behavior to issues of personal integrity and business ethics, rather than defining irresponsible conduct more broadly to include violations of the prevailing business beliefs and practices.

This chapter examines how the shared beliefs about control and learning influence new business creation (Table 6.1).

Many people believe that control is the antithesis of entrepreneurship and new business creation. Yet, contrary to popular belief, managers in companies with long track records of successful new business creation believe that appropriate control is the essential companion of entrepreneurship.[1]

Controls to test business convictions help new business creation[2]

Managers in companies with less experience in new business creation share the belief that the purpose of control is to enable corporate executives to make decisions regarding specific initiatives in the division, which de-motivates division managers and hurts new business creation. Greg Gibbons talked about how corporate interference had stifled new business creation at Xerox OPD before he took over as DGM:

> We had this incredibly bureaucratic system whereby the corporate committees and the corporate staff would evaluate everything the operating units did, and would slow the entire process down. And the corporate people were basically making the decision whether or not a division would move ahead on this strategy or bring that product to the marketplace.

In sharp contrast, managers in companies with successful track records of new business creation share the belief that the purpose of control is to test the business convictions of those engaged in new business creation. Corporate executives ask challenging questions to ensure that division managers are committed to new initiatives for sound business reasons, rather than to satisfy a personal ego or out of a sense of obligation to those who have invested their time and energy in these initiatives. These corporate executives do not tell a division to start a new program or

Table 6.1. *How shared beliefs about control and learning influence new business creation*

Hypothesis	Factor	Influence on new business creation
Shared beliefs of the management culture		
6.1	Corporate executives use controls to test the business convictions of the division managers	+
6.2	Corporate executives place a limit on the aggregate investment in the division but do not second-guess the division managers on their new business initiatives	+
6.3	Budget cuts and program delays might hurt new business creation, but they might also help it	+
6.4	Because failure is a normal outcome in new business creation, the focus must be on learning from failure	+

to drop one. However, only the most committed division managers can endure their unrelenting questions on initiatives that are off target.

For example, consider the Com program at 3M Micrographics which DGM Buddy March kept alive for eighteen years, with losses accumulating to $55 million. March described the kinds of questions he was asked on Com by 3M's corporate executives over the years:

Nobody told me to kill Com. Neither in one-on-one discussions with Ed Baker [EVP] or anything else. They don't quite do it that way, even on Com, with a $50 million cumulative loss. They keep asking, "Why do you keep it?" They don't say, "Drop it." They keep bugging you. Bugging the livin' daylights out of you. I think the culture here is that if you're in trouble with the program, they won't tell you to kill it but they just keep asking for more reviews and putting the pressure on or asking for special reports, until, finally, you get so goddamned tired of it, you say [chuckling] – "Kill it. We'll get rid of it." But I was very patient with Com, and stuck to it, because I really felt that it was necessary.

The shared belief that the purpose of control is to test the business convictions of those pursuing new initiatives is a necessary complement to the shared belief concerning the right to pursue one's business convictions (Chapter 5, Hypothesis 5.4). Only those with sufficient conviction about an initiative can pursue it; controls rein in the others and prevent "fake entrepreneurship" – the pursuit of an opportunity, not because there is any real conviction or passion about it, but because it is expected in one's job or because one thinks that *others* believe it is worth pursuing.

Limiting aggregate investment without second-guessing the division helps new business creation

New business creation is inherently risky.[3] Managers in companies without successful track records of new business creation share the belief that corporate executives must control the financial risk to the corporation by deciding the fate of specific initiatives in the division, which hurts new business creation by dampening divisional initiative.

In contrast, the management cultures of companies with greater experience in new business creation control the financial risk to the corporation by placing a limit on the total investment in the division, for example, up to a certain dollar amount, or up to a certain percentage of the division's profit or revenue.[4] Division managers are free to pursue their business convictions within this aggregate investment limit.

A balanced view of the impact of budget cuts and program delays facilitates new business creation

Each quarter, corporate executives ask certain divisions for cash and profit contributions over and above the budgeted amounts. The division might be forced to cut some new programs and delay others to comply with these requests for "quarterly giving." Shared beliefs that represent a balanced view of the impact of the required budget cuts and program delays ("this might hurt, but it might also help") facilitate new business creation.

Why "quarterly giving" is a fact of corporate life

Corporate executives ask some divisions to make additional contributions each quarter to compensate for anticipated shortfalls in the contributions of other company divisions and still achieve the company's expected financial results. This is done because of the perception that performance below market expectations will adversely affect the company's stock price. As president Jim McGuire of AMP said,[5]

I don't think there's any question we certainly do try to manage our operating performance. In spite of all the bad things you've read about quarter to quarter performance, we do try to do that. At the same time, we agonize frequently over whether we are making the proper tradeoffs between quarter-to-quarter performance and long-term performance.

DGM Ray Thorngate of 3M Engineering Products said the same thing: "I think that in the business community – at least in the financial part [chuckling] of the business community – consistency counts more than spectacular but unpredictable performance." President Jim Reilly of Monsanto offered a similar perspective:

The market doesn't like chemical companies, and within chemical companies they don't like Monsanto. Institutional investors are cautious. We surprised them and took a beating this quarter; yet we had the third best year in our history. "Tell us about your long term," securities analysts say, then get quickly to the short term. Investors don't feel we are a surprise-free company. We have some businesses that go up and down. Monsanto Agricultural Products is great when it is doing well; when it isn't, it's terrible. It's the surprise element that gets us.

Shared beliefs that represent a balanced view of the impact of budget cuts and program delays facilitate new business creation

Managers in companies with less successful track records of new business creation believe that budget cuts and program delays required for quarterly giving will *inevitably* hurt their new business initiatives, and they approach this task reluctantly and cynically. They tend to be superficial and mechanical in deciding where to cut and delay – for example, by asking each direct subordinate for proportionately equal contributions – which hinders new business creation.

Managers with greater experience in new business creation are not pleased to receive corporate requests for quarterly giving either. But they accept them as a fact of corporate life. DGM Buddy March of 3M Micrographics even viewed them as necessary to rid a large company of excess fat:[6]

They say, "You've got to turn in, next quarter, one million dollars more." If it is unreasonable, you just don't make it. But you try. And then the controllers monitor it – they want a report back in two weeks, what programs you're gonna do to get it. In other words, not just give it your best shot – what are the honest-to-God programs, and what will that amount to? . . . Primarily, I use such things as you might expect. Cut down travel costs – I can get a hundred to two hundred thousand dollars that way. We can cancel some advertising and pull half a million dollars out of that. Or there might be a sales meeting or two that we cancel, and save fifty to sixty thousand dollars. You could pull a million to a million and a half from all these things . . . Actually, you'll find that the quarterly requests for additional contributions are not ridiculous – they are real requests. They know how much waste there is in a year in this company. We never get it all out – tighten it up! The last recession, we tightened up fantastically. That's why you expect great returns as you pull out of a recession, because you're a hell of a lot slimmer company.

Managers in companies with long experience in new business creation undertake a careful review of all activity to decide if any new initiatives should be delayed or cut, and by how much. DGM Buddy March of 3M

Micrographics said he blocked out a whole week on his calendar prior to the expected call for quarterly giving for such a review:

When it comes to cutting specific programs, many times Ray [Thorngate, the technical director] comes up to me and says, "If you want this much, what do you want to give up?" And we go through the labs and work together on where to cut. Sometimes we cut out a whole program, or just delay a program. I prefer to cut when it is a very low priority – you have a champion there, but in your own heart you know [chuckling] it would take some unusual circumstances to succeed. And now you just make up your mind and say "No" . . . The next thing you can say is, "Okay, how many experiments can we cut out? Can you get the data out of fewer experiments?" We can cut out several programs in a pilot plant or make fewer prototypes. Sometimes we cancel outside research or lay off contract engineers. We can get a million to two million dollars from all these. Another thing we've asked is, "Can we find a substitute material that will give us a savings?" For example, we were buying a chemical which was costing us about two million a year. We found out that we could use a substitute chemical and I think we got a million and a quarter out of it that year. On that one, we generated maybe some lab expense to do it.

Managers with successful track records of new business creation share the belief that new program delays sometimes *help* by opening up future technology, product, or market options that might not be available if the initiative proceeded on schedule. That is what happened to the Coaxial Tap initiative in AMP Sigcom. The program delays caused by the FCC's regulations on allowable cross-talk and noise emission enabled the product to be redesigned to take advantage of technological breakthroughs that occurred later on, and this gave the eventual new product a better position in a bigger new market than if the program had not been delayed.

Experienced managers also know that *too much* money and other resources can hurt new initiatives as can too little.[7] A new initiative obviously starves without sufficient resources, but excess resources can lead to a proliferation of activities of questionable significance, dissipating energy and focus. Fewer resources impose greater discipline, generating focus and a sense of urgency. As Rick Smale, chief of staff and CFO of Xerox OPD, observed,

Having too many resources can kill you, because you tend to become fat and lazy with no management discipline. Managers in Xerox had a hard time understanding that. Their attitude for a long time during the glory years was, "If engineering needs more money, let's make sure they have it."

One former member of Xerox's Palo Alto Research Center (PARC) said this attitude hurt PARC's ability to translate advanced research into marketable products:

A corporate guy once told me, "You'll know when you have a development pro-gram for a real product. One day, you'll dig a bottomless pit out front. Come sunup, the trailer trucks will start arriving with dollar bills and dumping them in. Your biggest problem will be traffic control." Xerox drowned us in cash and the controls that came with cash.

A shared belief in learning from failure helps new business creation[8]

Managers with long experience in new business creation learn to expect fairly modest success rates. They share the belief that failure is a normal outcome in new business creation and focus their energies on learning from failure rather than on finding fault or apportioning blame. This helps to increase people's skill and competence, which helps new business creation.

For example, managers in 3M had learned that only about 40 per-cent of the new initiatives that were introduced to the market eventually succeeded. DGM Buddy March of 3M Micrographics said, "If we suc-ceeded at everything we tried, we would be the world's biggest company by now! Failure is normal. What is important is what we learn from it." This attitude toward failure can lead to second-generation initiatives, as this example given by DGM Ray Thorngate of 3M Engineering Products illustrates:

One of our divisions came up with the idea of making strapless brassiere cups. That was an outgrowth of non-woven technology, which was being developed for making decorative ribbons. And that became a project. And they started working with various manufacturers of ladies' garments. And it was an absolute failure. Then came OSHA [Occupational Safety and Health Administration, a US government regulatory agency]. Now we've got a whole goddamned business in composite facemasks built on that failure.

DGM Mike Walker of AMP Sigcom told this story to emphasize the importance of helping people to learn from failure:

As a development manager, I had a new product where all the rods kept cracking on me. When I quizzed people on what might have caused that, they said to me, "You know, Mike, it looks like they're making a lot more lots on the night shift," and that's the only thing they could see. So I said, "Who runs that?" And they gave me the name of the guy who runs it, so I showed up on the night shift and said to him, "Boy, you are doing a fantastic job. You're doing a lot of lots here. How do you do it?" He says, "Oh, well, everybody was telling me to keep these Plexiglas shields over the top and shine the infrared lamps through the shield to keep the plastic at a fluid-enough state so I could blend the powders in there." He says, "I found I could speed the whole thing up by taking the Plexiglas off." He was trying to improve productivity. And the reality was that the plasticizer from the plastic was volatilizing and didn't have the same plastic mix that was designed for the new process and that was what the problem was.

What Mike Walker did with this information is crucial. He said he used it to help his people learn from their mistakes, not to find fault or to pin the blame on someone:

If I'd gone in there and had the supervisor slap him on the wrist for making a stupid process change – it wasn't stupid to him. He was motivated to try to improve the number of lots he could get out on the night shift. And so I had to quietly educate him as to what the impact of that was and that took time because I had to go in and say, "All right we've got a big problem. For the time being, let's keep the Plexiglas on there and see what happens." The problem went away. So I went back on the night shift and I said, "Hey, I appreciate what you were trying to do but here's what happens." And I explained it to him. Oh, God, he felt chagrined. But he wasn't vilified and he wasn't torn apart amongst his peers. He got his pat on the back but he understood what the heck the problem was.

Mike Walker was impressed by the humble, down-to-earth pragmatism of AMP managers when he joined the company, and I had the same experience during my first visit. Jim McGuire, the president, and Ted Rigby, the corporate planner, had invited me to spend a day with them and some others so they could evaluate my proposal for this study. All the people I met were extremely courteous, but also extremely secretive, and I felt thoroughly checked out. But once McGuire gave the green light, the top managers who took me to dinner – George Sweitzer, VP of corporate technology, Ted Rigby, the corporate planner, and Jake Markley, the corporate VP of manufacturing – regaled me with stories about AMP's many *failures*, about the way they had messed things up from time to time. Without any provocation from me, they ribbed each other – "Remember the time you blew that one?" "Boy that was dumb, wasn't it?" – obviously enjoying the tales they were telling me.[9] At the end of the dinner, I thanked them for their hospitality and their unusual openness. George Sweitzer responded: "We were not trying to be funny, we were serious. We have to keep reminding ourselves how dumb we are because it's so easy to pretend, when things are going good, that I caused the thing to happen." The other two dinner hosts nodded approvingly and chimed in to say essentially the same thing.

At Xerox, the attitude was just the opposite prior to the time of the study in the early 1980s. There was complacency and arrogance as a result of past success, as a senior Xerox executive said.

Xerox skyrocketed to glory on the basis of essentially one blockbuster product – the Xerox 914 copier – and a set of patents that the competition couldn't get around until recently. Our massive sales and service network gave us another huge barrier to entry, and a near-monopoly position in the market. That's the truth. But the attitude here when things were going so well was to say, "Of course, look who's running the business! We are the world's best-managed company!"[10] But it wasn't brilliant management that gave us so much success, as the competition is now showing us.

Culture change

Management culture has a major influence on new business creation, so two points should be noted. First, it takes a long time to develop a set of shared beliefs and, once formed, they are resistant to change.[11] Second, management culture *can* change. Changes in leadership, or in the beliefs of people coming into the organization, or in people's experience in dealing with each other and the outside world, can bring about culture change.[12] For example, DGM Buddy March of 3M Micrographics indicated how the Tanaka Printer initiative, as well as some initiatives undertaken earlier by the current CEO and his predecessor, led to a modification of 3M's cultural taboo on external programs and acquisitions:

I think our Tanaka Printer licensing agreement was a benefit to the whole company in that they could see that it wasn't immoral or irresponsible or non-economic to go outside. MacNeil [the CEO] built his group that way as GVP. Jordan [the previous CEO] was doing it, starting with Filmsort [the company that Buddy March headed, which Jordan acquired]. But there weren't many others then. The whole company is doing well with external programs now.

Changes in the wind

The management culture of each of the four companies remained largely unchanged over the three years of this study. But a few individuals in some of these companies mentioned certain beliefs that were changing, which signaled potential future changes in their management cultures.

At AMP, two managers expressed concern that the company, while still highly innovative, was beginning to exert greater control from the group level, thus endangering autonomy and entrepreneurship in the division. Product manager Arjay Mason put it this way:

There has been a definite shift toward group control and group staff. The divisions are not as independent and stand-alone as they once were. There has been a tremendous change at the top. A lot of the old DGMs are now group directors [GVPs]. They either know their limitations, hence want more control; or know the limitations of their successors, hence want more control; or don't want to give up their previous style as DGMs, hence want more control ... Today it is much more a game of justification on paper, "Why do you want to hire people, facilities, etc.?" There is a lot of questioning by people who don't really understand your business. That happens in big companies. Small companies don't suffer that.

Development manager Jim Fitch of AMP Sigcom added this:

This company is now financially managed more than ever. Top management now thinks about outside investments, purchases, and acquisitions as perhaps ways to increase the company's shareholder value. This is against the founder's values and our legacy. We are now thinking of going in sixteen different directions.

In response to 3M's increasing product diversity and size, CEO John MacNeil reorganized the company into sectors and began allocating resources within and across them according to business life-cycle and portfolio theory concepts in order to spur growth and profitability. The company's unbridled faith in new business creation and the oft-heard admonition, "Don't use the term 'mature business' in this company," had softened by the end of the study.

At Monsanto, there was some evidence of a trend in the opposite direction. A few people believed corporate executives were making an attempt to give the DGMs greater autonomy and accountability for results. As DGM Ian McVay of Monsanto Engineered Products said,

The transition from Dan Stewart to me is not just a change in scope of the DGM job and a change in the management style. It is also a very fundamental change in corporate philosophy toward greater decentralization. People attribute changes they observe to changes in management style or changes in job scope, but it is also due to changes in corporate philosophy, that they don't see, as well.

The vast majority of those interviewed for this study did not perceive that the management cultures of these companies were changing; only a few people held the beliefs just mentioned. If these beliefs became more widely shared over time, however, the management cultures of these companies would change, with consequences for new business creation.

Summary

Many people believe that controls inevitably hurt new business creation. But managers in companies with long track records of successful new business creation know better. They share the belief that the purpose of control is to test the business convictions of those engaged in new business creation, not to make decisions for them. Corporate executives control the financial risk inherent in new business creation by placing a limit on the aggregate investment in the division, not by second-guessing the division on particular initiatives.

Quarterly results that do not meet the expectations of the financial markets adversely affect the company's stock price. To deliver the expected results, corporate executives in all companies ask selected divisions for additional cash and profit contributions, sometimes referred to as "quarterly giving," to compensate for anticipated shortfalls in other company divisions.

Managers in companies with less experience in new business creation believe that the budget cuts and program delays required for "quarterly giving" will *inevitably* hurt new business creation. Managers in companies with long track records of successful new business creation share the belief that cuts and delays might hurt new programs, but these actions might also *help* new business creation – because fewer resources might create a sense of urgency and increase the focus of surviving programs, and a delayed initiative might be better positioned to capitalize on future technology or market developments.

Experienced managers believe failure is a normal outcome in new business creation efforts. They believe in learning from failure rather than in finding fault or apportioning blame. This helps them to develop new knowledge and second-generation initiatives.

Management culture develops over a long period of time and is resistant to change. But it can change as a result of changes in leadership, changes in the beliefs of people coming into the organization, and changes in people's experience in dealing with each other and the outside world. Top managers must endeavor to change their managers' shared beliefs toward a management culture that encourages and supports new business creation.

Part III

The corporate executives

This part of the book examines how the corporate executives influence new business creation (Figure III.1).

Corporate executives pursuing the "bigger-is-better" corporate philosophy are focused on a few big opportunities, whereas those pursuing the "small-is-beautiful" philosophy are focused on many smaller opportunities. Each corporate philosophy has its advantages and limitations. It is difficult to pursue both philosophies simultaneously because of the fundamental difference in the scale of thinking, the duration of time, and the amount of resources needed to exploit bigger versus smaller opportunities.

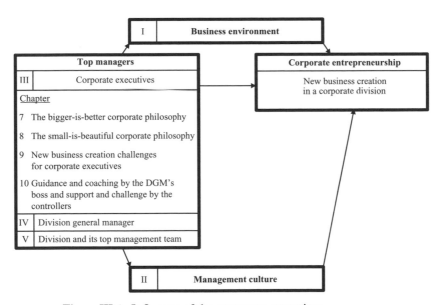

Figure III.1. Influence of the corporate executives.

Chapter 7 describes the bigger-is-better corporate philosophy – its principles, its limitations, and its implications for new business creation – and Chapter 8 does the same for the small-is-beautiful philosophy. Chapter 9 considers a number of challenges for corporate executives seeking new business creation, including the challenge of pursuing the bigger-is-better *and* the small-is-beautiful corporate philosophies simultaneously. Chapter 10 examines effective versus ineffective guidance and coaching by the DGM's boss, and effective versus ineffective support and challenge by the controllers.

The bigger-is-better corporate philosophy

This chapter examines how the bigger-is-better corporate philosophy influences new business creation (Table 7.1).

The attraction of the bigger-is-better corporate philosophy

The bigger-is-better corporate philosophy is focused on a few big opportunities rather than on many smaller ones. For example, Monsanto corporate executives perceived big, attractive opportunities in biotechnology, which they were attempting to pursue with huge investments – totaling several hundred million dollars – in corporate acquisitions, joint ventures, and research and development programs. Alf Hummel, VP of corporate planning at Monsanto, explained the logic of the bigger-is-better corporate philosophy:

> Monsanto is not opportunistic or entrepreneurial. We try to establish secure positions over an extended period of time. If we think we cannot do that, we leave it alone. Entrepreneurship requires repetitive creativity. If you can't do that, don't try to be entrepreneurial... 3M is entrepreneurial. It is constantly spinning off small new businesses from a common technological base. You can't translate that into Monsanto, or vice versa. They see their future in lots of smaller opportunities. We see our future in fewer, bigger opportunities, such as the two in Agricultural Products we are living off of right now. It is a difference in basic mindset... Clearing a new chemical today is no different than getting approval for a new drug. So this industry will *not* have the flow of new products as in the past when it was an unregulated growth industry. Our future lies in biotechnology.

President Jim Reilly of Monsanto said he couldn't get too excited about opening new doors that led into "a large closet." He was referring to a relatively small new business opportunity like Spray Guard, which was projected to grow to $100 million in sales, even though it was expected to deliver a 50 percent return on capital, one of the highest returns for any business within the company. Reilly said he was interested in new doors that opened into "a large ballroom," meaning a big new business

Table 7.1. *How the bigger-is-better corporate philosophy influences new business creation*

Hypothesis	Factor	Influence on new business creation
Five key principles of the bigger-is-better corporate philosophy		
7.1	Appoint a manager who fits the life-cycle stage of the division's business as DGM	+/–
7.2	Limited autonomy for the DGM	–
7.3	Specific marching orders for the DGM	+/–
7.4	Corporate executives review and control the division to ensure compliance	–
7.5	Corporate executives make decisions about new business initiatives in the division	–

opportunity, in the hundreds of millions of dollars, such as the one the company was pursuing in biotechnology:

I don't mean to put down Spray Guard, but it's not a big deal. I call it the "Flying Doormat" because I had a vision of these things on the back of a truck flying in the breeze! It has a terrific ROC [return on capital] but the biggest ROC this company ever had was in the vinyl siding business because there was no C [capital] needed for that business!... What I ask about a new initiative is, "Will it impact the corporation in a significant way?" If the answer is yes, it will get my personal attention. For example, when I put Prism Separator over there [under DGM Dan Stewart] I've been down to the west Texas fields looking at tertiary oil recovery for that business. I've been looking at the manufacturing, I've been reviewing step by step every piece of that business. Because that's going to lead to a large ballroom. Flying Doormat is going to lead to a large closet. And that's the difference.

This is a key advantage of the bigger-is-better corporate philosophy. One big win (e.g. success with a billion-dollar opportunity) can provide as much new business as many smaller wins (e.g. ten successes with one-hundred-million-dollar opportunities).

The limitations of the bigger-is-better corporate philosophy

The bigger-is-better corporate philosophy is risky and breeds arrogance

The bigger-is-better corporate philosophy is inherently risky because this is the flip side of the "home-run" advantage. As in baseball, big new business hits are less certain than singles.[1] For example, Monsanto had only two blockbuster successes (both in Agricultural Products) over the ten years prior to this study.

When they do occur, big hits can breed arrogance and a false sense of pride, hindering the learning so essential for new business creation. As Dan Stewart said at the time of the study in the early 1980s, after he became managing director (GVP) of Monsanto Agricultural Products,

We had two blockbuster developments, and we've been living on that ever since. We had a presentation yesterday from one of my guys in research and he was saying, "We're miles ahead of our competitors." Which is bullshit, because we have gone thirteen years without a major innovation. I said to him, "Number one, we've got this $200 million research center, and I hear that it's already of concern to other Monsanto people [because of the huge expenditure]. And number two, wake up. We are living on past success. When was the last time we had a big winner?"

Xerox was built on one very big winner – the 914 plain paper copier – that sustained the company for a period of twenty years prior to this study. Many observers both inside and outside the company at the time of the study in the early 1980s felt that this huge success had bred arrogance; Xerox managers seemed to think they had the "Midas touch" and were invincible. Several years of market share losses to Japanese competitors finally rid these managers of their hubris.

The bigger-is-better philosophy dampens new business creation in the division

The bigger-is-better corporate philosophy dampens new business creation in the division because of the fundamental differences in the scale of thinking, the duration of time, and the amount of resources needed to pursue bigger versus smaller opportunities. Even with $300 million in revenue and returns above the cost of capital, Fab Products was seen as a relatively small business by the Monsanto corporate executives. The people in the division felt that these executives were really not interested in the division or its initiatives. This bred cynicism and resentment, as DGM Ian McVay pointed out:

From the point of view of our corporate executives, the OPET bottle initiative is almost a junior achievement project – $4 million in capital and no downside risk. The attitude is, "Jesus, if OPET makes a big business, what is it? $75 million? Who cares!" Which is one of the frustrations of running a little business around here. To get people interested you've got talk in multiples of $100 million, and we don't have those kinds of businesses over here in Fab Products . . . But I happen to think they are wrong. I really do. I happen to think that we're doing some really neat things over here. And I happen to think that we can build a nice business out here and it ain't going to be the size of what they think biotechnology is going to be but they could be wrong about biotechnology too ... It concerns me when others in the division perceive the corporate mentality and say, "They don't give a shit what we're doing over here. It doesn't really have any significance to Monsanto."

It is also difficult for corporate executives pursuing the bigger-is-better philosophy to respond to attractive smaller opportunities fast enough, because of the fundamentally different mind-set.[2] Technical director Peter Dell of Monsanto Fab Products explained how this created delays in getting capital approved for the OPET bottle initiative:

Monsanto is a manufacturing company, and the mindset is hundreds of millions of dollars of capital investment. We are into "world-scale" plants, and we are increasing the capacity of existing plants to reach that scale. Now here comes little OPET asking for a measly $3.8 million to start with. They couldn't see that each increment is stand-alone. They didn't really hold it back. They simply went about it the routine way, as they would a $100 million new plant.

The five principles of the bigger-is-better corporate philosophy tend to dampen new business creation

The bigger-is-better philosophy assumes that corporate headquarters is the primary center for new business creation within the company. Its five key principles tend to dampen new business creation in a division because corporate executives: (1) appoint a manager who fits the life-cycle stage of the division's business as DGM; (2) give him limited autonomy; (3) give him specific marching orders to run the division according to the corporate game plan; (4) review and control the division to ensure compliance with this plan; and (5) make decisions regarding specific new business initiatives in the division.

The way in which Monsanto corporate executives managed the Fab Products division (and later the Engineered Products division of which it became a part) illustrates these basic tenets of the bigger-is-better corporate philosophy, and the implications for new business creation.

Principle 1. Appoint a manager who fits the life-cycle stage of the division's business as DGM: facilitates or hinders new business creation

Managers differ in terms of the life-cycle stage of the business that they are better at managing. The "good times" manager is better at managing the start-up and growth stages, when innovation and entrepreneurship are critical. The "hard times" manager is better at managing the maturity and decline stages, when asset management, including efficiency and cost reduction, are the keys to success. The "Renaissance" manager – one who excels in all the stages of the business life-cycle – is a rare breed.[3]

Corporate executives appoint a manager whose strengths match the life-cycle stage of the division's business as DGM. As Monsanto EVP Ed Costello said, "In areas of this corporation where entrepreneurship can spark great improvements, that's where you put your creative, motivational managers. Selection of the manager to fit the assignment is critical."

Managers become stronger at either asset management or growth management because of differences in personal inclination and training in their early careers. As they acquire the reputation for one or the other, they get called on to play to their strengths, which builds their strengths further. As Monsanto president Jim Reilly said,

People have particular tendencies that lead them to become more of a hard-times manager or a good-times manager. It's in character for most people to do one or the other. And their displeasure with doing the other shows up instantly... Every job has a component of each so it isn't totally black or white but here's the problem: you've developed certain tools over the years and if you never developed the tools to do the other kind of job it's unlikely that you are going to be able to do it, or even try to do it. You get twenty-five years in the company and you have never run a commercial development program of any consequence. And so you tend to work with what you have got good at... I see some people in an advanced stage in their career that finally try to change their image because they know you can't make it further without a broad image. Guys talking about new product development that don't have the faintest idea what they are talking about.

Managing director (GVP) Hal Courtney, to whom DGM Dan Stewart reported, compared him with his predecessor, Vic Thomas:

Dan Stewart's capabilities are more strongly oriented toward growth. Vic Thomas – his strength is to cut, prune down. If I had a chance to select, I'd select Stewart or Thomas depending on what I wanted to accomplish. It is only recently that we in MP&R [Monsanto Plastics & Resins group, of which the Fab Products division was a part] could afford to think about growth. So when Stewart arrived, it was the right time for a growth manager. Stewart had more faith in the product lines of Fab than Thomas did.

Thomas' perspective was consistent with that of both Reilly and Courtney. He said, "I can do both – grow or cut back – but I can do better walking into troubled waters and fixing it. Monsanto has called me in three times to do that."

Thomas was a better asset manager, with less interest and fewer skills in new business creation and growth. Stewart was a growth manager, with limited inclination to asset management. His successor, McVay, was a growth manager, with strong asset management skills. Their influence on new business creation varied accordingly.

The influence of the manager's boss   A manager's inclination can be reinforced or counter-balanced by the inclination of his boss, as well as that of the boss's boss. Alf Hummel, Monsanto VP of corporate planning, explained:

Personality is important. If a manager is development oriented, development will take priority. Stewart clearly was oriented that way; McVay [Stewart's successor] also happens to be; Thomas [Stewart's predecessor] was not... Stewart reported to Courtney, a balanced manager who understands growth and realism. Courtney reported to Allport, who is not growth oriented – his instincts are those of an operating man. McVay is growth oriented. He reports to Costello, who is powerfully growth oriented. Costello almost insisted on getting McVay as a condition for taking that job. When McVay came on board [as DGM of Engineered Products] all the signals were go, go, go.

Principle 2. Limited autonomy for the DGM: hampers new business creation[4]

Corporate executives pursuing the bigger-is-better philosophy grant the DGM only limited operating autonomy, and this hurts new business creation. For example, compare DGM Buddy March's efforts on the Tanaka Printer program at 3M Micrographics with DGM Dan Stewart's efforts on the OPET bottle program at Monsanto Fab Products. Both new business initiatives involved a licensing and marketing agreement with a Japanese company, both were opposed by higher-ups, and both DGMs felt confident (based on intuition more than analysis) that they had a great new business opportunity. Buddy March had the authority to negotiate the marketing agreement – he did need corporate approval for the cross-licensing of technology with the Japanese company Tanaka – and ended up with a big winner. Dan Stewart had no such authority to sign a marketing agreement, and was stalled for one year on corporate approval for the capital needed for the OPET bottle program.[5] Buddy March could have failed; the point is that he had the operating autonomy to move ahead on the basis of his intuitive understanding of the territory. Dan Stewart did not enjoy such autonomy, and he talked about this after he had been promoted out of Fab Products to become managing director (GVP) of Monsanto Agricultural Products:

They are going to spend a lot of time figuring out what the market for the OPET bottle is. I wanted to order that machine last August [when Stewart was still DGM of Fab Products]. I'm sure Owens-Illinois and the others are moving fast, and we're going to lose our lead-time advantage . . . We are not building a polystyrene plant for $100 million. We're talking about a minor capital investment to get in there and get our feet wet.[6] We have this unique OPET technology from the Japanese. They have done all the research, and they've done all the development and they handed it to us on a silver platter for $40,000 or whatever. I mean it was absolutely ludicrous. And we are standing here studying it, studying it, studying it. But, you see, that's part of our mentality.[7]

More autonomy for smaller and less important divisions   Although Dan Stewart's autonomy was limited, it was greater than what other DGMs in Monsanto enjoyed, because Fab Products was a relatively small and unimportant division for the corporation. As Stewart's boss, managing director (GVP) Hal Courtney, said,

Fab is an insignificant part of the company for the EMC [Executive Management Committee, composed of the top five corporate executives]. They are scaled to thinking in hundreds of millions of dollars of investment and pounds of chemical. Fab is very, very small and inconsequential for them.

Dan Stewart's successor, Ian McVay, made the same point: "My boss (EVP) Ed Costello is under the corporate gun because of the huge exposure on Silicon and Electronics that also report to him. I am a smaller part of his plate, so I enjoy a certain amount of autonomy."

Principle 3. Specific marching orders for the DGM: spurs or derails new business creation

Corporate executives pursuing the bigger-is-better corporate philosophy give specific marching orders to the DGM. Depending on what these instructions are, new business creation is either pushed forward or pulled back.

For example, corporate executives gave both the DGMs of Monsanto Fab Products – Dan Stewart and his successor Ian McVay – fairly specific marching orders to focus on the existing business, not on new business creation. President Jim Reilly recalled his instructions to Dan Stewart to "clean up house" when he took over Fab Products:

Clean up house to me is getting all the businesses to make money again. Get a decent return on capital – they didn't have it. There were some businesses that had been around a long time and everybody said they shouldn't be kept, so I asked Dan to sort that out.

Dan Stewart confirmed that both CEO Steele and president Reilly gave him the same marching orders when he was appointed DGM of Fab Products:

Anytime somebody made senior management, Steele had them over for dinner at his house. We went with Gossamer and his wife. We are sitting around in Steele's living room and Steele says to his wife, "Dan has just been handed a can of worms, and we have asked him to sort those out for us." And Reilly had said the same thing: "Sort it out. I am not sure we should be in any of these businesses. Try to figure out what businesses we should be in and what shouldn't we be in."

Stewart's successor Ian McVay was given the same marching orders. President Jim Reilly put it crisply: "I told him what not to do. I said that I didn't want him screwing around with Astroturf and running around selling to stadiums. I asked him to find me a theme for the businesses we should stay in."

> *Principle 4. Review and control the division to ensure compliance with the corporate game plan: hinders new business creation*

Corporate executives pursuing the bigger-is-better philosophy review and control the division to ensure compliance with their game plan. The specific goals vary depending on the game plan and the emphasis is on meeting these goals.

> *The division's goals vary depending on the corporate game plan* Monsanto corporate executives assigned different divisions different goals, depending on their role and contribution to the corporate game plan. DGM Ian McVay of Monsanto Engineered Products gave some examples:

It depends on the unit. In the case of D&P [McVay's prior DGM assignment] it was net income and the relationships with the Stouffers [a key customer]. In the case of Fab Products it is reducing our overheads, straightening out the businesses and getting some new things started if that's appropriate, and if not, getting back to the EMC and saying that it was not appropriate. As D Building [where the corporate executives sit] looks at it, the measurement is different for different businesses.

A division's priorities might vary from year to year. As commercial development director Joe Hurley of Monsanto Fab Products said,

The most important goal for the division changes each year. This year it is ROC [return on capital]. Last year it was cash flow. The year before that it was income . . . The budgeting process is where you really control new business development. And that's going to tell you what resources you have, both people and money, for next year. Fab Products' new product development goal last year was, "Ten percent of the business has to be from new products." We missed that goal.

New business creation requires a consistent emphasis from one year to the next; ever-changing goals and priorities do not help.[8]

Periodic corporate reviews   Corporate executives pursuing the bigger-is-better philosophy go beyond challenging the DGM to telling him what to do. For example, consider what DGM Ian McVay of Monsanto Engineered Products said:

I submit to EVP Ed Costello [McVay's boss] a series of reports every month. And he'll come back and usually ask questions. Here are the kinds of questions I get asked in a review: Why are you in the Astroturf business? How big would Astroturf ever be? Is that a realistic projection? What makes you think the business is going to be 2X in five years? What are the underlying premises? What's going to happen? That's a typical dialog. OK? They're testing, pressure-testing the strategy. The genius of an Ed Costello or a Jim Reilly is that they can ask the absolutely essential questions. They can sit down and in a matter of five minutes into a presentation pick out the two or three or four key issues and ask the right questions to get at that. If I have a point of view and Ed doesn't agree with it he might not say, "Ian I want you to go out and do this." He says, "I really think you should reconsider." That's a polite way of saying it.

Polite, yes, but the instructions were clear – *do as I say*.

Principle 5. Make decisions for new business initiatives in the division: impairs new business creation

Corporate executives pursuing the bigger-is-better philosophy view themselves as the real corporate entrepreneurs.[9] As such, they prefer to bet on their own judgments about specific new business initiatives in the division, rather than on the judgments of the DGM. This impairs new business creation in the division.

DGM Dan Stewart and his successor, Ian McVay, were not asked to kill any new initiatives in Monsanto Fab Products. But there was strong consensus in the division that if these initiatives had been losing significant sums of money, the corporate executives would have killed them. One top manager in Fab Products spoke for many others in the division when he said,

Spray Guard was included in the LRP [Long Range Plan] that was reviewed by the corporate executives, but we low-keyed the breakage problem. If all the facts had been known, they would have said, "Kill the sucker!" But since they didn't know too much about what was going on, and since the amounts involved were small fry, their attitude was, "Let the guys try."

The dysfunctional consequences of corporate vacillation in managing an important division

Because corporate executives pursuing the bigger-is-better corporate philosophy view themselves as the real corporate entrepreneurs, they become deeply involved in a division that has new business initiatives that are strategically significant for the corporation. When their micromanagement does not work, they swing the other way. They leave the division alone with little or no guidance, because they think this is necessary to foster entrepreneurship in the division. Or they do so because a powerful DGM succeeds in getting corporate executives to leave him alone. The experience of Xerox OPD illustrates how this can happen, and the dysfunctional consequences.

Minimum autonomy at Xerox OPD before DGM Gibbons

DGM Greg Gibbons said his predecessors suffered as a result of a lack of operating autonomy and corporate micromanagement: "One of the reasons why OPD was so very unsuccessful in the past is that it wasn't given any autonomy. Corporate financial people, product planning, and other corporate staff were trying to run this division and totally screwed it up."[10]

Maximum autonomy, no specific marching orders, and no rigorous corporate reviews led to excessive risk-taking by DGM Gibbons

Maximum autonomy   In a videotape message to Xerox employees, CEO Bill Nash said the company had learned not to expect any one individual to be both an entrepreneur and a professional manager. A corporate entrepreneur like Gibbons could not be questioned on every decision or expected to have a logical explanation for every action, Nash said.

I've become convinced that you won't find the entrepreneur and the so-called professional manager in one individual. I think for a time, fifteen years ago, Xerox tried to look for managers that would combine those. I think very few people combine being entrepreneurial and a professional manager. In fact, I know practically nobody. And I think there's a very logical reason for that. Because the so-called professional manager is really taught to be very objective, to question everything. And an entrepreneur can't be questioned at every turn of the thing. If we had been questioned logically, objectively, as to why we thought the Xerox 914 [the blockbuster product on which Xerox was built] would have succeeded, I think the answer was that it wouldn't have succeeded. We couldn't prove it was gonna succeed.

Gibbons was independently wealthy and had standing offers to return to Silicon Valley to do another start-up, which gave him tremendous clout with corporate executives. This is what he said at the start of his second full calendar year as DGM:

The venture capitalists who made an incredible amount of money on Shugart want me badly to do another start-up. They are willing to put up $35 million and give me 50 percent of the company. That's tempting. But I can't leave because of my commitment to the people here . . . When [Gibbons' boss, GVP] Jerry Tyson did my evaluation, he had many positives – knowledge of the business, leadership qualities, etc. – and on the negatives he had excessive risk-taking. I told Jerry, "If you took over a $200 million business that was losing $70 million, how could you ever have *excessive* risk-taking? What risk would be excessive?"

Despite GVP Tyson's concerns about excessive risk-taking, his powerful DGM came up with short-term and long-term plans that called for a dramatic boost in new business creation. Gibbons apparently felt that he had nothing to lose and everything to gain by shooting for the moon. He bet all he could get from the desperate but still deep-pocketed Xerox to try to make his mark as the Henry Ford or the Tom Watson of the "Office of the Future."

Gibbons explained why he fought so hard for his autonomy as DGM, including his insistence that he would not seek prior corporate approval for specific new business initiatives:

They call it the Product Review Committee – PRC – in Xerox. And every product, every program comes up to the PRC for approval. I fought very, very hard that that absolutely was the wrong way to do it. I maintain that these decisions should be taken down at the lowest possible levels in the organization. One, for speed; and two, for quality of decision-making . . . All these products – Star, Ethernet and PC – were done without the blessing of the PRC. It was just one of those things where I had to be prepared to be an asshole in front of the corporation and say to them, "You don't tell me what products to make. Here's my financial model; here are my plans for the next five years, how much I'm going to spend on research and development; here's my overall strategy. Now, goddamn it, I'm gonna go run a business down there. You're not gonna sit here and review every goddamn product I come up with and tell me where to put the help button on the product."

An example of how Greg Gibbons used his autonomy to implement his aggressive plans is the Saber program to produce the Memorywriter typewriter, which was conceived and designed as a breakthrough product. Without corporate approval, Gibbons authorized Tim Skinner, VP of manufacturing for Xerox OPD, to build a highly automated manufacturing facility for this new product to ensure the lowest possible manufacturing cost. Gibbons described how he commissioned Skinner for this task:

The Saber factory is the most impressive fully automated factory for this product in the world. And they didn't spend that much money on it. They spent $9 million, including all the material handling stuff which came to like $6 million. One of the problems in Xerox [at the time of the study in the early 1980s] is that we ask people to justify things that are very hard to justify.[11] And they spend all their goddamn time in trying to justify the son of a gun and never implement. I don't care if my payback is twenty years. I wanted the most highly automated factory, and they did an incredible job. And the way I did it is, I had one conversation with Tim Skinner. And I said, "Tim, I want the most automated factory that you can possibly build. I don't care how you do it; I don't care who you hire. I want it." And that was it. That was the sum total of the direction I gave him. Tim came back to me and said, "I need to have this signature. I need to spend $4 million." I signed and that was done. That's the way we got to do this stuff.

No specific marching orders   Greg Gibbons said he was not given specific marching orders when he was recruited to become DGM of Xerox OPD: "I didn't have any understandings up front. I just assumed that I could do anything I wanted to do. When the job was offered to me, I just took it."

No rigorous corporate reviews (periodic or ad hoc*)*   Since the corporate executives felt they were dependent on Gibbons, and were concerned that he might quit, the periodic corporate reviews of OPD's performance and the *ad hoc* corporate reviews of OPD's new business initiatives were not as rigorous or as challenging as they might have been otherwise.

Minimum autonomy at Xerox OPD after DGM Gibbons

After Gibbons left Xerox, the pendulum swung the other way. OPD was stripped of its operating autonomy and made a cost center that was responsible for just the Memorywriter typewriter, the PC, and the Fax Machine. The systems business – Ethernet and the Star professional workstation – was transferred out of the division. Gibbons' successor as DGM, Steve Carter, was given explicit marching orders to build on the one success of the Gibbons era – the Memorywriter typewriter – and to meet the division's sales and profit plan.

Xerox OPD went from very little operating autonomy for the DGM – with specific marching orders – prior to Gibbons, to a great deal of operating autonomy with no specific marching orders or rigorous reviews for Gibbons, to very little autonomy, very specific marching orders, and very tight review and control after he left. The extent of emphasis on new business creation varied accordingly, from limited to aggressive to none.

Summary

The bigger-is-better corporate philosophy is focused on a few, big new business opportunities rather than on many smaller ones. Its advantage is that one big winner can generate more new business than many smaller wins. Another advantage is that it enables the pursuit of opportunities that are beyond the ambition and/or capabilities of an existing business division.

One disadvantage of the bigger-is-better corporate philosophy is that success is less likely when pursuing one big opportunity than when pursuing several smaller ones, for the same reason that home runs are rarer than singles in baseball. Another disadvantage is that it tends to dampen new business creation in the division, because its key principles that corporate executives follow are: (1) appoint a manager whose strengths are well-suited to the life-cycle stage of the division's business as DGM; (2) give him limited autonomy and (3) specific marching orders, to run the division according to the corporate game plan; and (4) review and control the division to ensure compliance. Because corporate executives view themselves as the real corporate entrepreneurs, they (5) micromanage new business initiatives in the division.

Micromanagement is accentuated if the division has new business initiatives that are of strategic significance to the corporation. When their micromanagement fails, the corporate executives swing in the opposite direction to avoid stifling the division: they leave the DGM alone. This leads to excessive risk-taking by the DGM, without adequate corporate guidance or control, and with adverse consequences. The pendulum then swings back to limited autonomy, specific marching orders, and tight review and control of the division. The corporate vacillation makes it difficult to maintain the consistent emphasis needed for successful new business creation in the division.

8   The small-is-beautiful corporate philosophy

This chapter examines how the small-is-beautiful corporate philosophy influences new business creation (Table 8.1).

The attraction of the small-is-beautiful corporate philosophy

The small-is-beautiful corporate philosophy encourages the pursuit of many small opportunities because it assumes that the division, not corporate headquarters, is the primary center for corporate entrepreneurship. It is assumed that every business is a growth business,[1] and that innovation and entrepreneurship can create repeated waves of growth in so-called mature businesses. Corporate executives exit an existing business only when there is considerable evidence that the business cannot be profitably grown over the long term, as DGM Buddy March at 3M said when this study began:

Don't use the word "mature" in this company. We have grown huge profitable businesses from product lines that others called mature, by vigorously developing new products and new markets. We do divest businesses occasionally, but it is as difficult to convince corporate executives to divest as it is to persuade them to acquire.

The small-is-beautiful corporate philosophy also limits the financial risk to the corporation by requiring each division to self-finance its new initiatives. As Ray Thorngate, DGM of 3M Engineering Products, pointed out, "The tradition in 3M is that each division funds its own growth. Corporate is not going to give you any money."

The five principles of the small-is-beautiful corporate philosophy facilitate new business creation

Corporate executives pursuing the small-is-beautiful corporate philosophy follow five key principles in managing a division, which they regard

106

Table 8.1. *How the small-is-beautiful corporate philosophy influences new business creation*

Hypothesis	Factor	Influence on new business creation
Five key principles of the small-is-beautiful corporate philosophy		
8.1	Growth manager as DGM	+
8.2	A great deal of autonomy for the DGM	+
8.3	No specific marching orders for the DGM (but high expectations for short-term results *and* for long-term growth require a consistent emphasis on new business creation)	+
8.4	Corporate executives review and control the division to test the DGM's business convictions	+
8.5	Corporate executives allow the DGM to make the decisions about specific new business initiatives in the division (because he is viewed as the real corporate entrepreneur)	+

as the primary center for new business creation within the company:[2] (1) appoint a growth manager as DGM; (2) give him a great deal of autonomy and (3) no specific marching orders on how to deliver demanding short-term results *and* long-term growth; (4) review and control the division to test the DGM's business convictions; and (5) let the DGM make the decisions concerning new business initiatives in the division because he is the real corporate entrepreneur. The ways in which corporate executives managed the AMP Sigcom and the 3M Micrographics divisions illustrate these basic tenets of the small-is-beautiful philosophy and how they facilitate new business creation in the division.

Principle 1. Appoint a growth manager as DGM: promotes new business creation

Corporate executives pursuing the small-is-beautiful philosophy appoint a growth manager as DGM, and this promotes new business creation. AMP president Jim McGuire said the company typically selected a growth manager, but a turnaround manager was appointed when necessary:

Looking at the universe, I agree with the notion that different managers are best suited to different stages of the business life-cycle. Within our own company, we probably don't have many situations where we want to assign somebody to be a good caretaker or a good closeout guy. We're almost always looking for somebody who can manage the growth aspect of it ... On top of the general criteria, we tend to look at specifically what attributes would be important in *that* division manager's role, and who best possesses those attributes. Once in a while we have things that border on the turnaround situation. But that's the exception here. Generally, when we're confronted with that kind of thing, we tend to treat it a little differently. We rely on the ability of our staff people to help significantly in a turnaround area. Sometimes, we will move some people in at the level below the DGM. If we've got big manufacturing problems, we'll be more apt to put a more highly seasoned, proven manufacturing manager into that kind of a trouble spot.

DGM Clay Smith of AMP Sigcom illustrated how the manager's fit with the needs of the division played a role in managerial appointments:

I think the nature of the business dictates, too, what type of individual is needed. Because of the technology of our products, the performance characteristics and the applications, it requires more of an engineering background in this division. A manufacturing background would be more appropriate for one of our high tonnage divisions.

Principle 2. Autonomy for the DGM: helps new business creation

Corporate executives pursuing the small-is-beautiful corporate philosophy give the DGM a great deal of operating autonomy to run the business, and this facilitates new business creation in the division. DGM Buddy March of 3M Micrographics commented on the autonomy he enjoyed and how it allowed him to venture forth on a regular basis:

I don't have to go upstairs to get approval to start a new product program. Christ, if they had to review every new program that starts – there's dozens of them every month in this company. For acquisitions you always need corporate approval, no matter what size the acquisition is. For capital, I need to go up. But many of the programs don't need capital to get started. So they get started. My capital approval limit of one million dollars applies to one particular project. Now, we can play the game of splitting it up [chuckles] and we do that sometimes. Split 'em up into two and bring each one in under a million dollars. It still shows up in the annual budget, of course.

The marketing agreement I made with Tanaka [for the printer] didn't require any corporate approval because a general manager can sign it. Now, when I signed the first purchase order to buy those 200 units from Tanaka at $15,000 each [$3 million in total], we had to pay for half the order up-front so the immediate exposure was $1.5 million. But I could sign it without any corporate approval because all the up-front money went into inventory, not fixed assets. If the capital is in inventory, you don't need any corporate approval. It's just amazing; general managers here [in 3M] have more freedom than group vice presidents in many companies. We can sign for millions of dollars.

Buddy March recalled that both 3M and Xerox had wanted to acquire Filmsort, the company that he previously headed up. March said he chose 3M because of the autonomy the company gave to its DGMs, and he attributed the success of 3M Micrographics in part to the discretion he enjoyed as DGM. "I think 3M's environment of fostering and helping and planning these little embryo businesses without a lot of interference has been truly a blessing," he said. "Because I don't think I'd have gotten the same environment at Xerox to do the same thing. I really don't." Ray Thorngate also commented on his wide operating autonomy as DGM of 3M Engineering Products:

I'm finding that being a general manager is kind of a lonely operation. I'm discovering that the buck sort of stops here. That's the reason why maybe 3M retained a lot of people with entrepreneurial attitudes, because the guy who ran the business just kind of ran the business. You don't get a lot of second guessing by corporate staff – the corporate controller, the corporate technical people. Not in running the routine business. Now if you want to go out and acquire something, or you want to make a major investment and therefore you need a major concession in profits – these kinds of things bring that out.

Greater autonomy is not a license to hide   Corporate executives pursuing the small-is-beautiful philosophy give the DGM a great deal of operating autonomy because they trust him. But this does not mean that he can undertake new business initiatives without keeping the executives fully informed. The DGM has a great deal of freedom to explore new ideas, bootleg projects, and launch new initiatives without prior corporate approval. But these initiatives must be visible[3] to corporate executives when these projects reach a certain size, or have incurred a certain level of cumulative expenditure. As AMP's corporate VP of technology, George Sweitzer, said,

The divisions are free to pursue any avenue they wish, however small the initial business may be. When a program reaches $50,000 in expenditure, then it is reviewed in our project accounting system until it reaches profitable sales and is part of the ongoing business or is discontinued.

Principle 3. No specific marching orders for the DGM: permits new business creation

Corporate executives pursuing the small-is-beautiful philosophy do not give specific marching orders to the DGM, and this permits him to engage in new business creation unfettered by corporate dogma. Everyone understands that the game is short-term profitability *and* long-term growth, and the DGM is expected to make the trade-offs necessary to meet both of these demanding expectations.[4]

Corporate executives at AMP communicated their high performance expectations using what they referred to as "informal rules." For example,

40 percent gross margin (for short-term results) and 15 percent real growth every year (for long-term growth). Called "bogies," the analogous performance expectations at 3M were pre-tax profit equal to 20 percent of sales and 10 percent real growth every year. The division could not achieve short-term results by simply cutting back on investments, such as for research and development, because this would hurt long-term performance.[5] This encouraged the division to provide a consistent emphasis on new business creation.

Corporate executives in AMP and 3M used other informal rules and bogies to encourage new business creation. At AMP, one informal rule was that 9 percent of sales had to be invested in RD&E (research, development & engineering) each year, roughly *three times* the industry average. If an AMP division cut back on RD&E too sharply, the DGM was asked to explain why the division was so far from the norm. At 3M, a well-known bogey was that at least 20 percent of sales had to come from new products developed within the past five years. If a division was below this, corporate executives wanted to know why, and what was being done about it.

The informal rules, or bogies, varied somewhat from one division to another, based on industry and competitive realities. For example, DGM Buddy March of 3M Micrographics said he was given relief on the profit bogey because the division was growing faster than the industry average:

I wasn't growing at 10 percent; I was growing at 25 to 30 percent. Our growth rate forgave us some of our profit misses, because they [corporate executives] realized that we were investing in growth for the future. In a sense, when they bought the budget, they bought my lower profits on a year-by-year basis. But it wasn't a formal, explicit kind of thing where I went to them and said, "Hey, for the next five years, I'm gonna miss [the corporate bogey of 20 percent pre-tax profit] by 1 to 2 percent." It wasn't that kind of thing.

DGM Ray Thorngate of 3M Engineering Products, which served the 35mm market for engineering drawing and drafting applications, summarized how corporate expectations for growth encouraged new business creation:

Well, the corporate executives in 3M expect that you will grow at least 10 percent a year. And the degree to which you meet their expectations is proportional to the degree to which you get to run your own business. So it is very prudent to forecast that you're going to grow somewhere between 12 and 13 percent. Now, if the market is growing at a rate that allows you to do more, then you can forecast 15, 20, 25 percent growth. But when you're in a market such as Engineering Micrographics, where they're forecasting 8 to 10 percent growth, then forecasting 12 percent or thereabouts means figuring out what assets you've got that are gonna allow you to grow faster than the industry average. That means new products. Or acquisitions.

Avoiding the "managed growth" trap   GVP Mike Walker of AMP talked about the "managed growth" trap that a DGM must avoid:

The corporate executives' philosophy is the same as mine is – you try to do your best to plan the dang thing, but if you got an opportunity and you need more money then, damn it, you come to us and spend it. That's why I don't like the term "managed growth." That says, somebody set a cozy, what's a good enough growth level and you manage to that growth level. I don't believe in that. I believe that you've got to manage your growth in relation to what your market conditions are. We've got large operating divisions that are growing 55 percent per year. And we've got others that are growing 10 or 12 percent per year. Not managed growth, but growing and keeping ahead of the demands of the marketplace. Gaining market share, maintaining market share and all that. But I got to tell you there are people who will sit there and say, "What the heck's the company crying for? I'm growing 16 percent, that's all they want." That isn't all they want. What they want you to do is to maintain a strong position in the marketplace. Don't give an inch.

Principle 4. Review and control the division to test the DGM's business convictions: avoids "fake entrepreneurship"

Corporate executives pursuing the small-is-beautiful corporate philosophy challenge the thinking of the DGM in both their periodic reviews of the division's performance and in their *ad hoc* reviews of specific new initiatives. By testing the DGM's business convictions, these corporate executives deter "fake entrepreneurship" in which people go through the motions without any real commitment to the opportunities being pursued.

Periodic corporate reviews   Buddy March of 3M Micrographics indicated how the corporate executives challenged the DGM's thinking during the annual corporate reviews:

Each December, we have to give a review in front of the operating committee [the top corporate executives] of the company. You take along your team. That whole review is in writing, and they read it before the meeting. They use the controllers as a second channel of information. The technical auditing team also gives a review to the top people. So that's another channel of information . . . In that setting, they're more listening. They're asking questions about it, probing – this type of thing.

For example, I've seen forecasts where you've been running, let's say, 95 percent of forecast all year. Starting January 1 of the next year, all of a sudden you're gonna be making these forecasts. A very common question is, "What's gonna change in December?" Because history will tell you that things don't change that way, they change gradually. Because even if you're laying off a lot of people, it takes severance pay and a lot of other expenses for quite a while before you get the effect of laying people off... They're not telling you what to do; they are just challenging you.

There is nobody here that tells a general manager piece by piece what he should do or can't do. I've never heard them say, "You will." Never heard them say, "We want you to cut out this program." They may make it so uncomfortable for you that you finally do it... If the division is going along fine and no problems and so forth, that's the last you'll hear about it, until next year. But if you're in trouble – and there are always some divisions that are struggling with the forecast, profits and what have you – they call special reviews; we call them "selected opportunity reviews." I've been up more than once for Com, and we spent hours just on Com.

Ad hoc reviews[6]   The "selected opportunity reviews" conducted by 3M corporate executives were *ad hoc* reviews for new initiatives that had lost a lot of money, or were expected to lose a lot of money. Wim Williams, division controller of 3M Micrographics, indicated the selection criteria: "Programs that have lost more than $300,000 in the most recent year, or projected to lose more than $300,000 in the upcoming year are put on the selected opportunity list. Once on the list, programs remain on the list till they make a profit."[7]

Corporate executives invited other people within 3M whose knowledge of the technology, the market, or other areas could be helpful to provide their input. DGM Buddy March was challenged with questions such as these on Com over the years: "You said last time that the volume this year will be x million dollars – what went wrong?" "Why are you so sure this will be a viable business long term?" "Shouldn't manufacturing costs be going *down* if you made these changes? Why are they going *up*?" What was noteworthy was the absence of edicts from corporate executives to drop a particular program.

The content and tone of the questions the corporate executives asked indicated that they were trying to get the DGM and others in the division to consider all the evidence as objectively as possible. This was to ensure that these people remained committed to the opportunity for *business* reasons rather than because of personal ego or from a sense of loyalty to those who had invested their time and effort in the new initiative.[8]

Principle 5. Let the DGM make the decisions concerning specific new business initiatives: facilitates commitment to new business creation

All corporate executives must address one fundamental question: when there are disagreements – which are common in new business creation given the inherent uncertainties – whose instincts and convictions should carry the day? Corporate executives pursuing the small-is-beautiful philosophy periodically question the DGM about the progress of the division's initiatives, whether in brief exchanges in the hallways and in the elevators, or more formally in the periodic and *ad hoc* reviews. But he is the corporate entrepreneur, and the corporate executives are ultimately betting on *his* judgments and convictions rather than on their own.

If the corporate executives in AMP and 3M were really opposed to a particular program, they would question the DGM more frequently and at greater length, and the questions would become rhetorical: "Don't you think this business is too risky for us?" "Aren't we likely to miss the market window if your product is only on the drawing board?" But almost never was the DGM told to drop a particular program. As DGM Mike Walker of AMP Sigcom pointed out,

All they [the GVP and higher-ups] do is ask a lot of questions, but they never tell you not to start something or to drop something you have already started. You have to prepare well to answer their questions, and they are pretty insightful, but you don't need their approval. They questioned me a lot on the Commercial RF and the SMA F-Connector initiatives, but they never said "Yes, do it," or "No, don't do it." At the end it was always "Thanks, Mike. We appreciate it." At first I was incredulous, said to myself, "Is that all?" Pretty soon I realized it was up to me. I went ahead. I didn't need my GVP's approval on specific initiatives, but I did need profit forgiveness (equal to 5 percent of operating margin for two years) because of the large number of initiatives I was launching at one time. All he [Walker's boss, the GVP] could have done was deny me that 5 percent.

Only in very rare cases do the corporate executives pursuing the small-is-beautiful philosophy ask a DGM to drop a specific program. Even then, it is done not because they are trying to second-guess the DGM on a specific initiative but because they have made a more fundamental corporate strategy decision that rules it out. Examples are decisions driven by a concern about excessive liability exposure in certain industries, and decisions concerning the character of the corporation, e.g. "Are we a components company or are we a systems company?" As president Jim McGuire of AMP said,

I can recall only three instances when we *told* a DGM to drop a particular program. In two of these cases we had several special reviews before we finally told the DGM we were getting out. But even here, it was not the specific initiatives that were at issue. We just wanted to get out of that particular industry segment because the company's product liability exposure there was higher than we were willing to risk.

Mike Walker gave this account of how he had championed the Selective Signaling System for two and a half years when he was a new product manager in the Datacom division earlier in his career, and why AMP corporate executives canceled it at literally the last moment:

The Selective Signaling System was a big program for which I had field trials going on in California. The PUC [Public Utility Commission] had granted us the experimental tariff. The field trials were complete. The test reports were accepted. I was about to sign the first contract in the customer's office in California when I received a call from Patrick Ames, my DGM, telling me not to sign the contract because top management had just canceled the program. Right there in the customer's office I was told at literally the last moment! I sat down with Ames after I returned and I asked, "What are the reasons – I don't have all of them – why the program was canceled?" And he said, "You're free to talk to Jack Brimmer [the CEO] about it."

So I went in to see Jack and I told him we had this order coming in and all that, and he looked at me, and he said "Mike, I understand all that, but, we also have to add capacity if we go ahead with your project." And he said, "The way the economy is turning, we don't know how bad it's going to be, and we can't make that decision now. Furthermore, we've had to make some quick decisions on what kind of a company AMP really wants to be, and we've decided that the systems business is really not our game. We want to stay in the component business."[9] And I said, "Well, gosh, you guys never told me that." And he says, "Look, we know. And there's no reflection on what you and your team did. You did a heck of a job for us, for which we thank you, but, the decision is made. You're going to have to adjust to that and shape your strategies accordingly."

Such exceptional cases aside, AMP corporate executives let the DGM make the final decision on a specific initiative, as president Jim McGuire emphasized:

The purpose of the planning meetings is to give the DGM some exposure, give him a chance to tell us all the great things his division has been doing. It gives us a chance to become more knowledgeable about him and his business. We ask questions to try to help. Sometimes we have a piece of information or prior experience that might help the division. Other times our questions may help the division gain some perspective, some objectivity. But we don't tell the DGM what to do, because it is his show. Our philosophy is that we are betting on the manager, not on our own analysis of his business. In some cases we don't know enough about his business to sit in judgment on the specifics of a particular initiative. Where we do have some opinions, our inclination is still to allow the DGM to exercise his own judgment.[10]

Corporate executives pursuing the small-is-beautiful philosophy can use this approach because they have many irons in the fire – for example, about twenty divisions in AMP, and fifty in 3M, and several initiatives in each division. These corporate executives in AMP and 3M had learned from experience that with the right business, the right managers, and the right new business creation process, 30 to 40 percent of the initiatives that made it to the market would eventually succeed.

The limitations of the small-is-beautiful corporate philosophy

There are two limitations of the small-is-beautiful philosophy. One is the need for an underlying corporate capability to build on. Without it, the small-is-beautiful philosophy can yield a number of unrelated thrusts that lack critical mass and competitive advantage.[11] President Jim Reilly of Monsanto described this potential problem:

3M has a million cockamamie units. A guy saw a patent; a guy walks in off the street. That's how all those things get started at 3M. That's what I mean by cockamamies. People say, "Gee, if you just had those little entrepreneurial boutiques like 3M, you'd make it." But you look at 3M, which is always held up as the classic, and almost everything they do of substance flows from the ability to work with a common technology base. When they move very far away from that they fall right on their ass. I have competed with them in Agricultural Products and in Astroturf and they don't know what the hell they're doing. But they are good at running small businesses provided they have a common technology link.

Outside observers enamored with 3M's long track record of successful new business creation had not fully grasped this limitation of the small-is-beautiful corporate philosophy.

Another limitation results from the dictum of "every tub on its own bottom," meaning each division has to generate the cash flow needed for its new initiatives and other requirements. The financial risk to the corporation is thereby contained, but the flip side is that opportunities that are beyond the ambition and/or capabilities of the division, but well within the company's reach, are missed.[12] As DGM Ray Thorngate of 3M Engineering Products pointed out, "One of the issues we face is that, to get into these big markets such as Engineering CAD [computer-aided design], you couldn't possibly do it with your own resources."

Summary

The small-is-beautiful corporate philosophy assumes that the division, not corporate headquarters, is the primary center for corporate entrepreneurship. Corporate executives set high performance expectations for the division – both for short-term results *and* for long-term growth – and give the DGM a great deal of autonomy with no specific marching orders on how to meet or exceed these corporate expectations.

The DGM cannot deliver the demanding results expected in the short term by simply cutting back on investments, such as for research and development, because this will hurt long-term growth. This encourages the DGM to place a consistent emphasis on new business creation. The small-is-beautiful corporate philosophy also limits the financial risk to the corporation by requiring the division to self-finance its new initiatives.

In their periodic reviews of the division's performance, as well as in their *ad hoc* reviews of specific new initiatives, corporate executives challenge the thinking of the DGM but do not tell him what to do. Because the DGM is seen as the real corporate entrepreneur, these corporate executives are betting on his business convictions and judgments, rather than on their own.

The small-is-beautiful corporate philosophy has two limitations. First, it can lead the company in too many different directions without critical mass or competitive advantage. Second, it is not well suited to the pursuit of big, attractive opportunities that are beyond the ambition and/or capabilities of the division.

9   New business creation challenges for corporate executives

This chapter examines how the way in which the corporate executives deal with various challenges influences new business creation (Table 9.1).

It is difficult to pursue the bigger-is-better and the small-is-beautiful corporate philosophies *simultaneously* because of the fundamental difference in the scale of thinking, the duration of time, and the amount of resources needed to pursue bigger versus smaller opportunities. But with the right management approach it can be done.

How to successfully pursue the bigger-is-better *and* the small-is-beautiful corporate philosophies *simultaneously*

The challenge for corporate executives

With the small-is-beautiful corporate philosophy, the number of small wins needed to maintain the historical rate of corporate growth rises as the company grows. To take a very simple example, assume that a corporation needs to grow 10 percent from its new initiatives each year, and that a successful new initiative brings in on average $10 million in annual revenue. If the company's revenue is $100 million, it needs just one successful initiative ("win"), at $1 billion in revenue the company needs ten wins, and at $10 billion it needs a hundred wins.

For years 3M had been the model of the small-is-beautiful corporate philosophy for other companies, including AMP. But with more than $6 billion in revenue, 3M was experiencing increasing difficulty in securing the required number of wins each year with the small-is-beautiful corporate philosophy.[1] (AMP, with $1.5 billion in revenue when this study ended, had not yet encountered this challenge.) The "uninhabited" markets that the legendary CEO William McKnight wanted 3M to pursue were becoming inhabited, and crowded, as the company became very large. Ralph West, who had grown the 3M Imaging Products initiative into a department and then into a division and had become its DGM, commented on the problem:

Table 9.1. *How the way in which corporate executives deal with various challenges influences new business creation*

Hypothesis	Factor	Influence on new business creation
9.1	Successful simultaneous pursuit of the bigger-is-better and the small-is-beautiful corporate philosophies	+
9.2	Successful management of the volatility of new business	+
9.3	Avoidance of biased corporate perceptions concerning opportunities in the division	+
9.4	The right balance between clarity and ambiguity in the division's charter	+
9.5	Avoidance of a hidden corporate agenda for the division	+
9.6	Avoidance of too rapid a movement of managers (keep the DGM in place long enough to learn the business and contribute)	+

I've seen a change in 3M. While we still have entrepreneurial projects, we're a bit slower now to create them. One of the standards applied is that we don't really want to create a separate business or even a project unless it can grow to a division. And you have to find a new charter that would allow yourself a fifty or a hundred million dollar business in a market or a product line not covered by an existing division. We do now have fifty divisions, so among those they cover the market and the opportunities pretty well. So it gets a little harder to find something separate that might become a division.

3M's response to the challenge

A year before this study ended, 3M was reorganized. The company was split into four business sectors to create four "baby 3Ms" in an attempt to rekindle growth with the small-is-beautiful philosophy. Strategic planning, business life-cycle concepts, and portfolio theory for resource allocation were also introduced to try to address some of the limitations of the small-is-beautiful philosophy, and also to capture some of the advantages of the bigger-is-better philosophy. GVP Buddy March of 3M Business Products Group gave part of the reasoning:

I think John [MacNeil, CEO] felt that we were not organized enough, and were not using enough strategic planning, to grow from 6 or 7 billion in revenue to 30 billion and beyond. And he's been a great admirer of GE, which went into sectors quite early. So he wanted four presidents, if you will, or sector EVPs, so that his own operating committee wouldn't have so much stuff coming up to it.

Bill Lieberman, marketing director of the Engineering Products division, provided a complementary perspective:

The traditional 3M career path of project manager to department manager to division manager and on up to the top is becoming less common because we haven't developed enough innovative businesses lately. Is it a consequence of our size? Have we lost some of our entrepreneurial thrust? I don't know, but I think the break-up of the company into sectors is an attempt to regain some of that old spirit.

Manufacturing director Clay Renault of 3M Micrographics added this: "John [MacNeil, CEO] went to strategic planning because we were wiped out by the Japanese in magnetic recording [audio and video tapes]. We didn't have critical mass, didn't deploy sufficient resources." The 3M corporate reorganization attempted to address the resource limitation of "every tub on its own bottom" by charging the EVP with the responsibility of investing in opportunities that were beyond the ambition or capabilities of the division. GVP Buddy March offered this example:

The 3M Business Communications division in my group convinced us and Hubble [EVP and sector head] that they had to acquire Imagetel even though they did not have the resources to buy it. It will be supported by the sector. So we will encourage entrepreneurship that requires resources in excess of what the division can afford.

Another example was a new business opportunity that cut across the charters of two divisions that GVP March and his boss EVP Hubble were thinking of pursuing with a special inter-divisional task force.[2]

The concerns with 3M's approach

Not enough time had passed to judge the effectiveness of 3M's approach for getting the best of both worlds – small-is-beautiful and bigger-is-better – when this study ended, but four major issues had surfaced: (1) how to embrace strategic planning without stifling corporate entrepreneurship; (2) how to move from growth managers to business life-cycle managers; (3) how to acquire the resources needed for corporate executives to pursue bigger opportunities without squeezing the divisions dry of the autonomy and resources they needed to pursue smaller opportunities; and (4) how to ensure that corporate executives remained knowledgeable about the corporation's diverse businesses as the company became even bigger.

How to embrace strategic planning without killing corporate entrepreneurship[3]   Jill Pringle, 3M corporate director for technology planning, felt that strategic planning was counter to the 3M culture: "I think it can be good for mature businesses. We define mature as growing slower than 15 percent per year. But strategic planning is counter-culture to the niche mentality of 3M." Although he saw its benefits, DGM Ray Thorngate of 3M Engineering Products was also concerned that the new emphasis on strategic planning could hurt the company's entrepreneurial spirit:

Don't get me wrong; I think strategic planning can have some positive effects. In one part of your approach to things, you do a lot of creative thinking. But at some point in time, if you're ever gonna get anything done, you've got to back off and start doing some analytical thinking too. And I think strategic planning is highly useful in making sure that you've gone through and understood the background in which you have to operate. But the strategic planning requirements – a lot of financial analysis before you determine whether you've got anything – make it difficult to pursue the undiscovered need, what [legendary CEO] McKnight used to call an uninhabited market. It's pretty hard to do a financial analysis in the very early stages of it, other than to recognize it and to move in on it as quickly as possible.

GVP Buddy March of 3M Business Products Group also saw the benefits of strategic planning and was concerned about its adverse impact:

Strategic planning has helped us tremendously in those selective opportunities we see that do not strategically fit what we're trying to do in the division. We have moved some of these selected opportunities from one division to another because it fits their strategic plans and strategic profile much better . . . We have never had strategic planning – formally. You're always doing strategic thinking. We're formally reviewing strategic plans for the first time – we're only two years into it. But we're scared stiff. And I mean all of the top management. How are we going to do that without screwing up the entrepreneurship of this company? [CEO] MacNeil will tell you that we're gonna have to alter strategic planning from the pure theories to adjust to 3M. And we're still keeping our new product innovations and our pressure on new products and all the rest of it. Our bogies for performance – 10 percent growth and 20 percent pre-tax profit margins – haven't changed either.

How to transform DGMs from growth managers to business life-cycle managers   DGM Ray Thorngate of 3M Engineering Products felt frustrated by the notion of fitting the manager to the stage of the business life-cycle:

[CEO] MacNeil is saying we need different managers for different situations. He has been on videotape to talk about strategic planning and business life-cycle stages – embryo, growth, harvest, and exit. I buy that scheme, but I don't know any 3M managers who I would call harvesters or exiters . . . Since I've been with this division, in my opinion we've been in the harvesting mode. I don't think I have the temperament for harvesting. So they made a mistake when they appointed me DGM [laughter]. In fact, I feel very frustrated.

How to secure the resources needed to pursue bigger opportunities without squeezing the divisions dry of the resources and autonomy they need to pursue smaller opportunities 3M introduced port-folio theory for allocating resources across and within sectors with the intention of feeding the businesses that the corporate executives believed had growth potential, and starving the others. This was naturally re-sented by the DGMs of the divisions being starved, as well as by those whose divisions showed promise but happened to be in a troubled group or sector. For example, the 3M Engineering Products division, and the Micrographics division from which it was split off, were both performing around the corporate norms (real growth of 10 percent per year and pre-tax profit equal to 20 percent of sales), but were being starved of needed capital because they were part of the bleeding Business Products group. As DGM Ray Thorngate of 3M Engineering Products complained,

We've got so many problems in this sector. And the management [Alex Hubble, EVP] has made a decision that the major investment is gonna be in memory and optical technologies. Therefore, management has assigned, by virtue of that, roles in the sector. Electrical Products Group is the cash generator. The only thing they're asking of our group [Business Products, with Buddy March now the GVP] is to stop losing money [chuckling] and get profits up, at least to where we're not a drag on the sector. Now, there's a problem with that. We've got two major divisions in Business Products Group [Magnetic Recording – audio and video tapes – and Copying Products], whose sales dwarf Micrographics, that are making significantly sub-par profits – in fact they're losing money in some lines. And, in my opinion, we [Micrographics] are being harvested to keep those afloat. We're throwing good money after bad. And on the investments be-ing made in the memory and optical technologies, the concern, at least at the technical levels where I talk with some of my peers, has been, "Are we going to be at a competitive disadvantage as we are in magnetic recording, by only be-ing involved in the supplies, and not in the systems, in the hardware and in the devices?"

How to ensure that corporate executives remain knowledgeable about the company's businesses as the corporation grows even larger As 3M became larger and more complex, it was harder for corporate exec-utives to have a sufficiently deep understanding of the company's busi-nesses. They began to rely more on the financial numbers for guidance and control, as DGM Ray Thorngate lamented:

If you listened to McKnight [3M's legendary CEO], he always felt it was im-portant to have management that understood the business. But because of our growth, the company is now so large that we *de facto* have no chance but to run the company by the financial numbers. Jordan [CEO MacNeil's predecessor] was probably the last CEO to understand all the businesses. Today, no one in corporate top management really understands all our businesses.

Buddy March agreed partly with Ray Thorngate, but he was more optimistic about the ability of 3M's top executives to have a deep enough understanding of the businesses:

Knowledge of the business *is* important. Hubble [EVP] does get out in the field; he is one of the better ones. One other EVP knows his businesses well. The other two EVPs don't know their businesses that well but they are learning. John [MacNeil, CEO] and the EVPs really work at learning the businesses. So far, we have not gone outside for top talent.

A recipe for success[4]

Corporate executives who want the best of both worlds – the successful simultaneous pursuit of the small-is-beautiful *and* the bigger-is-better corporate philosophies – must take three key actions: (1) marshal the resources necessary to pursue the bigger opportunities without squeezing the divisions dry of the resources and autonomy they need to pursue the smaller opportunities; (2) replace strategic planning with an ongoing multi-level strategic dialog to ensure that the corporate executives remain knowledgeable about the company's businesses, and also to facilitate alignment and mutual reinforcement between entrepreneurship in the divisions and entrepreneurship at corporate headquarters; and (3) encourage and develop both "good times" managers and "hard times" managers without branding them as being one or the other.

Pursue bigger opportunities without squeezing the divisions dry of the resources and autonomy they need to pursue smaller opportunities   To pursue dual entrepreneurship successfully, that is, to ignite two engines of entrepreneurship, one at headquarters and the other in the divisions, corporate executives must demonstrate a deep commitment to the philosophy that the corporate executives *and* the DGMs need appropriate autonomy, resources, and controls to be effective corporate entrepreneurs.

Corporate executives must learn to follow the principles of the small-is-beautiful philosophy (Chapter 8) in managing the divisions. Some of the resources needed to pursue bigger opportunities may be obtained from the divisions – using the methodology successfully used for "quarterly giving" (Chapter 6) – by asking for an "annual giving" that does not squeeze the divisions dry,[5] does not tell the DGMs how to run their businesses based on portfolio theory and resource allocation concepts, does not second-guess the divisions on their specific new business initiatives, and keeps the DGMs in place long enough for them to deliver both consistent short-term results *and* long-term growth.

Who will provide guidance, review, and control for the corporate executives themselves, the real entrepreneurs for the company's big opportunities? The corporate board of directors must do it for them, just as the corporate executives must do it for the DGMs. This is currently not being done in most companies.

Replace strategic planning with an ongoing multi-level strategic dialog   The ills of strategic planning as practiced in the 1970s and the 1980s are well documented.[6] The current practice is to have a lean corporate planning staff to provide information and analysis for both corporate executives and division managers. These senior line managers are the ones who are responsible for crafting and implementing the corporate and business strategies.

But more than this is required for the successful simultaneous pursuit of the small-is-beautiful and the bigger-is-better corporate philosophies. First, corporate executives must have a sufficiently deep understanding of the company's businesses as the corporation grows. Second, the big new business opportunities being pursued by the corporate executives and the smaller ones being pursued by the DGMs must align with, and reinforce, each other. An ongoing multi-level[7] strategic dialog, involving appropriate corporate executives and division managers from across the corporation, is needed to facilitate this process.[8]

Encourage and develop both "good times" and "hard times" managers without labeling them   "Good times" managers are needed at the corporate and division levels to successfully pursue both large and small opportunities. "Hard times" managers are also needed to rescue businesses in trouble and restore others in maturity or decline. Although people tend to be one type of manager or the other, it does not pay to "brand" managers any more than it makes sense explicitly to label businesses as "growth" or "mature" businesses. Branding businesses or people – as "good times" managers and "hard times" managers – creates a self-fulfilling prophecy. It also kills creativity by categorizing a person or a business as fixed rather than flexible.

Anticipate and manage the volatility of new business

AMP Sigcom and 3M Micrographics – which had more experience and better overall records of new business creation – were *no better* than Monsanto Fab Products and Xerox OPD at delivering the forecasted sales and profits for new business.[9] *All four* divisions missed their new business forecasts by wide margins. This is not a surprise considering the high levels of technical, product, and market uncertainty new business must endure. Top managers who fail to anticipate and make allowance for the resulting higher volatility of results end up derailing new business.

More than 80 percent of AMP Sigcom's revenue, more than 90 percent of 3M Micrographics' revenue, and nearly all the revenue of Monsanto Fab Products, came from existing business. So each of these divisions had a large base of more stable business with which to absorb the volatility of their new business and still deliver their *division's* forecasted results. By contrast, only 50 percent of Xerox OPD's revenue came from relatively predictable existing business, so this division could not absorb the volatility of its relatively large base of new business. OPD's results were $100 million below the profit plan for Gibbons' second full year as DGM and $150 million below plan for his third year. Xerox corporate executives could no longer support Gibbons, and he left.

The Xerox corporate executives were apparently judging OPD's new business by the same yardsticks they used for their existing businesses, where results 5 to 10 percent below the profit plan were flagged for attention. But AMP and 3M – companies with long, successful track records in new business creation – experienced deviations of 100 percent or even more on their sales and profit plans for new business. If the Xerox corporate executives had known this, they might have expected OPD's planned $150 million in new business to be off plan by $150 million or more!

Unfortunately, Xerox corporate executives apparently did not anticipate this degree of volatility for OPD's new business and make sufficient allowance for it.[10] The irony was that at least one other Xerox division was reported to have experienced similar losses at the time, but, because these losses had been *forecasted* by the division and approved at the corporate level in advance, neither the division nor the DGM was said to have been adversely affected. However, Gibbons felt that if he had forecasted big losses he would not have been given the resources he needed to pursue his ambitious new business creation agenda.[11]

Avoid biased corporate perceptions concerning opportunities in the division

Corporate executives previously "burned" by a business opportunity or those unfamiliar with the product, market, or technology will perceive the opportunity as unattractive; they should recognize this bias and avoid it.

"We got burned"

Corporate executives who associate a new business opportunity with a bad prior experience will oppose it.[12] DGM Buddy March of 3M Micrographics said a senior corporate executive had opposed the division's licensing agreement for printers from the Japanese company Tanaka because he had been "burned" by similar deals with Sumo Electronics and with Takeda, both Japanese companies:

I don't think he ever thought he had exclusive distribution [for the US market]. But he thought he had an understanding that we'd get our machines at the same time that Takeda USA and Sumo USA got them. And the facts are, we'd get ours later. In fact, the Takeda selling program at one time was that, "Gee, I'm glad you're trying out a 3M machine. And if you'll notice, we're the manufacturer on that machine. But that's last year's model. Let us show you this year's model, with the newly lowered price!" We were going through dealers and Sumo was going directly [to the customer] – about a thousand-dollar difference.

Ray Thorngate agreed with Buddy March that the 3M corporate executive who was responsible for the division that made these deals felt burned by the Japanese. But Thorngate, who was then a technical manager in that division, felt it was the arrogance of the marketing people that led to the debacle:

Takeda didn't screw 3M so much as 3M wasn't astute in the negotiations. The guys in that division had a big ego. "No one is better than us." "We have a hell of a marketing organization." "We can run circles around Takeda in the US." They knew they had a non-exclusive agreement. They just didn't think Takeda was any match for them in the US market.

"What you see depends on where you stand"[13]

Executives who are not familiar with the technology, product, or market for a new business opportunity are likely to see it as less attractive than those who are familiar with it.[14] Stu Little, VP and GM of the Systems SBU of Xerox OPD, felt this was one of the main reasons why many Xerox corporate executives viewed the potential of office automation in general, and the Star professional workstation in particular, as far less attractive than did the champions within OPD:

At the dawn of the computer industry, Univac, of course, held all the cards in mainframe computing. But they thought that there was only a market for a hundred. And so IBM was able to make a real business out of that, and Univac, as they say, "snatched defeat from the jaws of victory." IBM, on the other hand, had the first opportunity to go into mini-computers, but they did not see that market, so Digital Equipment Corporation created it. And both IBM and DEC could have created the PC market, but they didn't; Apple did.[15] I could make a list of ten other examples where that turns out to be true. What that says isn't about luck. It says that your view of the market is very much formed by the market that you're in contact with. It has to do with what you can see from where you stand. Xerox is a major force in copying. And so it's very difficult, from within that context, to look out and see that, "Gee, there is this really new and different market for Star [the new-to-the-world professional workstation being launched by OPD]." Not any different than what happened to Univac–IBM or IBM–DEC, or DEC–Apple.[16]

Within Xerox headquarters, the CEO and the president were familiar with the office automation opportunity and became its corporate champions. They perceived it as far more attractive than did other corporate executives and corporate staff. As CFO Rick Smale of Xerox OPD observed, "There was no unanimity about whether we should be in this business. The advocates were [CEO] Nash and [president] Wind. The adversaries were the copier business and the corporate staff groups who felt we could do better in copiers."

Balance clarity and ambiguity in the business charter for the division

Corporate executives facilitate new business creation by striking the right balance between clarity and ambiguity in their divisions' business charters. Without clarity, divisions pursue any opportunity they like, resulting in chaos. However, if the divisional charters are made *too* explicit, opportunities begin to fall between the cracks.

There was sufficient ambiguity in 3M's business charters to encourage divisional entrepreneurship, and corporate executives avoided dysfunctional overlap and inter-division warfare with the following clear policy: every new product had to be cleared by a corporate marketing committee, which tried to insure that there was a coordinated thrust, without turf battles,[17] for any opportunity being pursued by more than one division. DGM Buddy March of 3M Micrographics explained:

The purpose of the business charter is to keep the tape division, for example, from going into the micrographics business; or the micrographics division from going into the copying business. So we do have a charter that says, "You will swim in this lake – the micrographics lake." And every once in a while, some big arguments come up. I'll give you one example. We had three divisions that developed imitation leather. One of them was in our group, Business Products. The other two divisions were in the Tape group. Our group was making leather sole, heel, that type of thing. The tape divisions were selling to regular shoe manufacturers and golf shoe manufacturers. Tape had a little better way of making the shoe tops; they could breathe a little better. Anyway, corporate management would not make a decision as to whose charter this was going to be. The net result was that the whole goddamned program failed. It wasn't big enough or strong enough to really get in the marketplace to do it. That's what led to this approach – the corporate marketing committee. That committee doesn't care how much you spend in the laboratories or in market research. Before you put a new product on the marketplace, it has to have their approval.

A hidden corporate agenda for the division hampers new business creation

Monsanto corporate executives were unclear and secretive about their agenda for the Fab Products division, and this bred confusion and cynicism that hampered its new business creation. A few corporate executives felt the division potentially had good long-term opportunities, "if we make up our minds and pay attention to the division," as one of them said. The division's continuous injection molding (CIM) technology was viewed as attractive, and the next-generation Cycle Safe technology was also seen as having potential if FDA approval could be obtained.

However, other corporate executives felt that Monsanto Fab Products had too many plants, too many people, and a cyclical business with only modest growth and profit potential. President Jim Reilly, who had been the DGM of Monsanto Fab Products many years earlier, was skeptical about the opportunities in that division. His favorite phrase for describing its prospects was: "You can't make money melting plastic!"

Dan Stewart answered a fundamental question concerning the survival of the division: "Why has Fab Products been allowed to continue so long, if [president] Reilly feels so strongly against it? And the answer is, it is such a minor irritant and he's got a lot bigger fish to fry." If someone could have divested the entire Fab Products division for a fair price, that would have been done. President Reilly said he did not believe in selling a business below its value simply because it did not fit with the company's strategic direction:

There is that marvelous phrase you see in the business press – "They disposed of a business because it no longer met their strategic direction." But those cases are so rare, unless the business was losing money on a cash basis – then it no longer met the strategic direction! Very few people just shut a business down or sell it at an outrageously low price for strategic reasons. People sell profitable businesses all the time, but for value. Selling a business under value because it no longer meets your strategy is a bunch of nonsense. Nobody does that.[18]

Because it could not be sold at a fair price, the corporate agenda that had emerged for Monsanto Fab Products was to use it as a training ground for general managers. President Reilly explained why this made sense:

I ran that business back when I was thirty-two years old, and I consider it the best training that I ever had. Look at the product mix we had at that time. We had Fomecor, Plastic Film; we were in the siding business – installing and selling siding in the home. We were in the scrap plastic business, we were in the garden hose business, boat covers, car covers – a whole lot of consumer products. You can do what you want and nobody is telling you every five minutes what to do.

Bright young managers with potential were appointed division general managers to see what they could do with the fairly complex business of Fab Products. This corporate agenda was a well-kept secret because it could de-motivate the people in Fab Products if they found out that the division was being used as a management training ground. President Jim Reilly and the VP of corporate HR, Rick Bentley, revealed this corporate agenda to me after I made several attempts to find out what Monsanto was really trying to do with the division. As Reilly explained,

There are limits to how badly you can screw up that business. So we are protected on the downside. At the same time, we can test the upside potential of both the business and the DGM by seeing what he can do with it ... I wanted to get Stewart out of Agricultural Products, where he had been in marketing, to give him a different exposure. So I said, "What's the worst that can happen if Dan Stewart screwed up Fab Products *totally*?" I felt it was more valuable to learn about him, and develop him, than to squeeze a few more bottles out of that business. It is an ideal mix of businesses to try people out.

None of the other managers who participated in this study knew this for sure, but they suspected that Monsanto Fab Products was being used as a management training ground. Whatever its merits for this purpose, this hidden agenda, and the corporate ambivalence about the division, had a dampening effect on new business creation. It bred uncertainty about the corporate direction and cynicism about corporate motives.

Avoid too rapid a movement of managers

Musical chairs: why a rapid movement of managers occurs

There are three main reasons why a rapid movement of managers occurs. First, if there is a shortage of management talent, the best managers are constantly in demand to tackle bigger problems and opportunities. As soon as one business is in reasonably good shape, there is another that urgently needs their assistance. Second, rapid movement occurs because of the assumption that this helps to accelerate management development. Finally, rapid movement can feed on itself because managers start judging their success in part by how quickly they are moved to the next assignment.

Rick Bentley, VP of corporate HR, said the rapid movement of managers at Monsanto was driven by the corporation's need to train large numbers of them quickly. He said it was done with adequate seasoned supervision, and with necessary support for the businesses, so that the risks to the corporation were minimized.

We think people development is terribly important, but it is not our primary objective. Otherwise I'd be the CEO! Our primary objective is to run our businesses for the best results, without unnecessary risk. So the trick is to do both – manage our businesses with acceptable risk *and* develop our people ... We had no management strength when Steele took over as CEO. We were forced to move people quickly in order to develop them. It's useful to go back to school, and we encourage that. But people develop by doing, by having to feel the sweat of responsibility roll down their backs. We get our managers used to greater and greater responsibility, so they are not overwhelmed by it, by moving them around. [President] Reilly and others were developed in this way ...

We do our best to contain the risk to the business by using the "sandwich technique" – the manager being moved around is supervised by someone who won't allow a disaster, and also the team reporting to the manager is kept the same to provide continuity. Electronics is a big risk for us, so we have kept the management team in place there for six to seven years now. You see Costello moving, but we kept electronics with him. Fielding [EVP] is on top of Monsanto Agricultural Products [the corporate crown jewel] even though Stewart now has it [as managing director]. Reilly was on top of Monsanto Agricultural Products when Fielding first got it, just as Bartley stayed on top of it after Reilly first got it. We also ask ourselves, "What is the worst that can happen?" ...

Do we move our managers around too quickly? Were Reilly *et al.* tested long enough? Someone in my shoes is always concerned about these questions, because when movement is too fast you risk mis-assessing the manager's contribution. It is not always easy to assess who succeeded and who failed. We try not to overlook one question, though: "Did the manager try to do the right thing?" ... We did not try to slow down the movement of people like Reilly, because Steele felt strongly that we had an obligation to develop a strong management team, so that we would never have to go outside again to recruit a CEO ... You create your own Frankenstein if you slow the rate of movement down. People think it is a reflection on them. So it is not that easy. We had good people clogged up in the middle, and we needed massive movement to get them out. We let that happen.

Confirming Rick Bentley's concern about slowing down the rate of movement, Ian McVay made the following remark one year after he became DGM of Engineered Products: "I am in the same lap of the race as Stewart and Gossamer. They are perhaps half a lap ahead. If I don't move from this position in a couple of years, I'll feel I am falling behind."

How a rapid movement of DGMs hinders new business creation

A rapid movement of DGMs hinders new business creation because managers are not in place long enough to learn the business, let alone develop the depth of knowledge necessary to identify the really attractive opportunities and pursue them with conviction. As DGM Ian McVay of Monsanto Engineered Products said,

We probably would be better off as a company if we didn't have so much DGM movement. When I was in Plasticizers, I saw a changeover of five general managers in four years. When I was in D&P [Detergents & Phosphates], I was the sixth general manager in seven years. I come over here and I am the third general manager in five years at Fab Products ... I happen to think that my greatest contributions to this corporation could have been realized had they allowed me to stay in D&P. We had some research programs and were developing some new products that could have revolutionized the detergent supplier industry. But the corporation didn't see it that way.

Stewart was equally critical of the game of musical chairs for Monsanto managers. He attributed this to (CEO) Steele and Premier Associates, the external consultants that Steele had retained. They apparently believed the company-wide systems being put in place permitted the DGMs to be moved around like interchangeable parts, Stewart said.

The logic for moving us around is to give us exposure to different businesses. I don't know if Steele really believes it, but the way it was articulated was – "We will have consistent direction because we will have the same management style and we're going to have the same management systems," brought to us by these wonderful consultants, Premier Associates. And so now we have these clones that we can move from this business to that business, and they work on the long-range plans in place, and we don't miss a beat. And, of course, that just defies human nature. If I come into a job I'm going to look at it differently. And if all I do is carry out what the last guy had, you don't need me.

Managing director (GVP) Hal Courtney of Monsanto's Plastics & Resins (MP&R) group, which included Fab Products, felt that the rapid management movement created confusion. Courtney said president Jim Reilly did not see the rapid movement of managers as a problem, however:

In the ten years before I took over, there were thirteen changes in either the managing director position or a DGM position in MP&R. So the people are continuously confused. The average DGM tenure in Monsanto today is two to three years; it is too short. Rick Bentley [VP of corporate HR] thinks the high turnover in the GM ranks is a problem, but [president] Reilly doesn't think so. The EMC is aware of this situation, but Reilly doesn't see anything wrong with it. He thinks two years is plenty of time, because he was moved thirteen times in fourteen years during his rise to the top ... I feel differently. I feel I am in a learning mode for the first two years.

Alf Hummel, VP of corporate planning, agreed with Stewart, McVay, and Courtney that the rapid movement of managers in the years preceding this study in the early 1980s had hurt Monsanto, and he was outspoken in his criticism:

McVay should have been left in D&P; he could have helped D&P. It is a clear failure by senior management to place people strategically. We have a parade of GMs through Plasticizers, again being run as a training ground. We have had seven or eight GMs there in the last few years. The training ground thing has been overdone at Monsanto. You can't move people around that fast. Leave them there long enough so they can learn and contribute. But [CEO] Steele believes he did train all these people; that was one of his high priorities ... In my opinion, we have jeopardized some businesses by doing this. And I am not convinced that rapid movement is the way to develop managers.

Keep the DGM in place long enough to learn the business and contribute

The unanimous opinion of these four Monsanto senior managers is consistent with the research on personal and professional development – people grow when they are challenged and have sufficient time and opportunity to learn new skills.[19] Moving managers around too rapidly is not a good way to develop them, and it is certainly not a good way to promote new business creation.

The DGM should be kept in place at least three to four years in most cases. If there is a pressing need for his help elsewhere within the corporation, capable outsiders must be recruited for that purpose. If this will take too long, insiders with proven contributions should be promoted, even though they may not be fully ready.

There is a risk in hiring outsiders or promoting insiders ahead of schedule, but there is also a risk in moving the DGM out too soon, which is typically not given enough weight. One reason for this is the mystique of the "superstar" DGM who might leave if not moved quickly enough to a bigger or more important assignment. Another is a belief in the "savior" whose help is deemed indispensable to revitalize a business or to put out a fire.[20]

Corporate executives fall into these traps, pretending that they are making painful but necessary trade-offs. Instead, they should confront a DGM's veiled threats ("I can always go elsewhere!") or their own fears ("There is no one else who can do it!") with fortitude. *No one* is indispensable. The risks taken with unknown outsiders or unproven insiders are not necessarily greater, and they bring new skills and fresh perspectives that could benefit the company.[21]

Summary

It is very difficult to pursue the bigger-is-better and the small-is-beautiful corporate philosophies simultaneously because of the fundamental difference in the scale of thinking, the duration of time, and the amount of resources needed to pursue bigger versus smaller opportunities.

Successful simultaneous pursuit of bigger and smaller opportunities requires corporate executives to be the real entrepreneurs for the bigger opportunities while allowing the DGMs to do the same for the smaller opportunities. This is easier said than done for it requires a great deal of skill and discipline for corporate executives to marshal the necessary resources for pursuing the bigger opportunities without squeezing the divisions dry of the autonomy and resources they need to pursue the smaller opportunities. An ongoing multi-level strategic dialog must replace strategic planning in order to align and mutually reinforce entrepreneurship at corporate headquarters with entrepreneurship in the divisions.

Strange though it may seem, divisions with a long track record of successful new business creation are not better than others at achieving the projected sales and profits for new business. All divisions miss their new business sales and profit forecasts by wide margins; deviations of 100 percent from plan are not unusual. This is not a surprise if one considers the high levels of technical, product, and market uncertainty that new business must endure. Corporate executives without a great deal of experience in new business creation review and control new business expecting results to be within the tolerances used for existing business – for example, deviations within 5 or 10 percent of budgeted sales and profits. Such unrealistic expectations derail new business creation.

Corporate executives previously "burned" by an opportunity, or those unfamiliar with the product, market, or technology, tend to perceive the opportunity as unattractive. Those who strike the right balance between clarity and ambiguity in their business charter for the division facilitate new business creation; a hidden corporate agenda for the division stifles it by breeding confusion and cynicism.

A scarcity of management talent within the corporation, and the desire to develop seasoned managers quickly, results in too rapid a movement of DGMs with too short a period of time in place to learn the business, make a contribution, and grow professionally. New business creation suffers as a result. This must be avoided by bringing in capable outsiders and promoting promising insiders into DGM positions.

10   Guidance and coaching by the DGM's boss and support and challenge by the controllers

This chapter examines how the DGM's boss and the controllers influence new business creation (Table 10.1).

The DGM's boss (typically a GVP) has the difficult task of providing guidance and coaching for the DGM without this being perceived by the DGM as corporate interference. It is a tall order, particularly when the DGM is engaged in new business creation, because the inherent uncertainties make it impossible to be sure who is correct or what the right thing to do is.

Ineffective guidance and coaching by the DGM's boss

DGM Buddy March of 3M Micrographics said he would have benefited from guidance and coaching from his boss, particularly during his early years as DGM:

> I would have liked to have a GVP who was a leader, a patriarch, who kind of guides you through the tough waters. I think the GVP should be well enough rounded, having been a general manager and so forth, so that he can help his general managers where they are weak. I would have liked, I think, more counseling and coaching on negotiations. And I would have liked more encouragement for some of the things I wanted to do – sometimes I was a little nervous. I came up through the technical route. And it took me a long time to be comfortable with marketing and sales, because I basically learned on my own.

Guidance and coaching by the DGM's boss is ineffective if (1) the GVP does not have sufficient time and interest, or (2) sufficient knowledge of the business to guide and coach the DGM; (3) the GVP micromanages the DGM, or (4) either leaves the DGM alone or gives him specific instructions rather than guidance.

Insufficient time or interest

DGM Dan Stewart's boss, managing director (GVP) Hal Courtney of MP&R group, had little interest in Fab Products, or time for it,

Table 10.1. *How the DGM's boss and the controllers influence new business creation*

Hypothesis	Factor	Influence on new business creation
Ineffective guidance and coaching by the DGM's boss		
10.1	Insufficient time or interest	−
10.2	Inadequate knowledge of the business	−
10.3	Micromanagement of the DGM	−
10.4	Either leave the DGM alone or give him specific instructions rather than guidance	−
Effective guidance and coaching by the DGM's boss		
10.5	Supervise "good times" DGMs and "hard times" DGMs differently	+
Ineffective support and challenge by the controllers		
10.6	Not knowledgeable about the business	−
10.7	Changes the budget without consultation	−
10.8	Does not provide assistance	−
10.9	Only interested in information for reporting and control	−
Effective support and challenge by the controller		
10.10	Knowledgeable about the business	+
10.11	Provides assistance	+
10.12	Requests information and provides challenge without presenting these as edicts	+

because he had bigger divisions that needed his attention. As Courtney said,

MP&R is 1.2 billion. Fab is 200 million and a relatively stable piece of MP&R. It is not a swing business for us. Some of my businesses were losing as much money in a month as Fab could lose in an entire year! So it didn't get my attention. It comes down to the problem of relative scale, to the question of human limitations, intellectual limitations, and time pressures.

Inadequate knowledge of the business

Buddy March was the industry godfather and knew more about the micrographics business than anyone in 3M, so it was difficult for his boss or others to challenge seriously Buddy's business judgment or counsel him regarding the business.

GVP Hal Courtney's group controller, Olaf Carlsson, said, "Courtney is not oblivious to what is going on in Fab Products. But he gives his

DGMs responsibility and he has faith in (DGM) Dan Stewart. Plus Courtney grew up in the other businesses in his group, and knows more about them." Commercial development director Joe Hurley said Courtney also had limited knowledge of the new initiatives in Fab Products:

The only time Courtney got involved with our new initiatives was when we had the second breakage on Spray Guard. He didn't have anything new in his group, so he said, "I'll risk another one and a half million on this." We slanted what we told him a bit, and we didn't tell him all the horror stories. We kept him in the dark for about nine months. But we gave him some information to defend himself, because [president] Reilly knew about the second breakage on Spray Guard.

Micromanagement of the DGM

Ian McVay described how he was micromanaged by his GVP in a prior DGM assignment at Monsanto:

I reported to an individual who had my job before he became GVP. He didn't have a full-time job as GVP, so he would try to fill up his day by coming down to my area and talking to my managers. One time he just walked into my office and he looked at me and he shook his head and he said, "You got *big* problems at the Arlington plant." One of my plants was in Arlington, Texas. And he just turned around and walked out! I said to myself, "What the hell is he talking about? I don't have any problems in Arlington." But he was right, we had one problem in Arlington which he picked up from one of the manufacturing managers. It was a temporary situation, but one of our plants was down for twenty-four hours down there. And there's your boss telling you this, and you drop whatever you're doing and you run around. He took delight in that; he thought it was the funniest damn thing, watching me run around like a chicken with my head cut off... He was in my office sometimes five or six times a day. He was reading my mail before it got to me. [Laughter] It's comical now but it was a nightmare at the time.

Either leave the DGM alone or give him specific instructions rather than guidance

It would have been difficult for any GVP to provide effective guidance and coaching for DGM Greg Gibbons because of his disdain for the GVP job. Gibbons had been GVP for Xerox Memory Systems before he became DGM of Xerox OPD; he said he thoroughly disliked being GVP and was bored to tears in that job:

I absolutely hated it. You're neither fish nor fowl. You've got generals you're re-porting to, but you have no troops. And you get to be a blocker for corporate, and that just doesn't turn me on. So one thing I learned is that I'd never, ever take a job as a group vice president – under no conditions. I went from like working twelve hours a day, six days a week, to like working five hours a day, four days a week [chuckling]. And I did more sailing than I ever did in my whole life, and I started a sailboat company and everything because I was just absolutely getting bored to death and I didn't know what to do. The reason why I'm telling you this is that I was absolutely crying to come down here as DGM of OPD.

GVP Jerry Tyson left DGM Greg Gibbons alone for the first year and a half as Gibbons cut the division's losses and launched exciting new initiatives. Unfortunately, Gibbons' second full calendar year as DGM ended with the division $100 million below the profit plan. Worse yet, losses were accumulating at an even faster rate by the end of the first quarter of Gibbons' third year as DGM.

Tyson then tried to rein Gibbons in by giving him specific instructions. In a strongly worded memo, Tyson directed Gibbons and Little, the co-champions on the Star professional workstation, to switch to a more conservative long-range plan for Star; specifically, to focus on in-house publishing and other "vertical" special-purpose markets, which he felt could yield a $500 million business five years out. But Gibbons and Little refused to budge from their plan to sell Star "generically" to the broader market, because they passionately believed this would yield a business that was twenty times bigger.

In an earlier period, under a different set of circumstances, Gibbons did accept guidance and coaching. As his business advisor, Joel Piedmont, said in the middle of Greg Gibbons' second full calendar year as DGM of Xerox OPD:

Greg made two to three million dollars when Xerox acquired Shugart. To what extent is the fact that he is wealthy a part of his risk-taking ability? Numbers would only be meaningful for him if he could make a big bundle. Xerox provides the bankroll . . . Early on at Shugart, Greg was different. He was a prudent risk-taker. I was the banker's guardian, and we did not – and we would not – allow Greg to do some of the things he has done at OPD. Shugart was a pivotal experience for Greg. He liked it and he was good at it . . . When taking over OPD, Greg said, "I'll change Xerox; they won't change me."

Steve Carter, who succeeded Greg Gibbons as DGM of Xerox OPD, described the kind of supervision he felt Gibbons needed:

Greg was on a crusade he thoroughly believed in. He was out to prove something. He didn't listen when he was counseled. Jerry Tyson, Joel Piedmont, and I all tried to counsel him. . . . You can't turn a guy like Greg loose – he has to be managed. To manage Greg, you have to give him what he must have, but don't give him everything that he asks for.

Effective guidance and coaching by the DGM's boss

As Buddy March said, he would have benefited from guidance and coaching, particularly in his early years as DGM of 3M Micrographics. The case of Greg Gibbons at Xerox OPD shows that it can be difficult to provide guidance and coaching for the DGM but that the solution is not to leave him alone. Tom Eldridge, a senior executive who had nurtured several successful corporate entrepreneurs within 3M, spoke about the kind of supervision they need:

What is the role of the entrepreneur's boss? The conventional wisdom says, "Leave the entrepreneur alone." Venture capitalists know better. How do you get the kind of discipline for the corporate entrepreneur that the bankers and the VCs provide for the independent entrepreneur? It's much harder to get corporate entrepreneurs to submit to that kind of discipline. The effective supervisor of the corporate entrepreneur leaves the entrepreneur alone, but is ready to step in when needed without seeming to. This will not work unless there is a common goal and mutual respect. I tell the corporate entrepreneur, "Don't confuse second opinions with second-guessing. Get those second opinions! Give everyone a chance to give you their insights so they cannot second-guess you afterwards and say, 'If only he had benefited from my insights!' "

Supervise "good times" DGMs and "hard times" DGMs differently

GVP Hal Courtney of Monsanto did not have adequate knowledge or sufficient time to provide guidance and coaching for DGM Dan Stewart of Fab Products, but he recognized that a growth manager like Stewart had to be supervised differently than a manager like DGM Vic Thomas who was involved in cutting and pruning:

At the time I took over as managing director [GVP], SRI and Premier Associates had completed their studies and concluded that we should concentrate on smaller opportunities rather than larger ones. That meant concentrate more on Fab Products. That was an interesting conclusion because we were doing a lot in large-volume opportunities – [president] Reilly had felt, if the business is not going to be $50 million, I don't want to look at it . . . I was interested in Fab as an opportunity for growth because I was not going to get that in Plastics [under DGM Vic Thomas]. I supervise Thomas, who is cutting and pruning, differently than I do Stewart, who is trying to create growth with new business initiatives. You got to put up with more failure there. You don't think in terms of win and lose. Rather, you encourage people to continue the process with the attitude, "If we do it long enough, it will work."

An example of effective guidance and coaching by the DGM's boss

GVP Mike Walker provided valuable guidance and coaching for Clay Smith, his successor as DGM of AMP Sigcom, without this being perceived by Smith as corporate interference. Walker was able to do this because of his deep knowledge of the division's business, a relationship of trust and respect with his protégé Smith, and sufficient time, interest, and skill to attend to the needs of both the division and the DGM. The following story told by Walker after he had been GVP for two years illustrates his approach:

Clay [Smith] was initially not objective enough to stand above his organization. For example, the group controller and I found that the scrap rate was much too high down at the plant level and manufacturing. We kept questioning him whether he had adequate supervision in the late shifts, but it took, I guess, until this past spring for him to finally face it. He was on a business trip and had to land in Baltimore and decided to stop in the plant on the second shift. When I saw him the next morning, he was flabbergasted. He said, "My God, I didn't realize it, I don't have any supervisors on the second shift, much less on the third shift." And so I said, "All right, what are you going to do?" And he said, "Shoot, I got to get a supervisor." And I said, "Fine, where's your requisition, I'll sign it." That kind of thing. He just looked at me, and I said, "Look, Clay, we can sit here and look over your shoulder all you want, but we got to lean back and let you find out for yourself and this is what we've been warning you about. We thought something was haywire. We couldn't tell you what, but all we could do is tell you the warning signs." I think it was a lack of involvement in the bowels of his organization. It was more wanting to sit in the office and get an overview. And take what his people were telling him.

Well you've got to do more than that. Walk-around management is a concept where you go out and get out on the floor, go down to the plant, you talk to people, you ask questions. Even after I became group director [GVP], Clay used to wonder how in the hell I found out about things. One time he pulled his staff together and accused them of having a leak in there who was telling me what is going on. I got a bunch of complaints on the damn thing and I said, "Well, fellas, I hate to tell you this, but Clay is the guy who told me." And so I talked to Clay and I said, "I understand you pulled your damn staff together and chewed their asses out." And I said, "You know who told me about what was going on?" "Who?," he says. I said, "You did." He said, "No I didn't." I said, "Yeah you did," and I told him the questions I asked him and the kind of wishy-washy answers I got and I knew exactly what the hell was going on. "You are just too damn much," he says. I said, "Well that's what your job is, to get perceptions. To tell, from the way people are telling you, what is going on."

The controller's dual responsibility

Large multidivisional firms, like the four in this study, have controllers at the division, group, and corporate levels. These controllers have a dual responsibility – to provide information, analysis, and other advisory services to line managers, and to provide their functional superiors in the control area with the information and analysis that higher-level management needs to review and control the division.

These dual responsibilities – "helper" and "policeman" – may appear to be in conflict, but good policemen are also helpers for good citizens! Research has found that the same is true for controllers. They can discharge both responsibilities effectively if they develop the necessary knowledge of the business, the right personal orientation, and the required interpersonal skills, in addition to the technical competence in financial analysis, reporting, and control normally expected of them.[1]

Ineffective support and challenge by the controller

Support and challenge is ineffective if the division managers perceive that the controller (1) is not knowledgeable about the business, (2) changes the budget without consultation, (3) does not provide assistance, and (4) is only interested in information for reporting and control purposes.

Not knowledgeable about the business

Arjay Mason, product manager for Cable Assemblies at AMP Sigcom when Mike Walker was DGM, was frustrated that the group controller's staff did not make allowance for the fact that his new business was more labor-intensive than other AMP businesses:

Every quarter, every month, when the budget is taken over to group, there is one magical thing – labor cost as a percent of billings. Labor is normally 10–15 percent of billings; it's now suddenly one-third because Cable Assemblies are very labor-intensive. Any historical numbers are irrelevant when you start shifting like that. But the group staff keep questioning us about labor cost as a percent of billings.

Changes the budget without consultation

DGM Clay Smith of AMP Sigcom was upset that GVP Jon Grover and his group controller were arbitrarily increasing the division's sales for the month without consulting him:

I may give a number, a value of sales I expect to ship this month, and if the group director [GVP] or the group controller does not agree, they'll change the darn number and that's what will be given to executive management. I was rather upset here about a week ago when that happened. I've accepted their number now and I'm going to have to violate the guidelines for what we call "reach" – how many dollars in the future I can go out, pick up, bring in, and ship this month (either in response to customer requests or at the discretion of the division) to meet that objective. But I have a concern that just arbitrarily they are going and altering my numbers. They're not my numbers any more, they become their numbers.

Does not provide assistance

DGM Dan Stewart of Monsanto Fab Products said that, with the exception of his group controller, Olaf Carlsson, the Monsanto controllers he had dealt with were not very supportive or interested in the division because it was not seen as strategically important to the corporation, and also because it had a set of businesses that they didn't really understand: "You got the feeling that they were trying to prove you wrong instead of trying to help you. Fab Products is a strategically irrelevant operation that they don't understand anyway. Why would they be interested?"

Only interested in information for reporting and control

DGM Ian McVay of Monsanto Engineered Products was not happy with the controllers either, but he said their influence had diminished over the past few years:

The financial community in Monsanto has lost favor in recent years. But under [CFO] Josh Curry, as recently as three or four years ago, it was the single most important function. They would go unleash an army of accountants on a capital appropriation request. And as part of that they'd come back with requests for data and information and everything would be very formalized. And this needs to be on so and so's desk at 12 o'clock on Friday afternoon, because Mr. Curry wants the information turned around over the weekend so that he could have it at 8:30 Monday morning. Not so much anymore, but believe me five years ago that was a real fact of life for those living in this corporation, and I never reacted to it very well.

Effective support and challenge by the controller

Support and challenge is effective if division managers perceive that the controller (1) is knowledgeable about the business, (2) provides assistance, and (3) requests information and provides challenge without presenting these as edicts.

Knowledgeable about the business

Support and challenge by the controller is effective if it is based on a good understanding of the business and on an overriding concern with trying to improve it. This requires the controller to go beyond the numbers to business considerations, both technical and human, that affect performance. The common stereotype is the controller who always says "no" to requests for more money. However, the effective controller makes a balanced assessment of whether the division is spending too much, *or too little*, and whether the monies are being spent too early, *or too late*, for best results. Hal Strauss, GVP Mike Walker's highly regarded group controller at AMP, described his approach:

Mine is a cold-hearted review. I have to look at it as a financial investment and return. But I don't get hung up with the numbers. I may ask, "Why haven't you got marketing input?" It is important to know what sales and marketing *believe*. It is not enough that the new product development manager thinks it's great – even if he is in fact right, and sales and marketing are wrong – because sales and marketing can make it a self-fulfilling prophecy of failure. So I look not just at the numbers, but whether it is a well-rounded plan that has the support of all ... My involvement is not about changing directions but about how investment might be altered. If the investment and engineering costs are too high, I ask, "Can we defer this into a later period? Will it affect the program, really?" I question the timing of expenditures. At the front end, I have to counsel the division not to invest too early in automated production, not until the design is frozen.

At other times I ask the opposite kind of questions: "Why can't we spend *more* money? Why don't we invest money *this* year versus two or three years from now?" So I frequently have to place timing in reverse, and propose earlier investments. I have asked this question several times this year: "Why aren't we investing in automated equipment for Cable Assemblies and Commercial RF, which are to-day hand-assembled, so we can reduce manufacturing costs?" Automation might also help to improve the reliability of the division. AMP Sigcom is at the bottom of most of our yardsticks on customer performance – how often they satisfy customers, how quickly, etc. They are the highest on past-due orders in the company.

My role is not to tighten the purse but to pursue what is sensible. My chance to influence is before they make the investments. I expect some good ones and some bad ones. There is no point in saying afterwards, "I told you so."

Provides assistance

DGM Dan Stewart of Monsanto Fab Products thought highly of his group controller, Olaf Carlsson, who served as a sounding board for him. Carlsson said he was happy to do some dirty work for Stewart:

Dan had me very much involved in his business. He relied on me to give him a perception of what his staff felt, and did, about their business. He used me as a sounding board. Sometimes it was easier for me to ask the tough questions; I became the javelin catcher! For example, when Yamada [the Japanese company] came along with OPET, our technical people said, "We are going to develop the bottle ourselves; let's not get into bed with Yamada." It was NIH [not invented here]. I could see us spending millions on internal development so I contributed to the murder of that idea. It wasn't my baby, so I could be objective and helped to kill it.

Requests information and provides challenge without presenting these as edicts

An effective controller has an open dialog with the division managers, and offers constructive challenge to their ideas and plans, without telling them what to do. Hal Strauss, GVP Mike Walker's highly regarded group controller at AMP, commented on this:

Sometimes I have to question the logic of continuing a program. "The numbers don't look good, why should we do it?" I don't say "Kill it." That's their call. I say, "Based on the numbers you have submitted, I can't see the financial return." I ask them when they intend to make a decision to discontinue the program or invest more. I may discuss this with my GVP. In some cases I meet with the DGM and the division controller before it gets to the GVP. I can have significant influence without issuing edicts.

Olaf Carlsson, DGM Dan Stewart's highly regarded group controller at Monsanto, emphasized the importance of an open discussion with the DGM, including an escalation to higher-level management if necessary to resolve any disagreements:

I want people to respect me, not to like me. I am not here to make the DGM happy. If I disagree with a DGM, I would rather tell him, I'd rather confront him. If the disagreement cannot be resolved, I'll go up to our mutual boss, the managing director [GVP], with the DGM present – belly to belly, not under the carpet. With Dan Stewart I never had a disagreement that we couldn't resolve.

An example of effective support and challenge by the controllers

3M's track record of innovation and entrepreneurship is widely admired; the impressive record of their controllers in providing support and challenge for line managers has not received the attention it deserves. 3M's experience shows that control is not the enemy of entrepreneurship. On the contrary, when it is *conceived properly* and *exercised skillfully*, control is an essential companion of entrepreneurship.

There is no magic in 3M's approach. It recognizes that new business creation needs to be controlled *differently* than existing business. This was discussed in Chapter 6 and more is said later (especially in Chapter 15). 3M's approach requires top management commitment to the development of strong controllers who are able to support and challenge line managers without being perceived as interfering.[2] The commitment to strong controls – and strong controllers – at 3M goes all the way back to legendary CEO William McKnight, who started his career as an accounting clerk, and who instilled in the minds of generations of 3M managers the notion that excellent entrepreneurship demands excellent controls.

3M had strong controllers at all levels – corporate, group, and division – and they were co-located on one floor of a corporate headquarters building. Division controllers walked to and from the offices of their divisions, which were located in other buildings of the 3M complex, with reams of computer output and reports under their arms! This channel of communication was used to pass information up and suggestions down, not to give orders to the DGM. It was clear that the DGM was running the show. Bart Breckner, the 3M corporate controller, talked about the controller's role as a conduit for consistent and rapid communication to and from the divisions, as well as the role of challenging the division managers without issuing edicts:

The controller's function gets strong backing from the corporate executives of this company. By sitting together and reporting up through the group controllers to me on a solid line, the division controllers provide the advantage of consistent communication to all the divisions, with fast reaction time. If corporate executives want something disseminated rapidly and consistently, they do it through us. If they feel additional price increases are needed, or if the divisions are not moving fast enough in some area, we bring that message home in one day . . . We are a service organization to the divisions. We give them the information they need to run their business. We are not detectives or policemen. Most of the controller's job is to *anticipate* problems before they happen. The division controller can argue and disagree with the DGM, but the DGM can overrule the controller. That avoids the DGM feeling stifled. If a corporate executive does not have the patience to roll with the ups and downs and intervenes in the affairs of a division, the DGM may feel stifled. But the division controller cannot stifle. If a DGM has a problem and it is highlighted, is that stifling? It shouldn't be seen as such by the DGM.

The division controller for 3M Micrographics, Wim Williams, helped DGM Buddy March to understand and accept 3M's strong financial control system and saved him from many embarrassments, particularly in the early days when he was still new to the company. For instance, March wanted to bury unfavorable variances, especially on the Com program, and play other accounting games, but Williams would counsel him against it: "I am sorry, Buddy, but this just won't fly in this company. I can't stop you if you want to go ahead, but you know I will have to let Bart [Breckner, the corporate controller] know about this."

Wim Williams said his solid line reporting relationship to the group controller and up to the corporate controller helped him to maintain the independence needed to challenge the DGM. He felt that the corporate pressures – for price increases and headcount reductions, for example – that were communicated to the division via the controllers were constructive and beneficial. But Williams repeated what Bart Breckner, the corporate controller, had said – neither the group controller nor the division controller issued edicts to the DGM:

The division controller reports through the group controller and the corporate controller directly to Garrison [CFO] – it gives us a little more authority to say what we want. As McKnight [the legendary CEO] used to say, "The accountants are going to report independently." Ever since, the controllers are expected to provide an independent opinion ... This is a very people-oriented company. As we like to say, "In 3M, people count." Since corporate executives watch headcount very carefully, the company wags say, "In 3M, count people." A large company can add people very easily, so every once in a while corporate says we are going to have to cut back. It is a way to get rid of deadwood ... I routinely pass along suggestions from corporate or group executives to Buddy [March, the DGM]: "Corporate (or group) wants us to see if we can increase prices on lines x, y, and z. What should I tell them?" Corporate keeps the pressure on the divisions to increase prices because inflation is eroding profitability ... I can only do so much when there is a disagreement. I don't argue with everything Buddy does. It is still up to him; he is the DGM.

Buddy March concurred with what Wim Williams said:

You get many messages from corporate executives through the controllers. "Your travel costs are too high." Or, "Your sales costs are running out of control." Wim [Williams] is constantly telling me the costs are too high. But he wouldn't tell me I could or couldn't do something. They don't have the authority to tell you that. He'd say, "The controllers are putting the pressure on us to raise prices." We do increase prices in small increments but more frequently than our competition, because we seem to have a better rapport with our customers.

Summary

The DGM's boss does not have an easy job. He must guide and coach the DGM without being perceived as interfering. This is particularly difficult if the DGM is engaged in new business creation, because the inherent technical, product, and market uncertainties make it impossible to be sure who is correct or what the right thing to do is.

Guidance and coaching is ineffective if the DGM's boss has inadequate knowledge of the division's business, or insufficient time or interest to attend to the needs of the division and its DGM. Micromanaging the DGM, or leaving him alone, or giving him specific instructions rather than guidance is also ineffective. The "good times" DGM and the "hard times" DGM must be supervised differently if guidance and coaching are to be effective.

DGMs do not like to be questioned or challenged by the controllers – the division controller working with the DGM and the group and corporate controllers working with the corporate executives. Both support and challenge are effective if the controller is perceived as having a good understanding of the business, if assistance in running the business is provided, and if information is requested and challenge is provided without presenting these as edicts. Controllers are ineffective if they are viewed as only interested in securing information for reporting and control purposes.

Part IV

The division general manager

This part of the book examines how the division general manager (DGM) influences new business creation (Figure IV.1).

The DGM has a major influence on new business creation.[1] Several specifics concerning the DGM are important: his personal assets, including his personality, experience, and leverage with the corporate executives (Chapter 11), his motivation and strategy for new business creation (Chapter 12), his building of corporate support for it (Chapter 13), and his leadership of the division for new business creation (Chapter 14).

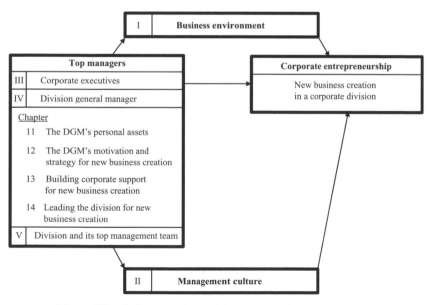

Figure IV.1. Influence of the division general manager.

11 The DGM's personal assets

This chapter examines how the personal assets of the division general manager (DGM) influence new business creation. These include personality, experience, and leverage with the corporate executives (Table 11.1).

Personality

The DGMs who participated in this study were requested to complete a set of personality tests because research regarding entrepreneurs suggested several important dimensions. These tests were chosen with two criteria in mind: (1) each test had to be relatively simple to administer, and (2) all the tests combined had to take less than one hour to complete. The DGMs were generous with their time, but there were limits to their patience with such tests. DGM comparisons based on these personality tests and the implications for new business creation are described below.[1]

Extroverted versus introverted

DGMs either were balanced between extroverted and introverted (March, Stewart, and McVay) or were extroverted (Walker, Smith, Gibbons, and Carter). This external orientation aided their capacity to perceive new business opportunities, and to gain the support of others in order to pursue them.

March's successor, Thorngate, was the only introvert. He realized that his introversion was dampening his capacity to perceive new business opportunities, as well as his ability to get others excited about these opportunities, and he began to force himself to visit more customers as the study ended.

Intuitive versus sensing

People who are "intuitive" have an inclination to look for possibilities and relationships whereas those who are "sensing" have an inclination

Table 11.1. *How the DGM's personal assets influence new business creation*

Hypothesis	Factor	Influence on new business creation
Personality		
11.1	Extroverted	+
11.2	Intuitive	+
11.3	Oriented to thinking (versus feeling)	+
11.4	Assertively self-confident	+
11.5	Low need for security	+
Experience		
11.6	Prior new business creation experience	+
11.7	Prior success from proceeding despite the skeptics	+
11.8	Prior success from proceeding despite opposition from higher-ups	+
11.9	Relevant prior experience in a different business setting	+
11.10	Knowledge of the business	+
Leverage with corporate executives		
11.11	Powerful corporate executive(s) support the DGM	+
11.12	DGM has credibility with corporate executives	+
11.13	Corporate executives feel dependent on the DGM	+
11.14	DGM is accepted in the management culture	+/−

to work with known facts. DGMs were either balanced between intuitive and sensing (Walker, McVay, and Carter) or were intuitive (March, Thorngate, Stewart, and Gibbons).

Since new business opportunities are by their very nature ambiguous, with few established facts to rely on, those who are intuitive are more likely to perceive these opportunities. After he became GVP, Mike Walker made the following observation about the importance of intuition for new business creation:

I like to see in a DGM somebody that really can move forward on his convictions, on his intuition. That, frankly, was my problem with Larry [one of the DGMs reporting to Walker]. Even though he had been in development, he was afraid to make the investments until they were absolutely proven and he had a customer who was willing to pay him money for it. He was too conservative. And you've got to have the kind of people that have the instincts to know when they should pre-invest so that they have capacity before that market develops, and stay ahead of the competition.

Walker's successor, Smith, was the only DGM who was more sensing than intuitive, but even he felt that intuition was important:

I don't analyze a program to death. I guess I go on more of a gut feel that the program looks like its going to be a potential winner. I'm not terribly bothered about coming to a lot of accurate conclusions as to how many dollars are involved in the sales and what percent the market share will really become and that sort of thing. There's some intuitiveness I like to see in projects.

Oriented to thinking versus feeling

People who are inclined toward "thinking" tend to base their judgments on analysis and logic, whereas the judgments of those who are inclined toward "feeling" are based more on their personal values. DGMs were either balanced between thinking and feeling (March, Stewart, McVay, Gibbons, and Carter) or inclined toward thinking (Walker, Smith, and Thorngate).

Those inclined toward thinking might be better able to control the pursuit of new opportunities when tough actions such as de-commitments and personnel changes are called for. Those inclined toward feeling might hurt the pursuit of new business opportunities by letting their personal values, rather than an objective analysis, guide their decisions.

Assertively self-confident [2]

DGMs displayed either moderately high (Smith, March, and Carter) or extremely high (Walker, Stewart, McVay, and Gibbons) assertive self-confidence. The only exception was Thorngate, whose score was considerably below the others.

Those who are assertively self-confident are better able to proceed on the basis of their own convictions regarding new opportunities, especially in the case of initiatives that are not supported by others in the corporation. Jane Langley, Buddy March's administrative assistant for many years, described him:

Well, he's stubborn. And there's usually an underlying reason that isn't apparent at the time he makes a decision. He really pushed that Beta acquisition. And oh, shucks, he got the whole company on his side. He talked them all into it. At one time they were all against it. They were all for getting rid of the whole Com thing; and Buddy said we had to have Com and we needed this Beta to keep moving with a new Com. Stick-to-it and doggedness – I guess that's a good word for it. Com didn't pay off in some ways. But Buddy accomplished what he was out for. We had a full product line.

Buddy March described himself:

> I guess I just don't have any fear. I've never experienced that – even when I was
> a little kid. And I don't know where that comes from, but my daughter is the
> same. I've never had fear of addressing bosses or presenting ideas to them. And
> that's not because of the 3M culture; there are people here that wilt when the
> Chairman comes in. No question about it [chuckling] ... I get nervous, but not
> scared, when the commitments get bigger than I think they might – and we make
> some damn big commitments, so you get nervous about whether you made the
> right commitment or not. How do you handle that nervousness? [Chuckling.] I
> get up several times a night!

Low need for security[3]

Those with confidence in their own talents, with a lack of worry over
the circumstances of their employment, have a low need for security. All
the DGMs had either a low need (March, Thorngate, Stewart, Gibbons,
and Carter) or a moderate need (Walker, Smith, and McVay) for security.
Here is what Mike Walker had to say:

> I've considered leaving the company to start my own business many times, but
> my conservatism, I think, always steps in the way. Up until the time my family
> was pretty much established, I felt the risk was too great to take at that crucial
> point in my son's life.

Ian McVay put it this way:

> I don't happen to be a security-driven individual. My roots are from a lower
> middle class family, and I hope I don't really need that much money. I wouldn't
> want for it to happen, but I could probably readjust to a job with half the salary
> I make now. I would have to change my lifestyle to a degree, but it wouldn't
> devastate me or anything like that.

All other things being the same, a lower need for security lowers one's
perception of risk, making it easier to pursue new business opportunities. This is particularly relevant in the pursuit of initiatives that are not
supported by higher-ups, because these initiatives tend to be personally
more risky.

DGM comparisons based on interview material

3M Micrographics: Buddy March versus Ray Thorngate   DGM
Buddy March and his technical director, Ray Thorngate, had complementary skills and personalities. March's intuition and aggressiveness
complemented Thorngate's analytical strength and more cautious approach. This created a powerful partnership for new business creation.

Thorngate later became DGM of 3M Engineering Products but, without March's entrepreneurial drive to complement his technical strength, his new business creation was not as strong and was less effective. One colleague compared Buddy March's street savvy and aggressiveness with Ray Thorngate's intelligent, cautious approach:

Ray is the complete opposite of Buddy. Ray is extremely intelligent – bookwise he is a near-genius – but streetwise he is naïve. Buddy has street smarts. He is intuitive, and has an unusual knack – imagination – to see far down, the ability to project the whole thing out, sales, marketing, etc. Ray can't do that. He has to have all the facts laid out to get to step one, then get all the facts to get to step two, and so on all the way out. Ray lacks the bombastic style; he is not an entrepreneur or a risk-taker like Buddy is. Ray is much better on control.

Monsanto Fab Products: Dan Stewart versus Ian McVay   Joe Hurley was the commercial development director when Stewart was DGM and also later when McVay succeeded Stewart. Hurley said the difference between the two DGMs was not their agenda for Fab Products but how they pursued it.

Ian McVay's philosophy is very similar to Dan Stewart's – better management of the existing businesses and growth via new business creation. The big difference between McVay and Stewart is the way they do things. Stewart is not as strong businesswise as McVay, who is perceived as very tough and business-minded. Stewart looked at the big picture most of the time; he was broad-brush. Whereas Stewart would let people get by with certain things, McVay doesn't let 'em do it . . . McVay is certainly upward oriented, not downward oriented. I honestly believe that if he received pressure from the top, let's say [EVP] Costello, and Costello was attacking me, he'd step aside. Or reinforce it. But Stewart would take the heat. Stewart is much more people oriented; McVay is more detached.

Stewart loved to work with people to bring out the best in them; he pursued growth via new business creation because he did not wish to lay people off. In contrast, McVay was more opportunistic, more politically savvy, and more tough-minded in squeezing the mature businesses to feed the new initiatives. Jason Singleton, the financial controller for Fab Products, said Ian McVay was much more selective than Dan Stewart in deciding what to pursue:

Ian is supporting OPET and Spray Guard but axed RCA Disk Caddy. Stewart had kept all three initiatives going and also had extensive investment in film and blownware. McVay thinks MAT [marketing, administration, and technical] expenses are too high in blownware and film, and he is looking to sell Astroturf.

Commercial development director Joe Hurley compared the two DGMs on the OPET bottle initiative. Hurley said Stewart was intuitive and perceived OPET as low risk whereas McVay was fact-based and analytical and decided to pursue OPET in spite of the higher risk he perceived:

It's kind of interesting to compare the risks. Stewart was proceeding almost on intuitive feel that there must be something in this. He didn't get into a lot of market analysis. He says, "Let's go out and see, after all $3.2 million of investment [for the hot-fill development line] is not such a big amount. And we'll find out if the market is there. We can always sell some bottles on it [as a cold-fill line] if it doesn't work out." And McVay goes through a detailed analysis, and by this time it looks not very good because you don't have any customers lined up. So, in a sense McVay is proceeding with more data but with a higher perception of risk. McVay became a believer on OPET *after* we presented the data.

Experience

Prior new business creation experience

DGMs with prior new business creation experience are more likely to pursue it, and do it well.[4] Mike Walker had been a new product development manager in three different divisions, and had enjoyed considerable success with new business creation prior to becoming DGM of AMP Sigcom. Reflecting on his career, Walker said,

Those early years shaped my style, my character, and my perception of how to get things done. I often have remarked to people since I came up to Harrisburg [Pennsylvania, AMP headquarters] as DGM of AMP Sigcom that this environment was a piece of cake. It was almost impossible to make a mistake. It was so easily compared to what I came from, the hard labor I served in Elizabethtown [Capitron division]. People don't realize the kind of place it really was down there in those years . . . I was able to do things very rapidly in new product development when I came here because I almost didn't have to put any energy into it, and I could do it right. My instincts were all there. And I had such good talent to work with that I didn't have down there (in Capitron) and so it was easy to get the extraordinary results out of it. The development people in AMP Sigcom didn't realize they could do it for themselves, but I did, and I looked for the talent that they had. They were working at such a slow pace; all I had to do is put a little bit of acceleration to it and it really achieved results.

Ian McVay had a great deal of prior experience in commercial development, and he said this helped him to pursue new business creation after he became DGM of Monsanto Engineered Products:

Early in my career, when I was in commercial development, I worked for six months on a project that would have gotten Monsanto into the dental care industry. I found an acquisition candidate, took the recommendation up, and it just died. And very soon thereafter, I was moved into another job and it just wasn't followed up on. That was a missed opportunity. It was an emerging field that has been profitable for a number of companies ... From this experience I learned how to sell projects – to look for where the leverage points are, who the sponsors might be, and how to cultivate those sponsorship relationships if you will. You know, I did it all wrong. I was a young commercial development manager trying to put through a program of corporate significance and you don't do that dealing with the relatively low levels that I was dealing with.

I think one thing that makes me unique as a general manager is the fact that I spent time in commercial development. And commercial development was in a way the most frustrating experience I ever had at Monsanto because, almost by definition, 95 percent of everything you work on is not going to come to fruition. It's going to terminate. You know that going in. But at the same time, it gave me a glimpse of how things can be strung together such that they can become legitimate business opportunities. I could pick out the best case scenario, as in the case of this food packaging thing, and try to insure that there's a low downside risk and the upside potential is enormous. And I find myself using that mechanism over, and over, and over again.

McVay also benefited from the training he received from a strong and effective R&D manager. As Alf Hummel, Monsanto VP of corporate planning, pointed out,

McVay was in the D&P division of Monsanto Industrial Chemicals. That division had the R&D director with the best track record in Monsanto, and McVay was trained by him. It was a beautiful team. I have seen McVay developed by a very strong and very effective R&D manager.

Prior success in proceeding despite the skeptics

DGMs are more likely to pursue new business creation if they have previously proceeded with new initiatives despite the skepticism of others and achieved success. DGM Greg Gibbons of Xerox OPD had co-founded Shugart, a successful entrepreneurial start-up that was later acquired by Xerox. Gibbons recalled that many observers had predicted Shugart would fail. Its success, despite the skeptics, gave Gibbons the confidence to stay committed to the OPD strategy – and to the controversial Star initiative – despite mounting opposition within Xerox. Gibbons said,

Any person who has a vision of what the world can be like will always find a lot of people who can't see that vision and share in it. And because a lot of it is kind of a gut feel, you have a hard time explaining that vision to them. I don't have a lot of business experience – a couple years at IBM and a couple years at Memorex – and then I was one of the founders and then president of Shugart. And I remember when we started Shugart, we had a very difficult time convincing the world that there was a real marketplace for our product. I remember our first business plan said that in five years we would build a cumulative total of 35,000 floppy disk drives. Shugart does 35,000 drives a week now. So the one experience I had was a marketplace I saw and nobody else agreed with it. And in that particular case, I happened to be right. I could just as easily have been wrong. If you believe in something, and if you have good intuition, I think you have to provide that vision to the people, and there will be many people who stand up and really question it.

Prior success in proceeding despite opposition from higher-ups

Not all DGMs have previously experienced new business success when proceeding despite opposition from their boss and/or higher-ups. Those who have done so (Walker, March, and McVay in this study) feel a special sense of confidence and satisfaction from this success. It encourages them to undertake other new business initiatives, including those not supported by superiors.[5] As DGM Buddy March recalled,

Dry Silver Paper may be the second most risky program for me personally after Com. Bennett Colt [GVP at the time, who later became CEO of 3M] was opposed to the program because his scientists said it was "kinetically unsound." Here we were with 2–3 percent profit margins on Dry Silver in the early days, with projections of 10–12 percent at best if we succeeded, at a time when our reader printers had 40–50 percent margins. But we stuck to it and today Dry Silver is our most profitable product... The thing that drives me is the great feeling of being right. It is not the "I told you so" feeling, but once you have tasted success, it is a big motivator... Maybe today I am being foolish on Com because of the success of Dry Silver – it took a long period of time and high investments before Dry Silver paid off. I don't think I am being blind on Com, but I have wondered about that.

DGM Ian McVay ignored his boss's instructions to achieve success with a new program in a prior assignment. He described that experience, and said similar experiences gave him the confidence to pursue the OPET bottle initiative despite opposition from above:

I'm not afraid to take on my boss if I think he's wrong, and I've done that many times. I've also defied specific direct orders... In a prior DGM assignment, I supported a new program that was very close to being killed. I put fourteen people on the program, because I thought it was extremely important, even though I was only authorized for seven, and I was caught. I maintained that as a general manger I had flexibility to move people around within a total headcount that was fixed, and that I just didn't think it was appropriate that every time we had a change on one of the basic R&D programs that I had to come back and check signals with my boss. So he and I got into a long discussion about what is delegated authority and what's not delegated authority, and my whole strategy in that session was to sufficiently obscure the subject matter so that he thought that maybe there was a misunderstanding. [Laughter.] My whole strategy was to confuse him. [Laughter.] When I went in, there was no doubt in his mind that I had directly defied one of his directives. He was right. But when we got out he wasn't so sure

[Laughter] ... Despite the fact that we had lots of technical problems to solve, and really a lot of pressure to cut our research cost, I believed in that product and I kept it going. I put seven guys on it and then fourteen and today it's got thirty-five people and the company is really excited about it. It's a major business opportunity for Monsanto. But it was – I don't want to over-dramatize this – a general manager with an idea, a game plan. OK? I kind of put this food packaging thrust with the OPET bottle in same area. I have a dream. [Laughter.] I can see this thing unfold before my very eyes. Just as I could see that program unfold before my very eyes. And it happened.

Relevant prior experience in a different business setting

DGMs with relevant prior experience in a *different* business setting have the benefit of contrast that enhances their new business creation capacity. For example, DGM Ian McVay could trace his decision to reorganize Fab Products into growth and mature businesses to his early training in the inorganic division. He believed it had taught him how to get the most out of both mature and new businesses.

Knowledge of the business

Depth of industry knowledge[6]   DGMs with deep industry knowledge are able to perceive and pursue new business opportunities that others cannot see or get excited about. DGM Mike Walker of AMP Sigcom had a great deal of industry experience that his predecessor, Chet Timmer, lacked. Walker said this gave him a relative advantage in new business creation:

Chet is more of a people type guy, and the CB thing worked because he liked the market manager involved. And so the two of them linked up and went out to Las Vegas to the consumer electronics show and began to see this thing. And Chet was smart enough to say, "Now this goddamn thing is going to grow like a son of a bitch, let me start doing something about it," and that's what they did ... He hit early, he built capacity fast ahead of demand, and he was the only one that could supply it that big. At that point in the game he must have had 80 to 90 percent of the market for the connector side of the thing. And the price went from 57¢ a connector down to 17¢ in that period of time. He made more gross margin at 17¢ than he did at 57¢ because he did the tooling job right, and he automated right. So I can't take a damn thing away from what he did.

Now what I would have done differently, I would have gone like hell to follow that CB success. I'd have pushed the heck out of Ribbon Coax, and tried to expand that new product development department. Chet didn't respect the development department. He didn't think he was getting his money's worth out of it. He didn't know why, but he just didn't think he was getting it, so all the development he was doing at that period of time was in product engineering [on product extensions]. So he was able to address the immediate opportunity [CB], but not the long-range direction the division ought to take. But you see Chet hadn't had the technical background I did at AMP. I could tell what was needed from a technical standpoint, and what the trends were telling me had to be addressed. So it gave me a sixth sense as to what the technology pressures were doing to the marketplace. I also knew the cadre of competitors over a long period of time so I had a pretty good idea of what their characters were like. And so I could kind of see all of the broader picture, I guess, than what he could.

Clay Smith, who was the development manager under DGM Walker before succeeding him, also had industry knowledge. But it was not as broad or as deep as Walker's. This affected the kinds of new business initiatives Smith felt comfortable pursuing, as he explained:

The Transmission Cable lines were new. So there was some learning relative to that product offering. It took me a couple years to really become comfortable in that marketplace altogether. And it's been a building experience as I've taken on additional responsibilities. The commercial products that we've been launching into we never produced before, such as the SMD product line. It's something we production-tooled without any known sales. And it was based upon, in my opinion, our successes that we've had in the Commercial RF product lines. At that time, back then, I would have avoided the SMD product line altogether. We learned how to take the manufacturing skills off of our competitors' turf and put it on our own turf where AMP's strengths were greatest. But it took some time before I felt comfortable with the SMD.

There are two special cases concerning knowledge of the business. Love of the business can lead to new insights and energy that spurs new business creation. But what is perceived as love could in fact be seduction! The focus shifts from doing what is necessary for business success to doing what is personally gratifying or ego-enhancing (e.g. first-class travel to exotic destinations, rubbing shoulders with celebrities, being in the limelight with the rich and the powerful).

Love of the business   Jane Langley, Buddy March's long-time administrative assistant, spoke about his love of the business: "I think it is his single biggest asset. I didn't think he would even take this job [GVP], because it would separate him from [being the DGM of] Micrographics." John Hypes, Buddy March's marketing director, said that March's position as the "industry godfather" gave the Micrographics division a competitive edge:

Buddy occupies a very special place in the micrographics industry, the total industry. He has a godfather image in the industry, and has been in the industry longer than any of our competitors. That has helped our image and reputation and given us a competitive edge. During the time that Buddy has been DGM here, Kodak [a major competitor] has had many DGMs. And Bell & Howell [the other key competitor] has had, seems like, twenty-five DGMs during this period – the last guy in there was a hell of a capable DGM; I am glad he was promoted within a year!

Seduced by the business   Buddy March's love of the micrographics industry gave his division a competitive edge, but even his supporters felt that March was seduced by the glamor of the customer events he sponsored, such as the golf tournaments and the track meets involving celebrities. Buddy March acknowledged that EVP Baker's criticism of these events and his executive decision to stop them was fair.

DGM Ian McVay said president Jim Reilly had warned him to guard against the danger of business seduction:

Fab Products is an unusual business for Monsanto. You can see a finished product at the end. And Reilly said to me when he commissioned me, "Don't get caught up in the fun." What he meant was, "Don't get caught up in the Astroturf business where you're flying around in the company plane and regularly visiting customers and all that." He was referring to the trap that many of our managers have fallen into [prior to the time of the study in the early 1980s] of becoming enamored with some of the more glamorous parts of this business. And all of a sudden they become part of the public relations scene and they are attending all the trade shows and the conventions and all that. That's what he meant. I mean, if he told me, "Go over there and don't have any fun," I would probably have turned it down. I don't work in environments where I don't have fun. That's one of the things that turns me on. If I don't have fun at what I'm doing, I leave.

The DGM's leverage with corporate executives

The DGM may enjoy one or more of these points of leverage with the corporate executives: (1) powerful corporate executives support him; (2) he has credibility with corporate executives because of his past record of delivering results and/or because his current results appear to be on track; (3) corporate executives feel dependent on him; and (4) he is accepted in the management culture. DGMs who have greater leverage with corporate executives are better able to bear the personal risks of new business creation.

Powerful corporate executives support the DGM

Support from one or more powerful corporate executives gives the DGM the direct benefit of their help and an important indirect benefit. *Others* who know the DGM enjoys the support of powerful corporate executives are inclined to cooperate with him! For example, DGM Dan Stewart was able to secure the support of corporate executives – even on matters that president Reilly himself was not so excited about – because they knew he was Reilly's protégé and *assumed* he had Reilly's support. As Stewart pointed out,

This is a terrible thing to admit, but I think people say, "Stewart is a protégé of Reilly. Let's not screw around with him." Blair [a corporate executive] had a reputation of being very tough. And I had an incident with him about the AR [appropriations request for capital] for a new facility. When I went to see him, he was a pussycat. And someone told me later, "Yeah, that's right. Blair knows that you are Reilly's boy and therefore he's not going to be tough on you. He's not going to screw with you." Even though I knew Reilly wasn't all that hot about our initiatives in Fab Products, people assumed he was!

The DGM has credibility with corporate executives

A DGM who has a track record of delivering results, and/or one who seems to be on track to deliver current results, has credibility with corporate executives. Greg Gibbons had credibility with the Xerox corporate executives because of his successful track record as president of Shugart, and the positive results he delivered in his first eighteen months as DGM of Xerox OPD. As he said at the end of his first full calendar year as DGM,

I took Shugart from $2 million in sales and a $9 million loss to 140 million in sales and 25 percent pre-tax profit within five years. So I had the credibility coming in, and we did better than anyone expected in the first eighteen months. They had seen a lot of positive things in terms of all these products being developed and so forth and we had a 50 percent revenue increase in my first [full calendar] year as DGM [from $200 million to $300 million].

According to Greg Gibbons, he began to lose his credibility with corporate executives as OPD's results fell below the profit plan during January, February, and March of his second full calendar year as DGM. But he felt his credibility was not harmed as much as it might have been because he could point to exciting new OPD products in the marketplace. The division now had something new to show the world and appeared to be on track, even if it was still unprofitable. As Gibbons said after he had turned in very disappointing results for the first six months of his second full calendar year as DGM,

You look at the numbers, but you don't only look at the numbers. You've got to look at: "Is there a strategy?" "Are the products coming out of it?" And they see all these new products coming out of development and out of manufacturing and so forth. So they can see some light at the end of the tunnel; they just hope it's not a locomotive.

Unfortunately, it *was* a locomotive. OPD's results continued to fall behind the profit plan as Gibbons' second full calendar year as DGM unfolded.

Corporate executives feel dependent on the DGM

Three previous DGMs had not been successful at Xerox OPD; Gibbons was the corporate executives' desperate fourth attempt to get OPD going. Knowing this, Gibbons was able to be far more aggressive with his initiatives than he could have been otherwise. By October of Gibbons' second full year as DGM, the division was $50 million below the year-to-date profit plan. But he thought he still had the support of the key corporate executives, in part because he felt they had no alternative but to stick with him:

I could have set a 20 percent growth plan for us this year and I could have made it. And we could have all been slapping each other on the back thinking we've done well, but to me that would have been like the Special Olympics (for physically disadvantaged athletes), because a 20 percent growth plan would have been far below the 50 percent market growth. And by the way, if they put somebody else in here, what would he do differently? That's always the key thing – what's the alternative?

In general, compared to the other DGMs in this study, the corporation was more dependent on Walker, March, and Gibbons – because of their special talents and industry insights – and this gave them greater leverage with corporate executives in pursuing new business opportunities.

The DGM is accepted in the management culture

A DGM with greater acceptance in the management culture has greater leverage with corporate executives. A DGM has greater acceptance if he is seen as an insider ("one of us") rather than an outsider (for example, an acquired manager or new hire). In general, a DGM who believes and behaves as prescribed by the culture has greater acceptance, but even outsiders and non-conformist insiders can gain acceptance if (1) the management culture tolerates deviants, (2) the timing is right, or (3) the DGM operates with cultural savvy.

The management culture tolerates deviants   DGM Ralph West of 3M Imaging Products pointed out that deviants were tolerated within the 3M management culture: "Buddy March is not charismatic, but that's not too important here. In 3M you don't have to have 'the managerial look' to become a DGM. 3M is a place for even a Buddy. He wouldn't be considered managerial elsewhere; 3M has less of that than most companies."

The timing is right   The timing also influences the DGM's acceptance in the management culture. As one manager in Monsanto Fab Products said, "Dan Stewart's timing was perfect. The company was growing less enamored with the centralized approach and more receptive to the kinds of things Dan was championing."

The DGM operates with cultural savvy   Mike Walker and Dan Stewart enjoyed a high degree of acceptance in their management cultures because they were seen as insiders who operated with cultural savvy.[7] For example, Walker and Stewart violated neither the dress code nor the culturally acceptable language and etiquette.

In contrast, Buddy March and Greg Gibbons were seen as outsiders who spoke and behaved in ways that were culturally offensive, and this diminished their acceptance within their management cultures. One member of March's management team had this to say: "The division [3M Micrographics] had some very flamboyant promotional activities, such as celebrity golf tournaments which had almost no relationship to our business, because Buddy loves celebrities and loves golf." DGM Ralph West of 3M Imaging Products gave a somewhat different perspective:

Buddy March has delivered the best results in this group [Business Products] but has the worst image. He got a reputation as a big spender because of the events we sponsored. But here's the background on that. I am a good amateur golfer and my name is associated with it. I am the godfather of the putt-out golf tournament where we would assemble customers for a couple of days to discuss technology and play golf. We did that in the early days of Com, and I believe that's an effective selling tool. It costs relatively little – a couple of thousand dollars. When one our most influential corporate executives became aware of this – he is a golfer – he suggested we do a celebrity golf tournament. The idea was to pay for it by taking some of the money we spend on advertising contests and sales incentives for winning dealers to go to Hawaii, etc. So for several years we did celebrity golf putt-outs at $20–35,000 per meet. First for Com, then for Imaging Products [when it was a department], then for 3M Micrographics in total. Was it worth 20–35 K? I could still argue that it was OK, since big customers were involved. However, the thing began to get publicity within 3M, and in addition to that the events got bigger, with a professional track meet added on, and the agenda began to get obscure. The technical content went down, the entertainment and the celebrity involvement went up. And the cost shot up to 200 K per meet – that was of questionable value. And people saw pictures of Buddy and the celebrities for all these contests in the newspapers. That gave him the reputation of a big spender.

Buddy March admitted that the golf tournaments and the athletic meets had gotten out of hand. "Baker [EVP] made us get out of all these kinds of events," he said. "It was fair criticism – it later on got out of hand."

Greg Gibbons' multi-millionaire status, his flamboyant style, and his use of provocative and earthy language irritated Xerox corporate executives who were accustomed to more conventional forms of presentation and discourse. Here is one example provided by Gibbons at the time of the study in the early 1980s:

Xerox is a very strange environment. No one ever says anything nasty about anybody else. You're always very polite within Xerox Corporation. And you're always very careful on the words that you pick. You never make a nasty comment to somebody or you never openly challenge somebody in an executive meeting, because it's just not done. You never create any ripples. But when the doors are closed, behind your back, all these things come out and they say: "Boy, that division is really crazy." "That's not gonna work." "That first year was just a flash in the pan." That kind of stuff.

I was in a meeting the other day – this is a senior executive meeting and all the DGMs and GVPs were there – and I made a presentation. Then one of the GVPs made a statement. And it was a very, very vague statement. And I said to him, "Max, I think you basically just told me I was full of shit. Is that correct?" And half the Xerox executives just kind of rolled under the table. Because you don't say that. [Laughter.] So Max went on and he explained it again. And I said, "Hey, Max, I still think you told me that I was full of shit." And finally Max admitted that that's what he meant. [Laughter.]

But see, that's not done in Xerox. All the staff work is done ahead of time. Somebody runs around and gets agreement from all these executives. So you go into this meeting and it all flows very nicely and it looks like the water's very calm and this corporation is just moving ahead. And nobody stands and says, "Hey, that's not gonna work." Or, "That's screwed up." Or, "We should do it this way." Never say anything openly. It's always done behind the doors... People either like me or they hate me and that's probably the way it should be. I mean, if you're really trying to make some very significant changes in a very large corporation, the people that want the change are gonna support you and the people that don't want the change think you're crazy.

Buddy March and Greg Gibbons were seen as outsiders to begin with. And they lost additional points because of their counter-cultural language and behavior in connection with matters that had little or no business significance. In contrast, Mike Walker and Dan Stewart were insiders, and they deviated from the management culture only where it was necessary in the interest of the business.[8]

Lower acceptance in the management culture enhances *the DGM's propensity to pursue counter-culture new initiatives*   A DGM who is viewed as an outsider, or an insider DGM who has low acceptance in the management culture, does have one advantage. He is better able to perceive and pursue counter-culture new business opportunities. Because others see the DGM as an outsider, or as an insider who does not believe or behave as prescribed by the culture, he has little to lose and much to gain by undertaking new initiatives that reinforce this impression but could produce valued results.

For example, despite a tolerant management culture at 3M, DGM Buddy March's acceptance was marginal because he was seen as an outsider, and he lacked the cultural savvy, and the desire, to compensate for this disadvantage. As a result, March did some things that were considered taboo within 3M and these turned out to be good things, as he pointed out:

I think we took a risk when we started working with Tanaka [on the printer licensing agreement] – just the fact that we'd go outside and work with a Japanese company versus what the 3M culture had been, certain and strong that we could do it all within. 3M had a big slogan when I came here: "Research is the key to tomorrow." And everything was centered on our laboratories to turn out the profits ... I was doing many things that were considered radical. Well, I didn't think they were radical, so I did a lot of firsts in those days, because I didn't know all of the culture of the company and didn't know what was right and wrong. We were the first division in the company to get its own marketing group. And I was the first to convince the vice president of Engineering to pull the product engineers, not the facility engineers, out of Engineering and into our laboratory.

Marketing director John Hypes agreed with Buddy March on this point: "Buddy is an entrepreneur, a dreamer and a risk-taker. His greatest asset is that he did not grow up in 3M. So he acquired product [Tanaka Printer] and leapfrogged technology [imaging and file management products] that others in the 3M mold could not do."

Buddy March, and Greg Gibbons too, were outsiders who had no hope or desire to become assimilated into their management cultures. A lower acceptance in the management culture did hurt their ability to gain the support of others in the corporation in the pursuit of their new initiatives. But it also helped them to champion and sponsor unpopular initiatives, including those that were counter to the management culture or counter to the preferences of powerful corporate executives, because a lower acceptance reduced their perceived personal risk in doing this.

Summary

The DGM's personality, experience, and leverage with the corporate executives are three important personal assets that influence new business creation.

A DGM who is extroverted, intuitive, oriented to thinking (versus feeling), assertively self-confident, and has a low need for security, is better able to perceive and pursue new business opportunities than a DGM who lacks these personality attributes.

A DGM with prior new business creation experience is more likely to pursue new initiatives; someone who has successfully undertaken new initiatives despite the skeptics, or despite opposition from higher-ups, is more likely to pursue unpopular or counter-culture new initiatives. An in-depth knowledge of the business, and relevant prior experience in a different business setting, are also personal assets that promote the perception and pursuit of new business opportunities.

A DGM who has greater leverage with the corporate executives is better able to bear the personal risks of new business creation. Leverage is greater if powerful corporate executives support the DGM, if he has credibility with corporate executives because of his past record of delivering results or because the current results seem to be on track, if the corporate executives are dependent on the DGM, or if he is accepted in the management culture.

It may appear counter-intuitive, but a *lower* acceptance in the management culture has one advantage. It *enhances* the DGM's capacity to perceive and pursue counter-culture new business opportunities because his perception of personal risk in violating the culture is *lower*.

12 The DGM's motivation and strategy for new business creation

This chapter examines how the DGM's motivation and strategy influence new business creation (Table 12.1).

A combination of business, organizational, and personal reasons motivates the DGM to undertake new business creation.

The DGM's motivation: business reasons

The DGM has extensive network of external contacts

All DGMs rely on their contacts with customers, suppliers, competitors, and other external sources to obtain information, ideas, and support. But the extent of their external network varies. A DGM with a wider network of external contacts is more likely to undertake new business creation for business reasons because he is more likely to have first-hand knowledge of customer needs and competitor actions that call for new initiatives.

DGM Buddy March of 3M Micrographics had spent his entire career in the industry and was known as the "industry godfather." March loved to travel. Even when he had slowed down during his later years, March was still away from his office about a third of his total time, most of it visiting customers. He was full of insights regarding customer needs when he returned from a trip, and he had ideas for new products. As Ray Thorngate, who had served as his technical director for many years, recalled,

Buddy [March] was the world's greatest traveler when he was DGM. He was active in the Micrographics Association committees and boards, and he was talking with customers. He would come back in from a field trip and he would just be bubbling over with enthusiasm. I couldn't get a word in edgewise before him telling me, "But what they really need is like this, and if we could do this it really would put us into a key position." And then he'd come back, and if you were cranking up or starting a project, he'd reinforce you with, "Boy, I talked to so-and-so and this is just exactly what they want." It's the coincidence of having the insight and the intellectual curiosity that he's loaded with. And that isn't always

Table 12.1. *How the DGM's motivation and strategy influence new business creation*

Hypothesis	Factor	Influence on new business creation
DGM's motivation: business reasons		
12.1	DGM has extensive network of external contacts	+
12.2	DGM sponsors or champions new initiatives	+
DGM's motivation: organizational reasons		
12.3	DGM pursues new business creation because his boss expects this of him	+
12.4	DGM pursues new business creation to produce results that the corporation values	+
12.5	DGM wants to avoid organizational layoffs by growing the division via new business creation	+
DGM's motivation: personal reasons		
12.6	DGM seeks industry or public recognition	+
12.7	DGM needs to prove something to himself or others	+
DGM's strategy for new business creation		
12.8	New products for an existing market	+
12.9	Existing and new products for an expanded redefinition of the market	+
12.10	Existing technology and production capacity for new market applications	+
12.11	New products for an emerging new market	+
12.12	Maintain or scale back new business creation	0/–

about products. It's about technology too. His understanding of technology is not deep, but he's very pragmatic in terms of what it can deliver . . .

One of March's major contributions, I've always felt, was that he really had his fingers on the pulse of the industry. And he had a very unusual, uncanny ability to sense directions and trends very early and give us an opportunity to move on them. He would perceive the need in advance of the product. And recognize the value and say, "Let's get ahead. Let's get moving on this." He kind of had the unique position of an observer who also had some power to get things done.

Buddy March had worked with his administrative assistant, Jane Langley, for twenty-four years, and he viewed her as a key link in his personal network of contacts. March said she knew hundreds of people in the customer and supplier organizations on a first name basis, and she would take care of customer complaints and requests and filter appropriate information to him.

DGM Mike Walker of AMP Sigcom also traveled a lot, as one project manager observed:

Mike Walker is a traveler. He visits a bunch of sales places, gets in to see customers at a pretty high level, and stirs up the market himself. Then he gets two or three people working on it. He loves to whip up a big deal himself. If we give up and de-commit on one idea, he has four or five others to keep us busy.

The DGM sponsors or champions new initiatives

A DGM with a wider network of external contacts is more likely to sponsor or champion new initiatives because more extensive external connections give him greater insight into which new initiatives are particularly important for serving the needs of customers, or for fighting competitors, and the degree to which these programs require his support.[1] Clay Smith said Mike Walker championed the Transmission Cable program when he was DGM of AMP Sigcom:

Mike tended to load some programs into our area [new product development] that he felt we needed to pursue. Transmission Cable was one example. He had a vested interest in that because he was responsible for convincing executive management to consolidate the efforts of three divisions under one roof, and that was the AMP Sigcom roof.

Product manager Arjay Mason described DGM Mike Walker's sponsorship of the Cable Assembly initiative:

Mike was not a "I know what is right, go do it my way" kind of manager. He would expect you come up with a story, and would support you if it seemed reasonable. So he bought my recommendation, even though it was counter to the AMP culture, that we assemble the product [Cable Assembly] and sell it to the customer and also that we license the Ribbon Cable to the competition. He ran into resistance with upper management on assembling the product, and he knew he would get flack from marketing on licensing to our competition. But Mike can sell something even when it is unpopular, and he knows how to get to the right people.

DGM Buddy March championed the highly successful Tanaka Printer program. His manufacturing director, Clay Renault, and technical director, Ray Thorngate, went along with the program, but they were not the champions. The Tanaka program encountered internal resistance because it used a new technology, plain paper, while the company was making fat margins on the old technology, coated paper. Many people told March that the program would sink the business as well as his career in the company, but he moved forward by changing the business model. As March put it,

I stole a page from Xerox – the machines [Tanaka printers] were not sold but were leased for a certain number of free copies per month, with additional charges for greater usage. Eventually, the machines were so much in demand that the profits from leasing far exceeded the profits from our traditional business model of giving away the machines [the razor] to make lots of money on the coated paper [the blades].

Buddy March was also widely seen as the champion on the Com program, as well as on the Beta acquisition for that program. As technical director Ray Thorngate said, "I don't think Beta went through a review with the Policy Committee [the division top management team]. That was one of those things Buddy did on his own."

The DGM's motivation: organizational reasons

The DGM pursues new business creation because his boss expects it

The DGM might undertake new business creation because his boss expects him to do so. DGM Clay Smith of AMP Sigcom emphasized new business creation while GVP Mike Walker was his boss, because Walker expected it of him. Smith said,

I generally found that if I disagreed with Mike [Walker, Smith's GVP], I disagreed long enough until I thought I made my point. And if he still disagreed with me, I accepted that, and I said, "OK, then we'll go your way." It's always been that way for me with my supervisor and my boss – I've got to satisfy him. So as long as it's not unethical or unprofessional, why then he's the one setting the direction. That was a rather common way of operating for me.

Smith stopped pushing new business creation after he got a new boss who expected him to improve manufacturing efficiency, reduce cost, and improve customer service instead.

The DGM pursues new business creation to produce results that the corporation values

A DGM might undertake new business creation in order to produce results that the corporation values. DGM Buddy March said he pursued new business creation to spawn new divisions for which he could become a GVP after a younger peer was promoted ahead of him and became his boss:

After Mike was made GVP over me, I withdrew – was not even rational for a year or so. I had nothing against Mike, but I felt deeply hurt. I would have done more to leave, but my wife didn't want to give up the retirement plan, and it has been a beautiful marriage for me . . . It took about two years for me to get comfortable [with the fact that March had been passed over]. The division's numbers got better after that. Our products' acceptability went up and started to pay off . . . I told my staff, "We'll work like hell, that's all we've got. We'll make it here. We will grow ourselves into a group." And we did grow, but they took away the Securities business from me, and they took away Imaging Products when it became large enough to become a division. If I had those, we would be the most profitable group in 3M today.

DGM Ian McVay of Monsanto Engineered Products said he defied his boss's specific instructions to pursue new initiatives in prior DGM assignments if he felt this would produce results that the corporation valued.

Well, I have thought of it this way. There were times when I was doing some high-risk things that had potentially adverse political and career consequences. But on the other hand, I felt almost that there was a higher calling, a higher purpose because if I know that my boss is wrong and if I can improve the business long-term, that's got to be better for me than if I followed his instructions and achieved ho-hum results. And I take a lot of pride in the fact that I made a lot of money for this damn company. And I've done it a lot of times through being able to persuade my bosses over to my point of view, and there were some times when I wasn't able to do that and I just did it my way – at some short-term risk but I think long-term benefit . . . My career anchors[2] are a combination of creativity and advancement in the corporation and, on reflection, more advancement than creativity.

The DGM wants to avoid organizational layoffs by growing the division via new business creation

A DGM who wants to avoid headcount reductions might try to grow the division out of its problems via new business creation. Dan Stewart said he pursued new business opportunities aggressively to grow the division out of its excess capacity and to give his people confidence that the division had a future:

What was driving my overall agenda at Fab Products? Maybe it's partly the "eternal optimist" point of view. Maybe it's partly the "too soft on people" issue. I think it's a combination of both. If you ask [president] Jim Reilly, he will tell you that I am not willing to make the tough decisions on people. I looked at the pruning thing [headcount reduction] as a pretty tough people situation, and so I wanted to find a way to avoid it. I may have over-emphasized new products, but I was doing it mostly to keep the division alive, and to let people realize that there was a future there.

The DGM's motivation: personal reasons

The DGM seeks industry or public recognition

After he was passed over for the GVP job, DGM Buddy March emphasized new business creation in part to get industry recognition. He said, "I decided to make my splash in the industry – took on more active roles in the committees and the leadership of the industry. And the accolades were coming from the industry. I felt 3M could lead the industry [if March's new initiatives succeeded]."

Greg Gibbons wanted to leave his mark as the pioneer of the Office of the Future. As he said at the start of his second full calendar year as DGM of Xerox OPD, "I am not satisfied with my career, because I haven't left my stamp as yet. I want to go down in history as a Henry Ford or a Tom Watson [legendary CEO of IBM] who revolutionized the world. I am not interested in the silver or the bronze medal; we are going for gold."

The DGM needs to prove something to himself or others

Greg Gibbons' emphasis on new business creation was also driven by his desire to prove to himself and others that his entrepreneurial success at Shugart was not just a flash in a pan. As he said at the start of his second full calendar year as DGM,

It's one thing to do a start-up and grow it to $200 million. It's another thing to walk into a $200 million division that you didn't start, that is all screwed up, and try to fix it and grow it. I wanted the experience of running a business in a large corporation. So I did it because of my interest in the office automation area, plus the challenge, just to kind of prove to myself that Shugart wasn't a fluke.

Dan Stewart pursued new business creation in part to prove to his mentor, president Jim Reilly, that he was wrong in his assessment of the plastics business. After three years as DGM, Stewart felt so personally committed to Fab Products and the new initiatives he had championed that he turned down an offer from Reilly to head up a much bigger division, Monsanto Rubber Chemicals. Reilly said he was not amused by Stewart's refusal:

I asked him to take it [DGM of Rubber Chemicals]. Personally. Because I didn't think he could move up from Fab Products with enough credibility to the next big managing director [GVP] job, whatever it was. So I wanted him to get into a large, stable, well-respected operation with all of the normal trappings, and then he could launch from there. I have almost never let anybody turn me down on something like that. Almost never. I was mad as hell.

Two years after this dramatic incident, and five years after becoming DGM of Fab Products, Stewart was promoted to managing director (GVP) of Monsanto Agricultural Products, the company's crown jewel. But even then, Stewart said he agonized over the decision before accepting the new position:

I spent an agonizing twenty-four hours deciding whether to accept. You may say, "You dummy, how could you give up a job to be a corporate vice president and managing director and a member of the CAC?" But I had been in Fab Products five years by this time, and I felt really responsible for it, personally. And there was the personal satisfaction, the learning experience, and a little bit of the pride in saying, "Hey, I want to ride these things out to success" ... If I had turned Reilly down a second time, that would have been the final blow. I mean, I think I would have broken the relationship, it would have been all done then ...

I never, ever convinced Reilly that Fab Products was any good. His experience with it when he was the DGM left him always saying, "There is no way you can make money melting plastic." ... I fought for Fab Products because they were the underdogs. And I said, "Hey, let's see if we can get this turned around." It's like in the movie *Twelve O'Clock High*, where the general played by Gregory Peck put all the losers within the squadron on one plane and called it "The Leper Colony." There was a little bit of that. I have to admit that there was a little bit of "Let's stick it to them. Let's show everybody." One of the things I really wanted – and maybe that led to my hesitancy in leaving Fab Products – was that I wanted to show Reilly that you *can* make money melting plastic. And I got close to it, but not close enough.

The DGM's strategy for new business creation

DGMs have strategies such as the following for new business creation: (1) new products for an existing market; (2) existing and new products for an expanded redefinition of the market; (3) existing technology and production capacity for new market applications; (4) new products for an emerging new market; or (5) maintain or scale back new business creation.

Strategy 1. New products for an existing market

3M acquired Filmsort, a company that Buddy March headed up, and merged it with an internal program to create the Micrographics division. The Aperture Cards from Filmsort and the Model 100 Reader Printer developed within 3M created a winning combination in the 35mm market for engineering design and drafting applications. March, who became DGM, focused the division's R&D effort almost entirely on catching up in the 16mm line, where Kodak was ahead, on the 105mm microfiche line, where Bell & Howell was out in front, and on the Com line, where Datagraphics was in the lead. He maintained the division's dominance in the original 35mm business by selective product acquisitions and licensing of new products, such as the hugely successful Tanaka printer. Technical director Ray Thorngate explained why this full-line strategy was risky:

> The risk was that we were taking resources out of a successful line [35mm] and putting them into lines where we were behind [16mm and 105mm], while absorbing the influx of the likes of IBM and Xerox into the 35mm business. The Tanaka printer was a necessity; we had to rely on external programs to keep our 35mm business. More than half the sales in that business today are from products we obtained from the outside. There was damned little internal development for that business.

Although it was risky and strained the division's resources, Buddy March said he pursued the full-line strategy in order to grow the division:

> The industry wasn't big enough where any one product line could generate what would be a reasonable 3M kind of business. They expect it to get up to hundreds of millions of dollars. That's what was driving this notion of a full-line strategy. My ambition was to be the biggest frog in a small pond [the micrographics industry] and help the pond grow. That's the only way to make a real 3M business out of it. And scoop the high-price, high-quality end of the market. And that means many new products. And that means a strain of resources.

During Buddy March's tenure as DGM over eighteen years,[3] the 35mm business grew from $12 million in sales to around $40 million, with a pre-tax profit of 20 percent of sales (the 3M norm for profitability). Although 3M had no position in the 16mm and 105mm microfiche lines when March took over, he helped to build a $120 million business in these lines with 23 percent in pre-tax profit. The losses on the Com program brought the division's pre-tax profit down to the 16–17 percent range. Buddy March described the challenge of developing a full line of products in a relatively small market:

> The micrographics market is only $2 billion worldwide. It is not big enough to justify the investments that are needed today to develop a full product line. We have to be in the file management market, which is $47 billion.

Buddy March felt confident about the future prospects for 3M Micrographics:

> When we began, Kodak and Bell & Howell had formidable positions and products that scared the daylights out of our salespeople. Having watched their products overtaken by ours has given me a lot of confidence. I don't get scared when

people talk about new electronics technologies outdating micrographics. What they don't realize is that we are not standing still either. We are marrying these technologies to get the best of both worlds for our applications[4] ... I have seen many companies lose direction because they don't have conviction about their vision. They get easily distracted. You have got to have conviction and keep your resources on track.

Strategy 2. Existing and new products for an expanded redefinition of the market

Since the division's business had a high market share in a relatively small market, DGM Buddy March was attempting to redefine the market from micrographics ($2 billion) to file management ($47 billion). DGM Ray Thorngate described how a similar market redefinition enabled 3M Engineering Products to grow from a department (consisting of the original 35mm business) into a division within two years. Thorngate got his division renamed 3M Engineering *Systems* toward the end of this study to signal the new, enlarged scope – not just stand-alone products but systems as well. He said,

There are many reasons for our success. Companies like Tera are romancing customers with integrated systems, and customers are demanding that some of our products, like the Tanaka printer, be included as part of the integrated system – such is the credibility we have in the marketplace ... We will be the system integrators – that's all we can do with the eighteen people I have in design and development. So I am looking to buy new products from entrepreneurial companies abroad, particularly in Europe, who find our huge US distribution system attractive. I signed a couple of exclusive marketing agreements very similar to the Tanaka printer agreement – in fact, I use Tanaka as an example of how a small company can work with us and win.

DGM Mike Walker also expanded the definition of the market – from coaxial cable connectors for RF signals to all kinds of cables and connectors for high complexity signals – and he got the division's name changed from AMP Coax to AMP Sigcom to signify the broader scope. Walker described how he worked with his divisional top management team in a business planning exercise to accomplish this, using his concepts of "measured" and "created" markets:

There are two kinds of markets. One is a "measured market" and that's simply the market that people are already selling into and you can measure each of your competitors' sales growth, your sales in it and add that up, and that's what our people had done. In their minds they felt they had about 80 to 90 percent of "the market." My view was, "No, I want to know the broadest possible definition of that existing market." And that is all the classes of product that are in that field that are sold in that market, whether we make it or not. So the first thing I had to do was disarm my team in thinking that, "Well, he's trying to figure out how bad a job we're doing," to "He's trying to find the opportunities for us to do a better job." A big concern to them was, "How do you get good measures of the market?" Because the data wasn't available. And I said, "Well, you've got to use intelligence. And you learn as much as you can. You read trade journals, you get little drops of data that you might find from a customer. You may find a guy that just left a competitor and you interview him. You get your own intuitive feel as to what the size of it is."

Now that really concerned them because they felt marketing [which was a separate division within AMP] was going to criticize them. And I said, "You did try to get the data from marketing, right?" And they said, "Well, yes." And I said, "But did they help you?" And the answer was, "Well, no, they don't know the size of the market either." Then I said, "Well, how are they going to criticize you?" "Well, they're going to think it's too big or too little." I said, "That's not good enough. What they have to tell you is *why* they think it's too big or too little, and in the process of telling you why you're going to learn more about that marketplace." So I said it's a constructive process, not a destructive process. That got things under a better climate.

A year later I added another dimension to the model because there is another kind of market – what I call a "created market." In other words, it was not attacking a market that existed where you were coming up with a strategy to gain market share from somebody that was already there. It was a market you were going to develop because the need wasn't fulfilled. That's how we developed the concept of the printed circuit board jack. That product didn't exist at that point. We created that market. And there are many major new product lines at AMP that we created using those kinds of principles and concepts.

Strategy 3. Existing technology and production capacity for new market applications

Joe Hurley, commercial development director under both DGM Dan Stewart and his successor, Ian McVay, said the two DGMs had essentially the same business strategy for Monsanto Fab Products:

Ian McVay positioned Fab Products in the mature businesses, and Dan Stewart had done about the same there. The driving force was to maximize cash, to run lean and mean. Dan's long-range plan called for $500 million in sales five years out, so we also had to emphasize a lot of growth in the division. Thirty percent of that $500 million, or $150 million, was to come from new products [Spray Guard and RCA Disk Caddy were each seen as $50–100 million opportunities] ... Ian McVay's strategy for Fab Products is very similar to Dan Stewart's; as far as new products, definitely.

Stewart, and to a lesser extent McVay, were pursuing new business creation in part to utilize the division's excess production capacity, Hurley said.

We were going to have 5 to 6 million square feet of excess capacity in our Pensacola, Florida, facility because we were putting new production machines in Europe. Spray Guard would pick up some of the excess capacity, but not all of it. The ski slope and landscape products, as well as the car floor-mats [three new initiatives that Stewart wanted to pursue], would have helped to get rid of the remaining excess capacity.

In fact, with the exception of the OPET bottle, all the new initiatives in Monsanto Fab Products were driven in part by the desire to utilize excess production capacity and avoid the unpleasant alternative of shutting it down and laying people off. This understandable desire becomes a trap if marginally attractive or unattractive opportunities are pursued as a result of it.

Strategy 4. New products for an emerging new market

Greg Gibbons defined the emerging office automation market broadly to include all computing, imaging, and information processing products and systems for improving the productivity of managerial, professional, and secretarial personnel in the so-called "Office of the Future." From a base of $10 billion, Gibbons expected the market to grow at least fivefold in five years.

Gibbons decided the division had to stop selling one or two units to lawyers, doctors, other independent professionals, and small business owners – what he referred to as "onesie-twosie" sales – and target the major corporations for sales in the *hundreds* of units. This major-account strategy brought Xerox OPD into head-to-head competition with IBM's Office Products Division. Gibbons said he was waging "total war" with IBM and that his objective, simply stated, was to knock the much bigger rival out of first place in the market within five years.

To compete with IBM, product prices were to be slashed as much as 25 percent, with major accounts qualifying for up to 35 percent discounts for volume purchases. For this to become a viable pricing strategy, development, production, and distribution costs would have to be driven down by a substantial amount.

Gibbons had developed a powerful weapon for the war with IBM – the Memorywriter typewriter, with a price/performance that he claimed was superior to IBM's legacy product, the IBM Selectric typewriter. Code-named "Saber," the Xerox Memorywriter had been conceived, designed, and manufactured from the ground up as a breakthrough product. Greg Gibbons explained:

IBM ships about a million typewriters a year. If you can get them to take a hit of $100 per unit, that's a hundred million dollars. The Office Products Division of IBM only makes $300 million in profit. So that hurts a lot. They're in the same position as Xerox in the copier business. Any tactical pricing decisions or strategic pricing decisions that Xerox made to keep the competition out hurt Xerox more than anybody else [because Xerox had the biggest share of the market] ... Now, strategically, this is a very important point. IBM's OPD has got 5,000 sales reps. They're out selling typewriters, copiers, and some portion of office automation. Now, if I can take the 5,000 copier sales people of the Xerox Corporation and send them into the typewriter market – that's the biggest profit generator of IBM's OPD – they have got to concentrate most of their sales force on protecting that profitable base. It hurts IBM's ability to sell copier products, which Xerox sales people love. And now the Xerox OPD sales force of 600 have got an open beachhead to sell office automation to the Fortune 500 companies.

People talk about the barrier to entry – these incredible investments in factories and so forth. It's also a barrier to exit. IBM has got such a huge investment in their typewriter factory, in that technology, that they will stay with that product and that technology well beyond what is reasonable, because nobody's willing to take this huge write-off for that factory.[5] But the technology they have is such that they can't be as competitive. Let me give you an example. Compare the IBM Selectric and the Xerox Memorywriter. Xerox has five lubrication points. IBM has 160. Xerox only needs three adjustments; IBM needs twenty-five. Ours is orders of magnitude better; a very significant product.[6] Steve Carter [VP & GM of the Memorywriter SBU] came from IBM's OPD. He understands the typewriter strategy inside out.

Greg Gibbons felt it was healthy to be scared of the competition, and he talked about his fear of IBM:

I am afraid of IBM. And it's important to be afraid – not afraid of all your competitors, but to pick out a couple of key competitors and really lose a lot of sleep over them. That's very good. What would scare me is if IBM came on the same tack that I was on. They dominate the word processor market, which is where office automation has been up to now. IBM's got about 18 percent; Wang's got about 18 percent; and Xerox OPD has 11 percent. So we've been sailing in their wake. We'll never pass them. All we'll do is burn up a lot of resources and make a lot of people unhappy. So we've gone on a completely new tack. We're going after the professional. Why? It's pure economics. If you look at where office automation has been, it's been word processing applications, particularly for clerical and secretarial personnel. Now, if you go after the professional – which is 80 percent of your cost structure – with a system that can automate half of their tasks, and you can get 20 percent productivity improvement, now you start to see some very, very significant economic paybacks that flow to the bottom line. So we say, "Office automation is not word processing." We even say, "Word processing is a joke." So now we've taken this tack in terms of professional productivity, and we've done it with a product that was designed from the ground up to go after the professional, which is our Star product.

Of course, we need the other products that fit in there so that we can be a complete vendor to a customer. But it's primarily this one product, Star [a new-to-the-world professional workstation, with the first commercial implementation of a graphical user interface and mouse]. Now, my hope is that I will be able to get far enough out in front of IBM before they finally make a decision that they've got to go after this marketplace. The development time on a product like the Star is three to four years; maybe they can do it in two and a half. What would scare me – because they got a faster ship than I do – is that they would tack immediately, and before I have a chance to get out in front and really establish that brand recognition, I've got IBM just coming down my tail. That would concern me.

After Gibbons left Xerox, Steve Carter, who was vice president and general manager of the Memorywriter SBU, became the fifth DGM of Xerox OPD in nine years. The Memorywriter had achieved acceptance and success in the marketplace, which gave Carter credibility in the eyes of the Xerox corporate executives. All other members of Gibbons' top management team had either left OPD or did soon after Carter took over. About six months after he became DGM, Carter gave his opinion about what went wrong at Xerox OPD under Greg Gibbons:

Greg's second [full calendar] year was the make-or-break year. He did believe he could deliver on that aggressive plan. The high point that year was that we were making "optical inroads" during the first half – the image of OPD in the corporation was improving, even though we were behind plan, because we got Ethernet adopted as an industry standard; we got the sales organization in place; we were really moving into the systems business. The Memorywriter typewriter was in the market by year-end... OPD did not make it [the division was $100 million below the profit plan that year] because of the major investments in the PC. We laid in a very large organization – we added eighty people – to manage the indirect distribution [dealers] for the PC... The $100 million shortfall was rationalized as an "investment" in new products. But Greg didn't present last year's picture well [his third full calendar year]. We came in $150 million below the profit plan. The penetration for Star was significantly below forecast. We put in 300 systems, but what was on the systems were the PCs, not the Stars... We did not properly assess software problems. We were overly aggressive; we should have put in a plan that was achievable. If not for the Memorywriter typewriter, and my credibility associated with it, this whole division would be down the tubes.

About six months after Gibbons left, Gibbons' boss, GVP Jerry Tyson, also reflected on the events:

The rest of the world cannot conceptualize the "Office of the Future." We are currently selling twenty networks [of office systems built around Ethernet and Star] per month, but we need to be selling sixty per month to be viable. We may not make it in the systems business, unless we can move up above forty per month before I run out of cash... The copier businesses are fighting overseas competition. As Xerox profits and cash have fallen, corporate reviews and caution are up. The fact that OPD missed the profit plan by $100 million [in Gibbons' second full calendar year as DGM], and then by $150 million [in the third year], has caused OPD to be seen as a total miscalculation – wrong business, wrong strategy, and wrong product. The PC, in particular, hurt a lot. It was rushed to market – with considerable investment in an indirect distribution organization – just as IBM changed the rules of the game by leaping to a 32-bit processor.

Strategy 5. Maintain or scale back new business creation

After Steve Carter took over as DGM, Xerox OPD was made a cost center; sales and profit responsibility for the Memorywriter typewriter was transferred to Xerox's copier sales force. Ethernet and Star, which were not selling anywhere close to the forecast and were together losing more than $100 million a year, were retained because the corporate executives viewed them as strategically vital to the corporation. These new products were designated as "investments," and the responsibility for managing them was transferred back to the West Coast. Steve Carter gave an update on where Xerox OPD stood and talked about his strategy for the division six months after he took over as DGM:

> What we have going for us here is the Memorywriter typewriter. IBM has responded aggressively and are going through dealers to compete with us. So we are slightly below plan for the first quarter. But in this second year of its life, we will sell 100,000 Memorywriters and turn in over $100 million in revenue and $25 million in profit. The rollout got national visibility, and we gained 20 percentage points in market share ... My mandate is to drive the development and manufacturing of the Memorywriter, the fax machine, and the PC worldwide. Our goal is cost containment – I have an overhead ceiling of $50 million. The strategy calls for 15–18 percent increase in profit and sales next year. The industry is growing at 40 percent. It should be a piece of cake.

GVP Jerry Tyson added this: "Steve Carter came from IBM. He understands IBM and he understands big companies. We should be able to move the Memorywriter and the fax machines. From $350 million this year, I am looking at OPD revenue of $800 million within three years."

The glamor of strategy and the hard work of execution

DGMs pursue new business creation strategies such as the five types described in this chapter. But the best strategies in the world will not produce the desired results without proper execution.[7]

DGMs understand the importance of proper execution, but some are better at it than others. Mike Walker and Ian McVay were the masters of execution, as subsequent chapters reveal. Greg Gibbons was at the other extreme; many of his people felt that he was so mesmerized by the appeal of strategy that he under-estimated the implementation challenges.[8] Xerox OPD fell further and further behind the profit plan during Gibbons' second full calendar year as DGM, but this is what he said in early June when the division was $40 million below the year-to-date profit plan:

You gotta have faith; that's the key. We have a strategy. And I feel confident in the strategy. And if the strategy is right, then we're gonna be successful. It's just a matter of timing. Of course, if the strategy is wrong, we don't deserve to be successful, okay?[9] So why worry about it? But it's a key point that if you really have a strategy that you have thought through and you're confident in, and it's strictly a matter of execution, then you don't needlessly worry when you find yourself behind plan or in a bind or what have you.

But it was a lack of proper execution that ultimately killed Greg Gibbons' strategy and sank the division, so his great emphasis on strategy and his relative neglect of implementation did not serve him well. Successful execution requires the DGM to build corporate support for his strategy of new business creation, and he must also lead the division appropriately for it. These topics are covered in the next two chapters.

Summary

The DGM is motivated to undertake new business creation for a mix of business, organizational, and personal reasons.

A DGM who has an extensive network of external contacts – with customers, suppliers, competitors, and other industry sources – tends to undertake new business creation for business reasons. Such a DGM also is more likely to sponsor or champion new initiatives because his wider external connections give him greater insight into which initiatives are particularly important for serving the needs of customers, or for fighting competitors, and into the extent these programs require his support.

One organizational reason for the DGM to undertake new business creation is that his boss expects this of him. Another is that, even though his boss may be opposed to it, he believes new business creation will produce results that are valued by the corporation. A third organizational reason is the desire to avoid painful personnel layoffs by growing the division out of its troubles via new business creation.

The DGM might be motivated to undertake new business creation for personal reasons. Two examples are his quest for industry or public recognition, and his need to prove something to himself or others. In some cases the personal reasons for new business creation are so compelling that the DGM is willing to put his job on the line for it, or refuse promotion to stay on to see his ventures succeed!

DGMs develop strategies for new business creation such as the five outlined in this chapter: (1) new products for an existing market; (2) existing and new products for an expanded redefinition of the market; (3) existing technology and production capacity for new market applications; (4) new products for an emerging new market; and (5) maintain or scale back new business creation. However brilliant the strategy, it will fail without proper execution – the subject of the next two chapters.

13 Building corporate support for new business creation

This chapter examines how the building of corporate support by the DGM influences new business creation (Table 13.1).

Support or opposition from corporate constituents

The DGM must build support with three corporate constituencies: his boss, top corporate executives, and relevant corporate committees and staff groups. Those who are opposed to the DGM's new business creation strategy and initiatives must be won over, neutralized, or defeated.

The DGM's boss and the top corporate executives

The DGM needs the support of his boss, typically a GVP, to get things done. It helps even more if the GVP's superiors – the EVP, the president, and the CEO – also support the DGM and his new business creation strategy. This is especially true for new initiatives involving substantial investment, or high risk, or excursions beyond the current corporate strategy.[1]

Buddy March said he had learned the importance of corporate support from his failure to obtain clearance for a key acquisition during his early years as DGM of 3M Micrographics.

I wanted to buy Sycor ten years ago, but I was turned down by corporate. I thought my GVP had sold it to [president] Bennett Colt. But he hadn't. Or maybe I did a poor sell upstairs. Anyhow, they turned me down. Said it was too risky. That was a poor decision because Sycor took off only a year later. I have learned from that. Today, I would sit down and personally sell MacNeil [CEO] and the two other top executives in such a case.

DGM Dan Stewart of Monsanto Fab Products felt he received no encouragement from his mentor, president Jim Reilly, to pursue new business creation. However, Stewart said his previous boss, GVP Ben Warner, and his current boss, GVP Hal Courtney, were both very encouraging and supportive.

Table 13.1. *How the building of corporate support by the DGM influences new business creation*

Hypothesis	Factor	Influence on new business creation
Support/opposition from corporate constituents		
13.1	DGM's boss	+/–
13.2	Top corporate executives	+/–
13.3	Corporate committees and staff groups	+/–
DGM's political power		
13.4	DGM reports to an EVP rather than to a GVP	+
13.5	DGM has a powerful corporate network	+
13.6	DGM has strong political alliances	+
DGM's political strategies and tactics		
Political strategy 1. Use reason and appeal		
13.7	Reframe the case for new business creation so it is perceived as less risky, more compelling, and/or more legitimate	+
13.8	Communicate effectively via persuasive presentations and memorable memos	+
13.9	Give people confidence in the new product or service by allowing them personally to experience it	+
Political strategy 2. Avoid or delay opposition		
13.10	Don't ask for permission; ask for forgiveness later if necessary	+
13.11	Use political timing to one's advantage	+
Political strategy 3. Overcome opposition with political power		
13.12	Use political power to overcome resistance	+

Warner and Courtney were the two guys to have because they were not political by nature [they were willing to support Stewart's new initiatives despite Reilly's skepticism]. Otherwise, it would have been very difficult. I would have had a lot of upward conflict. A lot more than I had . . . I don't think Reilly really supported me. I think he acquiesced [in Stewart's strategy]. It wasn't a big thing for him. It wasn't major dollars, and we were just doing it on our own. But I knew in his heart, and even today, he doesn't believe in it. He just had an intuitive feel that these were bad businesses. And time will tell; he may be right. If you look at last year's results, you'd say he was right.

DGM Greg Gibbons of Xerox OPD relied on the strong support of CEO Bill Nash, president Larry Wind and GVP Jerry Tyson – all of whom he referred to as his "corporate bodyguards." Without their support, Gibbons could not have defied the corporate committees, the corporate

staff, and the corporate culture of Xerox the way he did. Greg Gibbons
said he would never go around his corporate bodyguards:

There are always a couple people, hopefully at high levels, who like to see the
change that's developing, the new ways of doing things and so forth. And if you
piss those people off, you shot your bodyguards. Like if [president] Larry Wind
shot down my PC program, and I went to [CEO] Nash, well, then, I shot my
bodyguard. And Larry's just going to stand aside and let the coyotes come out
of the woodwork and eat me up. Likewise, if Jerry Tyson said, "Greg, you can't
do this," and I go to Larry Wind, then I've shot down Tyson. I would never do
that, even if I thought I was right. I would work through the system or I'd just say,
"Forget it." If I couldn't convince Jerry that I should go do this, it's either not
worth doing or I've done a poor salesmanship job. I'd probably leave the company
before I would go around Jerry Tyson and go to Larry Wind.

Gibbons respected his boss Jerry Tyson and he recognized that Tyson
was probably running corporate interference of which he was not even
aware:

Jerry may be doing such a good job of blocking for me that every time I get the
ball, I might run five or six yards and think I'm a great running back. But I may
have an incredible blocker out in front of me and I just don't know it. Jerry and
I communicate at the same level. We kind of are really in sync. I've always been
very honest with him and never play any games; and he never plays any games
with me. Pretty straightforward.

Corporate committees and corporate staff

Various corporate committees and staff groups review and advise the division on business and policy matters, and the DGM needs their support
for successful new business creation.

However, Greg Gibbons did not wish to engage in what he called "corporate politics" to cultivate this support. He said he had neither the patience nor the inclination for it. Because he felt he had the strong support
of his boss (Tyson) as well as the top two corporate executives (Nash
and Wind), Gibbons decided to fight what he viewed as the "corporate
bureaucracy" that did not understand the needs of the office automation
marketplace. He ignored the voluminous corporate policy manuals and
procedures, and refused to seek corporate committee approvals, because
he believed this was necessary in order to execute his strategy with the
required speed. When the corporate staff asked for reports and information that he felt were none of their concern, Gibbons would either ignore
their requests or, on occasion, return them without comment but with
the words "THIS IDEA STINKS" rubber-stamped boldly on the front
cover.

About six months after he became DGM of Xerox OPD, Gibbons conceived the idea of an OPD mascot, the Road Runner. The genesis of the idea came from watching television cartoons of the Road Runner and the Coyote with his two children on Saturday mornings. While acknowledging corporate's role as the banker, Gibbons insisted that "half-time people are not going to come down here and tell us how to run a full-time business." Gibbons said OPD managers were like Road Runners who had to be faster and smarter than the coyotes who laid roadblocks in their way:[2]

We're trying to be Road Runners. And anybody that gets in our way is a coyote, whether it be corporate or competition or what have you; and even the people internally within OPD that say it can't be done. There's a bunch of people at corporate who are coyotes – except [CEO] Bill Nash, [president] Larry Wind and [GVP] Jerry Tyson . . . Here is what I call "coyote shit." All pricing had to go up to corporate for approval. I mean, how the hell am I supposed to run a division down here and implement a strategy if I have to go up to them and justify all my pricing actions? So I absolutely refused to do that. The second thing is, they wanted to approve all product programs. I said, "That's a bunch of crap – here's my financial model; here's how much I'm gonna spend on development; here's my strategy. I'll come up and I'll give you my strategy once a year. Then the product program approval within that is my own prerogative. I'm not gonna come to you and go through all these gates on every damn program, every product I want to develop." Compensation for the sales rep was supposed to go up to corporate. And I said, "Bullshit, I'm not doing that." All advertising – you name it, everything goes up. If I wanted to promote somebody internally, that goes up to the corporate staff . . . There were also a lot of good people up at corporate, in the pricing organization and so forth, that really wanted to get the job done and they would really go out of their way to help us out. And we would give them a Road Runner Award. So it wasn't all negative . . . The biggest problem was enemy identification, trying to figure out who your enemies were and who your allies were. And then really playing up to the allies and saying, "Hey, we're not against corporate staff. We're not against having some controls. But all this bureaucratic stuff has to stop." So we just basically took them head on.

After president Larry Wind became CEO, he dismantled the corporate staff groups and committees to give greater decision-making authority to the business units. Gibbons said,

This company used to be run by the corporate staff – a very strong marketing corporate staff; a very strong HR corporate staff; a very strong financial corporate staff; a very strong strategy corporate staff. And they used to dictate everything. And that is all gone. There is no more corporate staff except in finance. And I agree that there ought to be a finance corporate staff. So I'm not so worried about the coyotes any more. I'm only worried about my own performance now, okay? That's some of the impact we've had on the big corporation as a result of some of the things we've done down here in OPD.

Gibbons admitted that, if not for CEO Wind's corporate reorganization, the corporate staff and the corporate committees that he had ignored
with impunity would surely have sought sweet revenge as OPD slipped
further and further behind the profit plan.

If the corporate staff had still been there toward the end of last year [Gibbons'
second full calendar year as DGM, when the division came in $100 million below
the profit plan], it might have been a real problem, because basically I had made a
lot of enemies. But luckily, the hunting expedition was very successful six months
before that, so there just weren't any coyotes around to eat the wounded Road
Runner.

Greg Gibbons' success in isolating OPD from the corporate committees and the corporate staff groups, as well as from the rest of the corporation, led others to misperceive the division and its strategy. As Gibbons'
successor DGM Steve Carter later pointed out,

Because Greg set OPD apart as an island, a lot of people in corporate and in
the copier group did not have direct first-hand knowledge about what was going
on here. So there was a mythology created, some of it dysfunctional, about what
OPD was up to. The mythology was, "OPD has no strategy," and "The markets
OPD is after are just not there." They got Greg's style mixed up with what was
his strategy. They did not see that his style was rambunctious but his strategy was
sound! When we began to integrate the sales force after I took over, the people
who came down here from the copier group and from corporate were surprised
to discover that there were a number of people here who actually knew what they
were doing!

The DGM's political power

A DGM with more political power is better able to build corporate support for new business creation, and neutralize or eliminate any opposition
to it.[3] The DGM's political power is based not only on his leverage with
corporate executives (Chapter 11), but also on his hierarchical position
within the corporation, his corporate network, and his political alliances.

The DGM reports to an EVP rather than to a GVP

DGMs are extremely sensitive about their hierarchical position, which
depends on the hierarchical position of the person they report to, because
this affects their political power within the corporation.

When DGM Buddy March was passed over for the GVP position a
second time, he and his colleagues were consoled that he would be reporting directly to an executive vice president (EVP), rather than to a
group vice president (GVP) as was typical for a DGM. Ian McVay, DGM

of Monsanto Engineered Products, also reported directly to an EVP and attributed the same degree of significance to it:

A lot of the games around here have to do with a guy building his power base. I report to [EVP] Ed Costello. That gives me the image of power because he is widely viewed as among the top four or five corporate executives. That is recognized by my people. They know that if they sell Ian McVay on something, that's it. In my previous DGM job, McVay was seen as necessary, but only one link in the chain. You've got to get by him in order to get to the next level. But you had to go to the next level to get what you wanted.

The DGM has a powerful corporate network

An individual's corporate network consists of his or her corporate contacts. The more powerful the DGM's corporate network, the greater the potential support for new business creation.[4] For example, DGM Clay Smith of AMP Sigcom compared his corporate network with the vastly more powerful one of his mentor and boss, Mike Walker:

My linkages with executive management are really limited to a couple of opportunities a year to really express my feelings and my needs and my concerns and so forth in our sessions with the planning committee. There are occasional opportunities a couple of times a year perhaps to get other communication or dialog going on a specific issue or what have you. But by and large it's got to be relayed up the organizational chain. And through a number of successive layers . . . Mike Walker was a little unusual as a DGM. He definitely had communication lines with key individuals in upper management that were not typical for a division manager. There definitely had been contact with those people earlier in his career at AMP when all of them were either division managers or group directors [GVPs]. And now that they were elevated to executive management level, there certainly was a rapport there that was developed years ago.

The DGM has strong political alliances

Strong political alliances are also important in cultivating corporate support, as DGM Ian McVay of Monsanto Engineered Products pointed out:

I think I'm aligned to the right people. I have good relationships with just about everyone within the senior management community. Particularly with guys like Tim Gossamer, Rick Porter [two of the rising stars]. I don't have as good a working relationship as I would like with some. Don Davis [an influential corporate executive] is a problem for me or has been. Unfortunately, he is important for me because he is such an influencer of Joe Payne [one of the top corporate executives] that I think that somehow my relationship with Payne is, or has been, damaged. Not to such a great extent that it can't be repaired, but it is probably not going to get any better until Don Davis retires from this company – which isn't going to happen for another year. So, I wouldn't give it a 95+ rating, but I think on balance I'm certainly 80–85 percent of where I would like to be. I work at it. I think that it's damn important.

In sharp contrast, DGM Greg Gibbons of Xerox OPD said he had no desire to put in the time and the effort necessary to create political alliances or build relationships with influential corporate executives beyond his three big supporters – GVP Tyson, president Wind and CEO Nash:

I don't play the political game well. I don't really have time to go do that. If I think people can be convinced or changed, I might spend some time with them. But a lot of these people I just basically have written off. And so I don't spend a lot of time, in terms of trying to smooth over the relationship and create this impression that, hey, we really can work together and so forth. I just think it's a waste of time, and I don't really have the energy or desire to go do something like that. And I basically think that these are the people that need to leave the business.

Independent entrepreneurs are ill-suited to corporate entrepreneurship

As in the case of Greg Gibbons, independent entrepreneurs often lack one of the essential ingredients for corporate entrepreneurship – the ability and willingness to navigate the political and cultural rapids of a large corporation to get things done – specifically, to get the attention and support new initiatives need to survive and succeed.[5]

Independent entrepreneurs have a tendency to venture forth on their own. Their lack of corporate experience equips them with neither the patience nor the skill required to build the corporate networks and the political alliances necessary to cultivate corporate support. Leon Milliken, head of R&D for Monsanto Industrial Chemicals, described the company's experience with a number of independent entrepreneurs and why they all had failed.

Rick Bentley [corporate VP of HR] created a task force on how to bring entrepreneurs into Monsanto. It cannot be done. Monsanto has tried from time to time to transplant outside entrepreneurs, and always failed. Take the entrepreneur we brought in to develop a nutritional drink. We were delighted to get him. He was with us three plus years but was simply ineffective. He tended to run with the ball and was terribly impatient with people. It was fun for him, but Monsanto couldn't find a way to work with him. He went back to LA . . . The odds of having a large company be home for an independent entrepreneur are very slim. This is not to say that there is not an entrepreneurial spirit in a large corporation. But I wouldn't use the same word to describe both types. We need a champion who stands out from the surroundings, but not the guy who will start out on his own . . . Monsanto is a complex society. You can't just come in here and operate like an independent. You need to understand corporate politics and how to get things done in this society. Outside entrepreneurs are like commandos. Entrepreneurship in a large corporation is like the D-Day invasion of Europe – coordination and control are critical.[6]

Political strategies and tactics

The DGM can build support for new business creation, and overcome any opposition to it, by using *reason and appeal*. Another political strategy for dealing with opposition is *delay or avoidance*. A third strategy is to overcome resistance by using *political power*.

Political strategy 1. Use reason and appeal

The DGM can try to reassure supporters and persuade opponents that his new business creation strategy and initiatives are eminently sensible, attractive, and worthy of corporate support.[7] This is the political strategy of reason and appeal, and it has three associated tactics: (1) reframe the case for new business creation to reduce its perceived risk and enhance its legitimacy and attractiveness; (2) communicate effectively via persuasive presentations and memorable memos; and (3) give others confidence in a new product or service by allowing them to experience it personally.

Tactic 1. Reframing the case for new business creation[8]   The perception of risk, the analysis, and/or the argument for new business creation can be reframed so that it is seen as a less risky, more compelling, and/or more legitimate activity that is deserving of corporate support.

Tactic 1A. Reframe the perception of risk (look – only upside, no downside!)[9]
The DGM can build corporate support for a new initiative by reframing it to show why it offers potential benefits without any risks. For example, Alf Hummel, VP of corporate planning at Monsanto, was opposed to the OPET bottle initiative because he viewed it as an incremental approach that was bound to fail:

There are two alternatives. One is to go in big and follow the experience curve and beat the pants off the competition, but that requires major investment. And the other is to hit and run – jump in with a $3.8 million investment, scoop the top of the market when no one else is there, and get the hell out. But what I see is an incremental approach. They are buying an option to play. But if the history of the plastic PET bottle is any guide, everyone will lose their ass in that market.[10]

DGM Ian McVay of Monsanto Engineered Products was able to gain corporate support for the OPET bottle initiative, despite opposition from Alf Hummel and others, by positioning it as a win-no-lose proposition that could become a significant business for Monsanto. McVay said,

Alf Hummel is one of the best corporate planners, and I have a tremendous respect for the man. There may be no fallacy in his argument. [Laughter.] What makes this OPET thing unique is the fact that the technology is protected for the next ten years. So we have more than just lead time here, we have a position that is sustainable. And I got Alf to buy into that. The second thing I said was, "Alf, who gives a shit if we piss away $4 million in capital on this – given the upside potential if it's successful. And we'll at least return the cost of capital for the investment by running this as a cold-fill operation. So, there's really very little downside risk." Now, is anybody going to be able to make any money? That's another one of Alf's very good questions. He says, "Who cares if there's a big packaging revolution coming, because the packaging industry has had a history of horrible profitability." And he's right. Once something is invented, hoards of competitors run in and emulate the technology and then start cutting the price. And nobody ever makes any money and that's exactly what happened with the PET bottle.

But if we were to get an early lead on our exploratory polymer program. If we were to get the FDA to come back quickly and approve Cycle Safe. And if we could get some interest immediately on the part of the beer packagers – because Cycle Safe is the only plastic container that could be used to package beer. You know, if three or four things happened we could be off and running. And Alf says, "Yeah, you're right. But it's the junior achievement syndrome. You're incrementalizing your way to nowhere." Well, yeah. But I'm a realist and I'm a general manager trying to make a buck and I'm not asking the corporation for $30 million for a new research program because I can't promise anything.

But in my own mind I have a plan, a perception, a road map, and checkpoints along the way. Now at any time if I see those checkpoints are flashing red I can stop at no real cost, no real damage, but if they continue to show green and if Cycle Safe comes back and we were to get along with OPET and, you know, we get something out of this modest little exploratory R&D program, well it starts coming together.[11] And then I can see the elements of a big business. I have that vision, I have that look to the future, and I have had them before. And most times they don't work out. But once in a while one of them does. Hummel and I have a philosophical difference on this incrementalizing technique. But if I'm right this could be a very substantial business for Monsanto.

Technical director Peter Dell felt that McVay had not only positioned the OPET initiative as a win-no-lose proposition for the business, but also for himself from the standpoint of personal risk: "McVay can almost say I saved this business, regardless of what happens. If it fails, he can say he limited the losses or even made a little money. If it succeeds, great!"

Tactic 1B. Reframe the analysis (from technical review
to marketing assessment)

DGM Greg Gibbons won a corporate political battle and brought the
Memorywriter typewriter program into Xerox OPD by reframing the
analysis, from a technical review to a marketing assessment. He described
how he did this:

When I came to OPD, I had to deal with three camps that wanted the Memorywriter – Diablo [a Xerox division], the Chicago Seven [a free-standing entrepreneurial unit that Gibbons had earlier helped to create], and the engineering
group within OPD here in Dallas. I clearly wanted OPD to have the responsibility for the Memorywriter because, if that's not a product for the Office Products
Division, I don't know what is. I was successful, but it was like trying to give
a tiger an enema in a phone booth, okay? [Laughter.] It was very dangerous.
[Laughter.] . . . Both Diablo and the Dallas group said that they could build that
machine for 600 bucks – best case. In the meantime, Steve Kendall, head of the
Chicago Seven, was jumping up and down, saying, "I can build it for 350. I can
build it for 350." And OPD down here says, "No, it's 600." And Diablo said it
was 600. Now if we're gonna build it for $600, we got to sell it for $1,800 – no
one disagreed with that. At that price point, you can sell 10,000, 20,000, 30,000
units a year. If I get the cost down to 350 dollars and I sell it for $1,200, then I'm
on the steep up-ramp of the sales curve and the program just blows out of sight.

So we went to the corporate PRC [Product Review Committee] meeting where
they looked at the Diablo proposal and they looked at our approach. And Diablo
wanted to make it a technical review. And I changed it into a marketing analysis.
And I said, "We're absolutely crazy to go to the marketplace with a $600 UMC
[unit manufacturing cost], because that will absolutely blow us out of the water;
IBM will come right down on top of us at $1,200. Which means we've got to cut
price and sell at two times the cost – and we're gonna lose our ass. What we need
to do is have a $350 UMC; the Chicago Seven product can beat $350 UMC,
and now the sales volume goes up dramatically . . . We just steamrolled Diablo on
the Memorywriter. And then we had to kind of integrate the Chicago seven into
OPD. That was easy to do because the Chicago group was an entrepreneurial
unit that Steve Carter was already coordinating. And when Carter came to work
for me, that whole group came. So we just bolted it in and made it an SBU under
Carter.

Tactic 1C. Reframe the argument (from performance/
competency to legitimacy/need)

DGM Mike Walker of AMP Sigcom got the Fiber Optics venture transferred to his division by reframing the argument that the DGM in charge
of the venture was making, that his division had better performance and
competency to manage it. Walker described a critical meeting in the office
of AMP's chief operating officer (COO) – whom he had pre-sold on the
transfer – in which he neutralized his opponent's objections by arguing
his case based on the legitimate needs of his division:

I had convinced Dave MacNeil [COO] we needed to do this and the meeting was in his office. Holmes [the division manager in charge of the Fiber Optics venture] went on a diatribe about how AMP Sigcom's technology and people were not as good. I had the impulse to argue with him, because I was in the early stages of understanding how to handle such situations. Fortunately, I decided to let him talk because he was digging a hole for himself. When he finally finished, I said, "Your technology and people are better, but our need is greater and it will have more impact on our product lines [fiber optics could one day replace coaxial cable]". . . At one point, Holmes said, "Your division has not been able to deliver profit." At which point someone else said, "That is not true. You are not being fair to Walker." And the tide turned. I said, "We are smaller, but we deliver more gross margin." Holmes then went on about how all the Fiber Optics guys were going to turn in their resignations rather than move to AMP Sigcom, and I said, "Dave [MacNeil], I can convince them; people won't leave."

Tactic 2. Communicate effectively   The political strategy of reason and appeal requires the DGM to communicate effectively. Persuasive presentations and memorable memos are two important means for accomplishing this.

Tactic 2A. Persuasive presentations

Presentations that are persuasive help to build corporate support for new business creation. Product manager Jim Fitch of AMP Sigcom contrasted DGM Mike Walker's persuasive presentations with the less effective ones of his prior boss:

Walker always has a very good story, all the i's dotted and the t's crossed. Politically, technically, and functionally. It is all mapped out. On paper. In very few words. I get counseling on some of this – how to write things for the first floor [the corporate executives]. Keep it simple and to the point. Don't go on with a lot of flowery, marketese kind of talk. Don't talk big, massive, fucking numbers. Talk in specifics. But talk in specifics that *they* [the corporate executives] want to hear – what do you need to be able do it, when do you need it, and when are we going to start making a profit from it. Done. [Laughter.] . . . It's quite a difference from my previous boss [Dennis Kay]. Massive. Massive. [Laughter.] Anybody that's schooled in computer programming does one of these diagrams with an input question and possible answers – yes, no, maybe. Right? Kay's had about seventy-five maybe's coming out of it. [Laughter.] Maybe's, could be's, should be's, would be's. For Walker it is yes or no. Binary. Now with the implementation you get into finesse. What do you want to do? Why do you want to do it? What's in it for us? How long is it going to take? How much is it going to cost? How many people are you going to need to do it? Done. Or not done. OK?

Tactic 2B. Memorable memos

Memorable memos command attention and enable people to see an initiative in a new, more favorable light. DGM Greg Gibbons explained the slow start of his second full calendar year as DGM to his key sponsors, Xerox president Larry Wind and GVP Jerry Tyson, hoping to keep other corporate executives and staff off his back. He sent them the following memorable memo, with copies to his division top management team:

To: Lawrence C. Wind
        Jerry N. Tyson

From: Gregory A. Gibbons
        Office Products Division

Before I go into the Guinness Book of Records as the shortest lived Corporate Vice President in the history of American Industry, I thought I would give you some insight into what happened in January and February.

The poor orders/installs for January and February resulted from the sales organization doing *exactly* what we told them to do – walk away from one and two unit orders! Last year, OPD had 60 Major Account Reps (MARs) out of a sales force of approximately 700. At the beginning of this year, we converted every sales rep (except approximately 75) to a MAR assignment, gave each one 10 to 15 focused accounts from the Fortune 1300 and directed them to concentrate on their focused accounts, even at the expense of walking away from business.

This is exactly what they are doing. They are walking away from business that ultimately will be the responsibility of dealers, and concentrating all of their efforts on their focused accounts.

Now, if the strategy is correct, we should initially see a drop in the scheduled backlog, which is all the Xerox systems can measure, and a significant increase in the unscheduled backlog. The attached chart shows how the unscheduled backlog has grown over the last year; note the significant increase since December. Note also that our "super products" (PC, Star and Memorywriter) have not hit the market yet!

The strategy, both product and marketing, is right. Don't panic! Don't lose any sleep over it either; I lose enough for all three of us. Have faith. And most of all, forget the fact that the entire future of this Corporation is riding on how well we do down here.

        Gregory A. Gibbons
        GAG. db

P.S. Don't help!

Copy to: Senior OPD Staff

Tactic 3. Give people confidence in the new product or service by allowing them to experience it personally   Another tactic for the political strategy of reason and appeal is to create confidence in a new program by giving people an opportunity to experience a new product, process or service directly. Managing director Dan Stewart of Monsanto Agricultural Products said,

My feeling is that [DGM] McVay's presentation [on the capital request for the OPET bottle initiative] got a pretty damn enthusiastic reception by the CAC [Corporate Advisory Council]. And cone of the reasons is he passed a bunch of bottles around. Which is a trick I always use. Give them a Spray Guard or show them the Drainage Mat. People can get excited about that, if they can see it and touch it and feel it. When I was in Fab Products, the board of directors went to the Anaheim, California plant and some of my people were worried about it. The board of directors loved it. They saw these little bottles come down the line, they saw these big film bubbles, and they saw Fomecor. Those are things that people can understand.

Political strategy 2. Avoid or delay opposition

Tactic 1. Don't ask for permission; ask for forgiveness later if necessary One avoidance tactic is to move ahead on a program that might be turned down if permission is requested. DGM Ian McVay explained:

I think all successful managers do this. There are times you sense you have an idea, a program, an agenda you want to follow, and if you asked the question you know what the answer is going to be. You understand enough of what's going on – the culture, the attitude, the mood – to know that what you're going to propose is unpopular and if you press it to a decision you'll be told not to do it. I am in that circumstance often so I just don't ask the question. I go ahead and do it. I've been caught. It's backfired. It's been embarrassing. But eight to nine times out of ten I'm successful with it. And I think that has led to a large part of my career success to date. I think every manager has an opportunity to take risk; successful managers are those who are willing to take those risks. They have developed a sense of it. After a while you just kind of know it – gee, if I go ahead and ask this question I know what the answer is going to be but I know what the result could be if I pull it off. And I know if I pull it off I'll be a hero; let's go ahead and do it.

Tactic 2. Use political timing to one's advantage   A DGM with a good sense of political timing can avoid or delay opposition to his new business creation strategy and initiatives. He knows when to move ahead and when to wait, when to argue and when to be quiet, when to swim against the tide and when to go with the flow.

When Ian McVay became DGM of Monsanto Engineered Products, the request for capital approval for the OPET bottle initiative was scheduled to go before the Corporate Advisory Council (CAC) in two months. McVay said he asked for a three-month delay because he felt he needed time to build corporate support for the initiative.

We had no conception of the political climate inside Monsanto. OPET is son of Cycle Safe. From the wonderful guys who brought you a $200 million loss [on Cycle Safe], four years later, here is another neat idea. It will cost you only $100 million this time! . . . Had we gone ahead on schedule to the CAC we would have been machine-gunned. No greasing of the skids had been done. We called together Rains [senior VP of process technology] and Schein [EVP of corporate technology] and presented informally to them. They asked about twelve devastating questions which we then went about trying to get answered. We sold Hummel [VP of corporate planning] separately. Three guys who could have blocked us in the CAC. The result was that we got excellent CAC support. Maybe Stewart [prior DGM] could have done it without laying all this groundwork; I would have been crucified.

Joe Hurley, commercial development director for Monsanto Fab Products, felt Ian McVay displayed an excellent sense of political timing by *not* asking for a second delay on the request for capital approval for the OPET bottle initiative:

Now there was a political thing that was involved here too. And McVay had a much better feel for it than I did. McVay's opinion was, "Hey, I have delayed going over to the CAC for the $3.2 million capital approval. The CAC knows that I've delayed. I don't want to delay again. I don't want to have to go back in April and say, "Hey I want to present it in August." Because then red flags start flying and all this kind of stuff, and he really didn't want to do that. And so, there's that political element that was involved also in going over there – I guess it was in April – even though we had not really done all our homework.

Political strategy 3. Overcome opposition with political power

Ian McVay fought two influential Monsanto corporate executives to implement his strategy of consolidating all the operations of the Prism Separator venture under one roof. Here is his detailed account of how he succeeded, but at some political cost.

The most recent incident with Don Davis [an influential corporate executive] had to do with moving the manufacturing of Prism Separator into a St. Louis plant. Davis saw an opportunity to consolidate more operations in that plant and pick up some idle capacity charges there. It would have been disastrous for the business but, as a short-term expediency, it sure as hell would have looked good on the books. His argument was that the business needed a strong infrastructure, and that could only be done at a plant that had a high skills base and maintenance and these other things. And to that I said, "Bullshit. This is not even a full-scale business. This is still a developmental product. We'll give up far more than we gain by moving to a strong unionized plant."

I've also dealt directly with Joe Payne [one of the top corporate executives] on this. He wanted to put a big polymer research center up in Springfield, Massachusetts and he wanted to have this Prism Separator venture in there so they could tap into all this polymer technology. And, you know, I took a position: "Well that's great. It may really help us about the year 2052 but it ain't going do a goddamn thing for us this year, and if we don't get this business off the ground and turn a profit there's not going to be any long-term business." ... It was coming down to all these political expediencies of putting people here and there and scattered all throughout the United States, and they were carving up the political carcass of the Prism Separator venture. And here I sit as a general manager responsible for that venture, and I'm not going to let that happen.

So I put together a little strategy that backfired – I took a recommendation to [McVay's boss and EVP] Ed Costello that we set up the manufacturing of Prism Separator at another site here in St. Louis in order to consolidate all the operations of the venture under one roof. I didn't realize that all such decisions had to eventually go to Don Davis [the influential corporate executive] for his concurrence. So it got back to Davis and he realized I was trying an end run around him. And you know, he just – it was a tough session. A tough session. But again, I report to the executive vice president; I convinced *him* and it was him and I going at it, but it was mostly him. Well, Davis is not going to stand up to an EVP and we won out. But at a little bit of a cost. [Laughter.] Cashed in a few chips and exposed some vulnerabilities that I think frankly within a year will not constitute any problems for me at all. But if Don Davis was forty-five years old and was not retiring next year, I probably would have created some problems for myself. And if he ever got a chance to take it out on who he *knows* was the architect of that strategy, it would happen. [Laughter.] Let's hope not.

Summary

The DGM must build corporate support for his new business creation strategy, and for the specific initiatives, in order to successfully implement both.

The DGM must gain the support of his boss and higher-ups, including relevant corporate committees and staff groups, and find ways to neutralize or overcome any opposition to his strategy and initiatives. He needs political power to accomplish this, which depends on his leverage with the corporate executives (Chapter 11), his hierarchical position, his corporate network, and his political alliances.

Three political strategies are available to build support for new business creation and neutralize or overcome any opposition to it: use reason and appeal to reassure supporters and convert opponents; delay or avoid opposition; and overcome opposition with political power. DGMs who are unable or unwilling to play this game of corporate politics are doomed to failure.

Building corporate support is hard work, but it only earns the DGM a ticket to play the game of new business creation. To win the game, a number of other important tasks must also be executed well. They are covered in Chapter 14.

14 Leading the division for new business creation

This chapter examines how the DGM's leadership of the division influences new business creation (Table 14.1). DGMs rely on three major levers to try to change the division's mindset and behavior for new business creation: getting people to buy into the vision and strategy for new business creation; educating and training them for the task; and motivating and supporting them appropriately.

These actions do not bear fruit fast enough without a parallel effort to properly assess, appoint, reposition, and remove people – especially the key players – when necessary. Some DGMs either consciously or subconsciously avoid this difficult task. DGM Mike Walker of AMP Sigcom stands out as the master to learn from in this area.

Changing the division's mindset and behavior

Getting people to buy into the vision and strategy for new business creation[1]

DGMs try to get the people in the division to buy into their vision and strategy for new business creation by various means: by getting them to buy in one person at a time, by involving them in creating the vision, by communicating the vision over and over again, and by reassuring them if the vision does not produce results as rapidly as expected.

Getting people to buy in one person at a time   DGM Mike Walker described how he was able to get a key player in AMP Sigcom on board by showing him why the strategy was important and how it could be sold to others:

We were putting together a strategy for having the company build us a screw machine plant for the anticipated growth in current business and new products. And Drew Nettle [the division manufacturing manager] was convinced at first that the company was not going to let us do that. Corporate purchasing didn't want to cooperate with him, and they wouldn't give him any purchase figures

Table 14.1. *How the DGM's leadership of the division influences new business creation*

Hypothesis	Factor	Influence on new business creation
Changing the division's mindset and behavior for new business creation		
14.1	Getting people to buy into the vision and strategy for new business creation	+
14.2	Educating, training, coaching, and mentoring people for new business creation	+
14.3	Motivating and supporting people for new business creation	+
Assessing, repositioning, removing, and appointing people for new business creation		
14.4	Assessing people for new business creation	+
14.5	Repositioning or removing people who are not performing up to standard	+
14.6	Appointing people who are right for the job	+

for screw machine parts because they were afraid we were going to cut out their vendors. And I finally got them to cooperate with us and got that data. And I said, "Drew, let's put together a study to show them why we need it." And we did. And he developed a five-year plan. And when they saw all the growth in demand for screw machine parts, and we still had to have over 50 percent of our purchasing from the vendors, they began to realize they got a capacity problem. They had to support us, not fight us. So they totally changed their terms. Then they became a help, and got us machines and space and all those kinds of things. And Drew learned how to sell a screw machine plant, not just pound fists. And then he became a believer [in the new strategy].

Involving people in creating the vision   The morale of the people in Monsanto Fab Products was at an all-time low when Dan Stewart took over as DGM. Commercial development director Joe Hurley described how Stewart involved his people in creating the vision and strategy for the division during those hard times:

When Dan Stewart came in, it was a very depressed group – they had been through some very difficult years. A lot of the technical guys had gone through the Cycle Safe crisis and felt let down by the shutdown and were saying, "We'll wait and see." And everybody was seeing things being spun off. We knew that Doormats was up for sale, Film was up for sale, Astroturf was being considered for sale. It was a survival culture and people were trying to get the hell out of the division to some other part of Monsanto [laughter] in a lot of cases... And Dan tried to turn that around and he succeeded to a great extent. What changed the culture and the vision, I think, primarily, was these task forces and organizational teams that got people talking to each other again and strategizing together.

And creating the spirit that we are all in the same trough, let's pull together. And Dan personally headed an awful lot of those teams. His presence was very important.

Communicating the vision over and over again   DGM Greg Gibbons of Xerox OPD constantly communicated his vision and strategy to OPD managers and employees – in face-to-face discussions, in management meetings large and small, and via management memos and videotapes. In everyday dealings, Gibbons' rapid-fire colloquial speech and breezy style communicated a sense of urgency and excitement that many people felt was contagious.

Gibbons viewed himself as a leader, not a manager. To Gibbons, leadership concerned the articulation of a mission that captured the imagination of the people in the organization and caused them to strive for more than they believed they could achieve:

If you want to do something very creative, very innovative, something very daring, you've got to be clear – you will either be a hero or an asshole. And you've got to be prepared to accept that. I think a lot of people really want to be heroes, I really do. And they really want to make significant changes. But they look at the down side and say, "Oh, my God." . . . I tell my people, it's better to have a disastrous failure than a mediocre success. The most dangerous place to be is the middle of the road. Get on one side or the other. It's either make the thing incredibly successful and put ourselves at the number one, number two spot or, if it fails, take the life support system off the thing and let it die peacefully so we can get on with the rest of our lives.

Reassuring people when the results are bad   Greg Gibbons explained the importance of keeping the organization committed to the vision and strategy, particularly when the results are bad:

When times are dark is probably when leadership is more important than when things are going well. And what you really need to do is become very, very visible and spend a lot of time with the troops, continuously explain why you believe the strategy is correct; continuously analyze, publicly, why things are not working well, what the failures have been; and just continually reassure them that you're on the right course and give them some statistics to back that up – we closed this account, we closed that account. Here is what the press is saying about us here, there and so forth.

Educating, training, coaching, and mentoring people[2]

Education and training   The implementation of Xerox OPD's new major account strategy had seemed simple enough. At the start of Greg Gibbons' second full calendar year as DGM, the old selling territories were redrawn and most of OPD's 700 sales representatives were assigned about ten major accounts each. However, implementation faltered badly because there was a big difference between selling one or two units to the local doctor or lawyer and selling hundreds of units capable of being interconnected into a *system* to a major corporate account. OPD sales people had to learn to interact with top-level executives and the office automation committees within large corporations, and effectively communicate to them the powerful appeal of OPD's strategy – a spectrum of versatile, modular, easily upgradable products that could be interconnected into an office system tailored to the customer's needs. Many OPD sales people felt they did not understand the specific product offerings, particularly the ones still in development, well enough to sell the system.

By the start of his third calendar year as DGM of Xerox OPD, Gibbons said he clearly recognized the importance of education and training for the sales force, and the magnitude of this challenge:

I have to convert that 500-person selling organization to selling systems and solutions versus selling stand-alone products on features and price. That's a tough job to do. I mean, we've had all our people in training for a solid week down in our training facility, and we're gonna have to continue that process through the year. I'm probably gonna lose another 30–50 percent of the sales force in that conversion to selling systems and applications to the professional.

DGM Ray Thorngate of 3M Engineering Products described how he addressed a similar challenge by providing proper education and training to his sales force:

It became clear why the 35mm business was not so hot – there weren't a lot of Micrographics sales people pushing those products. So we took the best sales people we could get [when Engineering Products was created by splitting the 35mm lines off from Micrographics] and put them through an intensive education and training program, including sales training in the field. Because the best we could get were order-takers. To sell systems that cost $50,000 to $100,000 requires the submission of proposals and other skills in systems selling . . . We tell our salesmen, "You do the financials; even if the guy is willing to go along with you, you do the financial analysis anyway. Because somewhere it's a capital expenditure, usually. So somewhere there's gonna be a guy who's a pencil pusher and he's gonna ask for it, and if you've done the financial analysis for the customer, you're just gonna save that much time in closing that sale."

DGM Mike Walker of AMP Sigcom emphasized education and training for his people in his daily work:

I look at staff meetings as an educational forum. I say, "If you don't understand *anything* that's being presented or why it's that way, you ask. I don't care what it is." I involve people deep down in the organization in the staff meetings. And my motivation is that if I'm building a growth operation, those people down at the lower levels are going to be up at the higher levels in a matter of a year or so. And if they don't understand the scope of the business, and what we're doing, and what the directions are, and how to tell whether the business is running right or not, then they're not going to be qualified to get that promotion. So I have people from the supervisor level up in those staff meetings.

Coaching and mentoring   Mike Walker expanded his division's new business creation capacity by coaching and mentoring his people not to think in terms of a fixed pie of time, money or other resources that required them to prioritize tasks. Product manager Arjay Mason described how Mike Walker did this:

Mike would say, "Don't tell me about priorities. That implies that you're only going to do one thing at a time." For example, somebody would come back from putting a job into the model shop for a new product, and Mike would ask, "What commitment did you get?" The answer was, "Well, the model shop said they'd have that for us in six weeks, unless some hotter job came in that would push it back." And Mike would say, "Don't let them tell you that. Get them to commit to a date when they will have it done no matter what." If you came back to Mike and you said, "Well, they can do it, but they have to stop working on the job we put in there earlier," he would say, "That's unacceptable. They are prioritizing. I need them *both*. Come back and tell me what he's going to do to make that happen. Is he going to work overtime? Is he going to hire more people? Is he going to contract the one out to another job shop? What's he going to do? Don't let them play the priority game." Mike Walker's point was to get your organization dynamic enough so that it can respond to everything in three weeks' time and have that dynamics include outside resources and overtime and all those things that can disappear instantly when the jobs aren't there to utilize those elements of your plan. And he tried to get that into everybody's thinking in *all* areas.

Two years after DGM Walker was promoted to group director (GVP), he was promoted once again. When his successor as group director, Jon Grover, began to talk about his priorities, the people that Walker had coached and mentored so well resisted the new emphasis. As Arjay Mason said,

And now under Grover, in the very first meeting he said, "Here are my priorities." I think Grover's perception of what needs emphasis is different than what Mike's perception was. I think, in this division, most of the managers have been around for a while. We don't prioritize as severely as we did five years ago. And so even though somebody comes along and says, "OK, here are my priorities – number one is safety, number two is quality," etc., it's going to take us a while to accept the fact that the very first consideration we make is safety. We'll still think, "Let's get all this done by the time that all these different things need to be done. And not prioritize." After we've worked under the new mentality long enough, we'll probably get back to the point where we do think more in terms of priorities.

Clay Smith, who succeeded Mike Walker as DGM of AMP Sigcom, viewed Walker as a coach and mentor from whom he had learned a great deal:

A lot of the concepts I believe in relative to development engineering, relative to risk-taking and growth and market analysis and so forth, were derived from things that I've learned from Mike. Certainly the building of teams, spirit of cooperation, dealing frankly and directly with people – a lot of those things I've tried to become conscious and aware of. Mike's influenced me in that way.

Mike Walker described his philosophy and approach for coaching and mentoring:

Dave MacNeil [retired COO] used to say, "You look *inside* a person." You sometimes begin to find things out about people they don't even know themselves. And there are people sometimes that are reluctant to take on something because they've never done it before and you develop kind of a sixth sense of whether somebody can handle that scope or not. So I really believe in that adage that your job is to try to get extraordinary results out of ordinary people. Sometimes it's just setting a goal out in front of them and having them drive toward it. Sometimes you have to put pressure on them to get it done. Sometimes you just keep expanding the role and they can't say no and suddenly they find out that they are doing it. You get people to articulate things, draw them out. You get them to put themselves in your shoes and say, "What would you do in my shoes?", and half the time the problem gets solved. When reasonable people are given a chance to think about it. To think it through.

Motivating and supporting people

Motivating people via a sense of destiny   DGM Greg Gibbons of Xerox OPD had fought hard to offer steep financial incentives for his top 30 managers, and strong financial incentives for the next 270 managers. He had used a company-wide incentive scheme, the Scanlon Plan, when he was president of Shugart, and he hoped to adopt it in OPD once the division was profitable. However, Gibbons felt it was very difficult to motivate the troops without a mission and a sense of destiny:

Profit should be an objective for myself, but profit is not an objective I can drive people to. Profit is a by-product of having the product strategy and the marketing strategy and the people strategy. If you try and do it the other way and say, "Okay, our only objective is profit," it can't be done. You can drive strategies down into the organization, and philosophies, but it's very hard to get people continuously motivated about making money for other people.[3] Now, you can obviously get them motivated about making money for themselves ... Profit is always a very short-term thing – next month, next quarter, for the whole year. But if you have a vision and a strategy, what you do is you create a sense of destiny. You've got to give people something to aspire to, like, "We want to be the number one office automation vendor in the marketplace. We want to absolutely cream Apple; we want to give IBM one hell of a run for its money." Right? "When people think 'office automation,' the first thing they're gonna think about is Xerox."

Motivating people via external benchmarks   Greg Gibbons also believed people could be motivated by providing them with externally focused benchmarks, such as his "Financial Model." For instance, 34 percent of the OPD sales dollar was currently spent on sales and marketing, versus 15 percent at a major competitor, Wang. The OPD goal in this area was thus set at 15 percent five years out, with intermediate goals for the interim years.

By focusing attention on the financial profile of an industry leader, Gibbons believed the Financial Model motivated people to "fight for a cause." It was, to him, a psychological energizer. Instead of wasting energy playing the budget game that Gibbons knew was a common occurrence in large corporations, the Financial Model constantly directed management's attention to the competition.

Motivating people by giving them freedom   People liked to work for DGM Buddy March of 3M Micrographics because he gave them a great deal of freedom to get the job done. His administrative assistant, Jane Langley, elaborated:

Anybody that's worked for Buddy is not real excited about working for anybody else. Ray [Thorngate, technical director] transferred to another division and he hadn't been gone six months when he called me one day and said, "Have you got any technician jobs open?" And he was very happy to get back to Micrographics as technical director . . . They like working for Buddy because he's not a detail man. Just the big picture, that's all he's interested in. You supply your own style. He doesn't want to be pestered about the little stuff. "Handle it," he says. And it's always been a pleasure for me to work with him.

Supporting people   AMP Sigcom product manager Arjay Mason described how DGM Mike Walker supported people when they pursued unconventional ideas and approaches:

There are a lot of people that are either positive or they're negative on an idea, and they take sides immediately. Mike was not like that. He recognized that for every action, there was some kind of a reaction, and therefore you had to look at the secondary effects, not just the primary effects. In other words, he would explore both sides of an issue. I think that allowed him to support people when they came up with new ideas. For example, when I presented Mike with the idea of licensing Ribbon Coax, he was not concerned that it was going to erode our existing business. Instead, he was interested in what opportunities that was going to open up.

Art Malone was marketing director for Astroturf, a Monsanto Fab Products business that had lost money consistently over the years. Many people believed it needed to be sold. Malone described how DGM Dan Stewart supported his efforts to try to save the business:

I completely changed the direction of the business by going to high pricing for high perceived value, indirectly saying to Dan, "Your past strategy was wrong." He was encouraging – always. "OK, I am open to that," was his typical response. Totally supportive. We may recommend liquidation of the business if we can't turn it around or sell it. But I don't perceive a personal risk, because of Stewart's support. Most bosses won't directly support you. They will say, "Sounds good. Don't fuck it up!"

Assessing, repositioning, removing, and appointing people

Assessing people

An organization needs to be diagnosed, and the strengths and weaknesses of its people assessed, before they can be positioned appropriately or removed if necessary. New business creation is facilitated when the DGM performs this task well.

Diagnosing an organization upon taking charge   Mike Walker was widely admired within AMP for his people skills. He described a three-step process for diagnosing an organization upon taking charge: getting a financial overview of the business; meeting people and visiting operations to get a sense of the strengths and weaknesses of the organization; and then digging deeper to get to the root causes of problems as well as discovering who the key players are and who needs to be repositioned or removed.

I guess your first report card is the financial health. That gives you an overview of how the organization seems to be meshing together. The second thing is, you do walk-around management. You meet people, you talk to people, you see what's going on, and you find out where the problems are. You attend engineering meetings and you find out what the caliber of the designs are. And how easy are they to produce. You go down to the manufacturing plant. You look at operating guys, and you look at the systems, and the methods, and the structure of management, and you can pretty well tell the stamp of the leader. You have obvious measurements of quality performance, but you also look at the ability of the quality guys in terms of analyzing customer complaints and helping the division solve their problems. So out of all that you develop a perception of the strengths and the weaknesses of what's going on in an organization. And, frankly, it doesn't take long. You develop first-line perceptions within a matter of days. Then in a matter of months you find the depth of the problem. You begin to find who your key players are. Names keep coming up. People that are in trouble – it's amazing they just try to avoid you. They want to get into a foxhole somewhere and just not be found. People who are doing a good job bring problems to you. So, it's not a difficult process but I will say this, though: you have to be looking for these things, you have to be willing to dive into an organization to find out what's going on. The organization will not do this naturally for you.

Performance appraisal and career counseling   DGM Mike Walker met for two to three hours with each of his top *seventy* people every year for a performance evaluation and career counseling session. He described his philosophy and approach after he was promoted to group director (GVP):

My philosophy in career counseling [when Walker was DGM] was a one-over-one-over-one type of an approach. The supervisor would write the counseling, write the evaluation. But when a manager reporting to me was counseling his people, I was there. They did it in my office. I was physically present. So it gave the employee a chance to be heard, not only in front of his boss but his boss' boss. And it gave the manager a chance to say something difficult to the employee and be reinforced by his boss. So it gave me a lot of insight into my managers and the people working for them. The salary reviews were done separately one-on-one without my involvement, but I did approve them of course. The typical counseling session took two or three hours. This is with three people present – the guy, his boss and me. I had about fourteen people reporting to me in those days and each of them may have five or so subordinates, so that's seventy people we are talking about. So you could get busy. But it was a very valuable process for me as a DGM to really understand my people and where they belong and where they didn't belong and how to get them in the right spot.

Repositioning and removing people

It is painful but necessary to reposition or remove people who are not performing up to the standard. DGMs who perform this task well help new business creation.

Mistakes in repositioning and removing people   DGMs commit two kinds of mistakes: (1) they are not tough enough on people, allowing non-performers to remain in their jobs; and (2) rather than removing the non-performers, they undertake "birdcage reorganizations" in which the same birds fly to different perches within the organization.

Not tough enough on people
DGM Buddy March of 3M Micrographics was not effective in weeding people out. He removed no one from his top management team for non-performance, and he was slow in repositioning failing managers.

DGM Dan Stewart said it was difficult to fire people in Monsanto (at the time of the study in the early 1980s), especially those over forty years of age – even for non-performance, for fear of being hit with age-discrimination lawsuits: "It is not easy to fire somebody in Monsanto. We give 'em six months to find a job, and you're really worried about firing anybody over forty. They're a protected class." Everyone agreed that this was a corporate reality, but Dan Stewart's colleagues said that his business optimism, and his innate desire to see the best in people and to help them develop professionally, made it especially difficult for him to be tough on non-performers. One colleague summed it up this way:

Stewart is Theory Y, clearly believes in people. Human nature tends to be negative – it is easy to see all the things that can go wrong. Dan is willing to look at the positives. He isn't worried about a few missed steps . . . Dan is smooth, a real nice guy. The people were so ecstatic when he came. He never likes to confront people. He is too easy-going, too permissive.

A former colleague echoed these sentiments: "Dan Stewart is a pretty neat guy. People felt they knew him on a personal basis. He walked the halls and saw people and he got down into the trenches with everyone. Because of these personal relationships, Dan had a difficult time with tough personnel decisions."

Birdcage reorganizations

DGMs who are either unable or unwilling to remove non-performers may try to get around the problem, or try to avoid the pain of confronting it, by undertaking "birdcage reorganizations" in which the same birds are moved to different perches within the organization. Such reorganizations create pressures to accept people who are not right for the job, as commercial development director Joe Hurley of Monsanto Fab Products lamented:

Some of the fallout of that stuff may affect me. I may have to pick up people that I don't want to pick up. Which I am not going along with as of now, but I may end up going along with it eventually. And that disturbs me because they are not development people.

The payoff from repositioning people who are not performing up to standard[4]   Dan Stewart's successor, DGM Ian McVay, got corporate approval for restructuring the Fab Products division and repositioning some of the people he inherited from Stewart. McVay said he had to fight hard to accomplish this:

In this company it is hard to change the team that reports to you. "Why do you want to make a change?" is what you hear. I mean, this restructuring [consolidating the marketing for the blownware, Fomecor and film businesses] that I'm sure looks so simple, it was a very difficult thing to do. The fact that Stan Reinhart is now a boss of two guys that were formerly his peers is no small thing to do. I mean I had to have that blessed and approved up the high levels of this corporation. It's just part of our culture.

DGM Mike Walker of AMP Sigcom felt strongly that if a person was not performing up to standard, it was management's responsibility to reposition the person into a job where he could perform well:

I have one outstanding philosophy, and that is, I don't believe that people deliberately go out to do a bad job. I think it cuts across the grain of human nature to do a bad job. So if somebody's doing a bad job it's not a deliberate thing; it is either something we're doing wrong in that we haven't provided them the right tools, or the right training or the right direction or they're in the wrong job. So if you approach your people's efforts with that kind of a philosophy, then you do what I do. That is, you search out what is the right role for them . . . It took me about six months to make the chess moves so we had the right people in the right places. Over three years, my entire management team was reshuffled. Some were promoted, some transferred out, and some are still on the team, but in a different role.

Repositioning can be painful, but everyone benefits when it is properly done. Consider this detailed account Mike Walker gave of how he counseled Ed Forrest, the development manager Clay Smith replaced, to step down and become a project manager again:

I had counseled Ed for two years. And I finally told him, "Ed, I'm going to make a change. I'm going to appoint you a project manager again." And I could tell it really was hitting him, but I had to lay it out the way it was. And I said, "Now I'll tell you why." I went through all that, and I said, "You're breaking your pick, you are trying hard and it's not working right. You were best when you were a project manager and developing new products, working with a small team of people. I'll give you whoever you want to work with, but I want you take this darn SMA project and I want you to succeed with it, and I want to get that RF line going. And I think you can do it. There's no change in salary, there's no change in bonus, there's no change in office, but I got to appoint a development manager that I think can work with all the personalities you got in that department. Take those headaches away from you, and also interface the marketing types and really get us moving in that area." I told him I was appointing Clay Smith in the job, and he was not too happy about it. I had already pre-briefed Clay that he was going to have to work to win Ed over and to make it work and develop teamwork.

It took Ed probably two years before he started to see exactly what I said was true and he started to relax. And he started to work with that little nucleus and he started to smile when Clay was having problems with the same people he had problems with. But he did see what Clay could do for him and really interface with marketing and get him exposed to the right kind of customer bases. And he was pleased to see a hierarchy get developed in there and, when he got his first designer, he just couldn't believe what could be done that way. So he really started being more productive . . . I always told Ed that I was working for this dual career path (technical and managerial) at AMP, and there was going to come a time when he would be properly recognized. And I was able to do that this past spring [after becoming GVP]. And he was one of the first guys to phone me after the announcements were made and thank me profusely because he remembered. And he said, "I guess I never really was honest with you and told you that you were exactly right." He said, "I have been so happy and so productive since [becoming a project manager again]." So you really have to work at this, you can't just make snap decisions and say all right, you're no good, boom, that's the end of it.

Appointing people

The mistakes DGMs make in appointing people, especially in key positions, hamper new business creation. There is a big payoff from finding the right person for the job.

Mistakes in making appointments   DGMs make two kinds of mistakes in appointing people: they hire in their own image; and they hire people based on friendship and loyalty rather than finding the best person for the job.

The trap of hiring in one's own image

After DGM Greg Gibbons left Xerox, several people said that one of the problems was that he hired his top team in his own image. Gibbons disagreed strongly with this assessment, but his critics maintained that he failed to bring in people who were strong in areas where he was weak, such as implementation skills. They felt that Gibbons needed more people who could execute well, as Steve Carter did with the Memorywriter typewriter.

The friendship and loyalty trap

Some people felt that Mat MacGregor was appointed program manager for Com because of his friendship with DGM Buddy March, even though he was not the right person for that job. DGM Ralph West of 3M Imaging Products, who was viewed as Buddy March's other good friend going back to when he was in the Micrographics division, offered this perspective:

Buddy formed friendships with some people; Mat and me for example. He looks after you; there is a special relationship there. Some people don't like such friendships. But I can be friends and still make business judgments. Buddy was not big on being harsh with anyone. I agree that Mat was perhaps not the right person for Com.

Buddy March agreed that he had erred in making the Mat MacGregor appointment, and he said his warm feelings for Mat had blinded him:

I'll readily admit it was a poor appointment. I think we pegged him in the wrong place. He's better pegged where he is now, as 3M country manager for Switzerland. And I admit that. I readily admit that it could have been my own warm feelings towards Mat that blinded me – I'm sure it did...There were plenty of people that didn't want the job [because it was seen as a very difficult assignment]. Mat agreed to do it. He saw it probably as a way to become DGM.

The payoff from finding the right person for the job   The appointments made by DGM Mike Walker of AMP Sigcom were widely perceived as excellent. Walker described how he made three key appointments – Arjay Mason as production engineering manager, and later as product manager; and Clay Smith as development manager:

I knew Arjay Mason could take our production engineering department from "Sleepy Hollow" to the state of the art, and he did that very quickly. Later on I moved him to become product manager for the Ribbon Coax and related lines because I sensed that, although he still had a bit of the introverted engineer in him, he would do well there. In fact, he has blossomed into a strong product manager. The thought of moving from Ribbon Coax to Cable Assembly, and licensing the cable to the competition, were his ideas and I supported him on that...I had to do some selling to get Clay Smith to become the development manager. I think Clay enjoyed what he was doing as a product manager for the existing RF line. I think Clay also felt, since he'd been in engineering management before, that it might not be necessary to become a development manager. I convinced Clay that until he had really started something from scratch, it wasn't totally clear that he could handle the full scope of an operating division [as a DGM]. Everything that I had seen Clay do in his career, both in General Products division and in Sigcom, somebody else had already discovered the market and he would perpetuate it. It takes quite a bit of somebody to find out if they have the vision and insight to find something brand new and get it going. There is a time when everybody's going to say, "Well, how do you know that's going to be big?" And you got to have a lot of self-confidence to proceed.

Mike Walker's selection of Jim Fitch as product manager, to replace Smith when he became development manager, was an especially risky move that paid big dividends. Walker said,

When I announced the product manager position [that Clay Smith was vacating] to the DAEs [district application engineers within AMP sales and marketing, a separate division], I did not have Jim Fitch in mind. I just took a shot in the dark. I said what the heck; put the floater out and see who picks it up. There is very little flow of people between the sales and marketing side of the corporation and the operations side [all the operating divisions, including AMP Sigcom]. Pretty much vertical career paths. We're trying to break those lines down, but there was a feeling of total disloyalty if somebody from sales and marketing ever jumped and went into operations. So I had a risk there that he [Jim Fitch] would be isolated. In fact, it happened for a while. There were some animosities that were established because he was considered disloyal to the sales and marketing side. There was also the risk of whether or not Jim was a good enough poker player to really run the business side of it right. I look at the art of negotiation as being the art of making the other person think you're willing to walk away from it if it's not right. And sales and marketing people make terrible negotiators because they aren't willing to walk away from an order. Fortunately, Jim does not do that. He *will* walk away from an order and he's perceived as being willing to walk away from an order, so he's a good negotiator.

Project manager Jerry Lange of AMP Sigcom commented on the success of the Jim Fitch appointment:

The Fitch appointment was an unusual move, and it upset some people in AMP Sigcom and in the sales and marketing organization. But it has worked out well for the division. Jim [Fitch] is not a methodical individual, and he went ahead and did what he wanted, and Mike Walker had to rein him in once in a while. But being the kind of character he is, Jim stirred up the pot, and he brought the interest of sales and marketing and the customer into the division.

Summary

DGMs rely on three major levers to change the division's mindset and behavior for new business creation. First, they get people to buy into their vision and strategy of new business creation. They do this one person at a time, and also by involving people in the process, by communicating their vision and strategy to them over and over again, and by reassuring them when the results are not on track. Second, they provide education, training, coaching, and mentoring for their people to learn the new attitudes and skills that are necessary for successful new business creation. Third, they provide the necessary motivation by giving people a sense of destiny, by using external benchmarks to challenge them, by giving them the freedom to pursue new ideas and initiatives, and by supporting them when they do so.

These actions are necessary, but they do not create change fast enough without a parallel effort to properly assess, appoint, reposition, and remove people – especially the key players – as warranted. DGMs must diagnose the organization upon taking charge, and assess people quickly but carefully to determine who needs to be repositioned or removed, and which positions need new blood.

There is much to be gained by repositioning those people who are not performing well because they are not right for their jobs. DGMs who are not tough enough on people fail to do this, and are also reluctant to remove non-performers. They engage instead in games of avoidance such as "birdcage reorganizations" in which the same people are rotated to different jobs. DGMs also fall into traps when making new appointments. They select people in their own image and are swayed by friendship or personal loyalty, which helps neither the organization nor, ultimately, the appointee.

DGMs avoid these difficult people-related tasks either consciously or sub-consciously. Those who face up to them and perform them well facilitate new business creation by finding the right people for the jobs, helping them to do their jobs better, and also helping them to grow professionally.

Part V

The division and its top management team

This part of the book examines how the division and its top management team (TMT) influence new business creation (Figure V.1). The DGM is, of course, the leader of the TMT and the division – so his influence will again be apparent – but Part V brings out the influence of other people in the division, including the TMT.[1]

New business creation requires that the people in the division generate, explore, specify, and commit to new business opportunities, despite the attendant technical and market uncertainties. Contrary to popular belief, a disciplined management system for doing this yields better results. These issues are considered in Chapter 15.

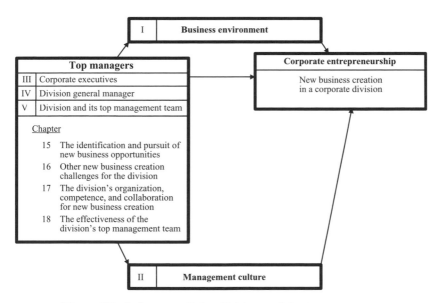

Figure V.1. Influence of the division and its top management team (TMT).

Other new business creation challenges for the division are the subject of Chapter 16. These include the dangers of "fake entrepreneurship," how others in the division can assist the DGM's efforts to build corporate support for new initiatives, and the challenge of managing the volatility of new business and the disruption it creates.

The next two chapters deal with organizational issues. Chapter 17 considers the pros and cons of various organizations for new business creation, as well as the management of competence, conflict, and collaboration for new business creation. Chapter 18 examines how the division's TMT deals with conflict, and the extent to which it compensates for the DGM's weaknesses.

15 The identification and pursuit of new business opportunities

This chapter examines how the identification and pursuit of new opportunities by the division influence new business creation (Table 15.1).

New business creation requires the generation and exploration of new business opportunities, their proper specification, and a commitment to pursue them despite the attendant technical and market uncertainties.

It pays to generate and explore a large number of new business opportunities in order find the most attractive ones to specify and commit to. A disciplined system for doing this – consisting of project phases, milestones, reviews, and technical audits – yields better results than less disciplined approaches.

Generation of new business opportunities[1]

New business opportunities can be generated by conducting market and competitor intelligence, by resurrecting discarded business ideas, and by using formal mechanisms such as a new product group or committee.

Conducting market and competitor intelligence

DGM Mike Walker of AMP Sigcom emphasized the importance of market intelligence:

My concept of business is economic warfare. *The Art of War* by Sun Tzu and *The Book of Five Rings* [by Miyamoto Musashi] are extremely pertinent. But first you need market intelligence – weather data, supply capabilities, the generals competing against you. You can know your marketplace, map out the battle plan, and make decisions [concerning threats, opportunities, and initiatives] by using intelligence. Read trade journals; talk to your suppliers, customers, and your competition. If a guy left a competitor, you interview him. You collect drops of data.

3M Micrographics had a small group of people who were responsible for conducting competitor intelligence. They collected and analyzed bits

Table 15.1. *How the identification and pursuit of new business opportunities by the division influence new business creation*

Hypothesis	Factor	Influence on new business creation
Identification and pursuit of new business opportunities		
15.1	Number of new business opportunities generated	+
15.2	Number of new business opportunities explored	+
15.3	Correct specification of new business opportunities	+
15.4	Commitment to pursue new business opportunities despite the technical and market uncertainties	+
A disciplined system for identification and pursuit of new business opportunities		
15.5	Consistent use of rigorous phase and milestone reviews	+
15.6	Tight screening of new opportunities prior to commitment	+
15.7	Independent and objective technical audits	+

and pieces of information as it came in from various sources: (1) analysis of bids submitted by competitors; (2) estimates of competitors' product costs obtained by dismantling and analyzing their products; (3) information from suppliers and other industry sources on what the competition was up to; (4) papers published and patents filed by the competition; (5) information picked up by people who were staying in motels frequented by the competition; and (6) anything anyone overheard about the competition while traveling in airplanes, on the road, or elsewhere. People in 3M Micrographics were told to keep their eyes and ears open for such drops of information, and their mouths shut to prevent similar information from leaking out. All these data were analyzed for early indications of both competitive threats and new business opportunities.

Resurrecting discarded business ideas

It is difficult to generate new business opportunities by re-examining discarded business ideas, because of the painful memories typically associated with them. Joe Hurley, commercial development director of Monsanto Fab Products, said DGM Dan Stewart tried to resurrect several discarded business concepts. Here is one example Hurley gave.

Dan and I had disagreements in some areas that I had worked in before, where he still felt that there was opportunity. One was landscaping with Astroturf. It was first begun many, many years ago. Dan knew this of course, but his comeback was, "Well, the Japanese are doing it, why can't we do it?" But the Japanese position the product entirely differently. They landscape very small sections of a garden and this type of thing. Very meticulous in cleaning it and things like that. Because it is a very small area. But when you get to any large areas, and with the sunlight that we have here, I mean it's a disaster. It turns brown on you and you can't install it properly and you can't clean it properly.

Joe Hurley recalled the pain associated with the failure of this concept (prior to the time of the study in the early 1980s):

I had to handle every one of the complaints that came in. And, you know, people would literally cry about it. Where they had put asphalt on their whole front yard to lay the Astroturf on, we'd take the asphalt out and put top soil back in. We ripped out total front yards, backyards, everything. And put grass seed down and said, "Goodbye." [Laughter.] I'm serious. I lived through all that stuff.

Although it is difficult to resurrect discarded business ideas, changes in technology or markets might make re-examination worthwhile. Dan Stewart said he went digging in the graveyard of discarded business concepts because he never got a convincing explanation of why they did not work in the past, and why they wouldn't work today:

The eternal optimist. [Chuckling.] That's me. Pollyanna. Yeah, I had some people look again at a number of opportunities. Why? Because I never got a straightforward answer as to why they failed. OK? Take the landscape product. That had proven to be a disaster, they said. But it was very successful in Japan. And theoretically – at least that's what Peter Dell [the division's technical director] told me – the technical reason for failure before had been overcome with new polymer technology. UV degradation had caused the product to change color and lose dimensional stability, but they had developed stabilizers for that.

Using formal mechanisms to encourage new ideas

A formal mechanism such as a new product group or committee is only as good as the thought, skill, and effort put into it. If managers go through the motions and use such a mechanism because it is politically correct to do so, it will produce little other than cynicism.

Dan Stewart said the NPD (New Product Development) committee, and its successor, the NPG (New Products Group), had not worked at Monsanto because "a lot of people are going through the motions: 'We know that [president] Jim Reilly likes new product committees, so if we do this he is going to like it.' It is just not very productive." President Reilly explained what he was trying to accomplish with the NPD committee:

I had several goals in mind. It was a way to involve senior managers in long-term research. It was a way to provide consistent funding, not fluctuating with our fortunes, and a visible focal point for new products. You can judge progress in a sophisticated way, with checkpoints. It's a forum to make sure generated ideas get encouragement. Monsanto Agricultural Chemicals had used this approach for a number of years and generated good products. I remember once [from when Reilly was there] that a guy wanted one and a half people; we gave him seventeen – his patents were running out.

DGM Dan Stewart's successor, Ian McVay, agreed with Stewart that the real constraint on new business creation in Monsanto Fab Products was a dearth of good new ideas, but he did not share Stewart's skepticism about the NPD/NPG approach, because of the actual results he had achieved with it. Instead, McVay viewed it as a useful formal mechanism for feeding and weeding the new business creation pipeline:

We have fewer opportunities than resources in Fab Products. I spent some time in commercial development and I have a feel for the number of projects that one has to initiate to have a success, or a reasonable statistical chance of success. And the rule of thumb that I use is, you are damn lucky to get to 10 percent, and 5 percent is a more meaningful number. Which says that to get five programs where you can be thinking realistically of resourcing them heavily, you got to screen a hundred ideas. I see it as a game of statistics . . . So, I'm pushing the hell out of my guys to come up with the ideas and let's keep this sequence going, let's get NPG revved up. Bring me more opportunities than we can possibly fund and let's decide as a group how we're going to pick and choose . . . Spray Guard, RCA Disk Caddy, and Drainage Mat all came to us from outsiders who had these ideas. I started the NPG to generate more ideas from within Fab Products. I had a NPG in the D&P division of Monsanto Industrial Chemicals [McVay's prior DGM assignment], and it worked. We got 132 suggestions from which we funded a couple of dynamite programs.

Exploration of new business opportunities

Market research can provide valuable information for the exploration of new business opportunities but, like all management tools, it can also be misused or abused. Exploration is aided by offering people discretionary time and money to explore new ideas, and by allowing them to bootleg projects they strongly believe in.

Conducting market research[2]

Caution: how market research can lie   DGM Dan Stewart of Monsanto Fab Products came up through the sales and marketing function, and he understood the importance of good market research. But he also knew that it could be fabricated to sell a preconceived position. For instance, Stewart did not believe the market research done to justify the OPET bottle initiative. He talked about this after he had been promoted out of Fab Products:

Their market research is beautiful, but I think it is pure bullshit. I don't even know if they believe it or not. I kid Joe Hurley [commercial development director] about that. He said, "We kept doing it until we got the right answer, and then we stopped." [Laughter.] . . . They said the consumer would pay more for the OPET bottle because of taste or perceived value. We had done some market research when I was there and it came back negative. But I didn't believe that either. I mean it was on the same basis. I think they called up fifty people and asked, "Would you pay more for a plastic bottle?" I thought the market research was poorly done.

Sometimes, market research can simply be wrong. Dan Stewart's group controller, Olaf Carlsson, gave one example: "I was the controller for Cycle Safe. We were convinced the consumer wouldn't buy a plastic bottle with a black base. They did buy it! So much for analysis and market research!" Stewart added that,

When we came out with the Cycle Safe bottle that had a shelf stability of three months, the market research said the customers needed a year [of shelf life]. We said that we could only give them three months, maybe six months. And they still went with our bottle. After the FDA banned Cycle Safe, the industry went with the PET bottle, which had a shelf stability of *six weeks*. So they told you they needed a year and PET gives you six weeks.[3] How many PET bottles do you see on the shelf now? There are billions of them on the market now.

Observational market research can help   Such examples are not exceptional. Traditional market research, where people are asked for their opinions – including in focus groups – can be misleading for new products, especially for new-to-the world products that are beyond the range of the customer's current experience. In such cases, it is better to let the customer *experience* the new product or service and study their *actual behavior*.

Offering people discretionary time and money

People in AMP Sigcom and 3M Micrographics were offered discretionary time and what was referred to as "mad money" to make it easy to explore new business opportunities.[4] At 3M Micrographics, those in the division's technical functions were given 15 percent of their paid time to work on new ideas of their own choosing. As technical director Ray Thorngate put it, "We say that you must allow sufficient leeway or sufficient soil for serendipity."

Bootlegging projects

People in AMP Sigcom and 3M Micrographics were free to start new initiatives without prior corporate approval. A project description sheet had to be filled out at AMP Sigcom, but results were not reported until the cumulative expenditures on a new program reached $50,000, at which point a three-year forecast of sales and expenditures was required. A program review was scheduled when the total capital and engineering expenditure reached $150,000. Development manager Jim Fitch of AMP Sigcom enjoyed telling me the following story to make a point – the division had considerable discretion in terms of both time and money for new programs, and how to account for them:

You keep coming back to the corporate financial people saying you want more money for things and they say, "Well, Christ, you're already working on twenty-one programs that we've given you money for; why do you need some more?" So you play the product extension game. You don't go to the well for more money, you just charge it off as extension engineering for work on a current program – even though it's a brand new technology advance, okay?... It was funny, we had a meeting just recently. All the development engineering managers in the company get together for a thing called DEMO – stands for Development Engineering Manager Organization – and once a year for the past six years we've had a meeting somewhere off in the woods, where we get drunk together and talk about common problems. And at the last DEMO session, they brought in the head bean-counter for all project accounting, a real good guy, Roger O'Connor. Down-to-earth kind of guy. And he was making this speech about how there are forty new programs that he was tracking, ten of which were marginally successful and the rest were absolutely goddamn problems. OK? And I started laughing in the back of the room. Roger and I know each other pretty well; we've had quite a few martinis together. And he says, "What the hell are you up to?" And I said, "Roger, your accounting system sucks." [Laughter.] He said, "Okay, smart ass. What's wrong with it?" I said, "You know goddamn well, you don't have a third of the programs that are going on in this company on your report." He acted dumb and he says, "No I don't know." I walked up and I handed Roger my business card and I said, "This is just to make sure that you know where to send me the pink slip for my termination." [Laughter.]

I turned around to the rest of the guys and I said, "Hey, I've got ten programs in my department that don't show up on his list." I said, "How many you guys got?" We took a poll. A hundred and thirty two programs are not on his list! [Laughter] He just about shit. He said, "Why am I doing all this?" I said, "I don't know – dart-board forecasting!" As it turns out, sitting in the back of the room is Jake Markley [the chief operating officer] listening to all this and everybody's kind of concerned that maybe they didn't do the right thing, you know? And Jake stood up and he said, "Well, what the hell." He said, "I'm glad to see things haven't changed since I've been in development."

It was also possible to bootleg projects in commercial development at Monsanto Fab Products. These projects were set up with their own accounts only when the investment got to a certain size, typically $100,000 to $250,000. Even as "hard times" DGM Vic Thomas was cutting and pruning the businesses, Joe Hurley was able to bootleg projects by using discretionary expenditures and informal connections. For instance, the Spray Guard program began as a bootlegged effort during that period.

Specification of new business opportunities

A new business opportunity might be specified incorrectly because of a lack of close customer contact. Misspecification could also result from a lack of clarity about whether a new initiative is best positioned as a new product or as a new process.

The importance of staying close to the customer[5]

Proper specification of a new opportunity requires close contact with the customer, as DGM Mike Walker of AMP Sigcom said.

My predecessor [Chet Timmer] had the philosophy that you keep your new product development bottled up in a closet and then when you're ready to show it, you show it. Well, the problem is you're isolating yourself from the users, so you may develop what you think is the perfect product. But until a user has worked at it, you don't know. So, the development engineers were not getting the exposure to the customer base and the marketing people that could help shape what they were supposed to do. I changed all that.

DGM Buddy March of 3M Micrographics recalled the mistakes on new product specifications that were made in the early days because he and his people did not stay close to the customer:

In the earlier programs, there were some miscalculations on the specifications that the market required. We wrote our own specifications without a lot of market study – it was a whim of the marketing manager and approved by me. And there were failures where we went up against an existing technology that we were trying to replace with a better mousetrap. The customers liked what we had to offer, but we miscalculated on whether the customer would be willing to give up some of the old features – they didn't want to give up some of the ones that they had gotten used to.[6]

The need for clarity – are we developing a new product or a new process?

It is important to be clear about whether a new business initiative is best positioned as a new product or as a new process, but this is not always easy to know at the outset. DGM Dan Stewart of Monsanto Fab Products said the RCA Disk Caddy initiative could have benefited from greater clarity on this issue.

In fact, we were developing a new process. The new product happened to give us a good motivation to develop the process. Had we been clear about this, we could have said to RCA, "All we want is the rights to the process to be able to use it for other products. You only want it for your disk caddy, which is fine. And hey, you'll save 25 cents on each disk caddy." Instead, we tried to assume full control of the patents and got RCA mad.

Commitment to new business opportunities

The division must commit to new business opportunities even though basic questions about market uncertainty and technical feasibility remain unresolved. Investments are needed to discover the market, and customer commitments must be made before technical solutions are found. The associated risks can be reduced if external partners with complementary competencies and resources can be enlisted, but such external programs carry other risks.

Making investments to discover the market

One of the challenges for the OPET bottle program at Monsanto Fab Products was that the food packaging companies needed 50,000 to 100,000 bottles to test-market the product for hot-fill applications. Such quantities could not be produced without a sizable investment – $3.8 million – in a new production line. DGM Dan Stewart talked about the "chicken and egg" problem this created:

Some people say, "Well, the delays on the OPET bottle haven't really hurt us because we don't have a customer yet." And you can go around and around on this, does the chicken come first or the egg? Do you need a customer before we make the bottle? What if we had a bottle; would we have a customer? I think that until we get that production line in there and start making bottles for that market we're never going to know. You need a test line to get enough bottles out there to do the test-marketing and get enough consumer reaction.

Making customer commitments before technical solutions are found

Bidding for new business without knowing how to make the new product Commercial development director Joe Hurley of Monsanto Fab Products described how the division made a commitment to deliver test samples of the Drainage Mat before they knew how to make it:

[DGM] Stewart was promoted and was leaving, like in November or December last, when we were negotiating with the State of Illinois to put in five miles. In December, Illinois came back and said, "We want to put it in the bid package for installation next June, but you have to let us know if you can make the product." Well, we really didn't know if we could make the product. It was an interesting concept, that's all. But we got a task force together – some manufacturing people and research people – and said, "OK. We don't know what the machine really looks like to wrap this stuff. But let's find a way to do it." We all had some ideas and we sat in a hotel room in Atlanta for a day and we finally came to the conclusion that, "By golly, we should be able to do it" and we were going to commit to Illinois. Even though we didn't know exactly how we were going to do it ... The cost of not making that commitment was not getting it approved in Illinois; but even more so, not demonstrating the total economics of the system. Because we are really selling an installed system, so the only way you would demonstrate those costs is by actually doing it. And then use that data in other States. So the cost of not doing it was probably an eighteen- to twenty-four-month delay. So we made a commitment and went to work and designed a piece of equipment to wrap it. The guys did an outstanding job, they really did. And we were off and running.

Thus, the pursuit of new business opportunities can be energized by making delivery commitments to customers before all the technical problems have been solved. This is what DGM Mike Walker of AMP Sigcom meant when he told his people: "Let's get into a lot of trouble."

"Do the quality control in the customer's shop" Customers may be willing to help debug a new product, but only if it offers new benefits they value, or if they are unhappy with the existing technology or product. Technical director Ray Thorngate of 3M Micrographics explained:

There was a mystique in the Business Products Group about moving quickly into the market because top management kept telling us, "Get it out. Do the quality control in the customer's shop!" It works when you have a product with new benefits that the customer values. When you are going up against existing technology and products that the customer is quite happy with, and you put out a new product that does not work, they don't want to mess with it. Then you need to get the bugs worked out internally.

Using external programs

The advantages of external programs   External programs, such as acquisitions, joint ventures, and the purchasing and licensing of new products from another company, enable commitment to new business opportunities by providing complementary resources and capabilities.[7] External collaboration also offers the opportunity to learn new skills from the partner. Such programs are a must if the division lacks the necessary competence to undertake new business creation on its own. Marketing director Bill Lieberman of 3M Engineering Products said DGM Ray Thorngate had to pursue external programs, despite their lower profit margins, because the necessary skills were not available in-house:

It may appear that Ray Thorngate has abandoned the traditional 3M emphasis on internal new product development, but he is using external programs – such as the duplicators from Wicks and Wolfson, the camera from Shout, and the System Integration Project with Tera – to get some new products in quickly while he does the stage-setting for internal development, because we have had no internal programs in the 35mm business for the last ten years. He is trying to breathe life into the organization by building it up with the skills we need in software and system integration.

External programs can facilitate new process development as well. When this study began, several managers in Monsanto Fab Products were concerned that some of the new process development work on the RCA Disk Caddy was being farmed out to so-called "development consultants." By the time this study ended three years later, there was consensus among the managers involved that this was beneficial – the outsiders moved faster than Monsanto would have, the development costs were lower, and the intellectual property remained with Monsanto.

A risk and a limitation of external programs   External programs can tempt the division to try unrelated diversification, which is more risky than diversification into related products, technologies, and markets. This higher risk should be explicitly factored into the strategy of new business creation; it should not be assumed that past success with external programs for related diversification foreshadows similar success for unrelated diversification. The success of the Tanaka Printer – a licensing and co-development program with a Japanese company for a related new product and technology – emboldened DGM Buddy March and others in 3M Micrographics to pursue *unrelated* new products and technologies using other external programs. But most of these programs failed.

A limitation of external programs is that they usually offer lower profit margins than internal programs. Ray Thorngate explained why:

It is difficult to achieve the kind of margins that 3M is looking for from the external programs because, frankly, somebody else [the external partner] is also looking [chuckling] for those high margins . . . From the Tanaka experience we know that we can pay no more than $40 for a product we plan to sell at $100. We need that 60 percent gross margin to deliver 20 percent pre-tax profit – because we always end up doing some development work on the products we buy, and then there are the selling, general, and administrative expenses. And that's assuming we use our own direct sales force. We make less if we use dealers, so I must keep at least 75 percent of the sales through our own direct sales force to make the margins 3M expects . . . We have to be really choosy with the external programs to get the margins we want. That's why you can't farm it out completely. If you do, you are vulnerable on purchase price. If you want high margins, you can't abandon internal development.

One way to buy a product from an external partner at a lower price is to negotiate a volume purchase agreement, often requiring global distribution for the product. But it might be hard to find someone who can make the right product at the right price for global distribution. The potential partner's existing distribution agreements are often a stumbling block.

A disciplined system for identification and pursuit of new business opportunities[8]

Description of a disciplined system: consistent use of rigorous phase and milestone reviews

The two divisions with the longest track records of successful new business creation had over the years developed a disciplined system – called the "phase system" in 3M Micrographics and the "review system" in AMP Sigcom – for encouraging and controlling the pursuit of new business opportunities.

The phase system at 3M Micrographics   Developed initially in the Micrographics division, the phase system had diffused to other 3M divisions and had become institutionalized company practice. Technical director Ray Thorngate of 3M Micrographics described its genesis and evolution:

We had already gone through some new products in the early days and I began to see that we were having problems recur. One of the first things we did that led to the phase system was to sit down and draw out a road map of everything that

Phase	Name	Description of the phase	Surviving concepts[1]
1	Business concept	Concept and discovery portion to identify and establish a market need, and its fit with the product and technical approach being proposed	100 (baseline)
2	Feasibility	To ensure that the new product meets the requirements of *technical* and *business* feasibility	50
3	Business development	To develop and document the product for the intended market, and the processes needed for its manufacture. This is the first major commitment of resources to the opportunity, e.g. prototype development	5
4	Production scale-up	To scale up the product and the manufacturing process, and produce a limited specified amount of the product for the market	3
5	Product standardization	To standardize and fully document the manufacturing process for the final product specifications	2
6	Business termination	To ensure an orderly withdrawal from the market	—

Note: [1]The data in this column are based on the experience of 3M Micrographics. For every 100 new business concepts examined, the number that made it to each successive phase is shown. No number is given for Phase 6 because the number varied depending on the product's duration in the market – all products eventually terminate.

Figure 15.1. Phase system used by 3M Micrographics.

you had to do to have a successful commercial product – made a list and then sequenced it. And it probably stretched the length of this room for a typical product that we produced. And there were about 270-odd items that were major . . . We provided that map to the program leaders and told them, "Look, this is what you use with your team." That was how we started. And then people kept looking at it and adding things and wiping them off, etc. We then took this map and began to group it into phases. And then other people started doing it, too, maybe parallel or otherwise, but it kind of spread. And then finally it got institutionalized. Now it's a 3M system.

Ray Thorngate went on to describe the benefits of the phase system:

The difference between a mediocre product and a good product is attention to nit-picking detail. And the phase system is a way of doing that. It really helps you because it gives you a set of guidelines and checkpoints. And you make the decision whether you ought to follow those or not, or whether that applies. But the point is, it ought to be a decision – not because you ignored it or went by it. Now, the biggest problem with the whole system is the degree to which you truly use it. Or do you give it lip service? And the system is only as good as the input. But if you've done the proper job, the new product is going to perform and will live up to the expectations.

The phase system consisted of six phases for reviewing and monitoring the progress of new business initiatives (Figure 15.1). The product champion or project leader was allowed to move his or her program through the phase system as rapidly as desired, but each phase had to be successfully completed before the next phase could be undertaken. As DGM Buddy March emphasized, "When the program moves from Phase 2 to 3, or 3 to 4, or 4 to 5, the Policy Committee [division top management team] reviews it. We will meet with them next week again if they want us to, but no program can skip a phase."[9]

Ray Thorngate described the purpose of each phase:

Phase 1 is concept; it is in the laboratory's bailiwick or in marketing. It's where people have an idea and they're free to pursue it. No formal authorization is needed to start work on a new idea or to do Phase 1, and it can be initiated by anyone in the division. Phase 2 is where we form a program team to show feasibility. There's a representative, usually, from every function. They're not all completely active at any one time, but as early as possible you try to get representation. Buddy [March, DGM] normally gets involved about the middle of Phase 2. But the big decision is Phase 3 – development. That's when you start pouring the money in; that's when you start going up the slope of people and dollars. That, in our division, usually takes a full-scale policy or operating committee [division TMT] review.

Phase 4, production scale-up, had two parts. The first was field-testing with prototypes. This was *not* primarily a test for reliability, or a test to determine whether the product was performing to specifications, but an attempt to learn from the customer's interactions with the product. Ray Thorngate elaborated:

Not all customers utilize the machine in the manner in which they're expected to use it. And in fact, some of the things that customers do, you couldn't think up if you sat there for thirty days trying to think up what they'd do. [Laughter.] And so what you're really doing in a field test is getting the effect of putting the thing in the hands of service people and customers. I generally like to make the customer pay something because then I know I'm getting an objective evaluation. So while we don't sell them the machine, we usually charge the customer for the supplies and for the service.

Customers with certain characteristics were sought to field-test new products, as DGM Buddy March explained:

Our sales force and our tech service people are very close to some companies. We try to pick those that are willing to accept the fact that it's a prototype machine and there will be problems. If the program is successful, they will buy a production machine like anybody else. We don't give them a discount or anything like that, but they get the first machines. Sometimes that is a month or more of lead time over their competitors. So they have a nice little advantage – but not on price; it's on delivery. And availability. We are also looking for customers who don't spill the beans, so to speak, who don't go and tell our competition what we're doing.

The second part of Phase 4 was a joint laboratory/manufacturing review to sort out if it was an "invention problem" or a "manufacturing problem," as Thorngate explained.

At production scale-up you'd get the thing into the factory and they'd run into problems and come back and say, "You haven't invented it yet." And one of the things we have worked out in Phase 4 is that a team from Methods Engineering will take a set of parts and the drawings and they put it together and qualify it. So that when you got done, everybody has agreed that if you had the parts to specifications and you followed the procedures, you could make a product that you could take through and test and it would pass the test. Once you've proven to everybody involved that it's been invented, now you can get to an objective problem-solving as you run into problems in the plant – and nine times out of ten it turns out to be parts that are out of specification.

Manufacturing was responsible for deciding when to move the new product into Phase 5 – standard production. Once the product was in Phase 5, it was under the control of manufacturing and no longer in the laboratory. Phase 6 was exit. It was the responsibility of manufacturing and product control – usually product control – to move the product into Phase 6.

The phase system – and the discipline and skill with which it was used – was widely believed to have contributed to the strong record of successful new business creation at 3M Micrographics. It had worked so well over the years that all external programs (licensing agreements, product and business acquisitions, joint ventures, etc.) began to be funneled through it. Although it was more difficult to get good, timely information for reviewing an external program, DGM Buddy March said the division had learned a few tricks to accomplish this effectively:

Now we put even the external programs through the phase system. We insist on it, even for an acquisition. And if they say it's in Phase 5, we want to see the data on testing and procedures. And almost invariably we find out it truly isn't in Phase 5; it's in Phase 4. Because the statements by the company – as to how far along things are technically – are usually a little exaggerated . . . It is a bit tricky to get good data on an external program because you don't own them; you haven't yet acquired them. And it may be in their interest to hide things from you. So how do you overcome those obstacles? Basically we tell them, "We need this data to get by the Policy Committee [division TMT]. We will send a team in to get it. You don't have to supply it. We'll work jointly to get the data." This is after you've gotten to where you know them well enough and you kind of agree that yes, you want to make this happen. You don't do that up front or you'll scare the hell out of them. And the problem is that it slows down the acquisition procedure. And we've lost some. But now that we are more sophisticated, we get provisional approvals quickly on the basis that "It's official when the facts are verified." So we get a handshake on the money part of it at least, and the rest of it on the verification. This approach has invariably revealed some problems we may not have caught otherwise. And we have walked away from some. In the past, we were terribly burned on inventory more than once. In the case of the Matrix acquisition, we really didn't get any software inventory. And if we had used this procedure we would have caught it.

Ray Thorngate added that service data, if available, also provided valuable information for a phase review of external programs.

The review system at AMP Sigcom   The people in AMP Sigcom followed their version of the phase system, which they called the "review system," and believed in it to the same degree as the people in 3M Micrographics. DGM Clay Smith described the review system:

In the first phase, idea generation, we have a new product sheet that asks about the product concept and how it will satisfy a market need. In the next phase, concept review, we create cartoons and models to show the customers. Does it look like a good idea? We like to show it to individuals in the customer organization and seek feedback. That helps energize the process and validate the concept.[10] We develop cost estimates. I tell our people to think about the following: "If the competition is entrenched, they could lower prices when we introduce our product. What is going to be our response?" At the next phase, business development, we create testable prototypes[11] in the model shop, with machining on soft [short life-span] tooling. In the final phase, design review, a meeting is held when the product is ready to leave the development house and pass on to the product manager and product engineering. This is an important checkpoint, and this is where it gets tough. The new product has to be relatively free of problems and satisfy other requirements, because it is getting ready to go to manufacturing. Nothing helps development along more at this phase than having a firm customer order, although we will go ahead and invest without a firm order.

Development manager Jim Fitch said the review system, although hard on the ego of his development engineers and himself, helped to flag design problems and brought forth suggestions for product improvement:

The development engineering guys, by their very nature, don't like to be criticized. I mean, it's hard keeping them from becoming prima donnas. And that includes their managers, and yours truly in particular, okay? [Laughter.] And to subject that kind of critter to a critical analysis is a sight to behold. [Laughter.] Well, I've seen guys out here sweating for three days prior to a concept review meeting based on what all those other bastards are going to do with his product concept. [Laughter.] . . . What I like to look for are those situations wherein a specific, viable question is asked and the only answer that is given by our guys in development is, "Trust me." They're the ones that will always get you. They're the ones we haven't thought about before, where we can't get there from here – a process doesn't exist to do it, it's not measurable, those kinds of things. And if the real honest answer has to be, "Trust me," then those items are areas for further investigation because we don't understand the problem. The other challenge is how to take a good idea from somebody else that our people have not thought about at all – it might be a total turn in the road – and somehow integrate that into the design, and that occurs quite often.

DGM Mike Walker of AMP Sigcom said he managed the crucial design review meeting to ensure that all the opinions were heard and the concerns addressed:

I want the die guy to say that the die can be built to make the part the way the guy wants it. I want the mold designer to stand up and say you can mold the part the right way. I want the machine designer to say it can be assembled that way. I want the quality guy to say that the process is capable of making the part that way, and I want the engineering managers to say that the engineering principles are sound and stand up on their own feet. And that's the purpose of the design review meeting.

Description of a less disciplined system: inconsistent and less rigorous use of phase and milestone reviews

The people in both Monsanto Fab Products and Xerox OPD used a system – procedures, checklists, milestones, and reviews – to pursue new business opportunities, but they had not used it long enough and with a large enough number of opportunities to develop the necessary consistency and rigor. A disciplined system would have helped them to achieve better results.

Xerox OPD   The early product failures at Xerox OPD led the division to conduct milestone reviews in product development, similar to those in AMP Sigcom and 3M Micrographics. Engineering development manager Keith Crawford said,

When engineering development for office products was established here five years ago, the philosophy was that if we put the Xerox label on a product, it will sell. They put a lot of faith in the Xerox brand name... The first word processor they put out was too late and too costly. The first fax machine was a disaster. These products had no good statement of requirements that was reviewed and challenged by engineering, marketing, human factors, etc.... Over time we developed a more systematic set of procedures and checkpoints for new product development.

Several of these product review checkpoints were bypassed or passed through hastily when the PC was brought from the drawing board to the market in a record nineteen weeks. As a result, knowledgeable people felt that the product's competitive potential had not been properly assessed. According to Steve Carter, who succeeded Greg Gibbons as DGM of Xerox OPD, "Some of the design problems that surfaced later could have been picked up at these checkpoints. As a 16-bit machine, its performance was better than most. But the minute IBM went to a 32-bit machine – they put $250 million into that effort – every 16-bit machine was obsolete."

Xerox OPD did not use its review system as consistently and as rigorously as AMP Sigcom and 3M Micrographics did, and this hurt its new business creation.

Monsanto Fab Products   The reviews of new initiatives at Monsanto Fab Products under DGM Dan Stewart were conducted at the discretion of commercial development director Joe Hurley, and were essentially updates to keep Stewart and the division top management team informed on progress. A rudimentary new product review system with six stages had emerged over the prior few years: (1) idea generation, (2) evaluation and screening, (3) business analysis, (4) product development, (5) product testing, and (6) commercialization. With more volume of activity through this "stage system" over a longer period of time, the division might have developed a more disciplined approach, like the one at AMP Sigcom or 3M Micrographics.

How a disciplined system could have helped Monsanto
Fab Products

The Spray Guard initiative ran into serious breakage problems in cold weather that should have been caught in their Stage 5 (product testing) review prior to commercialization. Instead, large quantities of product had to be recalled from the field, at a substantial cost and loss of customer goodwill. A firefighting solution was then developed in a crisis mode and it also failed, causing further havoc before the problems were rectified.

DGM Dan Stewart felt that he had moved too quickly and too broadly with Spray Guard, without adequate field-testing, because he and others believed it was a winner. Commercial development director Joe Hurley said the Spray Guard experience taught him a lesson that he had learned years earlier and had to re-learn – "Test what you're going to sell and sell what you test":

That's an old P&G [Procter & Gamble] slogan. If you market-test a product, by God that's the product you sell when you roll out in the marketplace. You don't change it. And we changed on Spray Guard. We changed the product from the time we field-tested in Oregon and New England [*glued* product] to when we went to the marketplace [*fused* product], without re-testing it.

A rigorous Stage 2 or Stage 3 review would have helped to clarify whether the RCA Disk Caddy initiative ought to be positioned as a new product or as a new process. Technical director Peter Dell said,

If we had conceived the initiative as a new *process*, we would have rewarded the getting of good data on the process, including early results that were negative. Since we conceived it as a new *product*, we rewarded the getting of orders. Because of the minimum sales threshold of $50 million and 30 percent gross profit, we set unrealistic goals and worked backwards from there. It made us shoot for a bigger target, rather than taking smaller steps to develop the process technology.

Peter Dell felt strongly that better checkpoints and controls would have helped this initiative and other programs as well:

The RCA Disk Caddy program was hidden. It needed to be exposed on results and status. Spray Guard got some of this attention because of the two breakage problems, and benefited as a result . . . The whole area of new product development didn't undergo reviews. We should have asked, "Which of the specs are absolutely sacred?" "Can we produce to those specs?" We could have recognized the shortcomings earlier and made the no-go decision sooner for the RCA Disk Caddy . . . What I have learned is, insist on continuous checkpoints and controls.

Description of a disciplined system: tight screening of new opportunities prior to commitment

AMP Sigcom and 3M Micrographics encouraged the generation and exploration of a large number of new ideas and then screened out most of them via systematic reviews in order to commit to the very best ones.[12] For example, consider the evidence for 3M Micrographics (see numbers for "surviving concepts" in Figure 15.1). For every new initiative in business development (Phase 3), twenty new business concepts had been generated and explored (100/5). For every successful initiative in product standardization (Phase 5), fifty new business concepts had been reviewed and examined (100/2).[13]

Monsanto Fab Products and Xerox OPD generated and explored fewer opportunities to begin with, and they were not reviewed systematically or screened tightly. Better opportunities could have been found by casting a wider net, and more rigorous reviews and tighter screening would have improved the success rate.

DGM Stewart's successor at Monsanto Fab Products, Ian McVay, had a great deal of experience in new business creation. He had learned the importance of casting the net widely for new product ideas and then screening them very tightly. McVay installed a new products group (NPG) for encouraging, reviewing, and screening new product ideas in a systematic way, and this was a step in the right direction.

How to reject new ideas without de-motivating the proponents   Dan Stewart remained skeptical about the effectiveness of the NPG after he was promoted out of Fab Products because he could not see how new business ideas could be invited and then rejected without de-motivating the proponents:

The tricky part, and I'm sure that they're aware of it, is giving people good, concrete, rational reasons why their ideas were rejected. You and I know that our idea is brilliant, and if anybody tells us it isn't, no amount of explaining is going to convince us that it wasn't a good idea. If the NPG is successful, they'll get fifty ideas every two months, and their problem is going to be to communicate back to people why their ideas were not accepted and doing it in a positive manner so people don't say, "Why should I send an idea to them if they are not going to accept it?"

It is indeed difficult to reject new ideas without de-motivating the people who propose them, but successful companies and managers learn how to do this. For example, managers in 3M Micrographics were amused that those writing about their company in the business press and in management books attributed the company's spectacular record of new business success to the company's presumed belief in never killing a new idea. As one of these managers said to me, "Maybe we shouldn't be telling you this, because it is such a well-preserved myth, but we do kill ideas all the time. Lots of them! We have a regular blood-bath of new ideas around here! The trick is in how you lay the idea to rest."[14] DGM Buddy March described how he did this:

I review the programs in the lab – about 150 people and perhaps 25 programs in various phases – four times a year. I take a full day to go through the lab and meet with the groups. When you do that, they want to show some progress. And they feel pretty good that I take the time to come out to look – that I am interested in the work they're doing, down on the bench.[15] Those visits are also an opportunity for us to de-commit projects. But we are as careful in de-committing them as we are in committing to them. They give us a progress review and even if they feel – or we do – that it ought to be de-committed, we go through the review. And then we present to them – to the whole team – why we are de-committing it. Because I think it's important that they know that it's not the end of their careers. Sometimes it's not their fault. Technology has just overtaken them, or the market has disappeared. They gotta know that. Because, Christ, they don't know what the big picture is. Otherwise, they get beaten to death . . . If a person on the team still feels it's hogwash, then he will become a frustrated individual, but we will not change the decision to placate somebody. The best we can do is to get this person busy with some other project as soon as possible.

Description of a disciplined system: independent and objective technical audits

3M had over the years developed a procedure for providing an independent, objective assessment of the technology being used in new programs. Ray Thorngate, long-time technical director for 3M Micrographics and later DGM of 3M Engineering Products, explained what the technical audits were, and their benefits:

They are conducted by a team of experts from the corporate labs and other parts of the company. They deal with the technical basis for programs – are the people keeping up with technology? Have they worked in the phase system? Have the people done their homework in terms of having a clear technical target? Is the expenditure in line with the return? – these kinds of questions ... In some cases their influence has been very strong because it gives the DGM an outside audit on those programs. And if the DGM is smart, he can utilize that as a lever to either terminate some things or add emphasis to some things, or to get priorities on things, etc. Sometimes, the group vice president has become involved because of those recommendations ... They audit the lab but they'll also comment on specific programs. And they compute probabilities of success which, in retrospect, have been pretty accurate.

Jill Pringle, 3M corporate director of technology planning was responsible for all technology audits within the company. She explained why the term "audit" was a misnomer and provided additional details:

We audit each 3M lab, once every two years, and all selected opportunities and other new programs as appropriate. We select projects that people are spending the most time and money on, as well as those they feel have the greatest potential. "Audit" is the wrong word, because we are not interested in what happened – only in what is *likely to happen* in the future. We actually estimate and put a number on two probabilities – the probability of marketing success and the probability of technical success. The probability of manufacturing success is factored into the probability of technical success. We should perhaps split that out in the future. We compute a joint probability of success by combining all these. Over the years, we have become pretty sophisticated in how we do this. For example, we know that people's estimates are biased. Most people don't rate below 30 percent or above 70 percent, staying in the safe middle zone when you are dealing with high uncertainty, so as not to upset colleagues. So we try to un-bias the estimates by making an adjustment for this "gentlemen's agreement." Our predictions have been closer to reality than the official forecasts, which don't adequately take the possibility of failure into account, because of normal optimism.

The technical audits at 3M were designed to provide constructive feedback to those involved in the project. Jill Pringle described the process:

The technical director, the chief scientist, our technical staff, and other experts all meet for a very open session. People's defenses are down at breakfast, so we begin over breakfast! There is no knifing of people; it is a very, very helpful, constructive thing. Some very good communication occurs at the audits. How often does a typical DGM take a day to really listen to what goes on in the lab? I used to wonder, initially, why doesn't the DGM already know what his people think? I have learned with experience that even if the DGM takes the time to listen, most people won't volunteer negative comments. But most people won't lie if asked opinions, especially in writing, by a third party. So the technical audits are non-controversial forums for getting *insiders'* opinions too ... We give our recommendations in writing, but they are non-binding. Sometimes we get set up – we don't mind if the lab manager or the program manager is using us [to support his position] and we will go along if we are in agreement.

At Monsanto, a corporate Technical Review Committee (TRC) composed of senior corporate technology staff and other experts conducted TRC reviews on a pre-planned basis. They put out a schedule of what they wanted to review, and fed the results to the responsible managing director (GVP) and to the Executive Management Committee. However, their primary purpose was that of a traditional audit.

Independent and objective feedback of the type offered by the 3M technical audits could have helped Monsanto Fab Products. As evidence, DGM Stewart recalled one helpful *ad hoc* technical review session in Florida, conducted at the behest of his boss, where experts from different parts of Monsanto provided constructive feedback on how the technical problems on Spray Guard might be fixed. Stewart felt that if this had been done earlier, the breakage problems that the program encountered could have been avoided:

Courtney [GVP] suggested we gather a group of our prominent scientists (most of them polymer chemists) and go down to Pensacola and review our Spray Guard research and make sure we have really thought our way through it. The guys went down there for like two days … The local guys didn't want that. Nobody wants to have somebody else come in and tell them how to do their business. But we did that after the second crisis – the second breakage after we irradiated the product. It should have been done earlier. Here we have years and years of plastics experience, and we didn't really utilize it effectively.

Skillful use of a disciplined system

Understanding the notion of a disciplined system for new business creation is one thing; learning to use it skillfully is another matter. AMP Sigcom and 3M Micrographics had developed their systems out of their own experience over a period of years. Top managers without experience in new business creation cannot expect to import such a system for immediate results. They will need to experiment with it, adapt it to their situation, and learn by doing. People must be educated and trained to use it consistently and effectively over a period of time.

Summary

It pays to generate and explore a large number of new business opportunities in order find the most attractive ones to specify and commit to.

New business opportunities are generated by conducting market and competitor intelligence, by resurrecting discarded business ideas, and by using formal mechanisms such as a new product development group or committee. The exploration of new business opportunities is facilitated by conducting market research, by offering people discretionary time and money to explore new ideas, and by bootlegging projects. A new business opportunity can be specified incorrectly if the people in the division are not close to the customer, or if there is a lack of clarity about whether the new initiative is best positioned as a new product or as a new process.

A commitment to pursue new business opportunities – despite the technical risks and the market uncertainties – requires the people in the division to make investments to discover the market, to bid for new business before they know how to make the new product, and to make promises to their customers without certainty that they can be met. External programs can facilitate commitment and reduce some of these risks by providing complementary resources and capabilities, but such programs carry other risks and have their own limitations.

A disciplined system – consisting of rigorous phase and milestone reviews, tight screening of opportunities prior to commitment, and independent and objective technical audits – can improve the identification and pursuit of new business opportunities. But simply copying the 3M system, or the AMP system, or some other system, will not yield the desired results. One can begin with such a system, adapt it to one's situation, and educate and train people to use it consistently and effectively over a period of time.

16 Other new business creation challenges for the division

This chapter examines how the way in which other challenges are managed by the division influences new business creation (Table 16.1).

Entrepreneurship is the pursuit of an opportunity because of a genuine belief in its attractiveness. It is what sustains a new initiative through the unexpected problems that are bound to occur. It is what motivates the search for creative solutions. But there is a danger that what is perceived and labeled as "entrepreneurship" is, in fact, fake. People pursue the opportunity not because of any real conviction or passion but because it is expected of them, or because *others* believe it is worth pursuing. Fake entrepreneurship must be recognized and avoided and real entrepreneurship detected and encouraged.

Avoiding fake entrepreneurship

The champion is not merely the principal driver of the new initiative. He is passionate about it. It is his baby. Unfortunately, there are far fewer real champions than top managers assume. What is viewed as corporate entrepreneurship is often fake.[1] One reason for this is that many corporations do not have a gene pool of innovators, as Monsanto president Jim Reilly pointed out:[2]

> If you think about it, innovators are by nature different. In a population of 1,000 live births I would guess there probably aren't 100 that have even a shred of creativity in them. At an early age you siphon off a great many of the really creative people to the arts and other places not available to industry. And within industry you siphon off a great many to the creative production side – advertising, and so on–who in most companies do not rise to the top of the corporation. They stay in the profession. So, what's left over is we retreads[3] . . . And so then we wake up and say, "My God. We don't have any innovators." But I don't think it's the climate so much. I just think that there's not very many [innovators] around.
>
> If we had the most free society here in this company I think you would improve the innovation. Improve it. I don't think that it would be light years different . . . I was out with our senior fellows, the cream of the scientific crop. They started talking about freedom to try things. "It's too stifling around here," they said.

Table 16.1. *How the way in which other challenges are managed by the division influences new business creation*

Hypothesis	Factor	Influence on new business creation
16.1	Avoiding fake entrepreneurship	+
16.2	Managing corporate perceptions and cultivating corporate support for new initiatives	+
16.3	Managing the disruption of existing operations	+
16.4	Managing the volatility of new business	+

I said, "Well, would you tell me one good idea you've had that was stifled or was not funded or you couldn't get a hearing." "Well, it's not us, it's those other guys that have the problem." So, I go to another group and say, "Tell me about all these marvelous ideas that are getting thwarted by the management that can't see past its nose. Or killed by some guy who came up the commercial side and doesn't understand research. All that stuff I hear. Could you give me an example of an idea that didn't get funded?" Well, you keep pressing and you finally get it down to, "We know that it won't get funded so we don't bring it up." I think it comes back to my observation that there aren't that many creative people in this world.

Fake entrepreneurship can be avoided by recognizing that the corporation may not have a gene pool of innovators, and by assuming there is only lip service rather than real commitment to entrepreneurship – unless there is compelling evidence to the contrary.

Will the real champion please stand up?

Managers who can identify innovation and creativity in others are valuable. President Reilly said,

There's another subclass that may escape notice, and they're extraordinarily valuable. And they are people who can recognize innovation instantly. And they do it so fast that it seems like they are innovators – and they probably have never had a creative idea in their entire life. But we're not in business to put people in categories; we are in business to get results. And they get results. They recognize creativity in other people instantly. And they're on to this thing so fast and so early that you swear that it's their idea.

Ed Costello, EVP responsible for Monsanto Engineered Products, liked to ask a question that top managers should ask: "My question is: are the 50 creative people out of the 500 doing what they should be doing? Even the Army produces a Patton." Several Monsanto managers said

DGM Al Stephenopolous had a talent for identifying the truly creative people. He said he did it by creating an environment in which the creative people "float up."

In my experience, 60 percent of the people are good citizens. They will innovate, but they are not going to shake the earth. Thirty percent I find are only implementers. Ten percent are the really creative ones. You can't select them because they are hard to identify. But you can create an environment where they rise. What does that mean? Ask for suggestions. Narrow the list to the best twenty or so. Pick one at random. Give the person three months off to work on the idea. See what happens. Our top scientist was identified through this float-up system. Today his unorthodoxy is tolerated because he accounts for most of the innovation in this division . . . One time I took over a plant and said to the people, "Take 10–15 percent of your time off to think of new ideas." One person came to see me later and said, "There is no way to take time off here." When I found out he had been there fifteen years I said to him, "Take two years off (with no cut in pay or status) to do what you have missed." He couldn't believe it, but I was serious. He came back three months later and told me, "I was wrong. I don't have any creative ideas. Please give my job back to me."

Top managers get the form rather than the substance of entrepreneurship because they assume they have real champions when in fact they have none, except perhaps themselves. People in Monsanto Fab Products viewed DGM Dan Stewart as the real champion on all the initiatives in the division, whereas Stewart looked to commercial development director Joe Hurley or one of his subordinates as the real champion. After he was promoted out of Fab Products, Stewart could see that he had been the only real champion in that division:

The champion should have been at [commercial development director] Joe Hurley's level or someone below him, but certainly not me. Maybe I usurped some of it a little bit and didn't allow somebody else to assume that role, because I was trying to keep hope in the division alive by pushing it so hard . . . How much better hiring and screening and all of this could we have done? I go back to the overall feeling about Monsanto. Maybe we just don't have the entrepreneur type. I've tried to think who could have done it. In retrospect, I don't think we had any . . . And I say to myself, "Geez, were the people's beliefs in these projects so fragile that when I left somebody could crumble them so quickly?" RCA Disk Caddy was one example of that. But I think Spray Guard too. Without the federal legislation [requiring spray protection for trucks], that would have been done too. So the whole thing is, "How much did I instill in people the belief and the optimism and all the rest, really?" And I have come to the conclusion that people really didn't believe in these things. That I was pumping them up and I was pushing it. But they weren't all that enthusiastic from their end of it. It was more or less, "This is what he wants and he is the boss so let's do it. If the next boss wants it fine and if he doesn't want it we'll do what he wants."

Top managers must avoid the trap of *assuming* that they have a real champion for a program because one has been appointed, a program team created, incentives provided, and activity generated. Instead of "appointing" entrepreneurs, they must create conditions under which someone who is both competent and committed to the new initiative will *volunteer* to lead it.[4]

The word *volunteer* might seem out of place, but intrinsic motivation is the real test of commitment. Top managers should wait and see who comes forward even though no special incentives are offered; the challenge of the entrepreneurial task will provide the necessary motivation for the right person. The champion should be allowed to recruit other believers who have the necessary skills, and must be given sufficient autonomy and resources to proceed.[5] DGM Ray Thorngate of 3M Engineering Products described how he did this:

To call a key person into your office and say "Gee, I've got this great assignment for you" is not the way to go. Because if he's convinced that he can't do it or he just isn't interested in doing it, etc., you get a second-class job. And if you have a really tough assignment, I have found that the smartest thing to do is to shop around until you get someone who takes fire with the problem or the assignment, and if you have confidence in him and he believes that he knows how to do it, you just buy in. But that's where I also say [chuckling] that he also gets himself the right – I think he has to lay out a program, etc. – but he also buys the right to make some mistakes and figure out how he's gonna do it. Because you can't have it both ways; you can't get people to feel ownership and also tell them this is the way it's got to be done. You can't micromanage the program and keep creative people too.

Managing corporate perceptions and cultivating corporate support for new initiatives

The people in the division assist the DGM's efforts (described in Chapter 13) to build corporate support for new initiatives. To do this well, they must be aware of how corporate executives perceive these initiatives. They must prevent premature or excessive corporate visibility for these programs and unrealistic optimism about them. And they must pre-sell executives and manage the godfathers to cultivate the necessary corporate support.

Awareness of corporate perceptions

A new initiative can be hurt by its perceived association with a failed program. It can also benefit if it is perceived to be associated with a promising or successful initiative. The corporate perception of a new program is either helped because the timing is right or hurt because of poor timing.

Guilt by association   A new program is perceived negatively if it is seen as a reincarnation of a prior program that failed. Commercial development director Joe Hurley of Monsanto Fab Products said, "The OPET bottle initiative was hurt by the Cycle Safe program's negative corporate image. That image is still very, very strong." Alf Hummel, Monsanto VP of corporate planning, elaborated:

Everyone knows that the father of OPET is Cycle Safe. We were producing 20 million bottles per month and had customer contracts worth $178 million when the FDA shut down Cycle Safe. We laid 1,000 people off, and wrote $200 million off the books. The core technical people were transferred to Fab Products, and they are now involved with OPET. So it is seen as the second coming and people ask, "Is this another Cycle Safe?"

Rick Smale, the CFO and chief of staff of Xerox OPD, pointed out that *customers* may also attribute guilt to a new program by associating it with a prior failure – for example, Xerox's exit from the mainframe computer business. According to Smale, "Some customers remember that. 'How do we know you are in word processors and PCs to stay?', they ask."

Benefit from association   A new initiative can benefit from its association with another program that is perceived to be promising or successful. Commercial development director Joe Hurley of Monsanto Fab Products felt that the Spray Guard initiative was helped by the fact that RCA Disk Caddy, a concurrent initiative, was seen as a parallel development with some promise:

The RCA Disk Caddy, which was running concurrently, was a very positive program at that time, so there was a fairly strong credibility. Both Spray Guard and RCA Caddy were seen as $50 million programs – big numbers and good ROC [return on capital]. It sounded good. So they sort of reinforced each other. They were sort of like companion technology. The fact that Spray Guard was associated with the Doormat business also helped, because it is a nice business with 50 percent ROC. That kept the optimism up.

Right or wrong timing   Timing can make or break an initiative. Poor timing hurt the OPET bottle because capital approval was being sought at a time when the blownware bottle business with which it was associated was having a terrible year. As one manager noted, the corporate attitude was, "Blownware is barely breaking even, and you want to put more money into OPET?"

Dilemmas in managing corporate perceptions

There are two major dilemmas. First, it might not be possible to justify the investments needed for a new program without an overly optimistic sales and profit forecast. But such unbounded optimism increases the risk that the actual results will fall short of the projections and cause the program to be questioned, slowed, or even stopped. Second, it is difficult to garner corporate support for a new initiative without giving it some visibility. But premature or excessive visibility creates unrealistic expectations about how soon the program will achieve success in the marketplace, which can hurt the program.

The risk of overly optimistic forecasts to justify the needed investments[6] DGM Greg Gibbons felt that Xerox OPD had to attain the first or the second position in the office automation marketplace for it to be a worthwhile business for Xerox. Enormous resource commitments were required to develop the new products needed to achieve such a market position quickly, because the market was emerging rapidly. These investments could only be justified on the basis of very aggressive sales and profit forecasts. This is one of the reasons why Xerox OPD's results came in so far below expectations – $100 million below the profit plan for Gibbons' second full calendar year as DGM and $150 million below plan for his third full year (he left in October).

When I interviewed GVP Jerry Tyson six months later, he said Gibbons apparently believed all would have been forgiven if the initial misses were followed by success. One celebrated general took a similar approach during the Civil War in the United States, Tyson said.

The general could have either been shot for violating the rules, or given a medal for winning the battle. He got the medal. And Greg Gibbons would have earned a medal too if he had delivered what he promised in his second year, or at least in his third year. Unfortunately, he didn't . . . I discounted the numbers Greg Gibbons gave me by 30–40 percent, but it was still not enough! He was way off the mark.

Avoiding premature or excessive corporate visibility   There is no corporate enthusiasm or support for a new initiative that is not visible to the corporate executives. But visibility brings scrutiny and an impatience for results. Peter Dell, the technical director of Monsanto Fab Products, was concerned about premature publicity for the division's new initiatives when Dan Stewart was DGM:

Dan Stewart made a gutsy decision to publicize Spray Guard and RCA Disk Caddy to the top 800 people at the Monsanto Management Conference. But Spray Guard is a premium product that may not sell as widely as we hope. What if it sells only $10 million versus $100 million that we are projecting? And RCA Disk Caddy has only a 50/50 chance of success. Why play it up?

Joe Hurley, commercial development director of Monsanto Fab Products, was concerned about the excessive corporate visibility that the division's new initiatives began to receive after Dan Stewart was promoted to managing director (GVP) of Monsanto Agricultural Products and became a member of the Corporate Advisory Council (CAC):

[EVP] Costello has more influence on the initiatives in Fab Products now under [DGM] McVay than [GVP] Courtney ever had when Stewart was DGM. And I'm really concerned because Costello gives a speech to the CAC once a month. It's supposed to be an upbeat speech, but the only damn things he ever talks about are Spray Guard and Drainage Mat and OPET [all three new initiatives in Fab Products]! He talks about nothing else. [Laughter] I'm getting exposure I don't want is what it amounts to . . . Stewart, who is now a member of the CAC, called me up recently and he says, "Boy, Costello really gave the CAC a great speech on Spray Guard the other day." He's laughing and he says, "Is it *really* that good?" [Laughter]

Dan Stewart saw this dilemma of corporate visibility for new initiatives as an inevitable one that needed to be managed:

That's just natural. You want to make a new initiative visible internally to people in the division to promote motivation by saying, "Hey, we are getting into new businesses." And also externally (to people in other divisions and at corporate headquarters) to say, "Hey, there are new things coming out of here. Here's a $100 million opportunity for us." But once you've done that then people begin to ask, "When is it coming?" And I guess that was a legitimate concern of a lot of our people in Fab Products: "Why don't you keep these things quiet until we are further down the pike?" But I said, "It was to keep us alive, baby." Without those promises we didn't have much to offer.

Cultivating corporate support

It is personally risky and politically dangerous to try to launch a major new initiative without the required corporate approval. So people in the division try to cultivate corporate support for such initiatives by pre-selling the executives whose approval is needed, and by managing the corporate godfathers.

The costs of proceeding without corporate approval   DGM Greg Gibbons supported the development of the PC, leased a new facility for manufacturing it, and built up $20 million in inventory – all without corporate approval! Gibbons said he had chosen to go ahead without any approval because the PC market was exploding. He felt that a quick entry was of the utmost importance. Indeed, the Xerox PC had been developed and produced in a record nineteen weeks; it normally took longer than that just to get on the corporate calendar to seek the necessary approval. Convinced that his decision had been correct from a business standpoint, Gibbons did not think he had used up too much political capital by proceeding without corporate approval. But he said he had used one of his "silver bullets" and would not do it again.

Pre-selling the corporate executives whose approval is needed   AMP and 3M permitted their divisions to undertake new business initiatives without prior corporate approval, provided the division had the resources to fund them. Initiatives that were outside the scope of the division's business charter, or beyond its technical or financial resources, needed prior corporate approval. Development manager Jim Fitch of AMP Sigcom was a master at pre-selling a new program to the key people whose approval was needed. He described how he got these people excited about it by presenting the big picture to them in a clear and compelling way:

This is an entrepreneurial spirit kind of thing. It has to be presented as if I was going to the bank for some money. Which means I write a business plan. People cannot very often visualize things in their head – you have to show it to them. Throw it up on a wall, multi-color, projectors and so on. Boom! And make a presentation. Say this is what it is. Here is what everyone is telling me, here are the people on those accounts that are telling me that, and here's when they told me that. And by the way here's verification on that. Bang. OK? And it's a very by the numbers – boom, boom, boom – kind of thing. When you are all said and done you have either overwhelmed them or got them on board...Who is "them"? The "them" varies. The "them" would obviously be the group directors [GVPs] of this world. Very often they'll drag in experts in certain areas to see if I'm bullshitting them.

But before presenting to the key people whose approval was needed, Jim Fitch said he pre-sold other people whose opinions they might solicit, as well as people in other parts of the company who might feel they have a stake in the new initiative:

You play Washington senator and you go to these various organizations, the order of which is very important because of the way that they relate to each other, oddly enough. These are all these VPs and associate directors and whoevers that individually would see me as an affront if I were to suddenly come screaming up with a program that may, on the fringes, have an impact on what they were trying to accomplish, but that they had not yet been able to do. You play that game . . . You kind of have to know who your group director [GVP] is going to work with too. Who he's going to reference off of. You know, who the credibility people are to him. And you get to these people too. OK? So that after you make the presentation to Grover [GVP] and he picks up the phone and calls one of these cats, he is told, "Oh yeah, I know all about that, and boy that's neat and ta da, ta da, ta da." Otherwise, Grover calls up and the guy says "No, I don't know anything about that and that sounds like a bunch of minutiae."

Fitch would proceed with the new product design and collect meaningful market information on it *before* a program was actually approved. This was both possible and necessary to get things done in a big company, Fitch said.

In the first meeting, the key people had a rough idea of what I was talking about because I gave them a rough prospectus. I said here's what I really think I want to go do. And here's about what I think it will cost. And now I hit them with a one-two punch and go to the specifics. I learned a long time ago that you don't go in with specifics from day one because then they are likely to shoot you down based on the numbers. So, you get them oriented to saying yes and then you go into specifics. "Here's exactly what I want to do. And by the way I want to get an electronics engineer and I want to pull this guy in." That gets pretty specific. But by then they've already pretty much said yes, so they say, "OK. Get started." And usually we've gotten started before that. Before we get the money. Because, it's really kind of a one-two punch as well. I get started because the philosophy around here is "go" until we say "no." So the smart approach is to go the formal route but also start the program before the formal lines ever ratify it. So you can very quickly plug in the reality after the formal approval. And it happens so soon after the formal ratification that they say, "Goddamn, these guys are fast!", you know? Right? That works pretty well. It's the only way to get things done in a large corporation.

Managing the corporate godfathers   The corporate godfathers – influential corporate executives who believe in a new program – are an important resource for cultivating corporate support. But their personal interest in the venture can become a liability if the reality diverges significantly from the way in which they have positioned it to their colleagues. At Monsanto, the Prism Separator venture had two corporate godfathers. Stewart, who was assigned responsibility for this venture during the second half of his five-year tenure as the DGM of Monsanto Fab Products, said they continued to play up the potential of this venture even though oil prices were falling, making it unlikely that the initial sales and profit projections would be realized. The program manager for Prism Separator said he was trying to manage the corporate godfathers by keeping them informed and working with them:

We entered the market with a splash and sold $12 million worth of equipment with 25 percent gross profit in the first year. Success has many fathers, of course, and these two powerful godfathers became very excited and started talking it up. Then the oil prices fell and with it our projections. But the godfathers have made public statements about a "$500 million business" and feel this business should be much bigger than the 200 million in ten years that we are now projecting. They have no formal authority over Prism Separator, but I have to keep them informed and work with them.

Managing the disruption of existing operations

Disruption and its dilemmas

New business can create a number of disruptions. Efficiency and quality are typically low until the people learn how to manufacture and sell a new product. If people who are skilled at manufacturing or selling existing products are reassigned to work on a new a product, their replacements must be trained. Then the quality and efficiency of *existing* products drops until the replacements have accumulated sufficient experience. AMP Sigcom's manufacturing manager, Dick Nottley, described some of these disruptions:

There's a continual problem that I have any time a new product comes in the plant. People don't like change – "Oh God, we can't do it. Everything's wrong with it." So acceptance is a problem before you get to the learning curve. We went through that on the Coaxial Tap. It wasn't that difficult but boy it was just horrendous. I went out and put the parts in it and said, "Now damn it, we're going to make them." And I sat there and we made them . . . Cable Assembly caused us a lot of chaos. Mainly because our policies require that we offer our Grade 1 labor the opportunity to move into the higher-pay Grade 2 for Cable Assembly. And train them for it. I'm talking about going from twenty people to eighty people. Like in thirty days. And all of a sudden you have eighty people and sixty of them are new to Cable Assembly. The newly hired Grade 1s now do all the existing products, and all of a sudden I am in all types of problems back in those products. And the efficiencies fall off, and the quality problems go up on new business *and* ongoing business.

The disruption caused by new business and the difficulty of getting the people to cope with it is not limited to manufacturing, of course, as DGM Mike Walker of AMP Sigcom emphasized:

Some of the jobs take longer to get going than what is originally projected. I'm afraid the teething problems are inevitable as new products come through from development to manufacturing to sales – even though we spend a lot of time strategizing how to make that smooth. And not everybody in the organization is willing to accept the disruption.

One project manager in AMP Sigcom expressed this concern: "We have so many new products, we do have the image with marketing and sales as not totally reliable on delivery commitments. They call us *Sick*com rather than Sigcom!" But the manufacturing manager, Dick Nottley, described the dilemma. Use of overtime to meet delivery commitments for new products hurt profitability, but attempts to maintain profitability by not using overtime and slipping on delivery commitments hurt customer service.

All new programs do not create equal disruption, of course. Programs whose demands outstrip existing capacity, those that are harder to automate than expected, or the ones that involve new materials that prove more difficult to work with than anticipated, cause more disruption.

Managing disruption

Flexible production and vendor management   One way to minimize the disruption to existing operations is to use flexible production lines that allow small quantities of a new product to be manufactured efficiently.[7] DGM Buddy March of 3M Micrographics explained how better vendor management can also minimize the disruption created by new products:

We're getting there, but we haven't learned to manage the changes that the vendors make that affect a new product. And all of a sudden, we find a problem in the field – for example, we've had motor manufacturers change their gears from steel or brass to plastic and didn't bother to tell us. We're getting better at managing that. We used to have 11,000 vendors that we bought stuff from. We're trying to get that down to 300 real big preferred vendors; we're giving them a hell of a lot more business and working with them more closely.

Cross-functional coordination   Smoother cross-functional project transfers reduce the disruption to existing operations. For example, neither the Spray Guard nor the RCA Disk Caddy programs at Monsanto Fab Products disrupted existing operations, as commercial development director Joe Hurley pointed out:

I invited Marshall [Babcock, the manufacturing director] to the major presentations. So that he was on board. I didn't surprise him one day and say, "Hey, OK. Now take this over and start making this for me." So there was an orderly transfer to manufacturing after the process was developed.

Managing the volatility of new business

The difficulty of achieving forecasted results for new business

The innate optimism of the proponents combined with the inherent technical and market uncertainties make it difficult to achieve forecasted results for new business. Consider the challenges in developing a new product as described by development manager Jim Fitch of AMP Sigcom:

Almost every one of the new programs overruns both in time and dollars! For two reasons. One is because the guy that wrote the thing in the first place is by definition an optimistic critter, so he's going to say you can do ten times as much as you can do. That's something you got to learn to live with. That's the way the guy's built. So you modify for him the book you keep on the program. The other one is the fact that if you are really pushing the frontiers, you are really going to run into problems that cannot be foreseen by the people involved, no matter how smart they are. And that's the one that hurts. And very often it stretches programs out three and four times what they ought to be in time and pain. Because by then you probably made commitments to other people too, so they're participating in the pain with you. Like customers.

Unanticipated difficulties in manufacturing can also play havoc with sales and profit forecasts for new business. AMP Sigcom product manager Arjay Mason described how this impacted the Transmission Cable program:

The initial cost sheets gave a distorted view of how inexpensively we would be able to assemble it. We didn't really have at that point a lot of experience in Transmission Cable and so we didn't really know yet what kind of yield you would get, what percent scrap you would have. Typically we figure 1 percent scrap. It has turned out to be many times that – in the 8 to 10 percent range. It's not difficult to get to 100 to 125 dollars extra for every thousand that you spend.

Because of the inherent uncertainties of new business creation, *all* divisions miss their sales and profit forecasts for a new initiative, often by wide margins. Here is an example from AMP Sigcom. During the first year that Coaxial Tap was in the market, actual sales were 93 percent below forecast (for a sales forecast of 100, the actual sales were 7) and pre-tax profit was 57 percent below forecast (for a profit forecast of 100, the actual profit was 43). During Coaxial Tap's second year in the market, sales were a bit more accurate (63 percent rather than 93 percent below forecast) but profit was way below forecast (2770 percent versus 57 percent). Actual profit was hurt badly because of unexpected product problems that had to be fixed quickly, with expensive methods, in order to retain customer goodwill. Coaxial Tap product manager Chad Blair provided the story behind these numbers:

Because of the FCC rulings on noise reduction, the insulation on the coaxial cable was beefed up and this made it more difficult for the tap to penetrate the cable. The cable is half the system; unless the cable is good, the tap is worthless. So we developed a test fixture to tell if the cable was *capable* of being tapped. How thick is the insulation? How well is the conductor centered inside the cable? In a last-ditch effort to solve the penetration problem, we developed a drilling kit, which emerged as the savior and allowed us to proceed...We got NEK [a big AMP customer] out of trouble and got lots of people off our backs. We lost a fortune in meeting this commitment because the materials we purchased cost $40–50 per tap, and the selling price of the tap was $29.50! We put in, oh, an extra $800,000 into the program.

In general, the actual sales and the profit for a new initiative tend to come in closer to the forecasted numbers as the organization gains more experience with the new business. For the first one or two years in the market, however, the sales and profits for a new initiative can be volatile, that is, the actual results can deviate widely from the forecasted numbers.

Achieving the forecasted results for the division

There are six main reasons why some division managers are able to deliver the forecasted results for their division, despite the inherent volatility of their new business: (1) they have a relatively large base of stable existing business with which to absorb new business volatility; (2) they factor the expected new business volatility into their sales and profit forecasts for the division; (3) they retain slack in the budget for the unforeseen expenditures that new initiatives typically require; (4) they have several new-initiative "irons in the fire," and at different stages of development and introduction into the market; (5) they target a variety of industries; and (6) they undertake a careful review of all new initiatives to decide which ones to cut and by how much, and where to delay, in order to deliver the division's forecasted results.

A relatively large base of stable existing business   A division with a larger base of stable existing business is better able to absorb the volatility of new business. At Monsanto Fab Products, Spray Guard was the only new initiative in the market, and its projected revenue, cash flow, and profit were small in comparison to the corresponding results for the division's large base of fairly stable existing business in blownware, film, and Fomecor. Thus, high volatility of the results for Spray Guard could easily be absorbed by the division.

Although Xerox OPD also had a large base of existing business in word processors and fax machines (revenue of about $300 million), it was less stable than the existing business of Monsanto Fab Products. In addition, the projected size of the new business was much greater at Xerox OPD – revenue from all the new initiatives (Star, Ethernet, PC, and Memorywriter) was projected to be as much as *50 percent* of the revenue from the existing business for their *first* year in the market. For their second year in the market, these new initiatives were projected to bring in revenue equal to 100 percent of the revenue from the existing business. Volatility on such a relatively large volume of new business could not be absorbed by the existing business of Xerox OPD, and this caused the overall results for the division to deviate widely from what was forecasted.

In contrast, the existing business at both AMP Sigcom and 3M Micrographics was relatively large and well established and provided a stable cushion with which the volatility of their new business could be absorbed. Ralph West, head of the Imaging Products department, explained how this allowed the 3M Micrographics division to achieve its forecasted results in recent years, and why results in the early years were less predictable. He said, "The more recent ventures were not a significant part of the division's sales of $200 million. Only the Com program lost a steady 3 million a year. But in the early years, when new business was a much larger fraction of the division's sales, the division's results were not as predictable."

Factor the expected new business volatility into the forecast for divisional results   Because it is difficult to predict sales and profits for a new initiative accurately, this uncertainty should be factored into the forecast for the division's results. DGM Ray Thorngate of 3M Engineering Products described how he modified the input he received from marketing to come up with a more realistic budget and forecast:

If we went upon what the marketing people initially said, we would forecast higher than we do for the first two or three years of our five-year sales forecast. In the last two or three years of that forecast, they're generally low. And they're generally low because they have a feeling of uncertainty as to whether any of these things are gonna come about. So as a net result, they're bullish in the short term and they're bearish in the long term. And it's a sort of a thing where they can't see what the product looks like and they feel uncomfortable forecasting sales for it. You get the best sales forecast when you've got a working prototype and they can come over and look at it. And if you're talking five years out, you don't have any prototypes. [Chuckling] And so those [longer-term forecasts] tend to run a little light, and we generally have to pump those up. But at the same time, I have a tendency to pull down the near-term forecasts, because they never take into account what could go wrong with the new products that they can see.

Retain slack in the budget for unforeseen expenditures   Because of the inherent technical and market uncertainties, it is impossible to prepare an accurate expenditure budget for new initiatives. Some degree of slack[8] must be built into the budget with the understanding that it will not be used if it is not needed. Commercial development director Joe Hurley of Monsanto Fab Products said both DGM Dan Stewart and his successor, Ian McVay, clearly understood the need for this:

Dan was tight with his own money, and he was tight with Monsanto's money. When it came to new business initiatives, however, he wasn't penny-pinching. He had the same philosophy I had, that we should always have some additional discretionary money when preparing the budget – this is like in August, for next year. Now when things got tight we would discuss it and he'd say, "Hey, do you really need that?" This may be in March or April or whatever and I'd say, "No, I think I can give it back to you." So, we had that type of relationship where I was very honest with him on the discretionary funds that I had. And he wouldn't call it up unless he really needed it. And I wouldn't spend it unless I had something that justified the expense . . . It didn't happen with Stewart, and it didn't happen under McVay either, on new products, but someone could look at $100,000 or $200,000 that is not specifically earmarked for a certain program and say, "That's ridiculous. We'll take that and put it on the bottom line." And it's just human nature to do that. I think a lot of managers are brought up to feel uncomfortable with development money that is not specifically earmarked for a program. But you are budgeting in July, August, for the next year and so you're talking as much as fourteen months out and it's just almost impossible to foresee what will be needed that far out. Opportunities arise so that you want to do something, or problems arise so that you don't want to do something. And it's just impossible to budget. We take our best shot and that's it. So I got my slush fund.

Have several new initiatives with staggered times for development and market introduction   Given the volatility of new business, it pays to have several new business irons in the fire because better than anticipated results on some initiatives can wash out worse than expected performance on others. And because initiatives that are in the market for a longer period of time deliver more predictable results, it also pays to stagger the development and market introduction times of new initiatives. As DGM Ray Thorngate of 3M Engineering Products said,

I think the thing that makes the difference is we have so many new programs. So on the average, it works. What throws you off is the first two years. Once you get to three or four years after market introduction, then you've gotten over those damned hurdles of what has gone wrong and all these kinds of things. So it's the third, fourth, fifth year that carries the day. But if you've got a big batch and they're all ones you just introduced, your forecast accuracy is lousy. What we've learned is to have a lot of balls in the air, and spread them out over time.

Target a variety of industries   Volatility of the division's overall results can be reduced, not only by diversification over several initiatives and
diversification over time, but also by diversification over industries. With
industry diversification, good results in booming industries offset poor
results in those that have become depressed, reducing overall volatility.
As Ray Thorngate said,

> We were reasonably successful at delivering the forecasted results for 3M
> Micrographics because we had three lines (35mm, 16mm, and 105mm mi-
> crofiche) that cut across so many industries and SIC [Standard Industrial
> Classification] codes. And we soon learned the game, that not everybody was
> in a tight economic situation simultaneously. And so when the airlines were fly-
> ing high we sold airline systems; when banks were flying high, we tried to get in
> the banking and financial area; when the Blue Cross/Blue Shield health insurance
> things started to boom, we took our goods and tailored our products and tried
> to get into that area; and we just kinda worked back and forth across where we
> thought the opportunities were.

Review all new initiatives carefully to decide where to cut and delay
It might be necessary selectively to delay new initiatives and cut expenditure levels for new programs in order to deliver the division's forecasted
results. DGM Ralph West of 3M Imaging Products described how he did
this:

> With some of these, it is allowing attrition to do the cutting, which is occurring
> in the case of Com – it is going through a phased withdrawal from the market.
> And rather than trimming a little off each program, we're just ending certain
> programs. We're diverting those people onto other programs, either within the
> division or, if we can't afford that, putting the people out to another division.
> We also tend to use contract people in 3M to some extent in our lab, and that's
> the first place we look to cut so we don't have to drop permanent employees.
> It's quite rare that we'd have to actually release a permanent laboratory em-
> ployee. You can normally find work, useful work, for them somewhere in the
> company.[9]

Ralph West added that, in his experience, new business creation rarely
suffered as a result of budget cuts and program delays. If anything, he
felt that some programs like Com were allowed to continue too long.

Summary

Entrepreneurship is the pursuit of a new opportunity because of a deep
personal conviction about its attractiveness and a determination to succeed against all odds. "Fake entrepreneurship" is the pursuit of a new
opportunity without any zeal or real commitment. People go through the

motions and parrot the right words because it is expected of them, or because *others* feel the new opportunity is worth pursuing.

Top managers fail to detect fake entrepreneurship because they focus on the trappings and miss the essence. They assume that they have unleashed entrepreneurship when a new opportunity is identified, a program team is created, a "champion" is designated, and appropriate incentives are offered. Only later, if ever, do they learn that they had no real champions, except perhaps themselves.

Fake entrepreneurship can be avoided by recognizing that the corporation might not have a gene pool of innovators, and by assuming there is only lip service rather than real commitment to entrepreneurship – unless there is compelling evidence to the contrary. Real commitment is revealed when a qualified individual *wants* to take on the assignment because of the *challenge* involved, not because he is told to do it or because of special incentives or other forms of extrinsic motivation.

People in the division must attend to the vital tasks of managing corporate perceptions of the division's new initiatives, and cultivating the necessary corporate support. They must be aware of how corporate executives perceive these initiatives, and prevent premature or excessive corporate visibility or unrealistic corporate optimism about them. To cultivate corporate support, they must pre-sell influential corporate executives and manage the corporate godfathers.

New business creation requires new ways of designing, developing, manufacturing, marketing, and/or selling a product or a service. This new activity disturbs proven ways of running the business. The disruption of existing operations and the associated dilemmas must be managed.

Divisions with a larger base of stable existing business are better able to absorb the greater volatility of new business. Volatility is also better managed by factoring it into the forecast of results for the division, by retaining slack in the budget for unforeseen expenditures that new initiatives typically require, by having several new initiatives that are diversified over time and across industries, and by selectively delaying new initiatives and cutting expenses to achieve the division's forecasted results.

17 The division's organization, competence, and collaboration for new business creation

This chapter examines how the division's organization, competence, and collaboration influence new business creation (Table 17.1).

Frequent reorganizations hamper new business creation

Xerox OPD had already endured several reorganizations when Greg Gibbons became the fourth DGM in six years. He reorganized OPD once again by breaking up the functional organization, "the silos" as he referred to them, to create strategic business units (SBUs) overseen by an Office of the President, which was subsequently disbanded. Whatever their merits, these frequent reorganizations created confusion and disruption that hampered new business creation.

Monsanto Fab Products also underwent several organizational changes in the quest for the right organization for new business creation. When Dan Stewart became DGM of Fab Products, he broke up the functional organization to create self-sufficient business units (BUs). His successor, Ian McVay, reorganized Fab Products into a matrix.

At 3M Micrographics, there was some organizational disruption when the 35mm lines were peeled off to create the Engineering Products department, but this was the normal 3M practice of "cloning" divisions once they became too large. AMP Sigcom and 3M Micrographics did not hinder their new business creation efforts with frequent organizational surgery.

A moratorium on reorganizations is not being recommended, but there is a lot to be said for less frequent organizational changes. The choice of organization does matter, and changes will be necessary from time to time, but here is the caution: because every organization has its limitations, it is best not to engage in a hunt for the "ideal organization." It is better to focus instead on the commonly neglected tasks of educating, training, coaching, and mentoring people to leverage the advantages and overcome the limitations of whatever organization is used.

Table 17.1. *How the division's organization, competence, and collaboration influence new business creation*

Hypothesis	Factor	Influence on new business creation
17.1	Frequent reorganizations	−
17.2	Business unit (BU) organization with dedicated cross-functional resources and clear accountability for new business creation	+
17.3	Competence for new business creation	+
17.4	Healthy competition to spur innovation	+
17.5	Resolving cross-silo conflict and achieving collaboration	+
17.6	Achieving cross-silo collaboration with a shared sales force	+

The business unit organization is well suited to new business creation[1]

Greater benefit justifies its higher cost

The dedicated cross-functional resources and clear accountability for results of the BU organization facilitate new business creation.[2] DGM Ray Thorngate described how the BU enabled 3M Engineering Products to grow from a department (consisting of the original 35mm business) into a division within two years:

Because we had put all of our development resources into the 16mm and 105mm microfiche lines, we had almost no new product development activity in 35mm – just variations on a theme. We had to make a decision whether to drop out of that market or to take advantage of the growth opportunities in that business. We decided that the business environment was promising and worth pursuing, but it required the focused attention of a separate department [semi-autonomous BU] with dedicated cross-functional resources. It worked. We grew faster than before and are more profitable today. We are also more profitable than we had projected when making this proposal to split off.

The dedicated cross-functional resources create duplication of effort that makes the BU organization more costly than a matrix organization, which utilizes shared resources, or a functional organization, which offers specialization to achieve efficiency. However, the benefits for new business creation offered by the BU justify its higher cost.[3] The top managers in AMP and 3M knew this, and both AMP Sigcom and 3M Micrographics had consistently used the BU organization. Their strong consensus on this point was aptly summarized by one of them:

I didn't say it was cheap to operate this way. It's costly to operate this way. It's expensive. But on balance we make a heck of a lot of more money this way. That's the key. The investment is higher, but the returns are higher yet.[4] But you got to accept that almost on faith, that the returns are higher. You can't prove it. But you can prove that the cost will be cheaper the other way. The easier approach is to cut cost. You can prove that.

All BU organizations are not created equal

Dedicated cross-functional resources for a BU are a matter of degree. At one extreme, Dan Stewart's Monsanto Fab Products had all the functions except manufacturing self-contained within its BUs. At the other extreme, Xerox OPD under Gibbons' successor, Steve Carter, had SBUs that were essentially engineering units with no other functional resources assigned to them.

The SBU organization that Gibbons had created at Xerox OPD was in between these two extremes. It was in fact a matrix organization based on shared resources and accountability, and for some very compelling reasons – since all three SBUs were targeted at the same major accounts to sell an integrated system that could be interconnected and upgraded, someone (it happened to be David Fond, VP of marketing) had to oversee and coordinate all marketing for OPD, and someone (Bill Baker, VP of sales) had to coordinate all sales into these accounts. Similarly, for reasons of coordination and efficiency, all manufacturing for Xerox OPD was under Tim Skinner, VP of manufacturing, and all engineering reported on a dotted line to Chris Godby, VP of engineering, who remained a "functional supervisor" of all the engineers within the SBUs.

Conditions for success with the BU organization

Two conditions must be met to achieve success with the BU organization: (1) the need for an executive champion who provides encouragement, support, and mentoring for the BU; and (2) the need for a critical mass of resources dedicated to the BU.

Consider the experience of 3M, long admired as the master of new business creation. Budding entrepreneurs within 3M sought recognition and advancement by trying to grow a new venture. Their aim was to meet the sales and profit thresholds required to get it designated first as a project, then as a department – a semi-autonomous BU with its own sales force and laboratory personnel – and finally as a full-fledged division. DGM

Buddy March spoke about the first condition for success with the 3M approach – the need for an executive champion to provide encouragement and mentoring for the entrepreneur and the others involved:

I think in their embryo stage, they need an overkill on endorsement and encouragement and this type of thing. I think they get despondent, as a group, quite easily. And I don't think you can cut them out, put them over here and say, "Okay, guys – run." Somebody's gotta champion it; not only the guy that's leading the project, but it needs a mentor, so to speak. It doesn't necessarily have to be the general manager – it's better if it is, but it needs some kind of a godfather.

Buddy March also described the second condition for success with the BU organization, that journalists and management writers enamored with the company's success had missed – newly created units had to have a critical mass of resources to withstand political attacks from those left behind in the parent division:

You'd think you'd get support for a new BU as you were splitting it off. But it's just the opposite. And until you get a big enough mass of people, resources, money, sales, and all the rest of it – so it can stand on its own two feet – it's very difficult to split those off. Because everybody around it who wasn't part of the people that split off attack it in various very funny ways; but it's attacked. I guess it's human nature; but I've seen it here, I've seen it in other divisions. When we split Com off, it was attacked like you can't believe ... Many more projects die here than succeed. You would expect that anyway, but my observation is that many of them would have flowered, had they had the support and all the rest of it, to make it grow ... Imaging was highly successful. But we didn't split that off until it was a pretty big business. We had all the rights to the Chicago Public Library and put a project on that and, Christ, the most popular guy we had was unpopular in a hurry because he got to head it up. Com was another one that we made a project too early. The critical mass is important. So that it can withstand the attack. Because the attack will come. I've never seen one where it didn't.

Limitations of the BU organization

The BU organization has two major limitations: (1) it is difficult to share resources and transfer skills across BUs to build the core competence of the corporation and pursue new opportunities beyond the ambition and capabilities of any single BU; and (2) it is not ideally suited to mature businesses, where the critical tasks are cost control and efficiency improvement.

The difficulty of sharing resources and transferring skills across BUs
The BU organization with its dedicated resources helps to unleash the entrepreneurial spirit, but this also makes it more difficult to share resources

and transfer skills across BUs.[5] Ralph West, who grew the imaging products project within 3M Micrographics into a department and then into a division and became its DGM, talked about this limitation of the BU organization:

It's possible that everyone might have benefited if we had not separated the Com program into a BU. The skills we were developing around this computer-type product might have been passed on more effectively to the microfilm business, and in particular the group product sales and marketing organization, and improved their ability to deal with a more sophisticated market . . . This issue keeps recurring. It's occurring now in my division, which has two or three separate businesses – in this case, they happen to be subsidiaries that were acquired and want to be separate. But the real benefit of these subsidiaries is if we can integrate them and share skills, share knowledge. So you're treading this line between allowing the managers the enthusiasm and spirit of a separate business, and yet sharing the know-how and also using the resources of the parent.

The BU organization is not well suited to mature businesses   A BU organization is not nirvana. It is an appropriate organizing principle for embryo and growth businesses, where the critical task is new business creation, but not for mature businesses, where cost control and efficiency are more important. DGM Ian McVay gave examples from the businesses of Monsanto Fab Products to explain why:[6]

Take Astroturf, which was set up as a semi-autonomous BU. There was a mentality that Astroturf was going to be in professional stadiums today, college stadiums tomorrow and high school stadiums right after that. And they were going to cover all the parks of the land with Astroturf. Well, it never happened and it never will happen.[7] Because Astroturf is a very expensive product that can only be justified in professional stadiums. And you cut it up any way you want and you're damn lucky to get 2 million square feet a year in volume and we have a dedicated sales organization equipped to sell 10. They don't need a dedicated sales organization. And I think a contribution I have made to this division is in getting people to accept and understand that we are not going to run our mature businesses like Astroturf the same as our growth businesses like Spray Guard. So we've got them separate. In Spray Guard I'm continuing what [predecessor DGM] Dan Stewart promoted throughout all the businesses. It has its own separate organization. They have their own marketing people; they have their own sales people. As we start other new businesses, for example our Drainage Mat program, they will be set up as separate BUs.

Joe Hurley, commercial development director of Monsanto Fab Products, agreed with McVay on the need to separate the mature businesses from the new programs. He commented on how the early field development work on the OPET bottle program suffered because it was assigned to the sales force for the mature blownware business:

Remember that OPET was initially positioned as a cold-filled bottle. It was targeted at a lot of existing customers, even though it was different technology. So the sales force was also made responsible for the field development effort. The results were very mediocre because here's the salesman who has got a buck to make in whatever year you want to pick. And then you're telling this guy, "OK. I want you to go out and also do this development work with these people on a new bottle," which is a two- to three-year program in most cases. It didn't work.[8]

Alf Hummel, Monsanto VP of corporate planning, also felt strongly about the need to separate new programs and mature businesses so they could be managed differently: "The most difficult thing you do in a large company is innovation. It requires full-time people. History shows that short-term drives out long-term. You need separate units within the division to look at longer-term programs."

Organization for new business creation: conclusions

There are six main conclusions and one overriding lesson about organization for new business creation. First, organization does matter. The BU with its dedicated cross-functional resources and focused accountability for results is more costly but better suited to new business creation than either the functional or the matrix organization. But it is not the best organization for mature businesses. So second, it pays to separate the start-up and growth businesses from the mature businesses and manage them differently.

Third, the BU organization needs an executive champion and a critical mass of resources to survive politically. Fourth, what is labeled as a BU or SBU organization may in fact be closer to a functional or a matrix organization. Even so, fifth, an organizational change to a BU with dedicated cross-functional resources is *not* necessarily recommended because frequent reorganizations hamper new business creation, and also because some sharing of resources might be necessary.

And sixth, the matrix organization generates strong negative reactions for some people because of its shared resources and accountability. But some sharing of resources and accountability is unavoidable if top managers want the best of both worlds – BU entrepreneurship and cross-BU collaboration to develop the core competence of the corporation and pursue new business opportunities that are beyond the ambition and capabilities of any single BU.

The overriding lesson to be learned is that it is best not to get hung up on the "ideal" organization for new business creation. Though choices exist and do matter, it is good to remember that the real payoff comes from attending to the neglected task of developing the competence of the people in the division for new business creation and enhancing their capability to work within and across the boundaries of whatever organization is used.[9]

Competence for new business creation

The best organization in the world will not generate new business if its people lack the necessary competence in technology, product development, manufacturing, marketing, sales, and other relevant areas.[10] Careful selection of people and their continuous education, training, coaching, and development are essential for creating and retaining the competence needed for new business creation.

We consider four specific challenges for top managers in this connection: (1) understanding core rigidities; (2) using technical resources efficiently; (3) achieving cost reduction; and (4) enhancing the image of new business creation.

Challenge 1. Understanding core rigidities[11]

Competence is far more specialized[12] and context-specific than top managers would like to believe. The rigidity of people's competence might make it difficult to redeploy them to pursue new opportunities, as commercial development director Joe Hurley of Monsanto Fab Products pointed out:

The OPET program is technically driven and it is strictly a bottle-type skill base. Those people could not be used in things like film, or rotary forming, or Fomecor. You could be theoretical and say, "I've put in half a million to a million dollars per year in OPET over the last five years. I could have taken that and done something else in a different business." Theoretically you could say that. Realistically it would have been very difficult to do because the skill bases that are involved are so different.[13]

Challenge 2. Using technical resources efficiently

Technical resources are more efficiently deployed by sequencing programs and moving people across programs as they evolve from one stage of development to the next. Ray Thorngate had years of experience doing this as the technical director of 3M Micrographics:[14]

You get the best efficiency out of the laboratory by running programs in sequence so that people move from one program to the next as the needs of the programs change. We always came out of those technical audits [conducted by

3M's corporate technology experts] with them telling Buddy [March, DGM] and our group vice president that we were spread too damn thin and that we were trying to do too many things. But Buddy knew what we were doing. Because they are looking at our top three programs over their full life; they are not looking at a point in time. And I'm balancing people across our programs at a point in time.

Challenge 3. Achieving cost reduction for new products

Top managers must drive hard to reduce new product costs in order to win in a highly competitive marketplace. This requires a dramatic change in the mentality and competence of the traditional product development organization, from "design to specification" to "design to cost." DGM Greg Gibbons of Xerox OPD described how he did this:

Big companies work backwards. First of all, they turn to their product planners to get marketing input and come out with the specifications. Now this goddamn specification has every bell and whistle in the world on it. And then they work backwards into a design, which represents some product cost. Well, that's the classic way of doing it. There is another way of doing it. You pick a unit manufacturing cost and you make them put as much function as they possibly can into it: "Guys, we do not have a program for a Memorywriter typewriter unless the UMC is 350 bucks. You tell me what I get for 350." And you can really motivate engineers to go do that.

I have to get into some technical things to explain the substantive difference between the $600 UMC our engineers had initially proposed for the Memorywriter and the $350 UMC we were able to achieve. They had proposed a closed loop server; we have an open loop server. They had a power supply; we went without a power supply and used an on-board regulator. We did it all on one printed circuit board, which they said we never could do. They had three printed circuit boards. It's all available technology – you've just got to be very creative and keep asking, "How the hell can I do that?" I've got to throw out all my old ideas on how things were done. I've got to throw out all the old Xerox specifications.

Chris Godby, VP of engineering for Xerox OPD, added this: "Greg [Gibbons, DGM] cuts the time you have to do something and makes you do it with fewer people. That forces you to find a better way to do it."

Challenge 4. Enhancing the image of new business creation

There is little chance that talent will flow to new business creation if it is seen as the wrong place to be. DGM Dan Stewart of Monsanto Fab Products offered his opinion about how the commercial development function within the corporation had been ruined over the fifteen years prior to the time of this study in the early 1980s:

I think Alf Hummel [Monsanto VP of corporate planning] tries to alert people to some of the problems we have. He's the one who stood up and said that we have ruined the commercial development function at Monsanto. We don't have one, it is nonexistent. It was eliminated fifteen years ago. We don't put good people in it; we put guys who are has-beens, those we don't know where to put. And that just tends to reinforce in people's minds that this is not a good function. He says that we got to put the best and the brightest here if we're ever going to grow.

In addition to functional competence, top managers must also address the challenge of developing people's cross-functional competence. This helps to resolve dysfunctional cross-silo conflict and achieve the cross-functional collaboration needed for new business creation. Before turning to this subject, let us pause to look at healthy conflict and its benefits.

Healthy conflict can spur innovation[15]

Healthy conflict is substantive and above-board; it can stimulate innovation. Dan Stewart recalled the conflict between the technical people and the manufacturing people over the best process for finishing blownware bottles when he was DGM of Monsanto Fab Products, and he viewed it as a spur to innovation:

We were developing a finished neck process internally when the RST alternative was available externally. Our technical people had a strong preference for finished neck, and manufacturing had a strong preference for RST, so there was a definite conflict. It wasn't beneath the surface. That was right on the table. But that's that inner competition that you want to foster in some ways. And I viewed that as inter-departmental competition that wasn't destructive.

Reasons for dysfunctional cross-silo conflict and poor collaboration

Organizational silos are departments, functions, divisions, and other organizational subunits to which people belong, and to which they feel greater identification and loyalty than to the larger organizational entity. Four major factors create or exacerbate dysfunctional cross-silo conflict and poor collaboration: (1) geographical separation; (2) emphasis on functional efficiency; (3) unclear task responsibilities; and (4) missing or ineffective mechanisms for cross-silo communication and collaboration.

Geographical separation

Geographical separation can exacerbate the conflict between functions, departments and other silos. CFO and chief of staff Rick Smale of Xerox OPD described how geographical separation between two factions within

Office Systems Division (OSD), the forerunner of OPD, brought new business creation to a standstill:

Perhaps the worst mistake was that, just as they were finally getting close to breaking even, the decision was made to have OSD in Dallas, Texas report to XBS [Xerox Business Systems] in El Segundo, California. It was done to keep John Lewin, a very talented executive we had on the West Coast, but he left anyway. His successor, Jacob Cowles, kept the VP of marketing and sales in Dallas, but moved all the other OSD leaders to El Segundo where XBS was headquartered. Marketing sent forecasts to El Segundo that never came back. The products were still priced 25 percent above the market, so to cut costs they cut sales commissions. Sales [personnel] turnover shot up to 60 percent and the business ground to a halt. The industry grew 50 percent; the division grew 5 percent.

Calvin Vinson, a Xerox corporate HR manager, added: "El Segundo dominated Dallas, and a schism developed between the two. It is fair to say that the stress and strain of that kind of marriage brought things to a standstill."

Emphasis on functional efficiency

A functional organization is efficient because it is specialized, but an emphasis on functional efficiency makes cross-functional collaboration difficult. One senior manager in Xerox OPD said there was pressure from corporate executives to break up and functionalize OSD: "Otterbein and Sandstrom [two influential corporate executives] were big on functionalization. They persuaded Jacob Cowles to split up OSD, with El Segundo as the headquarters and marketing and sales in Dallas. It was a disaster."

Calvin Vinson, the Xerox corporate HR manager, felt he had erred in his emphasis on functionalization: "I advocated breaking up OSD because I felt they needed to functionalize and get their house in order. That may have been a mistake on my part."

Unclear task responsibilities

Unclear task responsibilities lead to finger pointing and lack of collaboration. Greg Gibbons recalled the total absence of cross-functional collaboration when he took over as DGM of Xerox OPD:

I didn't know how bad things really were when I took over. I remember an early meeting in which I asked, "Who in this division is responsible for forecasting demand by product?" No one answered. I asked marketing, "Isn't it your responsibility?" They said, "No, that's finance." The finance guy said, "Bullshit. I don't do that." The guy running supply–demand was using two-year-old forecasts!

The order entry system was a joke. I expected to find good systems in a large company, but the systems were a disaster.

Missing or ineffective mechanisms for cross-silo communication and collaboration

As Greg Gibbons discovered at Xerox OPD, mechanisms designed to facilitate cross-silo communication and collaboration, such as a supply–demand system, might be ineffective or missing altogether. Peter Dell, technical director of Monsanto Fab Products, was critical of the lack of collaboration between the technical people working on the OPET bottle initiative and the blownware people who were responsible for marketing it.[16] He felt some mechanism was needed to improve marketing's input to, and involvement with, the technical people. He added:

The technical people should have received, way back, much more marketing input. The marketing people were reactive, not proactive. They could have been more involved, rather than being disinterested bystanders. This was a technology push effort and no one in marketing was getting on the bandwagon. I was by far the biggest pusher. Dan Stewart [DGM] was very supportive, but he was not pushing it on the organization.

The lack of collaboration between the technical people and the marketing people for the OPET bottle led to an embarrassing delay for a field test with Ocean Spray, a lead customer. They were very interested in the test bottle that they were shown, but were surprised that it looked like a "Howitzer shell." And they were shocked that the height of the test bottle was greater than the maximum $10\frac{1}{2}$ inches allowable for placement on retail shelves.

Resolving cross-silo conflict and achieving collaboration[17]

Cross-silo conflict can be resolved and collaboration achieved by (1) improving cross-silo communication, (2) creating cross-silo teams, and (3) providing strong leadership.

Improving cross-silo communication[18]

One way to improve cross-silo communication is to co-locate people from the different silos. The market researchers at 3M Micrographics were physically located in the technical area, and this facilitated cross-functional communication and collaboration. Another way is to hold regular cross-silo communication meetings, as DGM Buddy March of 3M Micrographics did: "Twice a year, there is a two-day meeting at which marketing makes an input on every product in the lab. And informal communication goes on all the time between marketing and the lab."

Confrontation meetings and team-building sessions with external facilitation can be useful if the conflict and lack of collaboration between silos is chronic or extreme. Chris Godby, VP of engineering, described how he used confrontation meetings to improve cross-functional communication within Xerox OPD:

I tried to open up communications with groups I depended on, primarily manufacturing. Tim Skinner [VP of manufacturing] and I made a pact that we would try hard to signal that we were getting along. We did some inter-group stuff. I said to his managers, "My managers think you guys are shit-heads. You guys undoubtedly think we are shit-heads. Let's write out the specifics on the board and work at it." It helped. Engineering and manufacturing began working together.

Periodic cross-silo visits by a top manager can also help to improve communication and collaboration. Joe Hurley, the commercial development director of Monsanto Fab Products, said he traveled back and forth between his commercial development people and the technical people, in order to manage their conflict on the Spray Guard initiative:

I can justify the technical position or I can justify the commercial development position, either one. But it did not really impact the program because there was a lot of interaction between commercial development and technology, and there still is. That's really one of the keys of new product development. You have to provide technology direction, have them understand the problems. I commute back and forth to Pensacola and the other technical groups where it is appropriate to develop this type of communication.

Creating cross-silo teams[19]

Cross-silo program teams facilitate collaboration, as DGM Ray Thorngate of 3M Engineering Products pointed out:

In the old days, marketing generated the product specs and did the forecasting for the business plan. They often predominated on features and bells and whistles and were always after the lowest price. So we began to do it in the lab. We had two or three marketing people in the lab who went into the customer installation because we couldn't get the marketing organization to do a good job on it. That led to some lab versus marketing sub-surface conflict which was a little dysfunctional. So we had to change how we did it. We created new-product marketing within the marketing function and got a program team to do the cross-functional coordination. That worked. Once we had agreed on what we were gonna grow to, then there was always a fair collaboration between marketing and the lab, trying to figure out whether we had the wherewithal to get there.

Providing strong leadership[20]

Strong leadership is needed to pull a cross-silo team together, especially one composed of members separated by geography. At Xerox OPD, the Saber program for the Memorywriter typewriter posed considerable cross-silo challenges during the commercialization stage. The skunkworks group in Chicago – the "Chicago Seven" – were on steep financial incentives to develop a breakthrough product design. But they had to work closely with the Xerox OPD product development and manufacturing people in Dallas, Texas, who were not on such incentives, to ensure successful final development and production scale-up. Luckily for Xerox OPD, the Saber program manager, Marv Chatsworth, proved to be a strong team leader. He described how he pulled the two factions together:

My biggest problem was getting the Chicago Seven to see Dallas' point of view. We got temporary quarters here in Dallas so that if we were working on a module, all the key people from the Chicago Seven and from here could be together for a week if necessary to work on it together...I began the practice of calling a meeting at 7 a.m. whenever the process was out of control or the two camps were not cooperating. I called it Sunrise Service – a short meeting at 7 a.m. to say, "Here is where we are and here is the plan for today." Some of the Sunrise Services were tough, tough sessions. But the problems got out sooner on the table, and they remained visible till they were fixed. Steve Kendall [leader of the Chicago Seven] took a lot of heat at the Sunrise Services, and at times would get really upset with me if he had to stay on in Dallas longer than he expected. But later on he apologized and told me I was right to put their nose into it and hold their feet to the fire...There was some resentment of the Chicago Seven among the guys down here: "These guys are going to make a million bucks, why should we help them?" But no one really knew how much they stood to make, and I killed that discussion anyway...There were three major things we did right. The skunk works came up with a breakthrough product design and did it very quickly; we put everyone in the same building, which greatly helped communication and coordination; and we conducted Sunrise Services.

Achieving cross-silo collaboration with a shared sales force

New and existing businesses within a division often use the same sales force, and several business units or divisions of the corporation sometimes have a common sales force. One reason for using a shared sales force is the promise of improved efficiency and enhanced professionalism, which require a critical mass of functional expertise. This is no different than the rationale for sharing other functional resources within the division or across the entire corporation, such as those for technology, manufacturing, or marketing. Some customers demand a single point of contact for all their purchases from a company, providing additional motivation for the supplier to create a common sales force.

A shared sales force hinders new business creation

A shared sales force hinders new business creation because the short-term focus that is necessary for selling existing products conflicts with the longer-term emphasis needed to explore new business opportunities with the customer, including products in development and products not yet developed. Persons responsible for selling existing products typically lack the product knowledge, the customer contacts, and the personal motivation to explore new markets. Even in the organizations of their existing customers, they typically lack the necessary contacts with the product development staff and others interested in new products or technologies, or those most knowledgeable about new business opportunities.

Consider the challenges for AMP Sigcom. The centralized marketing and sales division of AMP was organized by customer and industry segments and served all the operating divisions of the company. But the product lines of AMP Sigcom were at the high end of AMP's technology spectrum. The AMP marketing and sales people were less familiar with these technologies and products. Product manager Arjay Mason of AMP Sigcom highlighted a related problem:

An awful lot of what we get from marketing and sales is the here-and-now, we-need-it-yesterday kind of thing. It is user-driven rather than technology-driven innovation. The Coaxial Tap was started back before we had to have it yesterday – same with Fiber Optics and Transmission Cable. These are radically new products that could open up whole new markets. They did not come from sales and marketing.

Effective collaboration with a shared sales force can be achieved

The attitudes and capabilities for achieving cross-silo collaboration, described in the previous section, can overcome the difficulties created by a shared sales force. For example, DGM Mike Walker of AMP Sigcom relied on three main approaches for effective collaboration with the AMP marketing and sales division. First, he personally got involved in dealing with the key people in that organization. Second, he impressed on AMP's product managers and project managers the crucial importance of developing good working relationships with appropriate contacts in that organization. And third, he persuaded a well-regarded member of the AMP marketing and sales division, Jim Fitch, to join AMP Sigcom as a product manager.

Here is one illustration of how these approaches paid off. By working with the marketing and sales organization, AMP Sigcom successfully developed the SMA F-Connector as a beachhead product for creating a new market in the military, where the company did not have any business before. As Jim Fitch recalled,

It was counter-culture in AMP to go after the military market. Our marketing and sales folks didn't talk to those kinds of customers. They were afraid of them. They didn't understand them. They had no reason to. They weren't being pressured to. We had some of the finest performing products in the industry and they still were not capable of relating to that and in turn transmitting that to the customer. So we needed something – sort of a banner – to go sell this widget because it's so easy to sell that when they finally went and did that they gained a success that they otherwise would not have even considered doing. And once they got success in that area they said, "Gee whiz, if I'm successful there why don't I talk about this product which is so close to it as well," and the next thing you know they are selling those.

Thus, although AMP Sigcom under DGM Mike Walker's leadership also had difficulties with a shared sales force, these difficulties were overcome through continuous dialog across the organizational divide and the creative appointment of skilled managers such as Jim Fitch. To the extent that a shared sales force makes sense – for example, because several corporate divisions or business units within a division have the same customers or distribution channels – Mike Walker's success provides both encouragement and challenge to those managers who believe that a shared sales force is bound to kill new business creation.

This issue is similar in a way to the issue discussed at the beginning of this chapter in connection with frequent reorganizations. Managers prefer simple, structural solutions (that might not work), when the real challenge is more subtle and far more difficult. Strong leadership and interpersonal competence are critical, and these skills must be developed to enable people to resolve their conflicts and achieve cross-silo collaboration for new business creation.

Dysfunctional conflict and lack of collaboration can also plague the division's top management team. This is covered in Chapter 18.

Summary

Matrix organizations, based on shared resources and accountability, and functional organizations, focused on specialization, inhibit new business creation. The business unit (BU) organization, with clear accountability for results and dedicated cross-functional resources, is a better option for new business creation. Nevertheless, every organization has its limitations, and frequent reorganizations in search of the "ideal organization" create confusion and cause disruption that hurt new business creation. Better results are achieved by focusing on the commonly neglected tasks of educating, training, coaching, and mentoring people in order to secure the advantages and overcome the limitations of whatever organization is used.

Successful new business creation requires the people to have the necessary competence in technology, product development, marketing, sales, and other functions. Cross-functional competence and cross-BU collaboration is equally important.

Healthy conflict is substantive and above board. It spurs innovation. Dysfunctional conflict and a lack of collaboration across organizational silos hurts new business creation. Among the usual suspects are geographical separation, an emphasis on functional efficiency, unclear task responsibilities, and missing or ineffective mechanisms for cross-silo communication and collaboration.

Unhealthy cross-silo conflict is overcome and collaboration achieved with better communication across silos, use of cross-silo teams, and strong leadership. Managing cross-silo conflict and achieving collaboration is especially difficult when the division has no dedicated sales force. These difficulties can be overcome by maintaining an active dialog with the shared sales force, and by appointing people who are able to work effectively with them across the organizational divide.

18 The effectiveness of the division's top management team

This chapter examines how the effectiveness of the division's top management team (TMT) influences new business creation (Table 18.1).

Members of the TMT are not committed to new business creation[1]

Members of the division's TMT influence new business creation directly, and also, through their subordinates, indirectly.[2] Lack of commitment to new business creation on the part of a TMT member is therefore doubly destructive. Art Malone, prior marketing director for Astroturf, felt there was lip service but no commitment to new business creation among many of his former colleagues on DGM Dan Stewart's TMT at Monsanto Fab Products. Malone was highly regarded by Stewart and others; he spoke about this problem after he had been promoted out of Fab Products:

> There wasn't a lot of enthusiasm for new products and commercial development in that team. Spray Guard was kind of interesting, kind of nice, but there was a lot of skepticism... One key player was a cynic. Another tried to be a good soldier, but I don't think he understood what was going on. He didn't make a lot of waves. Several others on Dan Stewart's team didn't buy into the approach, didn't see the overall strategy. But they played along.

Unresolved conflict within the TMT[3]

Five patterns of unresolved conflict within the division TMT that hinder new business creation are (1) open conflict, (2) submerged conflict, (3) aversion to team conflict, (4) failure to achieve team consensus, and (5) no real debate or dissent permitted.

Open conflict

There were several open conflicts concerning new business creation in DGM Buddy March's TMT at 3M Micrographics. An early one centered

Table 18.1. *How the effectiveness of the division's top management team (TMT) influences new business creation*

Hypothesis	Factor	Influence on new business creation
18.1	Members of the TMT are not committed to new business creation	−
18.2	Unresolved conflict within the TMT concerning new business creation	−
18.3	TMT resolves conflict and develops consensus concerning new business creation	+
18.4	TMT compensates for the DGM's weaknesses concerning new business creation	+

on the Tanaka Printer, as March recalled: "Nearly everyone on my team was against the agreement. The only ones that were for it were the marketing people. They were the ones that were suffering (because we didn't have the right product)."

Submerged conflict

Conflicts might remain submerged. Ray Thorngate, the technical director on Buddy March's TMT at 3M Micrographics, said,

There were some people on that team whose approach was to polarize issues even to the extent of – oh, what's the term for it – adversarial relationships. I don't mean confrontational, where people have very strong views and are very open about it. I mean where a couple of people always suspected that somebody was trying to put something over on them. I don't think that was very productive.

There was submerged conflict between Joe Hurley, the commercial development director, and technical director Peter Dell at Monsanto Fab Products. The technical development of the OPET bottle was under Peter Dell, and he felt that Joe Hurley did not really believe in this initiative. Joe Hurley said the problems with OPET were the same as with Cycle Safe – the technical people wanted success so badly that they were not as objective as they should have been. He added that,

I've always had a disagreement with Peter Dell on OPET. It wasn't an open, vehement type thing. He's got a group of technical people in Bloomfield that is dedicated to the bottle business. And he's spending like $1.4 million in T [technical expense] on OPET. He desperately, desperately wants it to work. And so he's always been very enthusiastic in promoting it. All his OPET people come from the discontinued Cycle Safe program. It's the same people, and that scares the shit out of other people [because Cycle Safe cost the company $200 million when the FDA shut it down].

Aversion to team conflict

Some people avoid conflict like the plague. Hal Courtney, the managing director (GVP) to whom DGM Dan Stewart of Monsanto Fab Products reported, mentioned Stewart's aversion to conflict: "Dan tends to get a lot out of his people. He tends to optimize on people; get the best out of what he has to work with. Conflict bothers him more than it bothers some other people. He does not feel conflict is desirable."

Marshall Babcock, the manufacturing director, said: "Stewart wanted to get everyone together, and he didn't like conflict. He was willing to have conflict upstairs for you, but he did not feel comfortable with conflict on his team." Joe Hurley, the commercial development director, added this:

I don't know if we had a team. [Laughter] We had so many individuals in that team it was unbelievable. And Dan Stewart always wanted it to be a super-happy family. And if it wasn't, he was very concerned about it. He really was. He really didn't like that. I think that we were all conscious of that to a certain extent. And if we did have conflicts, we tried to resolve the conflict between ourselves rather than making it an outward display or something like that.

Failure to achieve team consensus

There was good personal chemistry in the TMT of 3M Engineering Products, but there were fundamental differences of opinion about how aggressively to respond to rapidly changing markets and technologies. DGM Thorngate was going to retire within a year. Therefore, he wanted a strong consensus within his TMT – particularly with regard to the long-term direction for the division – because they would be the ones to live with the consequences. Unfortunately, group dynamics was not Ray Thorngate's strong suit, and his TMT remained divided despite his attempts to arrive at a consensus. As technical director Tom Sonnenfeld said,

I think we have agreed that we are going to be in the engineering information management business, but we have not defined the precise steps that we must take in the next five years. Are we willing to consider products that are not micrographics? Do we go all the way back to CAD [computer-aided design]? Robotics? Factory of the future? Somewhere there is our goal. Ray [Thorngate] asked Lieberman [marketing director] and me to resolve this a year ago. We have made progress, but we need an operating plan. That requires real consensus. We meet a lot as a management team, and almost all our discussions involve differences of opinion.[4]

Ray Thorngate was surprised to learn that I had detected a lack of consensus on his TMT concerning the strategic direction for the division. He summarized what he thought his TMT had agreed to:

I thought I have said it often enough that we're too late for CAD. In my opinion, within two years, IBM is gonna be number one in CAD. There will be other biggies in the game too. If 3M really wants to get into that market, we should acquire Intergraph, which is well over $150 million and it's three times our size – because with anything else, you're buying a 2 percent market share. But such a major acquisition is not in the cards given the problems and priorities within our sector. The position that I have taken is that the most logical approach for us to take is to be in the engineering information management business, which is where we are, and where we have certain strengths. We should focus on satisfying, in the best way we know how, the needs of that market segment, and our acquisitions ought to be to augment our ability to retain our position in that area of the market. I have told them that there is an interest – and a feeling – that it's not too late for us in the architectural area. I personally question that. But I'm willing to see the data.

No real debate or dissent permitted [5]

Conflict remains unresolved when no real debate or dissent is permitted. Several people felt that DGM Buddy March of 3M Micrographics allowed no debate or discussion on the Beta Com acquisition. It was a *fait accompli* that turned out to be a disaster, one of his TMT members said.

The Beta Com acquisition was done emotionally and 100 percent separately by Buddy. He called the operating committee [the TMT] and told us, "We are going to do it." No discussion. That white elephant cost us $11 million – that's not in the losses you see for the Com program [$55 million], the internal losses over the years. And that doesn't count the enormous amount of management time we spent on it. But Buddy honestly feels his decision was right and his team didn't support him.

While acknowledging the contribution that DGM Greg Gibbons and his TMT made in bringing so many exciting products so quickly to market, several of those left behind in OPD after Gibbons left Xerox believed the division could have succeeded if real debate and dissent had been permitted. Greg Gibbons and Stu Little, VP&GM of the systems SBU, were seen as the co-champions of the Star initiative and emotionally committed to the division's strategy. According to the critics, those who raised fundamental concerns about the business and marketing strategy were labeled negativist and not listened to, and anyone who attempted to question their faith in Star or their strategy was disregarded. [6]

Several people knowledgeable about the industry said they repeatedly questioned Gibbons and his team about the market's readiness for large quantities of Star, which was a sophisticated product, but to no avail. Several salespeople had suggested a marketing strategy targeted at users who were technically sophisticated and familiar with such high-end products. However, Gibbons and Little had insisted on selling Star to a much broader market, the large corporate Fortune 1300 accounts. The "big two" had visions of the product taking off like Xerox's much-revered original breakthrough product – the Xerox 914 copier – on whose spectacular success the company was built. Because other members of the division TMT had concluded that Gibbons would not change his mind, they did not confront him on this issue, these observers said. As one of them put it,

Sure the Gibbons team yelled at each other a lot, but genuine dissent and thoughtful debate were missing. Otherwise the problems with the Star, the PC, and the implementation of the Major Account strategy could have been addressed and possibly overcome.

Another critic had this to say: "In contrast to the philosophy they publicly espouse about consensus management, a lot of entrepreneurs like Greg Gibbons are, in fact, autocrats – autocrats who have a hot tub."[7]

Gibbons maintained that he had an open mind on most issues when he was DGM of Xerox OPD. The one thing he would not waver on, he said, and the one thing he would not do differently, was his unbending commitment to his OPD strategy of selling systems to large corporate accounts, with Star as the lynchpin of that strategy. This is how Greg Gibbons responded to the criticism noted above after he had left Xerox to start up a new company with Stu Little:

I don't think I surround myself with people very much like myself. We had a lot of strong managers in OPD. I do not think I'm an autocrat in a hot tub. We had a lot of honest debate and a lot of decisions were reversed. The one area – and I guess that's the prerogative as well as the requirement of leadership – that I wouldn't bend on, is how I saw Star. Because I had a vision of what that product could do – not everybody else shared that vision. And in that particular case, if you want to call me an autocrat, fine. I would prefer to think of myself as having some vision, and therefore, I was gonna keep everybody in that line.[8]

TMT resolves conflict and develops consensus[9]

The division TMT can resolve conflict and develop consensus concerning new business creation with four basic approaches:[10] (1) help from the DGM; (2) help from other TMT members; (3) help from a process consultant; and (4) a clear understanding of who decides, if a disagreement persists.

Help from the DGM

DGM Buddy March of 3M Micrographics created a separate sales force for Com – reporting to program manager Mat MacGregor – as a way to control the conflict within his TMT concerning this program.[11] March said he tried to resolve other conflicts in his TMT by keeping an open mind, airing all points of view, and seeking consensus when a program was in trouble:

I think you have to be comfortable with conflict. Don't get angry; try to judge things on merit. Be open, and don't take sides till later, after all the views have been aired . . . I knew the outcome of today's meeting would be that the quality manager should report directly to me while we sort out some of our quality issues, but I allowed the discussion to go on because I was seeking consensus. Otherwise, Ron [the quality manager] would have had a fart's chance in church of succeeding.

Help from division TMT members

DGM Dan Stewart of Monsanto Fab Products credited manufacturing director Marshall Babcock with helping his TMT to confront some of their disagreements concerning new products. Jason Singleton, the financial controller on Stewart's TMT, gave the same assessment:

Overall, Marshall's influence was good. He was the check-and-balance guy. He would speak out, making people think about alternatives. For instance, Marshall agreed with the OPET licensing agreement, but was the devil's advocate on OPET's profitability. He said it is not going to be a financial success – it will take longer, and the volume will be lower than projected.

Joe Hurley, commercial development director of Monsanto Fab Products, explained how he helped to resolve a conflict with DGM Dan Stewart on the Spray Guard program:

Oh, I guess there was a mild disagreement with Dan on how we should take Spray Guard to market. He felt that maybe a direct field sales force would be better than dealer field representatives. We sort of put that to bed when we tested that technique. We took a Monsanto salesman, trained him, and then we put him on the job to sell Spray Guard for six months. It was a disaster. That convinced Dan.

Joe Hurley said Stewart's successor, DGM Ian McVay, did not like to be challenged when others were present. So Hurley said he would agree with McVay in public and resolve any disagreements later in private meetings:

"The trouble with Ian is that you cannot argue with him in front of five other people. So you say, 'Yes, we'll do it,' and then later on get back to him. When you come back one-on-one, it is more effective – much more effective."

Facilitation by a process consultant

At Xerox OPD, the division TMT met each month for an entire day, typically at DGM Greg Gibbons' home, in a shirtsleeves session to discuss operating issues. Jake Noonan, an organizational development professional, served as a process consultant[12] to help the TMT resolve conflicts and develop consensus.

I had the opportunity to observe one such all-day meeting at Greg Gibbons' home during the month of March in Gibbons' second full calendar year as DGM. Jake Noonan facilitated the meeting and helped the TMT raise three major concerns that day. First, the Office of the President was ineffective because a high-velocity environment needed more hands-on leadership.[13] Second, there was unresolved conflict between the SBUs and the functions. Third, sales and profits for the year might fall far short of the amounts promised to corporate. Although Noonan helped to get these issues on the table, no agreement was reached on how to resolve them.

Clear understanding of who makes the decision if disagreement persists

One way to resolve TMT conflict is to have a clear understanding of who makes the decision if disagreement persists. DGM Mike Walker of AMP Sigcom, and his successor, Clay Smith, expected TMT members to work out their disagreements on new initiatives, but gave the ultimate decision-making authority to the development manager. As DGM Clay Smith said,

Mike Walker's philosophy on that when he was DGM, and mine too for that matter, is that the development manager is the product manager of new products, and it is his idea and his vision and his belief as to what will hunt and what won't hunt. And so if there is a disagreement between he and the other members on my management team, he has the trump card so to speak. He is charged with bringing new products on stream so he's the entrepreneur that makes the decision.

Some DGM weaknesses

Like all people, DGMs have weaknesses too. The successful new initiatives of DGM Buddy March of 3M Micrographics – Aperture Cards and

Dry Silver Paper in the early days, and Tanaka Printer, Imaging Products, and File Management Products later on – made much more money than was lost on all the failures, including the disastrous Com program.[14] Nevertheless, Buddy March's personal style gave him the image of a flamboyant risk-taker within 3M, which did not help him or his division.

Several members of Buddy March's TMT felt that he was either too easily influenced by the last person with whom he spoke, or that he was pig-headed and wouldn't change his mind. Technical director Ray Thorngate offered a different insight:

> It's nice to know that Buddy is very open to input early on; but then he gets committed. And it's nice to know which mode he is in. That's one of the reasons I was in his good graces – I got to him *early*. Once he's made up his mind, you better get it done. A lot of people got into trouble because they didn't realize he was already committed.

DGM Greg Gibbons of Xerox OPD felt he had pretty good insight into his major strength, that he was a leader, and also his major weakness, that he was not a manager. Those who knew him and worked with him agreed with his assessment. According to Gibbons, leaders staked out high-risk, high-payoff positions. In contrast, he felt that managers attempted to minimize risk, opted for the safe course, and were concerned with "blocking and tackling" – such matters as goal-setting, organization, staffing, control, and performance appraisal. Chris Godby, VP of engineering for Xerox OPD, agreed with Greg Gibbons that he was a great leader but a poor manager. As Godby said in the middle of Greg Gibbons' second year as DGM,

> Greg is just a hell of a leader – can inspire with just the words he uses; people feel better, the fact that he communicates with the troops. A lot of old farts around here have gotten off their asses and improved their productivity after Greg Gibbons got here. But Greg is a shitty manager. He sets up all these performance targets but doesn't give any feedback. He does not like to talk about tough subjects. He has reversed lots of managers' decisions. He goes around his subordinates. And because he likes to solve problems while thinking on his feet in real time, the vocal ones – the bullshitters – do well.

TMT compensates for the DGM's weaknesses

Division TMTs have varying degrees of success in compensating for their DGMs' weaknesses. DGM Buddy March of 3M Micrographics and DGM Greg Gibbons of Xerox OPD were both outsiders who came to the company via an acquisition; it is instructive to contrast the support they received from their TMTs.

*Failure in compensating for DGM Greg Gibbons' weaknesses
at Xerox OPD*

Gibbons said he got good help from two external advisors who worked closely with him and his management team to address the team's shortcomings and his own weaknesses:

Joel Piedmont represented the venture capitalists as the chairman at Shugart and made me go do the financial model when I became CEO there. He said, "What do you want your financial profile to look like five years from now, and what's the plan to get there?" And the most important thing he said is that it had to be incredibly simple – I got to keep it on one sheet of paper. He didn't want some big, long, detailed financial analysis. Very bright, very practical guy. He's been CEO of a couple of hundred-million-dollar companies. He really asked some very fundamental questions as an advisor here at OPD. They are the kind of questions that drive you mad: "Who would buy this product?" "How do you know there's a marketplace for it?" [Laughter.] So I still use him as a mentor/advisor, and he comes down regularly to see me. He's helped me on setting up the Office of the President, and an organizational structure that can really help to drive the decision-making down. I use both him and Jake Noonan. Jake is the personnel, human resources end. And I use Joel [Piedmont] more for what I would call the business end, the operational end.

Greg Gibbons also said he understood the need to get strong managers to help in the areas where he was weak – for example, in follow-up and implementation. Tim Skinner, VP of manufacturing, agreed with this: "Greg is not threatened by strong people. He has a group of very strong individuals – with scar tissue – on his team."

Contrary to Skinner's view, many others in Xerox OPD felt that Gibbons did not have sufficient managerial strength on his division TMT. The critics maintained that, rather than helping Gibbons by challenging him and compensating for his weaknesses, many of his TMT members got on his bandwagon and relished their new-found role as corporate buccaneers.

*Success in compensating for DGM Buddy March's weaknesses
at 3M Micrographics*

DGM Buddy March's TMT colleagues did collectively manage to compensate for some of his weaknesses. For example, division controller Wim Williams helped March to work with the corporate procedures and controls, especially in the first few years after March joined 3M. Another TMT member said that he and technical director Ray Thorngate helped Buddy March overcome some of his weaknesses – flamboyance, an obsession with celebrities, and poor judgment concerning people and negotiations:

Buddy would tell the operating committee [the division TMT], "Nobody has any courage or imagination. This obviously can be done." He took a lot of personal pride in his initiatives; if it didn't work, he felt people were letting him down. He was continually getting into trouble with his management team. His flamboyant style irritated conservative people... Buddy's reading of people and his negotiating skills are pretty poor. One of the external programs failed because that partner was a con artist. He had dealt with Hewlett-Packard – played excellent golf and would tell Buddy, "You are cut out of the same timber as David Packard [legendary co-founder of H-P]." Unadulterated bullshit... Buddy needs strong people under him who disagree and do their own thing. Ray Thorngate [the technical director] is considered one of the most capable technical guys in 3M. I have the reputation of being a disciplined SOB. What we have done is, the poor business judgments Buddy makes, we wash out. Our talents overcome his shortcomings. Buddy doesn't set realistic targets either – that's not one of his strong suits. But he has people around him like us to bring him back to reality.

Ray Thorngate, the long-serving technical director under Buddy March, said the TMT was more analytical than March, and this compensated for some of his weaknesses. Thorngate also said that the organizational discipline – from mechanisms such as the policy committee, and the phase system for new products – as well as March's ability to learn and develop over the years led to greater consensus within the TMT and better decisions in March's later years as DGM:

A person changes over a period of twenty years. Buddy developed significantly in judgment and ability over time. That's also true of his management team. Development was possible because Buddy is not an autocrat. He has a reasonably high tolerance for disagreement. We evolved over time to a consensus form of decision-making, and the decisions got a hell of a lot better... The policy committee [for new products] evolved after we said to Buddy, "Hey, these things you get involved in affect us too! We should be involved." It was created to rein in the benevolent dictator [Buddy] and the "51 percent of the vote" that he said he controlled.

The phase system [the disciplined system for pursuing new business opportunities; Chapter 15] was, internally, the most effective way to bring things along at a measured pace, in a logical sequence. It also helped to keep Buddy informed as to whether things are going ahead, and how well they're proceeding... Buddy isn't analytical, but he's developed a backup team that is. And the other side of it is that he is smart enough to listen to them most of the time. Buddy has learned over the years that good decisions plus poor acceptance equals poor performance. You can make jumps and have discontinuities in your thinking, but you got to present it rationally, logically, and in a structured way to others. That is tremendously important, the rationalization that others buy into. That rationalization, buying in, took place in the policy committee. Poor decisions plus acceptance equals successful program.

Summary

It sometimes is assumed that members of the division TMT are committed to new business creation when in fact they are not. Division TMTs might have unresolved conflict concerning new business creation, at times submerged beneath the surface. Some of the TMTs are unaware of the submerged conflict; others are unwilling or unable to address conflict constructively. New business creation suffers as a result.

Division TMTs exhibit five patterns of unresolved conflict: open conflict; submerged conflict; aversion to team conflict; failure to achieve team consensus; and no real debate or dissent permitted. TMTs resolve conflict and develop consensus concerning new business creation by various means, with different levels of effectiveness: help from the DGM or other TMT members; facilitation by a process consultant; and a clear understanding of who makes the decision if disagreement persists.

Like everyone else, DGMs have their weaknesses. New business creation is facilitated to the extent that the division's TMT is able to compensate for some of the DGM's weaknesses.

Part VI

Putting it all together

The first five parts of the book examine each of the major influences on new business creation one by one. They are (1) the business environment, (2) the management culture, (3) the corporate executives, (4) the division general manager, and (5) the division and its top management team. This last part of the book considers their combined effect.

In Chapter 19, the focus is on understanding how the five major influences interact with each other to drive new business creation. This is illustrated for AMP Sigcom when Mike Walker was DGM. How the interactions changed to maintain and then reduce the thrust on new business creation under his successor, Clay Smith, is also described.

Chapter 20 highlights ten critical issues that cut across the five major influences driving new business creation. It also offers recommendations for top managers on how to manage these issues for better results.

19 How the five major influences interact to drive new business creation

This chapter describes how the five major influences examined in Parts I through V interact[1] to drive new business creation, and how these interactions change over time to increase, maintain, or decrease the thrust on new business creation (Figure 19.1). The experience of AMP Sigcom is used for illustration.

The interactions among the five major influences at AMP Sigcom when Mike Walker was DGM are considered first. This is followed by a description of how the interactions changed to maintain and then reduce the thrust on new business creation under Walker's successor, Clay Smith.

AMP Sigcom under DGM Mike Walker

The business environment

The external business environment of AMP Sigcom was characterized by low to moderate rates of change when Walker was DGM. Only customer buying requirements were changing at more than a moderate rate: customers increasingly favored products that were more standardized and yet more versatile in application. There were few technical developments and not a great deal of competitive activity in the area of new products. Thus, the external business environment had limited influence on new business creation.

However, the internal business environment did provide an impetus for new business creation. The existing business of AMP Sigcom was maturing, and its star product (the CB connector) was in rapid decline. Consequently, successful new business creation was needed to revitalize the division. And the fact that Walker's predecessor had brought the division into good financial condition made it *possible* for Walker to devote both time and resources to the task of new business creation. Combining the external and internal influences, the business environment provided a moderate impetus for new business creation.

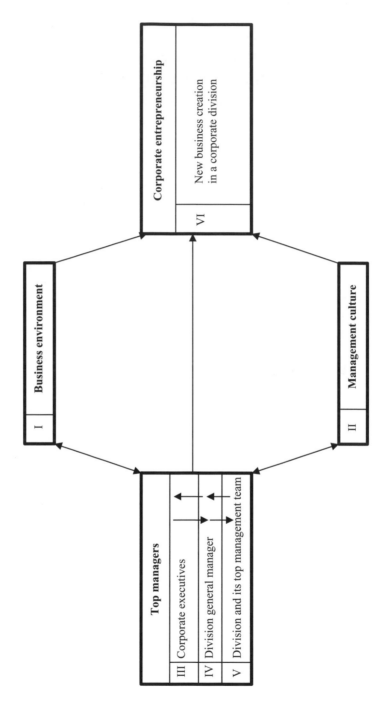

Figure 19.1. How the five major influences interact to drive new business creation.

The management culture

AMP's management culture valued new business creation. Many managers, including several of those at the top, had advanced in part on the basis of their entrepreneurial accomplishments.

The corporate executives

In their dealings with division managers, the corporate executives always inquired about new business opportunities, and they showed genuine interest in learning about promising new initiatives.

Financial incentives were not tied to new business creation. Instead, they were offered to the DGM and five or six other key people in the division on the basis of the *company's* earnings growth and the person's level of responsibility, and were computed as a percentage of the person's annual salary.

The division general manager

Mike Walker had bought into AMP's management culture, which valued new business creation. He knew the corporate executives expected not only short-term results but also profitable long-term growth, and he perceived the division's business environment made it possible to achieve this growth through new business creation.

Because of his prior experience and industry knowledge, Walker saw new business opportunities that his predecessor had missed. Four of the initiatives launched during Walker's tenure as DGM (Cable Assembly, Commercial RF, SMA F-Connector, and Tulip Plug) were counter to the management culture. Walker's boss and subordinates were not in favor of pursuing these initiatives. But Walker had conviction in respect of these opportunities and his extensive network of external contacts validated them. He was not afraid to pursue them because he had previously championed initiatives that others had suggested he drop, only to be eventually vindicated with big successes, as in the case of the Ceramic Filter in the Capitron division. Walker also had extremely high credibility with corporate executives and was able to get his boss to agree to a 5 percent reduction in the division's budgeted gross margin so that he could make the investments needed to pursue these opportunities.

Although the division was ill-equipped for new business creation on the scale that Walker envisioned, he had the skill to develop successfully several TMT members, and over time he replaced others with people who were more committed. He gave his people education, training, coaching, mentoring, and support to perform to the high standards he set, and he moved people around the division as well as into and out of the division to maintain and raise these standards.

The emphasis on new business creation did not mean controls were lax, however. As division controller Ben Keller put it, "As far as people are concerned, he is running pretty lean. The division has grown, but he has not added people – pretty tight control."

The division and its top management team

Commitment to new business creation was evident in the long hours that the people put in after the division was revitalized under Mike Walker's leadership. There was an air of excitement and a sense of intrinsic motivation that people felt in getting into and out of "a lot of trouble" with new business initiatives. The intra-divisional and inter-divisional meetings facilitated collaboration, problem-solving, and learning. On many an evening, impromptu groups came together to solve a particular problem, or to make a bid for a new program when quick action was needed.

Summary for AMP Sigcom under DGM Mike Walker

Despite only a moderate impetus from the business environment, the other four major influences drove new business creation to a very high level in AMP Sigcom under DGM Mike Walker: (1) AMP had a management culture that encouraged the pursuit of new initiatives and permitted unconventional ones if the DGM had sufficient credibility and business conviction to persevere; (2) the corporate executives were managing the division according to the small-is-beautiful corporate philosophy, and they had a great deal of faith in Walker and his new business creation ability; (3) Walker had the personal support of several corporate executives, including president Jim McGuire and COO Dave MacNeil, and he was able to persuade his boss, the group director, to buy into his vision and strategy for new business creation; and (4) the division and its top management team had developed the capability and commitment required for new business creation.

AMP Sigcom under Mike Walker's successor, DGM Clay Smith

When Mike Walker was promoted to group director (GVP), AMP Sigcom continued to report to him along with three other divisions. His development manager, Clay Smith, succeeded him as DGM. The forces at work after Smith took over were somewhat different than after Walker had become DGM.

The business environment

The economy had dipped into a recession during the last year of Walker's tenure as DGM and recovered a year or so after Smith became DGM. Competitive new business activity then intensified, and customer buying requirements began to change at a more than moderate rate. Because of AMP Sigcom's record of success and positive image in the marketplace, potential *customers* were coming to the division with ideas and requests for new products. Thus, partly as a result of the initiatives launched under Walker, the external business environment that DGM Smith faced demanded more new business creation than did the environment DGM Walker faced.[2] As Jim Fitch, the development manager under Smith, said,

The marketplace in general is also driving our new product activity. It's primarily customers. They come to see me, for example, without AMP marketing and sales [a separate division] even knowing about it. I inform my customers that they shouldn't do that so I don't get into a lot of trouble, and then they do come in with a sales engineer [from the AMP marketing and sales division]. But customers don't come in because they want to talk about sales. They come in because they want to talk about new product development. So it's acquired a momentum of its own.

The impetus for new business creation from the internal business environment, on the other hand, had decreased because the mix of the division's business had changed. There was now a bigger base of new business because of the success of two initiatives in particular (Cable Assembly and Commercial RF), which had the potential to yield greater profitability via cost reductions and production efficiency improvements. As DGM Smith noted,

We continue to invest in new products. But we had invested a lot of capital in lots of new products, and I decided to go for higher gross margin [32 percent when Smith took over as DGM versus 37 percent at the time of this interview]. For example, Cable Assembly, which is now 25 percent of our volume, had very high labor and material costs, hence low gross margins. We decided to manufacture our own cable to economize on costs because our suppliers were not reducing their prices sufficiently.

Other new business initiatives (Coaxial Tap, SMA F-Connector, and Transmission Cable) that had been introduced to the market when Mike Walker was DGM were still alive. Clay Smith was striving to ensure their success by introducing next-generation products to build momentum in the market (Coaxial Tap 3 and 4), adapting the initial product designs based on market feedback (SMA F-Connector), and achieving cost reductions and improvements in manufacturing efficiency and quality (Transmission Cable).

On balance, the impetus from the business environment for AMP Sigcom remained moderate under Smith, although the external environment – rather than the internal environment – was now the main stimulant for new business creation.

The management culture

The AMP management culture continued to value new business creation. Ted Rigby, AMP's corporate planner, put it succinctly: "Our culture emphasizes profitable growth. And that requires new products that command higher margins and new markets for growth."

The corporate executives

The corporate executives were influenced by their perceptions of the internal and external business environment, and their signals to the DGM had changed from the Walker era to the Smith era. As product manager Chad Blair said,

Mike Walker was DGM in an era when they [corporate executives] wanted to see this division expand, grow, blossom. And that was encouraged with a lowering of the expected gross margin. Now that pendulum has swung slightly and they say, "Okay, we've put all this money into it; now let's see some return." And some products are starting through that cycle now. Due to the economic changes on the horizon, profit has now become a driving force for the corporation.

Jim McGuire, president of AMP, agreed with this assessment:

When we get into a bad economy we know we have to make some calculated sacrifices long term in favor of short-term performance. Even in normal times we don't pursue every opportunity. Some management philosophies might have grown this company at a greater rate in terms of sales but probably would not have enjoyed the margins and therefore might have had considerable difficulty in financing that growth.

Walker remained DGM Smith's group director (GVP) for about two years and was then promoted to a critical overseas assignment, which led some people to speculate that he was being groomed to become CEO of AMP. Jon Grover, the corporate executive who succeeded Walker as group director, had expertise in manufacturing, and he began emphasizing safety, production efficiency, product quality, and customer service for AMP Sigcom. Smith commented on the switch in emphasis:

Grover has completely changed the whole direction of the group. We've moved completely off the realm of new product growth and optimism relative to expanding our markets to very definitely customer service, increasing inventories and quite a bit of emphasis now on aspects of quality. So a complete flip flop. My manufacturing costs are at 49 percent [of sales], so I am getting a lot of pressure from Grover and the group controller to reduce it to 45 percent. This is not a mandate, but Grover wants to know how I plan to get there, and to 40 percent eventually. I have directed the pricing manager to take the cost of the product and price it high enough to bring the manufacturing cost down to 40 percent of the sales price. That's a price mark-up of two-and-a-half times cost [two-and-a-half times 40 percent equals 100 percent]. This of course affects new business development, if we are not taking anything other than high mark-up business. And that bothers me, because you can start with low margins and then increase margins by riding down the experience curve [to lower costs]. We did that with the BNC connectors, ending up at 60 percent gross margins. So if we are not careful, we could adversely affect our ability to do this in the future.

The division and its top management team

Smith inherited a division and a top management team who were skilled in new business creation and committed to it. As product manager Arjay Mason observed, the division's development department was more capable of supporting this activity:

When Walker took over as DGM, the development department was not that big. He built it up. When Smith took over, he had the advantage of a large and strong development department in place, which he himself had supervised under Walker's direction. So as DGM, Smith inherited the many new product seeds that had been planted as well as the new product plant to produce more seeds.

The new product seeds planted during Walker's tenure as DGM led to several new product initiatives after Smith became DGM, including Miniature Ribbon Coax, Networking Devices, Coaxial Tap 3 and 4, Wafer Connector, and SMA Launchers. Smith explained: "The Coaxial Tap is radically different than the typical products that we've produced in this division, and Coaxial Tap 3 and 4 are new compact versions. Network Devices is new to the industry. Miniature Ribbon Coax is new to the industry."

After Jon Grover became the group director (GVP), some of DGM Smith's TMT members – who were by now much more committed to new business creation – began resisting Smith's efforts to redeploy resources from development into manufacturing to improve production efficiency, product quality, and customer service at the expense of new business initiatives.

The division general manager

DGM Clay Smith continued to invest his time and other resources in launching new initiatives while Walker was his group director (GVP). After Walker moved up and Grover arrived as the new group director, Smith shifted his emphasis to coincide with his new boss's priorities. Development manager Jim Fitch said,

> At one time development was everything. Or almost everything in terms of emphasis. And now you go from product development being everything to manufacturing and efficiency and customer service being everything. Which frankly is healthy, really, right now, because we had a long stretch there pumping out crap that didn't work. It's about time to make it all work now. [Laughter]

Product manager Chad Blair also commented on this shift from new product development to manufacturing:

> I think what we've done is taken a look at products that offer us good profitability and long-term manufacturability as compared to pushing the state of the art. Let's take what somebody else has already defined – the interface performance requirements – and now tool it in such a way that we can manufacture it much better, much more cost-effectively, and get it out for broad market coverage kind of a thing.

The manufacturing manager also agreed that Smith's relative emphasis had shifted from development to manufacturing: "I get the general impression that Clay Smith has let development stay at status quo. Whereas he's increased the horsepower in manufacturing. I don't see the number of new [product] programs that I saw before."

Comparing the DGM's influence: Mike Walker versus Clay Smith Mike Walker and Clay Smith were both inventors (each had several patents), and both had been (new product) development managers prior to becoming DGM of AMP Sigcom. Ben Keller, the division controller who had served under both these DGMs at AMP Sigcom, compared them:

> Mike Walker is the most astute manager I have worked with, and I have worked for several over thirty-two years. Smith went through a learning curve after he became DGM; Walker it seemed like had always been DGM! Smith took a year to find out what he was all about. Smith didn't come in with Walker's credentials or contacts; he had fewer contacts at the top and had to figure out what top management wanted.

Just as Smith was being pressured by group director Grover to improve gross margins, Walker, as DGM, was pressured by his group director, Hal Norris. But Walker succeeded in getting his boss not only to ease up the pressure but also to give him some profit forgiveness (5 percent of the division's gross margin) to enable him to make the needed new business investments. Arjay Mason, who was product manager under both Mike Walker and Clay Smith, contrasted the two situations:

> Walker was running a bit counter to what his group director, Hal Norris, wanted. Walker had to do a sell job to convince Norris that AMP Sigcom needed new product development; otherwise the goose that laid the golden eggs would die. Mike [Walker] is extremely persuasive . . . Clay [Smith] is more of a follower than what Mike was. If Grover had moved in over top of Mike, I'm not sure that Mike would have simply said, "OK, we're marching in his direction now."

In sum, their colleagues felt that the difference between Mike Walker and Clay Smith as DGMs was that Walker had stronger business conviction about what he wanted to do, and his credibility and contacts with corporate top management allowed him to get it done. Smith was motivated to pursue new business initiatives as DGM while he had the encouragement and support of Walker as his group director. But his colleagues said Smith did not have the conviction, the contacts, or the clout to continue emphasizing new business creation against what he perceived to be his new boss's (Grover's) different priorities.

Summary

This chapter showed how the five major influences examined in Parts I through V of the book *interacted* to drive new business creation in AMP Sigcom, and how these interactions changed over time first to maintain and then to reduce the thrust on new business creation.

Considering both its external and internal components, the business environment when Clay Smith was DGM provided about the same impetus for new business creation as when Mike Walker was DGM. The AMP management culture valued new business creation to the same degree during the tenure of both the DGMs. But because the economy had deteriorated, the corporate executives emphasized short-term profits more and placed less emphasis on new business creation by the time Smith became DGM.

Thanks to Walker's efforts as DGM, Smith inherited a division with much greater capability for new business creation and commitment to it than Walker did when he took over as DGM. Walker had deeper experience in new business creation and he had higher motivation to pursue it as DGM. But Smith enjoyed greater support for it from his boss, because Walker was the group director (GVP) to whom he reported. Thus, on balance, new business creation in AMP Sigcom was sustained under DGM Smith while Walker was his group director (GVP).

By the time Walker was promoted once again and Grover became DGM Smith's new group director, things had changed sufficiently to reduce the thrust on new business creation in AMP Sigcom. The corporate executives had shifted their emphasis even more toward profitability versus growth, group director Grover emphasized efficiency, quality, cost, and gross margin rather than new business creation, and Smith did not deviate from the direction his new boss had set.

20 Managing ten critical issues in new business creation

This chapter ties together what has been learned in Parts I through V. It considers ten critical issues that cut across the five major influences on new business creation examined in these parts (Figure 20.1). Recommendations are included for top managers on how to manage these issues for better results.

The ten issues are:

(1) How to know whether to pursue new business creation.
(2) How much emphasis to place on new business opportunities versus existing business opportunities.
(3) What organization to use for new business creation.
(4) How to select people for new business creation.
(5) How to motivate people for new business creation.
(6) How to evaluate and commit to new business opportunities that are highly risky and/or in need of quick action.
(7) How long to persist with a new initiative, how much to invest in it, and when and how to de-commit.
(8) How to manage the volatility of new business.
(9) How to stay within budget without hindering new business creation.
(10) What the appropriate controls are for new business creation.

Successful new business creation requires a *consistent* and *mutually reinforcing* set of philosophies, beliefs, and practices. Top managers must not fall into the trap of seeking quick-fix solutions by trying to change a practice here and a belief there. They should first think about how they currently manage these ten critical new business creation issues. Then they must decide which elements need to be changed or managed more effectively to create a consistent and mutually reinforcing approach for new business creation. Implementation requires attention to the five major influences and their interactions.

The recommendations that follow assume that the corporate executives are pursuing the small-is-beautiful philosophy, which is better suited to new business creation in the division. Those pursuing the bigger-is-better

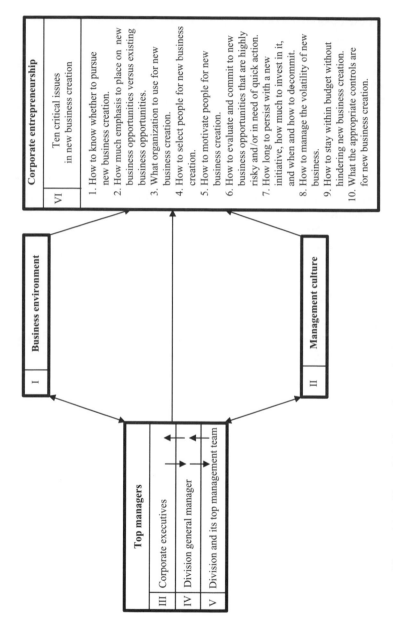

Figure 20.1. Ten critical issues in new business creation.

corporate philosophy, or both philosophies simultaneously, can also profit from these recommendations if they take two important steps needed to get the best of both worlds: (1) the resources required to pursue the bigger opportunities must be obtained without squeezing the divisions dry of the resources and autonomy they need to pursue the smaller opportunities; and (2) strategic planning must be replaced by an ongoing multi-level strategic dialog to facilitate alignment and mutual reinforcement between entrepreneurship in the divisions and entrepreneurship at corporate headquarters.

Issue 1. How to know whether to pursue new business creation

In addition to the potential direct benefits of additional revenue and profit from innovative products and new markets,[1] new business creation offers the promise of indirect benefits – both tangible and intangible – that are difficult to assess accurately, even in retrospect.[2]

There are three major indirect benefits from new business creation. First, new initiatives can boost *existing* business by enhancing the division's image in the marketplace and/or by complementing existing products. When Xerox OPD unveiled Ethernet as the electronic backbone, for example, it positioned the division as a credible contender in the emerging office automation market and this helped to sell the word processor, an existing product that could be connected to it. AMP Sigcom's lower-priced Commercial RF connector opened doors into new accounts that could not be penetrated with the more expensive regular RF connector; many of the new customers ended up buying the expensive connector because the less expensive one was not yet available in sufficient quantities! At 3M Micrographics, the Com program helped to sell the highly profitable reader-printer and the high-priced coated paper it used.

Second, whether they succeed or fail, new initiatives can lead to second-generation initiatives that open up new product markets.[3] The successful Coaxial Tap initiative at AMP Sigcom opened up new markets with second-generation products for point-of-sale terminals in supermarkets, department stores, and convenience stores. At Monsanto Fab Products, the lessons learned on the Spray Guard program about "sell what you test" helped the Drainage Mat initiative. The failed RCA Disk Caddy led to other applications, such as computer housings, that required tight tolerances but without the critical finishing step that killed the Caddy.

Third, both successful and unsuccessful initiatives can generate new knowledge that enhances the division's competitiveness.[4] The RCA

Disk Caddy taught the division how to make large three-dimensional sheets faster and with less material than its competitors. AMP Sigcom's Transmission Cable helped to develop the rolling wire technique, a high-reliability and low-cost method for making the cable used in many of the division's products. The Com program at 3M Micrographics brought electronic hardware and software skills that were later used in both mechanized and electronic retrieval devices for microfilm. It also taught the division the skills needed to sell systems in the data processing area.

Thus, new business creation must be undertaken to some extent on faith, not only because the direct benefits are uncertain – because of low rates of success for new initiatives – but also because it is impossible to predict what indirect benefits will accrue. And these might turn out to be substantial.

Issue 2. How much emphasis to place on new business opportunities versus existing business opportunities[5]

New business creation requires investment of time and resources that might be more productively deployed to improve the division's existing business. For example, investments in quality or manufacturing efficiency could improve the growth and profitability of the existing business. How should such trade-offs be made?[6]

The corporate executives

Corporate executives must allow the DGM to make this trade-off. They should emphasize both short-term profitability measures (such as a specified gross margin or return on capital or a pre-tax profit equal to some percentage of sales) and long-term growth measures (such as some percentage real revenue growth) to encourage the DGM to place a consistent emphasis on new business creation. They must also keep the DGM in place long enough (at least three to four years) to ensure that he is motivated to make this trade-off in the best long-term interests of the company.[7]

The short-term and long-term performance standards must be demanding yet flexible. Corporate executives must allow these standards to be bent by a DGM who has sufficient credibility and conviction about the initiatives in his division. They must also ensure that the DGM is committed to his new initiatives – not because of ego or an emotional attachment to them, but for sound business reasons.

The DGM

When the existing business is growing, there is a tendency to neglect new business creation. However, when the existing business starts maturing, or is under threat, new business creation is sought as a remedy. Unfortunately, new business cannot be created on short notice.

To avoid this trap, the DGM must place a consistent emphasis on new business creation and give it the continuity needed to achieve success. This also enables the conversion of both successes and failures into second-generation initiatives. And it leads to the generation of new knowledge that sustains new business creation and improves the performance of the *existing* business.

How much emphasis to place on exploration versus exploitation[8]   For a given level of emphasis on new business opportunities (versus existing business opportunities), what fraction of the available time and resources should be devoted to *exploration* – perceiving, defining, and screening of new business opportunities – versus *exploitation* – the conversion of the chosen opportunity into a commercial success? The greater the emphasis is on exploration, the greater will be the chances of finding more-attractive new business opportunities. However, the greater the emphasis is on exploitation, the better will be the chances of successful commercialization of the selected opportunities. How should this trade-off be made?

The DGM must place sufficient emphasis on the exploration of new business opportunities versus their exploitation so as to have a large enough pool of opportunities from which to choose the most attractive ones on which to bet.[9] AMP Sigcom under DGM Walker and 3M Micrographics under DGM March did far more exploration than others – not just in an absolute sense, but also relative to the emphasis they were placing on exploitation. Xerox OPD under Gibbons placed more emphasis on new business opportunities (versus existing business opportunities), but the division was doing *proportionately* less exploration.[10]

Exploration of new business opportunities must be conducted by knowledgeable people. In the divisions under Walker and March, exploration was done by people with considerable experience in the product market territory of interest. DGMs can encourage exploration by devoting an appropriate percentage of their personal time to this activity.[11] Walker and March spent a higher proportion of their personal time on exploring and screening new business opportunities than did the other DGMs, and this energized their division's new business opportunity pipeline to a higher degree.

A disciplined system for the identification and pursuit of new business opportunities, such as AMP Sigcom's review system or 3M Micrographics' phase system (Figure 15.1), also encourages the exploration of many new business ideas. These ideas can then be screened tightly to choose the most attractive opportunities on which to bet.

Issue 3. What organization to use for new business creation

Because of its greater technical, product, and market uncertainties, new business requires closer cross-functional coordination and a greater sense of urgency and focus than is necessary for existing business. What organization should be used for new business creation given these requirements?

The business unit (BU) organization is more costly (because of duplication of resources) but better suited to new business creation than either the functional or the matrix organization, because its dedicated cross-functional resources and clear accountability for results provide the required level of coordination, focus, and speed. But its higher cost might not be justified for mature businesses. It generally pays to separate the start-up and growth businesses from the mature businesses and use the BU organization for the former only.

An organizational change to get to a self-sufficient BU is *not* recommended if there has been a recent organizational change, because frequent reorganizations hamper new business creation. Also, a self-sufficient BU might not be practical if some sharing of functional resources is necessary. For instance, a shared sales force might be necessary if several BUs are serving the same customers or using the same distribution channels.

Some top managers hate the matrix organization because they do not buy its principle of shared resources and accountability. But some sharing of resources and accountability is unavoidable if top managers want the best of both worlds – the entrepreneurship of the BU organization, and cross-BU collaboration to develop the core competence of the corporation for pursuing new business opportunities that are beyond the ambition and capability of any single BU.

Top managers like structural solutions because they can be readily implemented, but it is best not to engage in a hunt for the "ideal" organization for new business creation. Though choices exist and do matter, it is good to remember that the real payoff comes from attending to the neglected task of developing the competence of the people for new business creation as well as their capability to work within and across the boundaries of whatever organization is used. Proper attention to education, training, coaching, and mentoring is essential if this is to be accomplished.

Issue 4. How to select people for new business creation

New business creation requires people who are capable of perceiving new opportunities and are committed to pursuing them despite the inherent technical, product, and market uncertainties. Product and general management champions who are ready to put their energy, talent, and credibility on the line for a new initiative are essential. How should people be selected to take on these challenges?

The corporate executives

Corporate executives can promote new business creation in the division by appointing a DGM whose personality and experience are well suited to the task. A sufficiently deep knowledge of the business and prior success with new business creation are strong personal assets.

The selection of the division's TMT also influences new business creation. The DGM should have a strong voice in the selection of his team, but corporate executives must ensure that the TMT has the required competence for new business creation and can compensate for each other's and the DGM's weaknesses.

Corporate executives fall into the trap of appointing a proven independent entrepreneur as DGM, typically one who has joined the company through an acquisition, in the hope that this will inject entrepreneurship into a corporate division that badly needs it. Instead, what they frequently get is chaos, excessive risk-taking, and a scary ride to nowhere. This is a common occurrence because independent entrepreneurs typically lack one of the essential ingredients for corporate entrepreneurship – the ability and willingness to navigate the political and cultural rapids of a large corporation to get things done. They tend to venture forth on their own, and their lack of corporate experience equips them with neither the patience nor the skill required to build political alliances and cultivate the necessary corporate support for new initiatives.

The recommendation for corporate executives is clear: do not appoint an independent entrepreneur as DGM of a corporate division, especially if this division is not the acquired company through which the independent entrepreneur came to the corporation – unless there is compelling evidence that God has blessed you with an exception to this rule!

The DGM

If he is not careful, the only real champion a DGM might end up with is himself! This happens all too frequently because there are far fewer true believers and real champions than the DGM might assume. What looks like corporate entrepreneurship is often fake. People talk the talk *and* walk the walk because it is expected of them. But the passion and the commitment that are the soul of entrepreneurship are often missing.

To avoid fake entrepreneurship, the DGM must resist the temptation to "appoint" a champion, create a program team, and exhort its members to entrepreneurship with the promise of financial rewards. Instead, conditions must be created under which someone who is both competent and committed to the new opportunity will *volunteer* to lead it. The challenge of the entrepreneurial task will beckon the right person to come forward. The champion should be allowed to recruit other believers who have the necessary skills, and the team must be given sufficient autonomy and resources to proceed.

Issue 5. How to motivate people for new business creation

High failure rates make new business creation risky, not only for the company but also for the individuals associated with it. How can people be motivated to undertake new business creation despite these risks?

There are two basic approaches. Both provide motivation by increasing the individual's perception of rewards from new business creation, relative to its perceived risks. One approach is to increase the numerator of this ratio, by offering financial incentives commensurate with the higher personal risk. This can work if the incentives are perceived by others as fair. But use of the Silicon Valley model of big financial incentives generates perceptions of inequity and feelings of resentment within the corporate setting, and is counter-productive except under the restrictive set of conditions described in Chapter 5.

The second approach, the one that works best for a corporation, is to offer plenty of recognition and career advancement as reward, and to reduce considerably the perception of personal risk – as the primary means of increasing the perception of reward relative to risk. The most effective way to do this is to create a mistake-tolerant management culture, as described in Chapter 5. But this takes time. In the meantime, top managers – both corporate executives and division managers – must reduce the perception of risk for those involved in new business creation by becoming their "bodyguards." They must lend their personal support to the people involved, rather than offer them the usual "Go ahead, but don't screw up!"

Issue 6. How to evaluate and commit to new business opportunities that are highly risky and/or in need of quick action

New business opportunities that offer the promise of higher payoffs generally carry higher risk. Also, a decision must often be made on whether to seize an opportunity on the basis of available information and analysis, or risk losing it by delaying action to secure additional information and conduct further analysis.[12] For example, the best time to get the lowest purchase price for a new technology or product acquisition is *before* either is proven in the marketplace. Once the technology is proven and the product starts selling, the buyer loses leverage. The Tanaka Printer was a highly profitable licensing agreement for 3M Micrographics because DGM Buddy March sealed the deal before the product was proven. How should such decisions be made? Who should make them?

The corporate executives

Corporate executives delay new programs for reasons such as skepticism ("this is too good to be true"), "not invented here," and the time needed for corporate approval. Corporate executives can also create delays if they have different conceptions of the opportunity. For example, president Reilly had questions about the OPET bottle initiative at Monsanto Fab Products because he did not believe it was an attractive long-term business for the company. Monsanto VP of corporate planning, Hummel, was arguing for a mass assault on the market, or a quick entry to skim the market and get out before the competition flooded in. DGM Stewart, and his successor McVay, were arguing instead for a toe-in-the-water incremental approach.

Corporate executives must give the DGM sufficient resources and autonomy to decide which risks to take and how quickly to move within agreed parameters. For example, at AMP all investments in excess of $75,000 (in current dollars, adjusted for inflation) required group level approval, and those in excess of $300,000 required corporate approval. Within these parameters, the DGM could initiate new business activity without the approval of higher-ups. This allowed him to undertake new business initiatives regardless of how risky or unattractive they seemed to others, including superiors. This autonomy also gave the DGM the flexibility to commit to a new business opportunity as rapidly as he saw fit. Corporate executives must also permit the DGM to pursue an initiative that is beyond the agreed parameters if he has sufficient credibility and can persuade them to support it. DGM Walker was able to get such support for both the Fiber Optics and the Transmission Cable initiatives.

For the corporate executives to feel comfortable granting such autonomy, they must appoint a manager with a proven track record within the company as DGM, and trust him to take prudent risks in the best interests of the company. This will also be in the DGM's self-interest if he is committed to the company, seeks advancement in it, and knows he will be in the job long enough to be judged on both short-term profitability and long-term growth.

The DGM

The DGM might have to commit to a new business opportunity relatively quickly, sometimes before solutions to the technical, product, or market problems have been worked out.[13] Quickness must not be confused with haste, however. A disciplined system for pursuing new business opportunities (Chapter 15) assures speed with rigorous assessment. After an opportunity has been analyzed to the extent possible, it might be necessary to act on the basis of intuition. Some failures are bound to occur, but *commitments to opportunities energize the search for new solutions* and lead to new knowledge and second-generation initiatives. This is what DGM Mike Walker of AMP Sigcom meant when he encouraged his people to "get into a lot of trouble!"

In making such decisions, it helps to view new initiatives as strategic options.[14] For the OPET bottle initiative at Monsanto Fab Products, president Reilly viewed the five-year plan to build ten hot-fill lines – six for the orange juice market and four for the apple juice market – as a $100 million investment in the bottle business that he was not willing to commit to. DGM Dan Stewart positioned it instead as a $3 million strategic option to discover the potential of the hot-fill bottle market. If it did not work out, the remaining $97 million would not be needed. Stewart's successor, Ian McVay, made the argument even more compelling by claiming that if things did not work out, the $3 million invested would be recovered by converting the lines to cold-fill, for which there was a proven market – a "win, no lose" proposition.

Issue 7. How long to persist with a new initiative, how much to invest in it, and when and how to de-commit

New business success comes from persevering, but how long is long enough? How much investment is too much? When should a decision be made to de-commit a program?[15] De-commitment is especially difficult when the write-offs associated with it cannot be absorbed immediately. This is the same reason sick manufacturing plants are sometimes not closed – because the shutdown costs are just too high. The Com project at 3M Micrographics was not killed earlier because, in part, the write-offs would have hurt the bottom line by $16–18 million when even a $2 million hit was considered unacceptable.

The corporate executives

Corporate executives should not ask the DGM to pursue a particular initiative, nor should they ask him to drop it. Commitment and de-commitment must be left to the DGM's judgment. This does not mean that the corporate executives should leave the DGM alone. Several techniques and forums – such as selected opportunity reviews and technical audits – should be used to spotlight the division's new business initiatives, particularly those involving major investments and those that have remained unprofitable for some time, and to question the DGM about these initiatives.

Thoughtful corporate reviews of new initiatives offer two principal benefits. First, they provide a broader perspective and a more detached assessment of the division's new initiatives that can help a DGM look at the situation more objectively.[16] Second, they increase the DGM's commitment to whatever decision he makes, because he is given the opportunity to think about it carefully *and decide as he sees fit*.[17]

The DGM

De-commitment poses a dilemma. On the one hand, it is possible to become so committed to an initiative that one persists and carries the associated losses for too long. On the other hand, it is possible to give up too easily. How should this dilemma be resolved?

The DGM must ensure that the technical people are not giving up too quickly. AMP Sigcom's technical managers favored dropping Fiber Optics because they felt it was impossible to produce the required precision molding. DGM Mike Walker, however, had sufficient technical knowledge and experience in dealing with technical people to recognize that they were too proud to ask for help, and were trying instead to solve the problem in a vacuum. He pulled a corporate–division team together with the blessing of the corporate VP of technology and, in a matter of six months, they had the technical problem solved. If he had allowed his people to drop the project, the division would not have later enjoyed the technological edge in precision molding that they did.

Success often comes from persevering even though others, including higher-ups, believe the initiative cannot succeed. Cable Assembly, Commercial RF, and Coaxial Tap were all examples of this for DGM Mike Walker of AMP Sigcom. Persistence pays off not only because of the proverbial "If at first you don't succeed...," but also because if you stay at it long enough, *unanticipated* developments in technologies, markets, or other factors might increase the odds of success. This was an important factor in the eventual success of the Coaxial Tap initiative at AMP Sigcom. FCC regulations on noise reduction gave this product a more attractive application in the marketplace. The higher-than-anticipated prices and volumes the product eventually commanded as a result of this allowed it to be designed and manufactured to yield a higher profit than originally estimated.

DGM Buddy March of 3M Micrographics also believed in not giving up too easily when technical difficulties were encountered. Even though he was viewed as the industry godfather, March's understanding of the technology was pragmatic, not deep as Walker's was. This made it more difficult for March to judge how far to push the technical people. However, he had the benefit of two technical judgments. First, he relied on the corporate technical audits, which had a track record of predicting success and failure that was better than the division's own record. Second, March relied on the judgments of his highly regarded technical director, Ray Thorngate.

The DGM should ask two fundamental questions in deciding whether to persevere or de-commit. First, as one of the participants put it colorfully, "Can the technical problems be solved without repealing the laws of physics?" If the DGM does not have the depth of technical knowledge to rely on his own intuition to answer this question – Mike Walker had the technical depth, Buddy March did not – he needs to rely on the best technical judgments available. If the technical problems can be solved, a second question must be asked: "Is the market likely to be big enough to justify the time and money required to solve the technical problems?" Again, the DGM must rely on those best qualified to make this judgment.

If a de-commitment is called for, it is best to allow an initiative that is already in the market to die with honor – a phased withdrawal in which existing customers are served while the product is priced out of the market. The Com program was discontinued over a two-and-a-half year period with this approach, along with a commitment to service the units for as long as the customer required it, at a price that was profitable to 3M.

Issue 8. How to manage the volatility of new business

It is more difficult to deliver the forecasted sales and profits for new business than for existing business. This is not a surprise if one recognizes that new initiatives face higher levels of technical, product, and market uncertainty. How should top managers anticipate and manage the higher volatility of new business?

The corporate executives

In reviewing a division's performance, corporate executives typically scrutinize results that are below the sales or profit plan by more than 5 to 10 percent; repeated deviations below plan are judged unacceptable. Such useful yardsticks for monitoring the performance of existing business are worse than useless for judging the performance of new business, because they are totally unrealistic and counter-productive. Even companies with long, successful track records of new business creation experience deviations of 100 percent or more from their sales and profit plans for new initiatives during their first or second year on the market because of the inherent uncertainties.

Corporate executives who do not anticipate and make sufficient allowance for this degree of volatility of new business end up killing it. They must consider whether a division has a large enough base of stable existing business with which to absorb the volatility of its new business and still deliver the total forecasted results for the division. If not, they should accept the division's decision to scale back new business creation so that its volatility can be absorbed, or be prepared to absorb its volatility themselves. This is not music to the ears of corporate executives, but they must listen to it and act on it.

The DGM

The DGM can take three steps to deliver the forecasted results for his division, despite the inherent volatility of its new business. First, he must factor the expected volatility into the sales and profit forecasts for the division. If the division does not have a large enough base of stable existing business with which to absorb the volatility of its new business, the new business must be scaled back appropriately; or the expectation of higher volatility for the new business must be negotiated explicitly with the boss and higher-ups.

Second, the DGM must retain sufficient slack in the budget for the unforeseen expenditures that new initiatives invariably require. It pays to have a portfolio of new initiatives that are at different stages of development and introduction into the market, and to strive for industry diversification as well.

Third, the DGM must undertake a careful review of all new initiatives to decide which ones to cut and by how much, and where to delay, in order to deliver the division's forecasted overall results. How to do this well is considered next.

Issue 9. How to stay within budget without hindering new business creation

DGMs must do more than simply achieve or exceed the division's revenue, profit, and cash targets. They also must comply with periodic corporate requests for contributions *beyond* the budgeted amounts. This is sometimes referred to as "quarterly giving," because these additional contributions (from as little as $100,000 to $2 million or more, depending on the division's "giving capacity") are typically made each quarter as corporate executives squeeze some divisions to compensate for underperformance by others in an attempt to deliver the forecasted quarterly results for the corporation as a whole.

DGMs can comply with these corporate requests without necessarily hindering new business creation if they do three things well. First, they must undertake the task with the attitude that budget cuts could hurt new business creation, but that they could also *help* it. Second, they must *not* make the budget cuts "democratically," i.e. with the intention of spreading the pain in an equitable manner. Rather, they should carefully review all their programs and make their cuts *selectively*. Third, they must avoid the temptation to advance customer billings or shipments to make the numbers look right.

Budget cuts and program delays can hurt or help

Top managers can be so eager to ensure the success of a new initiative that they bathe it in excess resources. But *too much* money and other resources, like too little, can hurt new business creation. Too much money can lead to a proliferation of programs of marginal significance that dissipate focus and drain energy from the more promising activities. Fewer resources can impose the needed discipline and help to achieve greater focus and a sense of urgency.[18]

For example, the technical director for the Cycle Safe program at Monsanto was convinced that too much money and too little control had contributed to the major losses on that program:

We went from bench to full production too fast because we feared Du Pont would beat us to it. There were no budgetary constraints – "Do it, and do it fast!" We put too much money into it. Had we been under more budgetary constraints, we would have done better. We had three plants and sixteen production lines before we had one plant that would run.

Whatever the potential for harm to new business creation from budget cuts and program delays, it must be weighed against potential benefits that can also accrue. First, the pressure to make these cuts and delays can lead to a more careful scrutiny of all the initiatives and their prospects. Second, the periodic discipline imposed by the need to cut and delay new business activity can force the division to make the tough choices on de-commitments. To the extent that such pruning is needed but is not being done, it can help the division focus on those initiatives that hold the greatest promise.

Make budget cuts selectively, not democratically, after a careful review of all programs

It is tempting but ineffective to spread the pain of budget cuts equitably, for example by asking each member of the management team to contribute proportionately equal amounts from their departmental budgets in order to come up with the total amount the division must contribute to the corporation.

The DGM must undertake a careful review of all programs to decide *where* to cut, and must then take the time to *communicate* the rationale to those affected so they understand his reasoning even though they might not agree with it. And he must reassign the affected people as quickly as possible to other programs to keep them motivated.

DGM Mike Walker of AMP Sigcom usually made his cuts in the following sequence. Travel and advertising were first to be cut. Capital expenditure cuts were next, but these were instituted only after a careful review of all the major programs, and discussions with the affected program managers. Walker tried to give these managers the big picture and his goal – "I tell them the truth and want truth from them," he said – and solicited their advice and opinions on how best to achieve the goal for the division.

Walker gave the people whose programs were about to be axed a chance to argue against the decision, and he gave them feedback ("I make sure they understand my reasoning, even if they disagree with it," Walker said). Once the decisions were made, those adversely affected were reassigned to another program already under way, one that seemed challenging to the individual ("The best way to get their minds off the old program is to get them excited about something new," Walker said). Managers whose programs survived were asked to be more creative about how to make do with fewer resources (for example, "Can we get away with only five test runs rather than fifteen?").

Avoid the temptation to advance customer billings

The DGM might be tempted to advance customer billings in various ways to stay within the budget. Customers can be billed before the product is shipped. If just-in-time delivery is not the norm and billings are tied to customer shipments, they can be brought forward by shipping product in advance of their delivery dates, or even in anticipation of customer orders. However, these actions can backfire. Customers might return the early invoice or the merchandise, for which the division has to pay freight and handling, and it also risks the ire of customers who do not expect or want early invoices or shipments.

Such procedures and other creative accounting games are never justified. They are unthinkable in the post-Enron era.

Issue 10. What the appropriate controls are for new business creation

In managing existing business, where uncertainties are much lower, control can be more readily exercised. For example, if manufacturing costs are too high, one knows where to look (materials prices, labor inefficiencies, etc.) and then decide what action to take. New business initiatives are hard to control in this way because cause-and-effect relationships are not well understood. When results are out of line with forecasts (as they invariably are), it is difficult to know what actions to take. How then should new business creation be reviewed and controlled?

New business creation should be reviewed and controlled with the aim of increasing the odds of success for *the total portfolio of initiatives*. Even though it is difficult to know what actions to take to achieve the desired results for a particular initiative, it is possible to control the total effort so as to increase the chance of getting some successes.[19]

There are four important dimensions to this "control the overall port-folio" philosophy. First, the controls must be tailored to fit the different phases of new business creation. Second, the purpose of controls is not so much to achieve the desired results on specific initiatives as to help those involved in new business creation gain perspective and objectivity regarding their initiatives, to increase their commitment to the actions they decide to take, and to promote new learning. Third, boundary controls provide the autonomy necessary for new business creation while limiting the risk to the corporation. Fourth, integrity of control is assured with the use of disciplined systems and effective controllers.

Tailor controls to different phases of new business creation

Exploration of new ideas and opportunities, and the testing of their fea-sibility, should be encouraged during the early phases of new business creation by making it easy to begin working on a new product idea or a new market opportunity (for example, the 3M Micrographics' phase system; Figure 15.1). Ideas and opportunities that show promise should be reviewed carefully and screened tightly to select the best ones on which to bet before major expenditures are incurred.

Projected profitability, but *not* market size, should be an important criterion in these decisions. As DGM Mike Walker of AMP Sigcom put it, "Experience has taught us that we don't know the real market – nobody does – till you get the product out." For example, their Cable Assembly and Coaxial Tap initiatives led to applications and markets that had not been initially foreseen, nor could they have been.

Review new business initiatives to promote objectivity, commitment, and learning

Once major investments are made (for example, in Phase 3 of 3M Micrographics' phase system; Figure 15.1), the initiative's performance and progress should be tracked and made visible to the DGM's boss and higher-ups, who in turn should question the DGM about it dur-ing their periodic reviews of the division without making any decisions. The questions, *and the way in which they are asked*, should convey sup-portive awareness, mutual trust, and a clear sense that it is the DGM's show. Selected opportunity reviews and technical audits provide special occasions for further review and feedback.

For example, the AMP corporate executives were knowledgeable about the division's business and its initiatives, and they wanted to hear about them in detail. They got this knowledge from the new business tracking system, from the group director (GVP), as well as from direct interactions with division personnel. These corporate executives probed deeply into the progress and prospects of the division's new initiatives during the semi-annual planning meetings. These demanding but sensitive reviews helped the DGM look at the situation more objectively than he might have done otherwise, increased his commitment to the decisions he subsequently took, and stimulated new learning. Both DGM Mike Walker and his successor, Clay Smith, expressed two sentiments about these meetings: "The corporate executives cannot be fooled," and "I can't let them down."

> *Use boundary controls to provide divisional autonomy while limiting the corporate risk*

To grant the division sufficient autonomy for new business creation, corporate executives must give it a big enough "ballpark" in which to play; the boundaries are the limits on the financial, technical, human, and other resources entrusted to the division.[20]

For example, DGM Clay Smith of AMP Sigcom said: "Corporate executives control the aggregate investment in the division, not how the total is allocated within the division. They say, 'You play the game.' Versus another style that is more hands-on and intervenes more on a day-to-day basis. Salary administration of people and authorization levels for capital expenditures are examples of the boundaries that are controlled."

> *Ensure integrity of control*

To ensure the integrity of control, top managers must encourage mutual trust and open communication between corporate headquarters and the division. Frequent face-to-face contact between corporate executives and staff and the division managers helps to foster a climate of trust and openness. A disciplined system of financial reporting and internal control, monitored and enforced by effective group and division controllers, is a must.

Summary

Ten critical issues must be managed well to facilitate the creation of new business within a corporate division.

Issue 1. How to know whether to pursue new business creation. New business creation must be undertaken to some extent on faith because success is uncertain and it is impossible to predict the substantial indirect benefits that might accrue.

Issue 2. How much emphasis to place on new business opportunities versus existing business opportunities. Corporate executives must give the DGM sufficient resources and autonomy to decide how much emphasis to place on new business creation, with the understanding that both short-term results and long-term growth are expected. This encourages the DGM to maintain a consistent emphasis on new business creation, which is beneficial. The DGM must place sufficient emphasis on the exploration of new business opportunities so as to have a large enough pool from which to choose the most attractive ones for exploitation.

Issue 3. What organization to use for new business creation. The BU organization, with its dedicated cross-functional resources and focused accountability for results, is best suited to this task. However, because interdependence is a fact of corporate life, too much focus on how the organizational boundaries are drawn is counter-productive. Frequent reorganizations are also harmful. It is more fruitful to develop the competence of the people for new business creation, and their capability to resolve conflict and to work effectively across the borders of whatever organization is used.

Issue 4. How to select people for new business creation. A DGM with the personality and experience suited to the task must be selected. It is generally folly to expect an independent entrepreneur to become an effective DGM of a corporate division. If a DGM is not careful, the only real champion he might end up with is himself. To avoid fake entrepreneurship, the DGM must resist the temptation to appoint a program champion; a competent and committed person must be allowed to volunteer for the task and given the opportunity to recruit a team.

Issue 5. How to motivate people for new business creation. Big financial incentives must be avoided; they create perceptions of inequity and resentment within the corporate setting that can derail new business creation. The challenge of the task, and the opportunity for recognition and career advancement, will provide the necessary motivation for the right program champion and his team if their perception of personal risk is reduced appropriately.

Issue 6. How to evaluate and commit to new business opportunities that are highly risky and/or in need of quick action. Corporate executives must give the DGM sufficient resources and autonomy for him to decide which risks to take and how quickly to move within agreed parameters. It helps to view new initiatives as strategic options.

Issue 7. How long to persist with a new initiative, how much to invest in it, and when and how to de-commit. Corporate executives must permit the DGM to make these decisions, while insisting on corporate reviews and technical audits of the division's major new initiatives to provide an independent and objective assessment.

The DGM can resolve the first two uncertainties by deciding whether the technical problems can be solved without repealing the laws of physics, and whether the market is likely to be big enough to justify the time and investment needed for solving the technical problems. If de-commitment is the right answer, it might be difficult to implement for emotional reasons, or because the write-offs associated with it cannot be absorbed immediately. Ways must be found to allow the new initiative to die gracefully, with honor!

Issue 8. How to manage the volatility of new business. The division must have a large enough base of stable existing business with which to absorb the volatility of its new business and still deliver the forecasted overall results. The expected volatility of new business must be factored into the sales and profit forecasts for the division, and sufficient slack must be allowed in the budget for unforeseen expenditures that new initiatives invariably require. It helps to have a portfolio of new initiatives that are at different stages of development and introduction to the market. The DGM has to undertake a careful review of all new initiatives to decide which ones to cut, and by how much, and what to delay, in order to deliver the division's forecasted overall results.

Issue 9. How to stay within budget without hindering new business creation. Budget cuts can hurt new business creation, but they can also help it. The key is to make budget cuts selectively, after a careful review of all the programs, and despite organizational pleas and pressures for equitable cuts across all the departments. The rationale for the budget cuts and the program delays must be communicated to the troops, especially to those directly affected, so they understand the reasoning even if they do not agree with it.

Issue 10. What the appropriate controls are for new business creation. Controls must be tailored to the different phases of new business creation. The purpose of control must be to ensure that new initiatives are being pursued because of a genuine belief in their attractiveness, not because of personal ego or because it is expected by superiors. Controls must promote the learning necessary for success. Boundary controls provide the autonomy and resources needed for new business creation in the division while limiting the risk to the corporation. A disciplined system for new business creation and effective controllers ensure integrity of control.

Notes

I   INTRODUCTION

1. "Managing for growth," *Economist*, July 31, 1999: 51–52. For a historical perspective, see Baumol (1986, 1993); Binks and Vale (1990); Greenfield, Strickon, Aubey, and Rothstein (1979); Kirzner (1979); Mueller (1971); Peterson (1981); Schoonhoven and Romanelli (2001).
2. Kent, Sexton, and Vesper (1982); Ronstadt (1982); Timmons (1994). Independent entrepreneurship is now part of the education curriculum of most business schools.
3. As Chesbrough (2000) points out, corporate ventures have several potential advantages over private venture capital: longer time horizons, larger capital investments, extensive coordination of complementarities with the firm's capabilities, and retention of learning from failures.
   Shane and Venkataraman (2000: 224) state:

   > Research in industrial organization has shown that entrepreneurship is less likely to take the form of *de novo* start-ups when capital market imperfections make it difficult for independent entrepreneurs to secure financing (Cohen and Levin, 1989). Entrepreneurship is more likely when the pursuit of entrepreneurial opportunity requires the effort of individuals who lack incentives to do so in large organizations; when scale economies, first mover advantages, and learning curves do not provide advantages to existing firms (Cohen and Levin, 1989); and when industries have low barriers to entry (Acs and Audretsch, 1987).

4. The relevant works are cited in these notes. The Preface acknowledges contributors who are cited most frequently.
5. Pinchot (1985) coined the term "intrapreneur" to spotlight the valuable role of the internal corporate entrepreneur, and his popular book *Intrapreneurship* helped to legitimize the notion of corporate entrepreneurship. Kaplan (1987) rebuts the charge that "management" is anti-entrepreneurial, and cites Drucker (1985a) on the entrepreneurial achievements of big business and Ramamurthy (1986) on public sector entrepreneurs in making his case.
6. Drawing on evidence from ancient Rome, medieval China, and the Middle Ages, Baumol (1990, 1993) shows that an economy of private enterprise does *not* have an automatic bias toward innovation, only toward profit. He argues that society's "rules of the game" drive the allocation of entrepreneurial effort between productive activities such as innovation, and unproductive activities such as organized crime. And executive crime, one might add today.

7. *Harvard Business Review* highlighted the importance of this subject by devoting an entire issue to it ("The innovative enterprise: turning ideas into profits," August 2002). Also see, "How can big companies keep the entrepreneurial spirit alive?" (*Harvard Business Review*, November–December 1995: 183–192). Teece (1987) argues that the large firm may be an ideal environment for innovation because of the availability of resources that could be combined in new ways. Pearson (1989) found that a firm's strategic orientation and organizational style were more important than its size as a guide to its entrepreneurial caliber.

8. See "The real internet revolution," *Economist*, August 21, 1999: 53–54; and "The big guys go online," *Business Week*, September 6, 1999: 30–32. Christensen (1997) argues that the incumbents must set up independent units, even completely separate firms, such as the virtual bank, Wingspan, set up by Bank One, to compete head on with the mother firm.

9. Burgelman (1983b: 65 [Figure 1]) offers an integration of the strategic management and corporate entrepreneurship literatures by proposing a new model of the strategic process in the large diversified firm. In their introduction to a recent special issue of scholarly work that integrates the entrepreneurship and strategic management perspectives, Hitt *et al.* (2001: 480–481) write: "Entrepreneurship is about creation; strategic management is about how advantage is established and maintained from what is created . . . strategic entrepreneurship is the integration of entrepreneurial (i.e., opportunity-seeking behavior) and strategic (i.e., advantage-seeking) perspectives in developing and taking actions designed to create wealth." Meyer and Heppard (2000) argue that strategy and entrepreneurship are really inseparable. Also see McGrath and MacMillan (2000).

10. Hamel and Prahalad (1994).

11. See Honda (A) and (B), Harvard Business School cases 9-384-049 and -050 for a case description, and Pascale (1984) for an analysis of these events. Burgelman and Grove (1996) present a framework for reconciling the strategic intent (top-down) and emergent strategy (bottom-up) views.

12. Based on a wide-ranging review of the literature, Peterson (1981) emphasizes the contextual view of entrepreneurship in which the significant blocks to entrepreneurship are legal, administrative, political, economic, and social, rather than a shortage of individuals with an entrepreneurial orientation. Using an entrepreneurial assessment instrument, Krueger and Brazeal (1994) found that the corporate pool of potential entrepreneurs is large – which is consistent with Peterson's (1981) argument.

13. Burgelman (1984a) has elaborated on four major sets of challenges that must be managed: vicious circles in the definition process; managerial dilemmas in the impetus process; indeterminateness of the strategic context; and perverse selective pressures exerted by the structural context on new business development.

14. Why do large old firms have difficulty creating and sustaining innovation? Dougherty and Heller (1994: 200–201) provide a very helpful review of two prevailing theories – Theory 1: Large old firms are too bureaucratic and inert to accommodate the learning and creativity necessary for innovation; Theory

2: Big old firms have difficulty innovating because they lack the necessary know-how or organization.

Dougherty and Heller (1994) then propose a third theory: "We develop the idea that, while managers may support 'innovation' in general, product innovation is in fact illegitimate at the level of everyday thought and action" (201). They found eight specific ways in which innovative activities were considered illegitimate, and observed three modes by which these activities were legitimized. Dougherty and Hardy (1996) found that product innovation is difficult because almost all companies (fourteen of fifteen they studied) had a strong "anti-innovation organizational configuration" of resources, processes, and meaning (1144–1146).

In addition to obstacles created by the marketplace, Krueger and Brazeal (1994) argue that the organization itself presents obstacles such as underestimation of capital needs, incorrect assessment of market demands, lack of contingency plans, impatience by top management, lack of top management commitment to innovation, and unrealistic expectations. Also see Mone, McKinley, and Barker (1998).

15. As is common in academic studies of this nature, I have used fictitious names for all the individuals in this study.

16. Based on the experience of Du Pont, Peterson (1967) was one of the first to point out that adherence to today's business is an obstacle to new business creation. Also see Drucker (1985a); Hanan (1976a, 1976b). Block (1982) argues that, as a company matures, the focus tends to shift from seizing an opportunity to protecting what the company has already acquired. He recommends that managers adopt a pluralistic management style that accommodates the needs of both new ventures and mature businesses. Burgelman and Doz (2001) indicate that top managers need to develop what they call "complex strategic integration" capability to address the challenges associated with exploiting existing *and* new business opportunities simultaneously.

17. A landmark contribution is the work of Burgelman (1983a, 1983b, 1983c, 1984a, 1984b, 1985) on the process of internal corporate venturing (ICV) in the diversified major firm. Following Bower (1970), Burgelman conceived the *core* processes of ICV to consist of the activities through which the new business becomes defined (definition process) and gains momentum in the corporation (impetus process). Two *overlying* processes characterize the context in which the core processes take shape – structural context and strategic context.

Bower (1970) originally proposed the notion of "structural context," which refers to the administrative mechanisms used to implement corporate strategy. Burgelman developed the notion of "strategic context," which refers to the political process by which middle-level managers convince corporate executives to redefine the corporate strategy in order to accommodate new initiatives that fall outside the current concept of strategy. Burgelman also contributed the concept of "autonomous strategic behavior" to describe activity that falls outside the current strategy (1983a) and provided a theoretical explanation for why such behavior emerges and why top management tolerates it (1983c).

For other work that emphasizes the process of new business creation, see Block and MacMillan (1993); Covin and Morgan (1999); Drucker (1985a); Kanter (1983); McGrath and MacMillan (2000); Noda and Bower (1996).

It should be noted that the core process of new business creation, which Burgelman and others have described, is *not* the focus of this book. Rather, the focus is on how top managers use the structural and strategic context, and other means, to influence, both directly and indirectly, the level of new business creation.

18. There is general agreement in the literature that the core process of new business creation is usefully conceived as a series of stages or phases, although their exact number and description varies (Dougherty and Heller, 1994; Galbraith, 1982; Guth and Ginsberg, 1990; Shane, 1995; Stopford and Baden-Fuller, 1994). Burgelman (1983a) pointed out that such stage or phase models need to consider the simultaneous influence of managers at different levels if they are to be usefully applied within the corporate context, and he fulfilled this need by utilizing the distinction between core process and overlying process (structural and strategic context determination). We examine the influences of managers at different levels separately before considering their joint effects on new business creation.

19. These three overarching and overlapping entrepreneurial tasks emerged from this study. The first two tasks follow the literature; the third task, the control of new business activities and the learning of new capabilities, has received less emphasis in prior work. The exceptions are Burgelman (1983c, 1984a, 1985) and Block and MacMillan (1993) who emphasized monitoring, controlling, and learning as integral parts of the process of new business creation (1993: 11 [Table I.1]); Zahra, Ireland, and Hitt (2000) found that learning can have a major effect on a new venture's performance.

20. This could be viewed as unrelated diversification because the new product-market is not related to the existing product-market. However, it could also be viewed as related diversification because Honda's move into automobiles was clearly related to the company's core competence in engines (Hamel and Prahalad, 1994).

21. Lumpkin and Dess (1996: 162) define the essential act of entrepreneurship as new entry (entering new or established markets with new or existing goods and services). They argue that new entry is a useful middle ground for the study of entrepreneurship, between too broad a definition such as Stevenson and Jarillo's (1990: 23) pursuit of opportunity regardless of available resources (which would include actions such as the purchase of a large supply of raw materials at bargain basement prices), and too narrow a definition, such as the creation of new organizations.

In their introduction to a special issue of scholarly work that integrates the entrepreneurship and strategic management perspectives, Hitt *et al.* (2001: 480) write: "entrepreneurial actions entail creating new resources or combining existing resources in new ways to develop and commercialize new products, move into new markets, and/or service new customers." Burgelman (1984b: 155) views such new business creation as related diversification that is achieved via incremental innovation; it is part of the induced strategic behavior loop and is driven by the structural context. He mentions new product development projects for existing businesses and market development projects for existing products as examples.

Leonard-Barton (1995: xiii) argues that the primary engine for development and growth of technological capabilities is the development of new products and new processes, with managers at all levels being the keepers of the wellsprings of knowledge. She points out that in some ways such incremental innovation is *more* of a challenge than radical innovation because, without the need to respond to technological discontinuities, there is no compelling reason to do it (1995: 17). As Utterback (1994: 228) states, "Thus a viable strategy for corporate renewal may be to build on established competences in marketing and distribution to renew a firm's line of business in a chosen market. Another might be to build on its strengths in product development and manufacturing to address new markets."

22. See the discussion of "new" innovation in Dougherty (1990, 1992a, 1992b) and the definition of degree of innovativeness used by Dougherty and Hardy (1996: 1128, 1153) – the number of ways in which the product is unfamiliar to the firm in terms of market, application, technology, distribution, and manufacturing.

23. Burgelman (1983c) has explained why autonomous strategic behavior which falls outside the current concept of strategy arises, why it is tolerated by top management, and how it requires middle managers to engage in a political process – strategic context determination – to convince top management to redefine the concept of corporate strategy to accommodate the new venture. We examine new business creation that falls both within and outside the current concept of strategy.

24. Burgelman (1994, 1996).

25. See Hof (1993) and Robello (1994) for the PDA story. Several authors have defined business that is new only to the company, not new to the world, as new business. For example, Zaltman, Duncan, and Holbek (1973) define innovation as any idea, practice, or material that is perceived as new by the relevant unit that adopts it. Baumol (1986: 163) suggests that entrepreneurial activities fall into two primary categories – initiating and imitative. And Van de Ven (1986: 592) states: "As long as the idea is perceived as new to the people involved, it is an 'innovation,' even though it may appear to others to be an 'imitation' of something that exists elsewhere." As Ahuja and Lampert (2001: 541) put it, "Prior research has identified three basic strategies for entrepreneurship in large firms (Lant and Mezias, 1990): fixed (nonentrepreneurial), imitative (searching domains new to the firm), and adaptive (searching domains new to the population)."

26. D'Aveni (1994) argues that companies in hypercompetitive industries ought to pursue cannibalization. CEO Lew Platt of Hewlett-Packard referred to this competitive necessity colorfully as "eat your own children" (Deutschman, 1994a, 1994b). Markides (1998) argues that fear of cannibalization is an obstacle to strategic innovation.

27. There is some question as to whether new business creation in established and emerging business divisions – the subject of this book – can lead to successful

unrelated diversification. For example, the corporation "Gamma" studied by Burgelman (1983b) had little success with this approach prior to establishing a new venture division. Similarly, in their study of forty product innovations in fifteen companies, Dougherty and Hardy (1996: 1128) found that only five innovations were clearly successful two years later and all of them were from among the twenty-seven innovations that represented low to medium levels of innovativeness; none of the thirteen innovations with high levels of innovativeness (unfamiliar in four or more ways) was successful.

Two points should be noted. First, although there are contradictory findings (Grant and Jammine, 1988), a number of studies have indicated the attractiveness of related over unrelated diversification (Biggadike, 1979; Porter, 1987; Rumelt, 1974; Shelton, 1988). Second, a sustained emphasis on related diversification can lead the corporation over time into product markets that are significantly removed from the original base of business. Well-known examples are 3M, Procter & Gamble, and Johnson & Johnson (Porter, 1987). MacMillan (1987: 445) provides an excellent illustration of how consistent expansion into adjoining markets with existing products or services, and the creation of new products or services for existing customers, can lead to the development of significant new skills and competencies and substantial diversification over time.

28. Mergers and acquisitions have been in vogue from time to time, partly as a recipe for growth. However, from the standpoint of the health of the economy, corporate competitiveness, job creation, and innovation, mergers often do not produce the claimed synergies. The available evidence on mergers should give pause to thoughtful managers and policy-makers (Porter, 1987). Hitt *et al.* (1996) found that firms engaging in acquisitions and divestitures emphasize financial controls, de-emphasize strategic controls, and thereby produce less internal innovation.

Some have argued that recent merger mania is driven by a different set of motivations than in the past: the search for scale, brands, and distribution channels to gain efficiency, competitiveness, and access to new markets, rather than for growth *per se* as in the past (Lipin, 1997). Nevertheless, the planned synergies are often hard to realize (Sirower, 1997), and the acquisition price frequently constitutes an up-front payment for the hoped-for synergies that may never materialize (Oster, 1994: Chapter 7).

29. Deeds and Hill (1996) observed an inverted U-shaped relationship – as the strategic alliances increased, the number of new products developed first increased (up to about twenty-five alliances), then decreased. These authors attributed the U-shaped relationship to the limited ability to manage alliances and hypothesized that, after a certain number of alliances, diminishing returns set in. Rothaermel (2001) analyzed strategic alliances between large pharmaceutical firms and providers of new biotechnology and found that the former were able to learn from the latter and thereby enhance their own new product development.

30. The challenge of managing a joint venture between firms with complementary skills is succinctly stated by Utterback (1994: 227): "New firms in technology product industries are often closer to the frontiers of progress than

are established firms, while established firms have the financial, manufacturing and distribution clout that the new firms lack almost entirely. The flaw
in the seemingly idyllic marriage of these parties is the substantial cultural
differences that set them apart."

31. Siegel, Siegel, and MacMillan (1988) studied corporate venture capitalists
(CVCs) and noted the distinction between "pilots" (CVCs with substantial independence from the parent corporation) and "copilots" (CVCs who
were highly dependent on corporate management with respect to venture
funding and decision authority). Pilots produced not only financial returns
(no surprise) but also strategic benefits (something of a surprise), whereas
the copilot model, with its primary emphasis on strategic benefits, encountered more obstacles. 62 percent of the sample were organized as copilots –
not a preferred mode given the results. Also see Winters and Murfin
(1988).

32. The new venture division (NVD), a breeding ground for *unrelated* new businesses, has had a checkered history. Several well-known companies including
Du Pont, General Electric, Monsanto, and 3M tried this approach during
the 1960s and the 1970s but abandoned it by the late 1970s (see Fast, 1979).
The inherent difficulties of the NVD, the general disenchantment with unrelated diversification (Biggadike, 1979), the drive to "stick to your knitting"
(Peters and Waterman, 1982), and the resulting retrenchment back to the
core business all played a role in its decline.

Burgelman (1985) has argued that the difficulties with the NVD reflect
top management's inability clearly to recognize that it is best suited to ambiguous situations – when both the strategic importance of the venture and
its operational relatedness to other businesses of the corporation are unclear.
Top managers must attend to structural and strategic context determination
to succeed with NVD when it is the appropriate design for entrepreneurial
activity. Chesbrough (2000) describes the New Ventures Group (NVG) created by Lucent Technologies in 1997 – a hybrid between internal business
development and private venture capital – to avoid past difficulties with the
NVD (43 [Table 4]).

33. See Roberts (1980). Burgelman (1984b) provides a framework to determine which organizational arrangement (spin-out, direct integration, etc.)
is recommended based on operational relatedness and strategic importance
(1984b: 161 [Figure 2]).

34. It could be argued that some of these activities, such as mergers and acquisitions, are not entrepreneurial activities since they represent the buying,
selling, and merging of existing businesses, rather than the creation of new
business. However, these activities could also be viewed as entrepreneurial
since they do involve the pursuit of new business opportunities for the
corporation (see Schollhammer, 1982). I prefer this broader view of entrepreneurship because it covers the "buy" versus "make" decisions which
managers face in all business activities, including new business creation.

35. Based on years of bad experience with the new venture division (NVD)
and other centralized venture groups, Block (1982) recommends that ventures should be located within existing operating divisions so that they are

supported by the local management, skills, and facilities. Along the same lines, Sykes and Block (1989) urge companies to shift most of their new venture development responsibility to their operating divisions, as GE and 3M have done.

Systematic evidence on what percentage of the corporation's new business creation activity takes place at the division level is hard to find, but a study of diversification and decentralization in 291 manufacturing firms by Vancil (1979: 14) provides a very rough indication: 64 percent of all R&D expenditures occurred in the business divisions and 42 percent of the firms sampled conducted all their R&D at the business-unit level (1979: 55). Given the prevalence of such activity, Hambrick and MacMillan (1985) call for more direct inquiry into innovation at the business-unit level.

36. Block and MacMillan (1993); D'Aveni (1994).
37. Baum, Locke, and Smith (2001) point out that researchers in the field of entrepreneurship have proposed that individual, organizational, and environmental dimensions should be considered simultaneously to provide a more comprehensive prediction of venture development and growth.
38. The constant comparative method is explained by Eisenhardt (1989); Glaser and Strauss (1967); Hammersley and Atkinson (1983); Miles and Huberman (1994); Silverman (1993); Strauss (1987); Strauss and Corbin (1990).
39. In her study of 136 internal corporate ventures, Day (1994: 156) made the same argument: "The vast majority of the ventures in this database were launched between the mid-seventies and the early eighties. Given that the economic, behavioral, and political processes underlying championing are generally timeless, the data's age should not be a problem."
40. Innovation is unlikely to occur in established organizations without champions (Schon, 1963). Also see Kantrow (1980); Maidique (1980). Shane (1994a) argues that a champion – someone who takes a personal risk to overcome organizational obstacles – is critical for innovation within established companies. Based on survey data provided by 4,405 champions and non-champions in 43 companies in 68 countries, Shane (1994b) describes four innovation-championing roles – the organizational maverick, the network facilitator, the transformational leader, and the organizational buffer. Each of the four roles is critical at one stage of the innovation process, and the presence of champions who undertake these roles improves the innovative activity of a firm. Shane (1995) argues further that uncertainty-accepting societies may be more innovative than uncertainty-avoiding societies because of the greater legitimacy of these roles in the case of the former.
41. With two notable exceptions, the literature does not explore the role of corporate executives and division general managers as *venture champions*. Day (1994) argues that the prevailing theory of bottom-up championing is not the only valid path to corporate entrepreneurship. Her data suggest that top-down championing is important for visible, costly, and strategically reorienting or risky ventures (168).

Maritan (2001) conducted a field study of twenty-nine capital investment decisions in one large paper and pulp firm and found that the received "bottom-up" theory (proposed initially by Bower 1970, and developed further by Burgelman 1983a) was confirmed for the sixteen investment decisions that were related to maintaining or adding to the firm's *existing* capabilities. However, contrary to the prevailing "bottom-up" theory, the senior corporate and division managers got directly involved in initiating and developing almost all (twelve out of thirteen) investment proposals relating to *new* capabilities.

42. Day (1994: 148).

43. "He" will be used to refer to a generic person; "he or she" or "one" will generally not be used, to ease the reading.

44. AMP and Monsanto were acquired in the late 1990s, and 3M and Xerox are no longer in the businesses that were the focus of this study. AMP was acquired by Tyco, and Monsanto by Pharmacia. At the time of writing, Pharmacia was being acquired by Pfizer, and Monsanto was being spun off as an independent agricultural biotechnology company ("Monsanto faces pure-play biotech future," *Wall Street Journal,* August 20, 2002: C1, C3).

45. Unless specifically indicated, the figures for revenue, profit, and cash flow presented throughout the book are the actual amounts, *not* adjusted for inflation. To get an approximation of their magnitude in today's dollars, these numbers should be doubled.

46. Christensen (1997) found that such technology hybrids eventually lost out to the newer, disruptive technology.

Appendix: A theory of corporate entrepreneurship

47. Three notable exceptions are the studies of Burgelman cited in the bibliography; MacMillan (1987); and Noda and Bower (1996).

48. A special issue of scholarly work in this area (Drazin and Schoonhoven, 1996) indicates the need for research on how senior managers influence new business creation: "Although the behavior of top management teams has been a topic of much interest to organizational scholars, little work has been done that links senior executives' behavior to the innovation process. This appears to be a fertile area for future innovation research" (1071). These authors also state that there is a need to "examine multiple levels of analysis when researching the role of organizational context on innovation and, in particular, to develop links between corporate strategy, top management behavior, organization design, and the psychological antecedents of creativity as bases for innovation" (1072). We examine all these connections.

As Utterback (1994: xxviii) concluded,

> How is it that a large and powerful firm can respond with great creativity in its defense while rarely exhibiting the creativity required to embrace the new and abandon the old? After sifting the evidence we believe this is primarily the result of the habits of mind, commitments and strategy, or patterns of behavior of the organization's elite . . . to sustain its success and renew its products, the firm must focus not on the products but on the people involved!

49. Lumpkin and Dess (1996: 164) suggest that future research should use fine-grained methodologies (Harrigan, 1983), such as intensive field research and case studies, to provide insight into the role of culture (Barney, 1992) and other complex social processes associated with entrepreneurial orientation.

2 WHY A CONSISTENT EMPHASIS AND APPROACH FOR NEW BUSINESS
CREATION IS BENEFICIAL BUT DIFFICULT TO ACHIEVE

1. Drawing on the theory of self-organizing systems, Burgelman (1983c: 1360) argues that a consistent emphasis on new business creation is needed:

> If top management of large, complex firms cannot specify the content, or even the precise direction, of entrepreneurial activity in advance, it *can* determine the overall level – how much – of entrepreneurial activity . . . Top management needs to make a firm commitment to support this level of activity independent of fluctuations in nonrelevant variables – e.g., variation in sales volume due to the business cycle (emphasis in original).

   The importance of a sustained commitment to new business creation is also documented in a survey of 168 companies from the Fortune 1000 conducted by Hisrich and Peters (1986). Stopford and Baden-Fuller (1994: 527–528) examined more than fifty mature European companies and discovered that entrepreneurial capability can only be built up with a consistent emphasis on it over a long period of time: "There was no evidence of successful metamorphic change, though some tried."

2. PIMS stands for Profit Impact of Market Strategies (Buzzell and Gale, 1987).

3. Biggadike (1979).

4. O'Hara-Devereaux and Johansen (1994); Schrage (2000). Thomke (2001) provides guidelines for using new technologies, such as computer simulation and rapid prototyping, to make experimentation cheaper and faster and enable companies to innovate more quickly. He describes the gains achieved by Toyota with this approach in the 1990s.

5. This is supported by the findings of Amburgey and Miner (1992) on strategic momentum. Momentum can become *excessive* (see Miller, 1990), but AMP Sigcom and 3M Micrographics avoided this problem because they also emphasized appropriate controls for new business creation, as described in subsequent chapters.

6. The disruption created by frequent management changes was one of the reasons for the lack of sustained innovation in a study of forty product innovations in fifteen companies conducted by Dougherty and Hardy (1996: 1142).

7. As Burgelman (1983c) observed,

> The firm studied oscillated in its emphasis on new venture activity . . . In other words, when things were going well in the mainstream areas of the business, only lip service was paid to diversification. When prospects looked not so good, top management seemed to be ready, as one manager put it, "to jump into just anything" . . . From the perspective of top management, corporate entrepreneurship is not likely to be a regular concern, nor an end in itself. Rather it is a kind of "insurance" against external disturbances or a "safety valve" for internal tensions resulting from pressures to create opportunities for growth (1355).

> Burgelman concluded: "The 'safety valve' or 'insurance' approach is probably not a very productive one for the firm in the long run, and almost certainly not for the development of its entrepreneurs" (1361).

8. Dougherty and Hardy (1996: 1144–1146) argue that managers must change their "anti-innovation organizational configuration" of resources, processes, and meaning to achieve sustained product innovation.

PART I: THE BUSINESS ENVIRONMENT

3 THE EXTERNAL BUSINESS ENVIRONMENT

1. Porter (1980); McTaggart, Kontes, and Mankins (1994).
2. Von Hipple (1978, 1988) shows how new product ideas often come from customers. Christensen (1997) provides compelling evidence on the power of customers in driving a firm's innovation toward sustaining technology and away from disruptive technology.
3. As Van de Ven (1986: 596) states,

   Richard Normann observed that well-managed companies are not only close to their customers, they search out and focus on their *most demanding customers*. Empirically, von Hipple (1978) has shown that ideas for most new product innovations come from customers . . . In general, we would expect that *direct personal confrontations with problem sources* are needed to reach the threshold of concern and appreciation required to motivate people to act (emphasis in original).

   Porter (1990) found that demanding customers spur innovation, and advised firms to seek out such customers around the world to remain globally competitive.
4. Von Hippel, Thomke, and Sonnack (1999) describe 3M's lead user process for developing breakthrough products. Lead users are companies, organizations, or individuals whose needs are more demanding than those of the average user. The central idea of the lead user methodology is to identify such companies and individuals and learn from them. The article describes an application of this methodology by 3M's Medical-Surgical Division.
5. As Utterback (1994: 210) states, "Why were firms willing to pay hundreds of millions of dollars for incremental changes and not a few million dollars for a new frame size? Because the new frame size did not address the *needs of their established customers* . . . A good analogy is the car companies [the customers] discouraging Goodyear, Firestone and others [the suppliers] from introducing radial tires because they did not want to change the design of the suspensions on their cars" (emphasis in original). Christensen (1997) discusses the trap that traditional customers pose because of their reluctance to support disruptive technologies. Bower and Christensen (1995) caution that companies that stay too close to their current customers may fall short of addressing their next-generation performance needs.
6. As is common in academic studies of this nature, I have used fictitious names for some of the companies in this study.
7. Porter (1980) demonstrated three main approaches for gaining competitive advantage: low cost, focus, and differentiation. Porter (1990) found that the intensity of rivalry among direct competitors spurred innovation. In more recent work, Porter (1996) elaborates on the importance of avoiding "me too" strategies and clearly differentiating one's offering from those of rivals to create a sustainable strategic position. Also see D'Aveni (1994) on innovation created by hypercompetition.
8. The influence of other external factors in the environment on the organization in general, and on entrepreneurship, innovation, and new business creation

more specifically, has been extensively examined in the literature, e.g. Aldrich (1979); Barringer and Bluedorn (1999); Baumol (1990); Bower (1970); Burgelman (1983a); Child (1972); Covin and Slevin (1991); Drucker (1985a); Jackson and Dutton (1988); Jarillo (1989); Kanter (1983); Lumpkin and Dess (1996); Miller (1983); Miller and Friesen (1983); Normann (1971); Zahra (1991); and Zajac, Golden, and Shortell (1991).

9. Baumol (1990, 1993) examines how entrepreneurship could take an unproductive path in today's society owing to the damaging effects of litigation and tax evasion. Corporate executives devote much of their time and energy to lawsuits, and litigation is used to blunt or prevent excessive vigor in competition. Because of huge rewards by the courts, it may be tempting for the entrepreneur to select his closest advisors from lawyers rather than engineers. Also see Covin and Slevin (1991).

10. Cooper and Schendel (1976) found that firms continued to make substantial commitments to existing technologies even after sales had begun to decline. Also see Abernathy and Clark (1985); Smith and Cooper (1988).

    Utterback (1994) defined discontinuous change or radical innovation as "change that sweeps away much of the firm's investment in technical skills and knowledge, designs, production techniques, plant and equipment" (200), and observed: "As a general rule, competence-enhancing innovations come equally from established firms and from outsiders. Competence-destroying innovations nearly always come from outsiders" (184).

11. Cooper and Smith (1992) observed that early commitments and divided loyalties posed significant challenges for firms planning to enter an emerging industry from a threatened established base.

12. Christensen (1997) distinguishes between two very different types of new technology. *Sustaining* technology is new technology that is needed by existing customers in known markets. *Disruptive* technology is new technology that is not desired by existing customers, because it is currently inferior in terms of the performance dimensions most valued by these customers. However, disruptive technology is attractive to a *new* set of customers who value the dimensions of performance that the new technology makes possible – typically products that are smaller, cheaper, more reliable, or more convenient to use. Christensen provides compelling evidence that "good management" in several industries disregarded disruptive technology because the firm's existing customers did not currently value it. This was generally a fatal mistake for the incumbent firm because the disruptive technology, pioneered by non-competing firms in new markets, eventually improved and invaded the incumbent's home market where customers who initially rejected the disruptive technology now found its improved price/performance irresistible.

    Although it was difficult to foresee in the case of Xerox, electronic imaging technology did not turn out to be disruptive technology that displaced chemical imaging; on the contrary, computers and the Internet increased the demand for copying!

13. Henderson and Clark (1990) found that even relatively minor shifts in technology architectures (the ways in which components are integrated into a system) could have disastrous consequences for the industry leader. Arend

(1999) shows how *competent* incumbents who devote resources to achieving high current efficiency lose competitive advantage to entrepreneurs who devote resources to tomorrow's opportunities.

Levitt and March (1988: 322) suggest that a "competency trap" occurs when "favorable performance with an inferior procedure leads an organization to accumulate more experience with it, thus keeping experience with a superior procedure inadequate to make it rewarding to use."

14. Day and Schoemaker (2000) recommend that incumbents attend closely to signals from the periphery of their markets, encourage a diversity of viewpoints that challenge prevailing mindsets and myopic views of new ventures, maintain flexibility by adopting a real options perspective for new ventures, and organizationally separate the new initiative that is based on the emerging technology from the firm's mainstream activities. Also see Foster (1986); Foster and Kaplan (2001); Leifer *et al.* (2000); Stringer (2000).

15. This is an example of *disruptive* technology (Christensen, 1997) – plain paper copying eventually overtaking the incumbent coated paper copying technologies.

16. This is an example of *sustaining* technology (Christensen, 1997) because AMP was pursuing the new technology to address the evolving needs of its *existing* customers. Particularly noteworthy is the evidence provided by Christensen that leading incumbents overcame the common difficulties of new technology – and even the most challenging problems of architectural or radical innovation that destroyed the incumbents' current capabilities – as long as it was *sustaining* technology, i.e. valued by existing customers.

In sharp contrast, even incremental or competence-enhancing disruptive technology was not pursued, for the reason that it did not make strategic, financial, or career sense to the managers of the incumbent firm because their existing customers simply did not value it. This led Christensen (1997) to the important conclusion that the attacker's advantage (Foster, 1986) enjoyed by a new firm derives from strategy and human psychology, not from technology. An incumbent firm that properly executes the strategy to pursue a disruptive technology, even though it is ignored or even discouraged by existing customers, can gain the attacker's advantage.

17. See related literature on environmental *hostility* (Block, 1982; Miller, 1983; Miller and Friesen, 1983; Normann, 1971; Slevin and Covin, 1990; Zahra and Covin, 1995), environmental *turbulence* (Naman and Slevin, 1993), environmental heterogeneity and *dynamism* (Zahra, 1991), environmental *discretion* (Finkelstein and Hambrick, 1990; Hambrick and Abrahamson, 1995; Hambrick, Cho, and Chen, 1996), and *scarcity of resources* available from the environment (Jarillo, 1989; Zajak, Golden, and Shortell, 1991).

4 THE INTERNAL BUSINESS ENVIRONMENT

1. As pointed out by Utterback (1994: 163), "Established firms also carry the burden of large investments in people, equipment, plant, materials, and knowledge, all of which are closely linked to the established technology. It takes a rare kind of leadership to shift resources away from areas where one

currently enjoys success to an area that is new and unproven." Sharma (1999) indicates that it is a challenge for large firms to protect innovative activity from the pressures of ongoing business.

2. As Utterback (1994: 223) found, "Established firms with massively profitable businesses are almost invariably more conservative and risk-averse than are fledgling competitors with none."

3. Markides (1998, 2000) points out that companies neglect strategic innovation and new business creation when the existing business is growing.

4. Burgelman (1983c) observed a bell-shaped relationship – at one end, when the core business was doing very well, there was no desire to get new business, since the challenges of growing the core business took up all the time of top managers. At the other end, when business was really failing and in a turnaround mode, there were no slack resources for internal corporate venturing (ICV), hence very low ICV. In the middle, when the core business was slowing and about to go bad, top managers wanted ICV in a hurry, which led to a proliferation of bad ventures (see, especially, Figure 2 in 1983c: 1356–1357).

5. Burgelman and Doz (2001) argue that top managers need to develop what they call "complex strategic integration" capability to balance the challenges associated with exploiting existing *and* new business opportunities simultaneously.

6. Charan and Tichy (1998) maintain that any business can be transformed into a growth business by creatively redefining existing markets.

7. The tendency to avoid moves that risk the base business leads to missed opportunities (Block, 1982). Teece (1987) argues that fear of cannibalization is an obstacle to innovation – for example, Xerox's incentive to respond to low-price Japanese plain paper copiers was dulled by the possible cannibalization of its profitable higher volume machines.

8. As Christensen (1997: 21) states, " . . . if new technologies enable new market applications to emerge, the introduction of new technology may not be inherently cannibalistic. But when established firms wait until a new technology has become commercially mature . . . and launch their own version of the technology only in response to an attack on their home markets, the fear of cannibalization can become a self-fulfilling prophecy."

9. Both tangible and intangible resources are important. Williams, Tsai, and Day (1991) found that a "high corporate image" for a firm launching a new venture gave it a competitive advantage. Lounsbury and Glynn (2001) argue that "cultural entrepreneurship" – which involves the telling of stories to enhance the entrepreneurial firm's reputation by building legitimacy with potential investors, customers, and even competitors – is an intangible resource that can be used to leverage the firm's other resources in the quest for the survival and success of a new venture.

10. Stevenson and Gumpert (1985); Stevenson and Jarillo (1990).

11. Ahuja and Lampert (2001) found that although many firms would like to emulate the invention leaders, they are unable to do so for lack of slack resources to get started and this locks them into a vicious circle rather than getting them going on a virtuous circle. This is similar to the "poverty trap"

and the "rich get richer" arguments in sociology and economic development. Also see Wender (1968).

12. As Utterback (1994: xvii–xviii) summarizes,

> the rate of product innovation in an industry or product class is highest during its formative years. This is a period called the "fluid phase," during which a great deal of experimentation with product design and operational characteristics takes place among competitors ... The period of fluidity, according to the model, typically gives way to a "transitional phase" in which the rate of major *product* innovation slows down and the rate of major *process* innovations speeds up. At this point, product variety begins to give way to standard designs (emphasis in original).

Also see Abernathy (1978) and Nystrom (1979) on managing the tension between efficiency and innovation.

13. "Masters of innovation: how 3M keeps its new products coming," *Business Week*, April 10, 1989: 58–63.

14. In working with managers around the world, I have encountered a widely held perception that the Japanese have a natural advantage, a "cultural bias," toward process innovation. Yankee ingenuity, it is felt, favors product innovation. The Europeans seem to fall between these two poles. I am not aware of any systematic research on this question, however.

15. Gilbert and Strebel (1988) describe strategies to outpace the competition by periodically switching the emphasis from product innovation to process innovation.

PART II: THE MANAGEMENT CULTURE

1. Although earlier work has viewed culture as part of the structural context (Burgelman, 1996: 205), we examine its influence separately because culture takes much longer to change than the structural context (Sathe, 1985a; Schein, 1985). This is supported by Leonard-Barton's (1995: 45) description of the increasing difficulty of changing the four dimensions of capability: physical systems are easiest to change; managerial systems come next, followed by skills and competencies; and beliefs are the most difficult to change. The influence of culture is considered in Part II; the influence of the structural context, managerial systems, and skills and competencies is covered later.

2. Judge, Fryxell, and Dooley (1997) identified organizational culture as a key driver of innovation in R&D departments. Jassawalla and Sashittal (2000) found that effective leaders of new product development teams are more likely to emerge in cultures that look favorably upon change and view product innovation as a high-priority organizational activity.

3. The many definitions of culture, reflecting the many different assumptions about the nature of organizations, cluster into two fundamentally different schools of thought (Smircich, 1983) – those who view culture as an organizational variable (something an organization *has*) and those who see it as a root metaphor for conceptualizing the organization (something an organization *is*). Each view has its place, depending on one's purpose. The view presented here is that of culture as a variable; specifically, culture as shared beliefs and assumptions as proposed by Schein (1985) and adapted by Sathe (1985a).

4. Deal and Kennedy (1982); Martin (1992); Sitkin (1992).
5. Since only one division was studied in each firm, it is not clear whether this represented the culture of *all* the managers in the firm.
6. Schein (1985) explains how a group of people with a shared history develop a set of shared beliefs and assumptions. Chattopadhyay *et al.* (1999) found that executive beliefs were influenced to a greater extent by the beliefs of their colleagues (social influence) than by their own past or current functional experience (functional conditioning) – which is consistent with Schein (1985) on the importance of shared history.

5 SHARED BELIEFS ABOUT REWARDS, RISKS, OPPORTUNITIES, AND RULE-BENDING

1. Palmer (1971: 34) points out that economic factors alone cannot explain entrepreneurial behavior – cultural differences and social-psychological factors are important. Knight (1967) is an early attempt to link the contributions from economics, psychology, and sociology to the innovation process.
2. Shils and Zucker (1979).
3. Ronen (1983); Shane and Venkataraman (2000).
4. Brockhaus (1980) found no significant differences between entrepreneurs and managers in terms of risk preference; both preferred a moderate level of risk. Busenitz (1999) also found that independent entrepreneurs did not have higher risk propensity, and did not view themselves as being more risk-adventurous, than a comparable sample of middle managers in large organizations.
5. Burgelman (1983c) points out that corporate entrepreneurship involves new resource combinations that are at least to some extent related to the larger resource combinations constituted by the firm. In fact, if this is not the case, the corporate venture should be spun off. As Burgelman argues cogently, "Such dependencies also create 'information impactedness' (Williamson, 1975) problems, which make it difficult to communicate clearly what the new business opportunity is, and how it will evolve, to outsiders. This would seem to constitute an important theoretical reason why the venture capitalist's approach, if adopted by large, complex firms, is unlikely to resolve their corporate entrepreneurship problems" (1983c: 1354).
6. Others rely on their perceptions of the situation, as well as on their personal relationships with the individual, to make this assessment (Sathe, 1985a).
7. Block and Ornati (1987) found that CEOs agreed on the types of incentives that improve venture performance – milestone bonuses, equity, and/or options in the new venture. However, the primary obstacle to installing such incentives was the concern over internal equity. Burgelman (1988: 84) has argued that measurement and reward systems must recognize that success in particular ventures may depend on earlier, often failed efforts of other individuals. Also see Nonaka and Takeuchi (1995).
8. For perceptions of inequity to be minimized, incentives must be tied to contributions that are unambiguously associated with the individual or the group in question. For the dysfunctional consequences produced by perceptions of inequity to be limited, the individual or group on steep incentives must be minimally interdependent with the activities of the rest of the organization.

9. Based on a study of thirty-seven new ventures, Sykes (1985) argues that extrinsic rewards such as money should *not* be relied on to motivate corporate entrepreneurship. Block and Ornati (1987) found that most companies did not provide different incentives for venture managers versus other managers, nor did the respondents believe that special incentives for venture managers affected the percentage of successes and failures.

   Krueger and Brazeal (1994) emphasize the crucial role of intrinsic rewards for motivating entrepreneurial behavior. Judge, Fryxell, and Dooley (1997) found that pure economic incentives are not always as effective as intrinsic rewards in R&D departments. Others have argued that creativity is motivated primarily by the challenge, the interest, and the satisfaction from the work itself (Amabile, 1998; Csikszentmihalyi, 1996). The findings presented in this book indicate that both intrinsic motivators, such as the challenge offered by new business creation, and extrinsic motivators, such as recognition and career advancement tied to successful entrepreneurship, drive new business creation.

10. Levinthal and March (1993: 107) point out: "In general, however, organizational arrangements seem to be more effective in removing downside risks than in providing extremely rich rewards for great success."

11. Levinthal and March (1993: 108) make an important distinction: "Studies of risk taking suggest that there are two major ways in which beliefs affect risk taking. The first is by influencing *risk preference*, the propensity to engage in apparently risky behavior. The second is by influencing *perceived risk*, the estimates that decision makers make about the riskiness of the alternatives they consider" (emphasis in original). The management cultures of AMP and 3M reduced *perceived risk*.

12. The literature is ambiguous on the effects of job security on innovation propensity because security is necessary for risk-taking from the social psychology perspective (Amabile, 1988; Walton, 1987) but job security offers no incentive for risk-taking from an economic perspective (Quinn and Rivoli, 1991).

13. As Thomke (2001: 72) states, "3M is another company with a healthy attitude toward failure. 3M's product groups often have skunkworks teams that investigate the opportunities (or difficulties) that a potential product might pose. The teams, consisting primarily of technical people, including manufacturing engineers, face little repercussion if an idea flops – indeed, sometimes a failure is cause for celebration."

14. The importance of tolerating mistakes in order to promote creativity and entrepreneurship has been emphasized in other studies (Amabile, 1998; Hisrich and Peters, 1986; Kuratko, Montagno, and Hornsby, 1990; MacMillan, Block, and Narasimha, 1986).

   Thomke (2001: 72) states: "Failures, however, should not be confused with mistakes. Mistakes produce little new or useful information and are therefore without value. A poorly planned or badly conducted experiment, for instance, might result in ambiguous data, forcing researchers to repeat the experiment. Another common mistake is repeating a prior failure or being unable to learn from that experience. Unfortunately, even the best organizations often lack the management systems necessary to carefully distinguish between failures and mistakes." One reason for this is that the terms "mistake" and "failure" are used interchangeably in the literature and in everyday use."

15. This shared belief helped AMP to avoid one of the learning myopias identified by Levinthal and March (1993: 101) – the tendency to overlook mistakes and failures.

16. Based on research on creativity in scientists, Simon (1986: 16) points out that the opportunity to fail can seldom be separated from the opportunity to be creative.

17. Economists use the term "moral hazard" to denote the concern that people will take excessive risks if they are not penalized for failure.

18. The problem may be formally stated as follows. If they are to be encouraged to take risks, people must be insured against bad luck. Given the great difficulty of distinguishing between bad decisions and bad luck, this means that they must also be insured against bad decisions. And therein lies the moral hazard – since they will not be punished for bad decisions, people will become sloppy or irresponsible.

At the heart of this deduction is the assumption that people are inclined to be sloppy and irresponsible unless they know they will be punished for such behavior – what McGregor (1960) called a "Theory X" assumption. To the extent that it is a valid assumption, there are two ways to address this problem. One is to devise methods for separating bad decisions from bad luck, and to insure people against the latter only (Arrow, 1980). Another solution is to insure people against both bad decisions *and* bad luck, but to try and find ways to limit sloppy and irresponsible behavior. The management cultures of 3M and AMP were based on the latter approach, as described in this chapter following this note.

19. Krueger and Brazeal (1994) describe situations that are conducive to entrepreneurship: (1) a "nutrient-rich" environment (where nutrients include social and cultural support, information and tacit knowledge, and tangible resources); (2) credible information; (3) credible role models; (4) emotional/ psychological support; and (5) opportunities to attempt innovative things at relatively low risk.

20. Dutton and Duncan (1987) argue that beliefs about *risk preference* are important because they act as a filter through which management perceives the realities faced by the firm. Sapienza (1984) found that top managers perceived, defined, and acted in response to environmental change so as to protect their core beliefs. See Donaldson and Lorsch (1983); Noda and Bower (1996).

21. In his review of the edited book *Entrepreneurship as Strategy*, Michael (2001: 134) writes:

what is the limit to empowerment? All the authors state that the firm should desire individuals to be risk taking, adventurous, and curious. Such behavior might lead to impressive results, such as Post-it Notes, but it might alternatively lead to the total collapse of the organization, as it did at the Barings Bank. The obvious answer – empowerment within limits – is true but not very useful, and the various authors do not identify the limits as clearly as a reader might like ... It is certainly an opportunity for further research by these authors and others to identify rules that encourage and channel creativity appropriately.

We identify two meta-rules – that is, rules by which all other rules are governed – embedded in the management cultures of AMP, and of 3M, that channeled creativity appropriately by: (1) permitting rule-bending to give *prescribed* behavior the flexibility necessary for creativity; and (2) enlarging the space for creative behavior by limiting *proscribed* behavior to violations of personal integrity and business ethics. These two meta-rules are consistent with Van de Ven (1986: 603): "Institutional leadership thus involves a choice of limits (issues to avoid) rather than a choice of ends...As a result a space of possible actions is defined which leaves room for innovative ideas to develop and to be tested against these constraints." These meta-rules are also consistent with Simons (1995), who argues that boundary systems, such as formally stated rules and proscriptions tied to sanctions, allow individual creativity within defined limits of freedom.

22. Nemeth (1997) argues that company cultures that support innovation are diametrically opposed to those that encourage clear norms of appropriate behavior, cohesion, and loyalty.

23. See Sathe (1985a), Chapter 4, on homosocial reproduction.

24. Dougherty and Heller (1994) discovered ways in which new product development activities were found to be illegitimate. People whose products were more innovative described more instances of illegitimacy (210). They conclude: "Perhaps the most important next research question is to explore the change in managerial ideology that may be necessary for product innovation to become truly legitimate, that is, truly a part of the institutional order of large firms" (216). The two meta-rules embedded in the management cultures of AMP and 3M (see Note 21 above) helped to legitimate product innovation in these two companies.

25. Shane (1994a) found that individuals with championing experience are more likely than individuals without championing experience to prefer champions who break organizational rules in the interest of innovation. Shane, Venkataraman, and MacMillan (1995) found that the following differences existed across national cultures (using the analytical dimensions proposed by Hofstede, 1980): (1) the more uncertainty-avoiding a country is, the more people prefer champions to work through organizational norms, rules, and procedures to promote innovation; (2) the more power-distant a country is, the more people prefer champions to gain the support of those in power; and (3) the more collectivist a country is, the more people prefer champions to secure cross-functional support.

6   SHARED BELIEFS ABOUT CONTROL AND LEARNING

1. Cameron (1986) has argued that extremity in any criterion of effectiveness creates linearity and dysfunction. Some balance must be present in opposition. "For example, effective organizations demonstrate both proactivity and entrepreneurship as well as stability and control. However, too much action

and innovation can create a loss of direction, wasted energy, and a disruption of continuity. An overemphasis on control and coordination can produce stagnation, loss of energy, and abolition of trust and morale" (549).

Miller (1990) shows how entrepreneurial momentum becomes dysfunctional when not opposed by countervailing force. He analyzes the forces that lead to excessive momentum, e.g. leaders with big egos, overconfidence, and defense mechanisms (Chapter 6), and offers an excellent example of excessive risk-taking at Alcoa (242). Along the same lines, Leonard-Barton (1995: 34) describes how success leads companies to overshoot the target. Miller (1990) describes how some companies recovered from excesses, and others avoided excesses and remained excellent (Chapter 8).

Stopford and Baden-Fuller (1994: 524) state: "Renewing organizations surmount challenges which had previously appeared impossible; often a creative process of resolving internal dilemmas. Schumpeterian entrepreneurship is about combining what had been regarded as mutual opposites and harnessing the outcome as innovation in the market." Also see Poole and Van de Ven (1989).

2. The literature considers the important question of *type* of control – financial versus strategic – but ignores the more fundamental question of the *purpose* of control – to educate and empower managers to make their own decisions versus telling them what to do – which Peter Drucker first emphasized fifty years ago (Drucker, 1954).

Although tight financial controls associated with large diversified firms can lead to a short-term, low-risk orientation (Hoskisson and Hitt, 1988), Barringer and Bluedorn (1999) were unable to confirm this – they found support for their Hypothesis 5A that strategic controls are positively associated with greater entrepreneurial intensity, but not for the predicted negative relationship between emphasis on financial controls and entrepreneurial intensity (Hypothesis 5B). Strategic *and* financial controls seem to be necessary for new business creation. I also argue that top management's *purpose* in exercising control (both strategic and financial), and the *skill* with which it is exercised, influence new business creation.

3. The unpredictable and chaotic nature of the innovation process has been carefully documented by Van de Ven and his colleagues (see Cheng and Van de Ven, 1996; Garud and Van de Ven, 1992; Polley and Van de Ven, 1996; and Van de Ven and Polley, 1992). Woo, Daellenbach, and Nicholls-Nixon (1994) argue that we know more about the initial conditions and the factors that are important to an understanding of entrepreneurship, much less about the process by which these initial conditions and factors lead to entrepreneurship. They consider the importance of experimentation and learning, and random effects.

4. The higher the corporate expectations for new business creation in the division, the more favorable the view of its industry and competitive environment; the better the track record and performance of the division, and the higher the credibility of the division managers involved, the greater the aggregate investment in the division.

5. McNulty (1962) was one of the first to document the pressures felt by top management to meet the profit norm, and to avoid the extra risks associated with going above the norm.

6. These quarterly requests produce important unintended benefits. They provide what Gersick (1994: 40) calls "temporal pacing," which generates a predictably timed alternation of attention from "momentum" to "change" by creating opportunities for assessing progress, inventing adaptations to keep moving ahead, as well as providing a check against escalating commitments to failing courses of action.

7. Nohria and Gulati (1996) found an inverse U-shaped relationship between slack and innovation – both too much and too little slack hurt innovation. With too little slack there is no room for experimentation, but too much slack can lower the needed discipline over innovation projects.

8. Stopford and Baden-Fuller (1994) found that *learning capability* was one of the five key attributes shared by firms that had developed entrepreneurial capability. They state: "Corporations that go far in developing corporate entrepreneurship can be expected to make sustained *investments* in facilitating the learning environment" (emphasis in original, 1994: 524).

   Floyd and Woolridge (1999) argue that when failed initiatives provoke disapproving response by the senior managers, organizational members will be less likely to participate in related initiatives. Alternatively, if failed initiatives are viewed as important steps in the organizational learning process, employees are likely to remember routines, maintain the social contacts associated with the initiative, and develop new initiatives based on the earlier experience.

9. This attitude helped AMP to avoid a learning trap identified by Levinthal and March (1993) – "failure myopia," the tendency to overlook failures, which breeds overconfidence.

10. As Levinthal and March (1993: 105) point out, "Research on individual attributions of causality to events indicates that individuals are more likely to attribute their success to ability and their failures to luck than they are to attribute their successes to luck and their failures to ability (Miller and Ross, 1975)." It appears that Xerox management did what most individuals do, whereas the managers at AMP developed a set of shared beliefs that were counter to the normal human tendency to take credit for success and to blame luck or others for failure (also see de Charms, 1968; Rotter, 1966).

11. This is why it is important to keep separate the influence of the management culture and the influence of the structural context and management practices, and not lump the two together (see Note 1 for Part II: The management culture).

12. Sathe (1985a, 2000); Sathe and Davidson (2000); Schein (1985).

PART III: THE CORPORATE EXECUTIVES

7 THE BIGGER-IS-BETTER CORPORATE PHILOSOPHY

1. For example, Apple Computer invested hundreds of millions of dollars in the unsuccessful Newton PDA in the early 1990s in the hope of repeating the

company's huge success with the Macintosh computer in the mid-1980s. Burgelman and Grove (1996: 15–16) point out that "CEO John Sculley was clearly in front of his organization when he pushed the strategy of developing personal digital assistants (PDAs) and personally championed the Newton operating system. Sculley's strategic intent stretched beyond Apple's available innovative capabilities and the market's readiness."

2. In connection with the difficulties faced by Xerox Corporation in the late 1990s, Gary Pisano of Harvard Business School states: "You can't pursue small opportunities in big organizations" (*Business Week*, June 19, 2000: 221). But Paul Allaire, CEO of Xerox Corporation in the early 1990s, wanted this "win-win" formula: "We want the best of both worlds – the creativity of small units and the strategic vision of a big corporation" (Howard, 1992: 107). Also see Goold, Campbell, and Alexander (1994).

3. See Kotter (1982) and Lorange (1999).

4. Singh (1986) observed a negative direct relationship between performance and risk-taking in organizational decision-making. However, the indirect relationship, mediated by decentralization and organizational slack, was positive – suggesting the importance of both operating autonomy and slack resources for entrepreneurship and new business creation. Zajak, Golden, and Shortell (1991) found that slack resources and operating autonomy were positively associated with the innovativeness of internal corporate joint ventures (1991: 177 [Figure 1]).

5. Burgelman (1985) argues that corporate executives need to find ways to promote more autonomous strategic behavior – both the need for strategic adaptation to respond to global competition in a rapidly changing business environment and the need to retain entrepreneurial professional and managerial employees would seem to dictate this.

6. Ahead of his time, Dan Stewart was arguing for a real options approach (Amram and Kulatilaka, 1999; Luehrman, 1998; McGrath and MacMillan, 2000). However, discounted cash flow analysis was the only game in town at the time, and it hurt the OPET program.

7. In this case, Monsanto was clearly resource-driven rather than opportunity-driven (Stevenson and Gumpert, 1985; Stevenson and Jarillo, 1990).

8. Amabile (1998) argues that clearly specified strategic goals enhance creativity. Freedom could be mismanaged if managers change goals frequently or fail to define them clearly – employees may have "process freedom" without knowing where they are headed. Also see Judge, Fryxell, and Dooley (1997).

9. Day (1994) found that ventures that needed legitimacy (see Dougherty and Heller, 1994) and significant resource commitments were championed by corporate executives.

10. Judge, Fryxell, and Dooley (1997) found that too little operating autonomy hurt innovation. Also see Lorange (1999).

11. Teece (1987) has argued that entrepreneurs without authority cannot take the necessary leaps; their justifications before the fact will always turn out to be inadequate if choices are made by people who do not fully comprehend the proposals presented to them.

8 THE SMALL-IS-BEAUTIFUL CORPORATE PHILOSOPHY

1. Charan and Tichy (1998).
2. Based on years of experience with entrepreneurial management, Sykes and Block (1989) argue that the operating divisions must be the centers of corporate entrepreneurship.
3. As Rosner (1968) found, activity control hurts innovation, but controls designed to increase the visibility of consequences help innovation.
4. Amabile (1998) argues that people should be given freedom concerning the *process* but not necessarily about the *ends*.
5. Abell (1993) discusses the importance of a dual strategy for encouraging and managing both today's businesses and tomorrow's businesses.
6. Dougherty and Hardy (1996) urge senior managers to build innovative organizations by "increasing the strategic meaning of innovation" (1148), by making the activities of product innovation more meaningful to people throughout the organization. These authors also recommend actively and deliberately engaging in open strategic conversations around product innovation so that "processes can begin to link the right people and emphasize the right criteria, and resources can begin to flow to the right places" (1149). The "selected opportunity reviews" conducted by 3M, and similar *ad hoc* reviews at AMP, provided opportunities for increasing the strategic meaning of innovation as recommended by Dougherty and Hardy (1996).
7. This is "event-based pacing" which facilitates persistence and generates momentum, with the potential to gain the rewards of pursuing a course of action until the desired events indicate success (Gersick, 1994: 41).
8. Data from 2,994 independent entrepreneurs collected by Cooper, Woo, and Dunkelberg (1988) revealed unbounded optimism about their chances for success – 33 percent saw their odds for success as 10 in 10! Those who were poorly prepared and less likely to succeed were just as optimistic as those who were better prepared and more likely to succeed. The authors advised independent entrepreneurs to form relationships with board members and other professional outsiders who can be more objective in diagnosing problems and assessing the chances for success. The corporate executives at AMP and 3M played this role for their corporate entrepreneurs. Also see Shane and Venkataraman (2000: 223).
9. This is a case where autonomous strategic behavior (Burgelman, 1983a) forced the corporate top management to re-evaluate and clarify the corporate strategy – that AMP was a component company, not a systems company – rather than redefining it to include the new initiative.
     Burgelman (1996) argues that Intel's corporate top management's strategic capability allowed them to draw conclusions about what they were *not* (memory company) as well as what they were (microprocessor company). "One important manifestation of corporate capability is the company's ability to adapt without having to rely on extraordinary top management foresight" (1996: 208).
10. Such an approach is consistent with the recommendations of Burgelman (1984b: 158), because the division general manager in this book corresponds to a middle-level manager in his conceptual scheme:

There is a tendency for top management to rely on corporate staffs, consultants, and informal interactions with "peers" from other companies to make assessments of new business fields. Such information sources have merit, but they are no substitute for efforts to understand the deeper substantive issues involved in a specific proposal. The latter efforts should be based on requiring middle level managers to "educate" corporate management and to encourage middle level managers to "champion" new proposals based on their own substantive assessments. Such *substantive* interaction between different levels of management is likely to improve top management's capacity to make strategically sound assessments, making them rely less on purely quantitative projection [emphasis in original].

11. This is consistent with the argument of the "core competence" school of strategy (Hamel and Prahalad, 1994).
12. Schwartz (1973) found that the size of the attempted innovation was proportional to the size of the division.

9 NEW BUSINESS CREATION CHALLENGES FOR CORPORATE EXECUTIVES

1. Christensen (1997: 133) points out that small markets do not solve the growth needs of large companies. Regarding the widely held view that Apple Computer's pioneering Newton PDA was a failure, Christensen writes: "Apple sold 43,000 Apple II computers the first two years they were on the market (1977 and 1978) . . . Apple sold 140,000 Newtons in 1993 and 1994, its first two years on the market . . . [W]hile selling 43,000 units was viewed as an IPO-qualifying triumph in the smaller Apple of 1979, selling 140,000 Newtons was viewed as a failure in the giant Apple of 1994" (1997: 134–135). Porter (1996) provides an excellent discussion of the "growth trap."
2. Burgelman and Doz (2001) distinguish between "scope" (the extent to which pursuing a new business opportunity requires the collaboration of existing business units given the corporate strategy) and "reach" (the extent to which developing a new business opportunity requires changing the existing corporate strategy). They discuss the difficulties faced by reach-driven companies such as 3M in pursuing scope-driven strategic integration:

Strongly decentralized companies that traditionally have emphasized corporate entrepreneurship and organic diversification around core competencies tend to be reach-driven. Johnson & Johnson, 3M and Hewlett-Packard (before the arrival of CEO Carly Fiornia) are classic examples . . . Pursuing scope-driven integration often requires strong top-management intervention. That was the case at 3M and Johnson & Johnson during the early 1990s, when the CEOs sought to increase cross-business collaboration in their entrepreneurial, strategically fragmented companies (2001: 33).

Burgelman and Doz (2001) argue that top managers should be neither overly ambitious nor overly cautious and should strive for the maximum scope and reach, what they refer to as the "maximum strategic opportunity set," that is consistent with the realities of both internal and external constraints.

3. See Mintzberg (1994). Burgelman (1983b) has argued that this challenge can be addressed by recognizing that strategic planning is focused on opportunities that fall within the current concept of strategy; autonomous

strategic behavior and strategic context determination allow the corporation to pursue opportunities that fall outside the current strategy, leading to its retroactive redefinition.

4. Top managers need to develop what Burgelman and Doz (2001) call a "complex-strategic-integration" capability in order to address the related challenge of exploiting existing *and* new business opportunities simultaneously: "Developing a complex-strategic-integration capability involves two important challenges for executives: first, managing the evolving tension between reinforcing the company's core business and redirecting strategy; second, managing the sharing and transferring of resources among business units" (2001: 32).

   Based on the experience of energy giant British Petroleum (BP), Hansen and von Oetinger (2001: 108) discuss the need for what they call a "T-shaped" manager: "one who breaks out of the traditional corporate hierarchy to share knowledge freely across the organization (the horizontal part of the 'T') while remaining fiercely committed to individual business unit performance (the vertical part)."

5. Raynor and Bower (2001) argue that corporate executives of multi-divisional companies such as Sprint, WPP, Teradyne, and Viacom (which they studied) need to balance the competing demands of divisional autonomy in the present with divisional cooperation in the future in order to create strategic flexibility that enables the corporation to exploit opportunities that require cross-division collaboration. One way to do this is to impose strategic constraints on the division to insure that future integration with other divisions remains possible. Nevertheless, these authors emphasize the importance of granting the division a considerable degree of operating autonomy: "The use of strategic constraints should not be confused with routine intervention by the corporate office. To create strategic flexibility, divisions must still enjoy considerable operational autonomy and remain competitive as stand-alone businesses" (2001: 95).

6. Mintzberg (1994).

7. Ireland *et al.* (1987) found that managers' perceptions of a firm's strengths and weaknesses, and of environmental uncertainty, varied by managerial level. The implication is clear: the strategy formulation process must involve groups of managers from the top, middle, and bottom levels to incorporate and resolve differences in perception; the typical process involving managers one level at a time (top, then middle, then bottom, then back up to top) is inadequate.

8. As argued by Raynor and Bower (2001: 100), "Monthly or quarterly reviews of operations are necessary, but the focus of the executive meetings has to be the strategic opportunities that markets offer, regardless of divisional lines. In addition to formally scheduled meetings, corporate and division executives should have frequent conversations that are not cluttered up with operational issues." The case, "Sharp Corporation: Corporate Strategy" (Harvard Business School Case 9-793-064, 1994), provides one illustration of how this can work.

9. Christensen (1997) compared forecasted results with actual results for new disk drives during the first four years after commercial shipment. He obtained these data from *Disk/Trend Report* and aggregated the results for all companies in the industry to find that:

Over all, *Disk/Trend* has a remarkable track record in forecasting the future of established markets, but it has struggled to estimate accurately the size of new markets enabled by disruptive disk drive technology . . . its estimates were off by 265 percent for 5.25-inch drives, 35 percent for 3.5-inch drives (really quite close), and 550 percent for 1.8-inch drives. Notably, the 1.8-inch drive, the forecast of which *Disk/Trend* missed so badly, was the first generation of drives with a primarily non-computer market (1997: 149–150).

10. Christensen (1997: 147) states: "Markets that do not exist cannot be analyzed: Suppliers and customers must discover them together. Not only are the market applications for disruptive technologies *unknown* at the time of their development, they are *unknowable*" (emphasis in original).

Forecasting is also treacherous when the customer base is assured but the *customer's* products are targeted at an emerging market. This was the case with the RCA Disk Caddy initiative at Monsanto Fab Products – RCA's videodisk did not sell nearly as well as RCA had anticipated, and the Disk Caddy suffered as a result. Christensen (1997) provides a similar account of Hewlett-Packard's revolutionary 1.3-inch Kittyhawk disk drive for customers such as Motorola, IBM, Apple, Microsoft, and H-P itself, all of whom were targeting the PDA market which did not materialize as rapidly as had been forecast by these elite customers. H-P executives made the same mistake as their counterparts at Xerox of expecting accurate forecasts for an emerging new market.

11. Van de Ven *et al.* (1989) found that the fear of not obtaining start-up capital led new business entrepreneurs to commit themselves to a set of highly optimistic expectations by investors and corporate sponsors that were very difficult to meet. When these expectations were not met, the confidence of key sponsors and investors was shaken, resulting in external interventions that often misdirected the new venture.

12. Wender (1968) and Schein (1993) describe habits of avoidance learned from painful past experience that tend to persist well after the painful stimulus has been removed. What is most interesting, and of great practical significance, is that this *learned anxiety* remains "conserved" when it should have been "extinguished" over time after the removal of the painful stimulus.

13. Dutton and Jackson (1987) explain why organizations in the same industry respond differently to the same environmental events and trends. They argue that labeling an issue – as either a threat or an opportunity – affects both the motivations of key decision-makers and their subsequent information processing: "Specifically, the 'opportunity' category implies a *positive* situation in which *gain* is likely and over which one has a fair amount of *control*; in contrast, the 'threat' category implies a *negative* situation in which *loss* is likely and over which one has relatively *little* control" (emphasis in original, 1987: 80). Denison *et al.* (1996) found that global business experience, firm size, and perceived capability are significant predictors of the perception of threat or opportunity for organizations in the same industry. Sarasvathy, Simon, and Lave (1998) found that successful entrepreneurs see opportunity in situations where other people see risks.

Shane and Venkataraman (2000: 222) state: "Human beings all possess different stocks of information, and these stocks of information influence their ability to recognize particular opportunities . . . Even if the person possesses the prior information necessary to discover an opportunity, he or she may fail to do so because of an inability to see new means–ends relationships."

14. Christensen (1997) provides provocative evidence that unfamiliarity with an emerging new business can cause managers to view it as *more risky* than a familiar business (such as an existing business) even though the objective probability of success in the unfamiliar business may be *higher*: "the findings presented in Table 6.1 . . . showed a stunning difference in the posterior probabilities of success between firms that entered new, emerging value networks (37 percent) and those that entered existing value networks (6 percent)" (1997: 158). Christensen cites the research of Amos Tversky and Daniel Kahneman to explain this anomaly – people tend to regard propositions that they do not understand as more risky, regardless of their intrinsic risk, and propositions that they do understand as less risky, again without regard to intrinsic risk (1997: 162 n8).

15. Although IBM was not the first mover in personal computers, it did come from behind to set the PC standard that revolutionized the industry and made Apple irrelevant.

16. Elder (1989) critiques and compares two books, (1) *Blue Magic*, the story of the IBM PC, and (2) *Fumbling the Future*, the saga of the Xerox Alto computer – the predecessor of Xerox OPD's Star professional workstation – to reveal additional constraints and limitations faced by IBM and Xerox. IBM was in a good financial condition in 1980, and understood the threat of the personal computer to its core business; Xerox had other concerns in the mid-1970s (government antitrust investigations, emerging Japanese competition, and indigestion from the SDS acquisition) and did not see the personal computer as a threat to its core business, but rather as an opportunity. As Elder states, "there was no immediate danger to Xerox sales if the Alto was delayed or scrapped" (1989: 154). This is anecdotal evidence on how stimuli from the environment command more management attention if they are perceived as *threats* than if they are perceived as *opportunities*.

17. Nokia, a Finnish forest products company, entered the mobile phone business by assembling components purchased from different divisions of the global giant Philips Electronics. Nokia went on to become a world leader in mobile phones, while the Philips divisions fought turf battles about which division had the right to pursue the mobile phone opportunity for the company! (*Source*: Personal interviews with several Philips corporate executives.)

18. This is contrary to the advice of Goold, Campbell, and Alexander (1994), who recommend getting out of businesses that the parent cannot add value to.

19. Csikszentmihalyi (1996).

20. Khurana (2002) examines the the myth of the "savior CEO" and its dysfunctional consequences.

21. Subramanian (1998) found that migrating executives transmit knowledge from one organization to another. Executive migration helps new product

development by bringing new skills, new knowledge, and relevant industry experience. Young, Charns, and Shortell (2001) found that top management migration led to the diffusion of innovation – directors who had prior exposure to total quality management (TQM) were inclined to adopt this innovation at hospitals they joined.

10   GUIDANCE AND COACHING BY THE DGM'S BOSS AND SUPPORT AND CHALLENGE BY THE CONTROLLERS

1. Sathe (1982).
2. An education and training program for the development of strong controllers is outlined in Sathe (1982: 145–146).

PART IV: THE DIVISION GENERAL MANAGER

1. MacMillan (1987) compares the behaviors of CEOs of major divisions of corporations – DGMs in this book – five of whom were successful at new business development versus four who were unsuccessful. Several of the findings in this book corroborate MacMillan's findings and recommendations: forge a venturesome culture by insisting that the entire division pursue new business (1987: 440); no specific extrinsic rewards for new business creation (442); sustain the commitment for a long, long time (443); expand from the existing competence base (445); build momentum (446); the need for discipline (446–448); the management of failure (449–450); and shoot the wounded (450).

11   THE DGM'S PERSONAL ASSETS

1. The first three comparisons – extroverted versus introverted, intuitive versus sensing, and thinking versus feeling – are based on the DGM's self-reports using the Myers–Briggs Personality Type Indicator (Myers, 1976).
2. Assertive Self-Confidence was measured by the Public Image Factor Scale (Kahn *et al.*, 1964: Appendix G). Ratings were obtained by averaging the scores for each DGM as reported by the "common subordinates" (those who worked directly for DGM 1 and later also for DGM 2). As Shane and Venkataraman (2000: 223–224) point out, "Researchers have argued that people with greater self-efficacy and more internal locus of control are more likely to exploit opportunities, because exploitation requires people to act in the face of skepticism of others."
3. Need for security was measured via the Self-Description Inventory (Ghiselli, 1966). Hanan (1976b) mentions low need for security as one of the characteristics of entrepreneurs.
4. MacMillan, Block, and Narasimha (1986) found that experience in venturing resulted in improvement in venturing performance, but only after several venture attempts. Woo, Daellenbach, and Nicholls-Nixon (1994: 510–512) also indicate that the entrepreneur's past experience influences

venture performance. As Shane and Venkataraman (2000: 223) point out, "the transferability of information from prior experience to the opportunity (Cooper, Woo, and Dunkelberg 1989), as well as prior entrepreneurial experience (Carroll and Mosakowski, 1987), increases the probability of exploitation of entrepreneurial opportunity because learning reduces its cost."

5. Shane (1994a) found that individuals with championing experience prefer champions who violate the organizational hierarchy to develop an innovation.

6. On the basis of research on creativity in scientists, Simon (1986) examines the implications for *managerial* creativity. To become a world-class expert (e.g. a chess grandmaster) requires at least ten years of immersion and 50,000 "chunks" of knowledge. It follows that depth of knowledge – about the industry, the company, and the business – as well as about human behavior in organizations, and about how organizations operate, are critically important for managerial creativity (1986: 15).

Sykes (1985, 1986) found that the level of the venture managers' prior experience in the venture's target market area, and the level of prior general managerial experience, showed a strong positive correlation with financial success. Sharma (1999) found that good judgment about the feasibility of a new technology, and the readiness of the market, only comes with years of experience in the business.

7. Sathe (1985a), Chapter 8.

8. Sathe (1985a), Chapter 10.

12 THE DGM'S MOTIVATION AND STRATEGY FOR NEW BUSINESS CREATION

1. Day (1994) defines product champions as those who provide impetus and advocacy for the venture, and organizational sponsors as those who give it resources and legitimacy. When top managers become both product champions and organizational sponsors, she refers to them as "dual-role champions" (1994: 153). The information and power asymmetries that occur when product champions are at one organizational level and their organizational sponsors are at another level (Schon, 1963) are avoided in the case of dual-role champions. Day (1994: 148) defines the "principal champion" as the one whose involvement is viewed as the most crucial in the transformation from concept to commercial business.

2. Schein (1978).

3. In a study of all major Hollywood studio heads between 1936 and 1965, Miller and Shamsie (2001) argue that performance first increases due to increased learning and then decreases as executives become stale: "an increasing rigidity and overconfidence commits them to archaic product lines" (2001: 727). This is consistent with the evidence on Buddy March. The performance of 3M Micrographics increased during the first ten years of his tenure, and then leveled off, primarily because March continued steadfastly to support the "archaic" Com program as it lost $55 million over eighteen years.

4. Christensen (1997) found that such hybrid products created by the marriage of sustaining and disruptive technologies rarely succeed in the end; products

based on the disruptive technology eventually win out. Examples of hybrid products that lost the race are the Hydrohoe excavator, combining the traditional cable technology with the new hydraulics technology, and trans-oceanic steamships outfitted with sails, combining the traditional wind technology with new steam technology (Christensen 1997: 68).

5. Utterback (1994: 160–161) writes about the technological developments in the typewriter business:

> When the next wave of innovation hit that industry – electrics – it was not one of the giants of the typewriter business that pioneered its development or growth. It was the outsider, IBM. Still later, when computer technology moved into the document-processing business, the innovating came from unknown hardware companies, such as Wang, Apple and Tandy, and dozens of software firms. IBM would eventually acquire its share of the hardware business, but as a follower, not as a technical leader... One is tempted to say that *because* of their [incumbent's] great investments in the established forms of the business, they were impeded from making the industry-altering innovations" (emphasis in original).

6. Such orders-of-magnitude improvements in certain performance characteristics are typical of disruptive technologies (Christensen, 1997).

7. As CEO Percy Barnevik of ABB observed,

> Companies readily talk about their strategies but are not as likely to reveal the true inner workings of their operations. Developing and articulating a strategy is often more intellectually exciting than doing the daily, repetitive work of making a company and its employees function better. When asked to explain the reason for a successful endeavor, I often disappoint the questioner by admitting that it can be attributed to no spectacular, hidden strategy but to the execution... When I am asked how I split my time between strategy formulation and execution, I answer 10 percent and 90 percent, respectively (Barnevik, 1994: xii).

Also see Klein and Sorra (1996).

8. According to Elder (1989), Xerox OPD's Star computer workstation was seen as strategically significant. But it was designed without direct knowledge of customer needs and the competitive environment, and collaboration with marketing was also lacking.

9. Contrary to Greg Gibbons' belief, Christensen (1997: 159) has pointed out that the initial strategy for successful new business initiatives is typically *wrong*:

> Research has shown, in fact, that the vast majority of successful new business ventures abandoned their original business strategies when they began implementing their initial plans and learned what would and would not work in the market... Guessing the right strategy at the outset isn't nearly as important to success as conserving enough resources (or having the trusting relationships with trusting backers or investors) so that the new business initiatives get a second or third stab at getting it right. Those that run out of resources or credibility before they can iterate toward a viable strategy are the ones that fail.

13 BUILDING CORPORATE SUPPORT FOR NEW BUSINESS CREATION

1. When the new initiative falls outside the current corporate strategy, the DGM has to persuade corporate executives to redefine the corporate strategy so as to accommodate the new initiative. This is what Burgelman (1983a) called "strategic context determination."

2. The use of symbols and language to portray the corporate bureaucracy as the enemy may have helped to galvanize the troops within OPD (Aronson, 1976), but it undercut corporate support for the division.

3. Kanter (1983: 216) states: "What it takes to get the innovative organization up and running is essentially the same two things that all vehicles need: a person in the driver's seat and a source of power."

4. Dougherty and Hardy (1996) found that product innovation took place because of individual initiative and skill, as well as personal networks and power.

5. Sharma (1999) argues that the main impediment to successful innovation in large firms is not so much the bureaucracy, but the lack of experience and judgment at reconciling new ideas in the context of pre-existing corporate interests.

6. Citing the economist Schumpeter's emphasis in his early work on the role of independent entrepreneurs in seizing opportunities to innovate, Utterback (1994: 193) states:

   In later years (1942) Schumpeter began to place greater stress on the role of larger enterprises in innovation, seeming to believe that as scientific knowledge accumulated there was a threshold investment in R&D below which a firm could not be an effective player. I have always been troubled by this conflict in Schumpeter's views. The present analysis suggests that the former hypothesis is true for areas of emerging product technology . . . while the latter hypothesis might well hold for process innovation, for many nonassembled products, and for firms producing standard products and large systems.

7. As Van de Ven (1986: 604) concludes,

   Thus, a key measure of innovation success or outcome is the currency of the idea, and a basic research question is how and why do some new ideas gain good currency while the majority do not? Based on the work of Schon (1971), Quinn (1980) and others, we believe the answer requires longitudinal study of the social and political processes by which people become invested in or attached to new ideas and push them into good currency.

8. Mike Walker of AMP Sigcom pulled the Fiber Optics and the Transmission Cable programs into his division using this tactic. Dan Stewart of Monsanto Fab Products tried to bring the Fomecor business into the division using the same tactic after he took over as DGM, but president Jim Reilly would not give it to him because he did not want to reverse a decision he had just made – Reilly gave the Fomecor business to Stewart two years later. These are attempts by DGMs at "strategy building" (Burgelman, 1983a; 1988: 80).

9. The *modus operandi* described in this section appears to be consistent with all three modes of legitimization discovered by Dougherty and Heller (1994).

10. Sharma (1999) found that all firms struggled with this dilemma – make a new product available in small quantities in order to minimize the financial risk or in large quantities to maximize the payoff from market success? The dilemma can be addressed by viewing investments in new business initiatives as part of a strategic portfolio of real options (Amram and Kulatilaka, 1999; Luehrman, 1998; McGrath and MacMillan, 2000). In this case, Monsanto VP Alf Hummel did not think the OPET option was worth buying.

11. This is the essence of viewing strategy for new business creation as a portfolio of real options (see Amram and Kulatilaka, 1999; Luehrman, 1998; McGrath and MacMillan, 2000).

14 LEADING THE DIVISION FOR NEW BUSINESS CREATION

1. In his book review of *Entrepreneurship as Strategy* (Meyer and Heppard, 2000), Michael (2001: 133) writes:

   The unifying theme of the book is to uncover, for firms large and small, the components of an entrepreneurial dominant logic ... two components emerge across the chapters. The first involves a focus on the development of the dynamic core competency of inventing new products faster or better than others [the subject of the next chapter] ... The second component involves development of structures to support this competency. Information regarding market opportunities cannot be centralized and communicated at the necessary speed to top management. Therefore employees at all levels must be empowered to act ... Such empowerment requires a complex combination of freedom, rules, and vision, created by top management and transmitted down through the ranks. Managers must unite employees through a common vision of aggressively seeking new opportunities.

2. In his review of *Entrepreneurship as Strategy*, Michael (2001: 134) writes that the authors "describe the role of top managers in entrepreneurial management as setting a strategic vision for both content and process. Managers should monitor less and instead help develop individuals' skills and provide those individuals opportunities to use these skills." Schuler (1986) describes human resource practices for fostering and facilitating corporate entrepreneurship.

3. These comments are consistent with Drucker (1954) and Ellsworth (2002) on business purpose.

4. Amabile (1998) argues that a good match between employee abilities and the job is required because appropriate expertise and skills ignite creative thinking. To achieve such a match, managers need rich and detailed information about their employees. Good matches are rarely made because such information is difficult and time-consuming to gather.

PART V: THE DIVISION AND ITS TOP MANAGEMENT TEAM

1. Hambrick and Mason (1984) argue that the top management team is crucial to the success and sustainability of the organization. Tushman and O'Reilly

(1997) discuss the vital role of the executive team in creating ambidextrous organizations that can manage both incremental and radical innovation. Also see Alderson (1993); Eisenhardt, Kahwajy, and Bourgois (1997); Hambrick (1987, 1995); Katzenbach (1997, 1998); Nadler, Spencer, and Associates (1998).

15 THE IDENTIFICATION AND PURSUIT OF NEW BUSINESS OPPORTUNITIES

1. Drucker (1985a, 1985b) identifies and discusses seven sources of innovation (areas of opportunity). Three of these are within the company: unexpected occurrences; incongruities; and process needs. Four are from outside the company: industry and market changes; demographic changes; changes in perception; and new knowledge.

   Krueger and Brazeal (1994) argue that "self-efficacy" (the perceived ability to execute entrepreneurial action) is a good predictor of opportunity recognition (1994: 94, 102). This has important implications for practice because perceptions can change with experience and training, i.e. entrepreneurs are not "born" but "made."

   O'Connor and Rice (2001) examine how new-to-the-world innovations are triggered through opportunity recognition: "the individuals in positions to see opportunities aren't always as motivated as the champion literature would lead us to believe" (109); "the literature has not identified those who recognized opportunities but elected *not* to champion them, which is something we identify in this work" (emphasis in original, 116 n30). O'Connor and Rice (2001) present a set of approaches for improving opportunity recognition capabilities. Several mechanisms that senior management can use to encourage radical innovation are identified.

2. Block and MacMillan (1993) emphasize the importance of market research. Without it, investments are based on assumptions that might prove totally wrong.

3. Christensen (1997: 161–162) argues the need for "agnostic marketing" in these cases:

   Such discoveries often come by watching how people use products, rather than by listening to what they say. I have come to call this approach to discovering the emerging markets for disruptive technologies *agnostic marketing*, by which I mean marketing under the explicit assumption that *no one* – not us, not our customers – can know whether, how, or in what quantities a disruptive product can or will be used before they have experience using it (emphasis in original).

4. Several authors have pointed out that sufficient time, money, information, and other resources must be available to permit the exploration and learning necessary for new business creation (Hisrich and Peters, 1986; Kanter, 1982; Kuratko, Montagno, and Hornsby, 1990). Amabile (1998) argues that managers often keep resources tight, which pushes people to channel their creativity into finding resources but not into developing new products or services.

5. Maintaining good communication with external constituents, especially customers, facilitates the flow of information and other resources that are critical

for new business creation (Barringer and Bluedorn, 1999; Fiol, 1996; Hornsby *et al.*, 1993; Kanter, 1982; Lumpkin and Dess, 1996; von Hipple, 1988; Zahra, 1991). See Christensen (1997) and Utterback (1994) on the danger of allowing the customer to dictate innovation.

6. Christensen (1997) found that the customer's most important buying criterion must be satisfied before the customer will consider the differentiating advantages offered by a new product (see, especially, his Chapter 8, on the evolving basis of competition).

7. Quinn (2000) recommends outsourcing any part of the firm's innovation chain – research and development, new product development, testing and production, or distribution – that is not essential for maintaining and further developing the firm's core competence.

8. Based on twenty-nine years of innovation experience at General Electric Company, Steele (1983) describes eight common misconceptions concerning technology. Misconception 7 is that discipline and control hurt innovation. Also see Drucker (1985a, 1985b).

   Block (1982) argues that new business losses can be held to affordable levels if the existing business planning methods are replaced with event milestones which test the basic assumptions of the new venture. Block and MacMillan (1985) describe ten such milestones for new business – including concept and product testing, first financials, market testing, production start-up, and analysis of competitive reactions.

9. In the conceptualization of Gersick (1994), this is "event-based pacing" which facilitates persistence and generates momentum, with the potential to gain the rewards of pursuing a course of action until the desired events indicate success (1994: 41). The "*ad hoc* reviews" (Chapter 8 in this book) and the "technical audits" (described later in this chapter) also generate event-based pacing. On the other hand, the periodic corporate reviews (Chapter 8) and the calls for "quarterly giving" (Chapter 6) represent temporal pacing (Gersick, 1994: 40) which provides an opportunity for reorientation and change, as well as a check against escalating commitments to failing courses of action. Thus, these management practices enabled the top managers of 3M and AMP to regulate the balance between continuity/momentum and reorientation/change.

10. The use of "boundaryless" cross-functional new product development teams with good market input from both customers and non-customers helps to create robust product designs that do not need to be reworked in later stages of development after substantial resources have been expended in development and production. In general, shifting the relative allocation of time, effort, and resources toward the *early* phases of new product development reduces the overall cost and development time – which translates to increased cumulative profit for the new product.

11. Schrage (2000) describes how companies model, prototype, and simulate to innovate. Thomke (2001: 68) argues the benefits of a system for experimentation: "All development organizations have such a system in place to help them narrow the number of ideas to pursue and then refine that group into what can become viable products. A critical stage of the process occurs when

an idea or concept becomes a working artifact or prototype, which can then be tested, discussed, shown to customers, and learned from." Thomke (2001: 73) reports that Toyota strives to solve at least 80 percent of all design-related problems before the first prototypes are made.

12. Sharma (1999) argues that firms must develop an ability to distinguish the productive seeds from the weeds among the ideas and proposals. Two approaches for doing this are identified: (1) Experiment and Explore – giving autonomy and discretion for individuals to maximize the chances of generating new ideas, and (2) Discipline and Streamline – new ideas are gradually developed and are held to strict outcome criteria at predetermined stages.

13. Thomke (2001: 74–75) provides data on survival rates in the pharmaceutical industry: "Typically, for each successful drug that makes it to market, a company investigates roughly 10,000 starting candidates. Of those, only 1,000 compounds make it to more extensive trials in vitro (that is, outside the living organisms in settings such as test tubes), 20 of which are tested even more extensively in vivo (that is, in the body of a living organism such as a mouse), and 10 of which make it to clinical trials with humans."

14. As eloquently put by Van de Ven (1986: 600–601), "the management of innovation must also be the management of termination, and of transitioning people, programs, and investments from commitments in the past toward the future. In common social life, funerals and wakes are used to commemorate and bereave the passing of loved ones and to make graceful transitions into the future."

15. Raychem's CEO Paul Cook has pointed out that management must show genuine curiosity about what's happening in the labs. People need both pressure and encouragement to put a brilliant idea into practice. Cook maintained pressure by an extensive personal involvement that he calls "management by calling about." He personally reviewed and supported new ideas and product plans (Taylor, 1990).

16 OTHER NEW BUSINESS CREATION CHALLENGES FOR THE DIVISION

1. Slevin and Covin (1990) make an analogous distinction between entrepreneurial and pseudo-entrepreneurial firms.

2. Amabile (1998) points out that managers often fail to hire creative people because they focus on technical expertise and ignore creativity and intrinsic motivation. Block (1982) argues that if a company promotes compatible individuals, it may lose the innovators; the company must accommodate "boat rockers" to promote innovation.

3. Kirton (1980) argues that adapters (Reilly's "retreads") tend to operate cognitively within the confines of the consensually accepted paradigm; innovators are more likely to treat the paradigm as part of the problem to be solved.

4. Burgelman (1983c: 1361–1362) observes: "entrepreneurial initiative is abundant, and the level of corporate entrepreneurial activity is a function of demand rather than supply for it ... Corporate management thus need not encourage entrepreneurship; it need only make sure not to suppress it. In

fact, 'encouraging' entrepreneurship may create games and lead to misguided opportunism." Also see Peterson (1981).

5. Block (1982) points out that the entrepreneur and his team must avoid two common traps: (1) a venture fails if the venture's managerial needs outgrow the entrepreneur's capabilities; and (2) failure can result because the venture team does not have the necessary mix of disciplines, which could lead to the classic problem of technical success and market failure.

   David (1994) observed three modes of venturing: (1) the R&D phase was followed by a venture manager, but there was no entrepreneur; (2) there was an entrepreneur who became the venture manager; and (3) the entrepreneur and the venture manager were different people. Success rates were highest in the second category, moderate in the third, and least in the first. This suggests the importance of intrapreneurs who see the venture through to completion.

6. Van de Ven et al. (1989) found that business plans were used as a tool to obtain resource commitments from corporate sponsors, rather than to develop realistic alternative scenarios. The entrepreneurs acknowledged that parts of their business plans were overly optimistic, but they did not propose a more realistic timetable for fear of losing funding.

   Discovery-driven planning (McGrath and MacMillan, 2000), which calls for managers to identify and test the assumptions and aspirations on which their business plans are based, is a useful planning approach for new business creation.

7. Dougherty and Hardy (1996: 1148) cite Jelinek and Schoonhoven (1990) as showing that "manufacturing can emphasize both cost efficiency and product innovation if manufacturing managers are rewarded properly and given the resources needed to work out the complex interfaces; for example, they need money to fund pilot lines and enough staff to oversee the connections between old and new products."

8. There is a large academic literature on this subject. See Nohria and Gulati (1996).

9. To overcome the negative consequences of downsizing on product innovation, Dougherty and Bowman (1995) argue that managers should support innovation sponsors and champions, retain old-timers who are part of the key network, bolster the network by building more connections between departments, and between new and established businesses, and incorporate innovation directly into the firm's strategy.

17 THE DIVISION'S ORGANIZATION, COMPETENCE, AND
COLLABORATION FOR NEW BUSINESS CREATION

1. Based on the experience of Du Pont, Peterson (1967) highlights the advantages of the BU organization – singleness of purpose, simplicity of communication, and direct accountability.

2. Van de Ven (1986: 599) argues that the concept of a hologram as proposed by Gareth Morgan (1983) is the appropriate metaphor for designing an organization for innovation: "the brain, with its incredible complexity, manages that complexity by placing the essential elements of the whole into each of its

parts – it is a hologram . . . the hologram metaphor emphasizes that organization design for innovation is not a discrete event but a process integrating all
the essential functions, organizational units, and resources needed to manage
the innovation from beginning to end."

3. Others have argued this position, particularly in terms of being able to move
   quickly against the market (Drucker, 1985a; Hamel, 1999).

4. Child (1977) maintains that when human diseconomies of scale are factored
   in, diminishing returns occur with increasing size much earlier than predicted
   by traditional economic analysis.

5. Hamel and Prahalad (1994) refer to this difficulty as "the tyranny of the SBU"
   and call for the SBU's demise. However, Leonard-Barton (1995: 17) argues
   that core capabilities can be usefully conceived at the division or business
   unit level, and cites Johnson & Johnson and Hewlett-Packard as examples.
   Sharma (1999) found that all firms struggled with the dilemma of whether
   the new venture should build its own capabilities or share the capabilities
   already existing in the company.

6. Block (1982) indicates that two problems arise if new ventures are not separated from mature businesses: (1) destructive conflict occurs between the
   formal needs and policies of the established firm and the needs of new ventures; and (2) new ventures are misdirected because of the imposition of
   irrelevant and often damaging corporate management practices. Hisrich and
   Peters (1986) also point to the importance of such separation. Strebel (1987)
   argues that successful organization for innovation requires decoupling from
   the mainstream organization. Foster (1986: 210) favors a separate organization for radical innovation: "the attacking and defending ought to be done by
   separate organizations." Also see Galbraith (1982); Drucker (1985a).

7. It is interesting to note that this strategy for Astroturf was fifteen to twenty
   years ahead of its time. The new and improved Astroturf and its competitors
   are now finally finding their way into high-school football stadiums and city
   parks. Dan Stewart could therefore say to Ian McVay, "Never say never!" But
   injuries to athletes who play on artificial turf versus natural grass remain a
   concern. ("Fake grass is always greener, cheaper, but it's harder, too," *Wall
   Street Journal*, June 24, 2002: B1–B4).

8. As Burgelman and Sayles (1986) observed, a new venture's access to the market was generally controlled by a salesperson representing the firm's established product lines. This can lead the firm to develop new products desired
   by these customers (although this is by no means assured, as the case of the
   OPET bottle at Monsanto Fab Products illustrates). But such a salesperson
   was unable to identify new applications for new technology. Also see Christensen (1997).

9. Leonard-Barton (1995: 20) coined the term "T-shaped skills" to emphasize
   the importance of both depth and breadth of skills – the stem of the "T"
   denotes depth of skills; the crossbar of the "T" denotes the breadth needed
   to interface with other skills. Also see Hansen and von Oetinger (2001).

10. Burgelman (1988: 84) argues that such capabilities evolve over a long period
    via careful selection and nurturing. Leonard-Barton (1995: 4) distinguishes
    between supplemental capabilities (which add value but can be imitated),

enabling capabilities (which are necessary but not sufficient for competitive advantage, e.g. world-class quality), and core capabilities (sources of competitive advantage, built up over time, which are hard to imitate), and argues that *activities* – not goals or rewards or even skills (until they are activated) – create the firm's capabilities. She examines how the activities pursued in the course of developing new products and processes build on, and further develop, the firm's core technological capabilities (1995: 8–9). Eisenhardt and Martin (2000) define "dynamic capabilities" as a set of specific and identifiable processes, such as product development.

Utterback (1994: 223) summarizes forcefully:

we can see that the idea of developing and balancing core competences as the key to success seems more credible than any number of current management philosophies and fashions ... In summary, the most important change of all would seem to lie in top management's renewed appreciation of the people who build and sustain their firms and in their ability to learn and to adapt to changing and challenging circumstances.

11. Leonard-Barton (1995: 30) found that core rigidities result when the activities that create core capabilities (1995: 19 [Figure 1.3]) are not well managed. One of the pathologies leading to core rigidities is insularity, bred by arrogance and defensiveness at the top. She points out (1995: 41–44) that core rigidities are most dangerous when the company is on the brink of a technological discontinuity, and provides examples of how Apple, GM, DEC, IBM, Kodak, NCR, Sears, and Westinghouse stumbled.

Dougherty (1995) compares successful and failed new product ventures in four large firms and finds that success requires a link between the venture and competence – which is difficult to achieve because of core incompetencies – and discusses how to break out of this bind.

Galunic and Rodan (1998) argue that competences may become institutionalized and less susceptible to alteration because they transform into social values beyond their usefulness. When personal identities are strongly associated with a competency area, the probability to resource re-combinations, and thus possible innovation, will be diminished.

12. The question of how narrowly or broadly a firm should build its core competences is addressed by Utterback (1994: 221): "Like other living organisms, the firm that becomes too highly specialized – too keenly adapted to the peculiarities of its environment of technologies, production processes, and markets – is in danger of extinction if that environment changes even slightly."

13. Christensen (1997: 209) supports Joe Hurley's view:

the capabilities of most organizations are far more specialized and context-specific than most managers are inclined to believe ... organizations have capabilities to take certain new technologies into certain new markets. They have disabilities in taking technology to market in other ways. Organizations have the capability to tolerate failure along some dimensions, and an incapacity to tolerate other types of failure.

14. One of the most common syndromes in new product development is *firefighting*, an unplanned allocation of resources to fix problems discovered late in

the product's development cycle (Repenning, Goncalves, and Black, 2001). These authors offer two recommendations for developing the capability to avoid firefighting: (1) manage resources *across* as well as *within* projects; and (2) cancel projects with inadequate concepts before they reach the design phase. 3M Micrographics did both and avoided firefighting.

15. In their study of the process by which Canon created the personal copier, Nonaka and Yamanouchi (1989) argue that the self-renewal of the firm is stimulated by deliberately creating a climate of turbulence and creative conflict within the organization. This fosters dynamic cooperation between different divisions and task forces, leading to a restructuring of knowledge (1989: 313 [Figure 3]). Nemeth (1997) also argues that organizations can limit complacency and fuel innovation by creating healthy conflict.

16. Mone, McKinley, and Barker (1998) found that innovation is relatively rare in organizations because it requires coordination across organizational subunits, and implementation of innovative products may be resisted by those who perceive they will lose power or resources as a result.

17. Suggestions for resolving cross-silo conflict and achieving collaboration include: change the culture (Kanter, 1983); institutionalize innovation by tying it systematically to every unit's performance and evaluation (Jelinek, 1979); and use heavyweight product managers (Clark and Fujimoto, 1991a, 1991b).

18. A long line of research has found that more flexible and organic structures, characterized by open communication, lateral relations, less hierarchy and bureaucracy, and broader roles and responsibilities, all facilitate innovation and new business creation (e.g. Burns and Stalker, 1961; Hornsby *et al.*, 1993; Kanter, 1982; Kuratko, Montagno, and Hornsby, 1990; Lawrence and Lorsch, 1967; MacMillan, Block, and Narasimha, 1986; Miller and Friesen, 1983; Slevin and Covin, 1990).

As Burgelman (1984b: 159) argued, "Often, internal entrepreneurs will weave together pieces of technology and knowledge which exist in separate parts of the organization and which would otherwise remain unused." Shane (1994b) found that champions establish informal communication channels to promote innovation. West and Meyer (1998) observed that a flatter organization structure is not sufficient to foster entrepreneurship in established firms; good organizational communication is needed to enhance the production of new ideas.

Hoopes and Postrel (1999) define a "glitch" as a costly error that occurs only because knowledge is not shared within the firm; they demonstrate that shared knowledge is an important source of integration for superior product development performance.

Nonaka and Takeuchi (1995) emphasize the importance of both *explicit* knowledge that can be codified in the form of drawings, writings, or formulae, and *tacit* knowledge, the know-how embedded in employees' hunches, ideals, and skills. Open communication and collaboration are needed to share tacit knowledge.

19. Kanter (1982) describes the characteristics of an organization that supports creativity – frequent and smooth cross-functional contact and a tradition of working in teams and sharing credit widely. Amabile (1998) argues that managers must recognize creative work by teams and support creativity by

serving as role models, persevering through tough problems, and encouraging collaboration and communication. Also see Leavitt and Lipman-Blumen (1995) on "hot groups" and Katzenbach and Smith (1993) on the qualities that differentiate performing teams from other working groups.

20. Jassawalla and Sashittal (2000: 35) make the following observation regarding leadership for new product development (NPD): "simple knowledge of what leaders *ought* to do does not produce an effective team leader. The transformation in team leaders' thinking, learning and doing – and the similar transformation they affect [*sic*] within their teams – lies at the root of effective leadership, effective teamwork, and accelerated NPD processes" (emphasis in original). Jassawalla and Sashittal provide specific examples of the actions team leaders need to take to transform themselves and their teams (2000: 37 [Table 1]). The "knowing–doing gap" (Pfeffer and Sutton, 1999, 2000) created when managers substitute "smart-talk" for action can thus be avoided.

18   THE EFFECTIVENESS OF THE DIVISION'S TOP MANAGEMENT TEAM

1. Hambrick (1987) and Finkelstein and Hambrick (1996) have argued that the top management team is a key to the firm's success. Hambrick (1995) found that the most serious problem that CEOs have with their TMT is fragmentation – the situation in which team members pursue their own agendas with a minimum of communication and collaboration. He argues that this may work in a stable environment but is maladaptive in a changing environment.

2. Hitt *et al.* (1999) indicate that elements of team context, such as top management team support, have a more significant influence on the success of cross-functional teams engaged in the development of new products than internal team characteristics.

   Jassawalla and Sashittal (2000: 45) found that effective team leaders "overcome what the literature uniformly regards as the principal challenge of product innovation – namely, the challenge of fostering inter-functional collaboration and the common vision among diverse participants – largely because they are set up to succeed by senior management."

   Hisrich and Peters (1986) noted several important ways in which top managers supported entrepreneurial activity: by supporting proposals, helping to resolve conflicts, providing direct budget allocations in terms of funds and staff on a long-term basis (10–12 years), and providing indirect budget allocation to ensure that other departments commit resources.

3. Cyert and March (1963) view unresolved conflict as the inevitable outcome of political activity by organizational participants. Alderson (1993) presents some empirical data on how top management processes (e.g. degree of openness versus sensitive issues not discussed) impacts performance.

4. Eisenhardt, Kahwajy, and Bourgois (1997) argue that insistence on consensus can lead to endless haggling.

5. Burgelman found that Intel's ability to exit the memory business without having to rely on "extraordinary foresight" by top executives is explained in part by the tradition of open debate that allowed Intel managers to speak freely (1996: 205).

West and Meyer (1998) argue the importance of idea diversity within the top management team. Nemeth (1997) points out that cohesion and loyalty support implementation of an idea but do not stimulate idea generation. Openness and welcoming of dissent stimulate creativity. The "trick" is to balance coordinated group activity with an openness to differing views – to create unity in the organization without uniformity.

Dooley and Fryxell (1999) found that greater levels of dissent improved both decision quality (strategy conception) and decision commitment (strategy implementation) when team members' competence and loyalty were perceived to be high – but greater dissent *decreased* decision quality and commitment when competence and loyalty were perceived to be low.

6. Bowman (1999) argues that ventures die for one of two reasons – natural causes or lack of entrepreneurial insight. His examples of the latter are the belief that the venture has unique order-winning value when it does not, or the failure to recognize that the causes of past success may not deliver current advantage. Rather than learning from setbacks, others (competitors, customers, sales people, employees, etc.) are blamed instead for the decline of the venture.

   Guth and MacMillan (1986) found that one reason for poor implementation is the lack of buy-in by middle managers. These authors offer two specific recommendations for general managers (GMs) if their middle managers do not believe in the strategy being pursued: (1) commit to listening to what middle managers have to say. Can the GM restate middle management's concerns? Can middle managers restate the GM's position?; and (2) insist on full identification of the risks associated with the strategy being resisted.

7. Kets de Vries (1985) describes the "dark side" of several entrepreneurs he studied – their need for control, sense of distrust, desire for applause, and other pathologies – that ruined their ventures and harmed their organizations. Shane (1994b) found that the influence of champions was not always beneficial. They could abuse their power, fail to follow up on their initiatives, or actually hurt the innovation process.

8. Greg Gibbons' bold vision for office automation has a perfect parallel in the bold vision for electronic distribution of entertainment that turned out to be so disastrous for media companies at the time of this writing:

   Enthralled by the possibilities posed by the Internet, brash, young executives rose to the top promising to transform their organizations. At AOL Time Warner Inc., Vivendi Universal SA, and Bertelsmann, the young guard figured the Web would revolutionize the distribution of music, books and movies and enlarge the market for entertainment products ... [they] may yet be proven correct about the impact of digital technologies. But their refusal to rein in their visions and pocketbooks in the face of market reality gave them formidable trouble (*Wall Street Journal*, July 29, 2002: A1, A10).

   The young guard resigned, or were reassigned, and the media companies retrenched to their traditional businesses – no different than what happened at Xerox about twenty years earlier.

9. In a conceptual piece that attempts to link the strategic management and entrepreneurship literatures, Sandberg (1992) argues that not much research attention has been paid to top management conflict and its resolution.

Stopford and Baden-Fuller (1994: 529–530) found that "Inertia and lack of teamwork at the top were common obstacles to progress ... Sustainable progress did not start until the top team was committed to a common direction and was prepared to undergo the pain of reexamining their fundamental values."

Eisenhardt, Kahwajy, and Bourgois (1997) stress the importance of healthy conflict within the top management team. It leads to a better understanding of available options, creates a broader range of choices, and helps to make effective decisions. Unfortunately, healthy conflict can turn unproductive because it can degenerate into dysfunctional interpersonal conflict and destroy members' ability to work as a team. Also see Katzenbach (1997); Reich (1987).

10. Knight *et al.* (1999) found that greater demographic diversity within the TMT made the achievement of strategic consensus more difficult. However, TMTs that avoided emotional or person-oriented interpersonal conflict (versus task-oriented interpersonal conflict), and TMTs that worked together to reach agreement, achieved greater strategic consensus.

11. Ware and Barnes (1983) discuss three options for managing conflict – bargaining, controlling, and confrontation. Buddy March's action illustrates the second option in this case; specifically, controlling conflict by preventing interaction or reducing its frequency.

12. Schein (1969).

13. Eisenhardt and Brown (1998).

14. It may be that the successes experienced by Buddy March in one domain – internal new product development – led him to inappropriately generalize this experience to another domain – external programs such as acquisitions and joint ventures – where many of the failures occurred. See Levinthal and March (1993).

PART VI: PUTTING IT ALL TOGETHER

19 HOW THE FIVE MAJOR INFLUENCES INTERACT TO DRIVE NEW BUSINESS CREATION

1. Woodman and Schoenfeldt (1990) propose an interactionist model of creative behavior at the individual level that incorporates antecedent conditions, personality dimensions, cognitive styles and abilities, and contextual and social influences (1990: 285 [Figure 1]). Woodman, Sawyer, and Griffin (1993) extend this model to explain organizational creativity as the outcome of the interaction of individual characteristics, group characteristics, and organizational characteristics (1993: 309 [Figure 2]).

Based on a review of the literature, Hornsby *et al.* (1993) present an interactive model of intrapreneurship as a conceptual contribution. Building on the work of Shapero and Sokol (1982) and Bandura (1986), Krueger and Brazeal (1994) develop a model that shows why prediction of potential entrepreneurs on the basis of demographics, personality, or other static criteria is unlikely to be fruitful. These authors argue that potential entrepreneurs surface when "credibility" (perceived feasibility and desirability) meets propensity to act.

Shane and Venkataraman (2000) point out that entrepreneurial behavior is not an individual attribute but rather the outcome of an interaction between person(s) and the situation. The same person(s) may exhibit entrepreneurial behavior in one situation but not in others. Similarly, while some person(s) in a particular situation may exhibit entrepreneurial behavior, other(s) in the same situation may not. Also see Bird (1988); Bird and Jelinek (1988); Lumpkin and Dess (1996).

2. Stopford and Baden-Fuller (1994) propose a progression of increasing corporate entrepreneurship with three stages: (1) individual entrepreneurship, including intrapreneurship and internal corporate venturing; (2) organizational renewal or transformation of a business, involving more than a few individuals or teams engaged in intrapreneurship; (3) frame-breaking change that transforms not only the enterprise but also the competitive environment by changing the industry's competitive rules (1994: 527 [Table 2]). Also see Baden-Fuller and Stopford (1994). DGM Mike Walker took AMP Sigcom to stage 3.

20 MANAGING TEN CRITICAL ISSUES IN NEW BUSINESS CREATION

1. Subramaniam and Venkatraman (1999) indicate that the capability to develop and introduce new products to the market is a primary driver of a successful global strategy. Ireland *et al.* (2001) argue that an important value-creating entrepreneurial strategy is to invent new goods and services and commercialize them. Zahra, Kuratko, and Jennings (1999) point out that corporate entrepreneurship adds value not only by utilizing resources in new ways but also by creating new resources. Also see Capon *et al.* (1992); Floyd and Woolridge (1999); Greene, Brush, and Hart (1999).

   There are two pieces of research evidence that corporate entrepreneurship is associated with better financial performance. First, Zahra and Covin (1995) found that corporate entrepreneurship (CE) does have a positive impact on financial performance. The relationship is modest for the first few years, but then increases over time, suggesting that CE may indeed be a good leading indicator of long-run financial performance. CE was found to be a particularly effective practice for firms operating in hostile environments. Second, Roberts (1999) found that high innovation was related to superior profitability.

2. Burgelman (1983c: 1355) has pointed out that the true benefits of entrepreneurship may be systematically underestimated because the focus is usually on the financial costs of failure, whereas the benefits of failed attempts remain hidden. Mone, McKinley, and Barker (1998) point out that innovation is relatively rare in organizations because it is difficult accurately to predict the costs and benefits of a new product.

   Research evidence on the indirect benefits of corporate entrepreneurship includes these two studies: (1) Pearce, Kramer, and Robbins (1997) found strong support for the hypothesis that managers who are entrepreneurial have a positive impact on their subordinates. As entrepreneurial behavior increased, employee satisfaction increased too; and (2) Birkinshaw (1997) found that entrepreneurship at the subsidiary level of multinational corporations has the potential to enhance local responsiveness, worldwide learning, and global integration, a much broader set of potential benefits than previously envisioned.

3. As Zahra and Dess (2001: 8–9) point out,

> Many entrepreneurial efforts succeed and lead, in turn, to the formation of new ventures and wealth creation for both entrepreneurs and investors. More typically, of course, ventures fail. However, as suggested by McGrath (1999) in her innovative perspective on "entrepreneurial failure," many of the intangible resources associated with new ventures may lend themselves to new resource combinations (Kogut and Zander, 1992), thus lessening the risk of irreversible commitments. For example, entrepreneurs (or intrapreneurs) who develop knowledge and skills that can be readily redeployed in other ventures can more safely enter into new markets, products, or technologies. Similarly, consistent with the real options literature, entrepreneurs (or firms) can use new ventures as "platforms" for future investments (Genadier and Weiss, 1997).

4. Henderson (1994) found that the knowledge generated by a failed project could be utilized in other areas of the company. Floyd and Woolridge (1999) examine how corporate entrepreneurship mediates between inertia and learning. Lynn (1998) describes how knowledge capital develops from new product team learning. As Zahra and Dess (2001: 9) observe, "It is not a coincidence that countries and companies that promote entrepreneurial activities are also among the most proactive in developing and nurturing their human capital (Fukuyama, 1995). Of course, the relationship between entrepreneurship and human and intellectual capital is dynamic, with each affecting the other over time."

5. As Shane and Venkataraman (2000: 220) state, "Entrepreneurial opportunities differ from the larger set of all opportunities for profit, particularly opportunities to enhance the efficiency of *existing* goods, services, raw materials, and organizing methods, because the former require the discovery of new means–ends relationships, whereas the latter involve optimization within existing means–ends relationships (Kirzner, 1997)" (emphasis in original). Also see Burgelman and Doz (2001).

6. Several scholars have reached the conclusion that established firms need to strike a balance between engaging in activities that use what they already know and challenging themselves to embark upon new activities and opportunities to revitalize themselves (Ahuja and Lampert, 2001; Floyd and Woolridge, 1999; Leonard-Barton, 1995; Levinthal and March, 1993). Ahuja and Lampert (2001) argue that one mechanism for striking this balance is to experiment with novel, emerging, and pioneering technologies to overcome the learning traps of familiarity, maturity, and propinquity that established firms face.

7. Having long-term managers who "still have to be here and answer", as president Jim McGuire of AMP said, helped AMP and 3M avoid one of the problems pointed out by Teece (1987) – that entrepreneurial managers may select and support projects that show near-term gains but long-term losses, on the assumption that they can leave the firm or division if the project does not generate promised returns.

8. March (1991) argues that organizations divide attention and other resources between two different kinds of activities – exploration (the pursuit of new

knowledge) and exploitation (the use of existing knowledge). He points out that the basic problem confronting organizations is to engage in sufficient exploitation to ensure its current viability and sufficient exploration to ensure its future viability. Along the same lines, Ghemawat and Ricart I Costa (1993) explore the tension between static efficiency (refinement of existing products, processes, or capabilities) and dynamic efficiency (development of new products, processes, or capabilities).

9. Levinthal and March (1993) state: "Sometimes exploration drives out exploitation. Organizations are turned into frenzies of experimentation, change, and innovation" (105); "the more common situation is one in which exploitation tends to drive out exploration" (107). Reaching a similar conclusion, Ghemawat and Ricart I Costa (1993: 72) observe that, with increasing environmental change and increasing organizational inertia, dynamic efficiency deserves more attention. Fiol (1996) indicates that one reason for inconsistent results in innovation research is that studies have not considered the distinction between the capacity to absorb innovative inputs and the capacity to produce innovative outputs. Fiol states (1996: 1018): "You can't squeeze out more than you've got." Trying to do so implies too much emphasis on exploitation and not enough on exploration.

10. Cooper, Folta, and Woo (1995) found that experienced entrepreneurs searched equally extensively in familiar and unfamiliar fields. This probably helped them to avoid two of the learning traps found by Ahuja and Lampert (2001) – the tendency to favor the familiar over the unfamiliar (familiarity trap), and the tendency to look for new solutions near old solutions (the nearness or propinquity trap).

11. Rather than rely on superhumans to create innovation, Van de Ven (1986) offers a more realistic view based on the limitations of people in handling uncertainty, overload, and complexity, and he examines how these impact innovation. Van de Ven notes that crises, dissatisfaction, tension, or significant external stress command attention (1986: 595). Therefore, the management of attention is critical if these natural tendencies and problems are to be overcome. Van de Ven argues that "*direct personal confrontations with problem sources* are needed to reach the threshold of concern and appreciation required to motivate people to act" (emphasis in original, 1986: 596). This argument supports the external orientation at AMP and the dictum to "walk the territory" at 3M.

12. Reinertsen (1983) reports that, in the case of printers, cumulative profit was 31.5 percent lower for new products that were six months late to the market.

13. Block (1982) argues that the focus in early stages of commercializing a venture must be on responding to the changes needed rather than on achieving efficiency and return on investment, because new ideas usually require modification and adaptation before they are commercially viable.

14. Amram and Kulatilaka (1999); Luehrman (1998); McGrath and MacMillan (2000).

15. In their study of why two companies in the same industry (telecommunications) responded differently to the same business opportunity (cellular), Noda and Bower (1996: 186) found that better than expected early results at

BellSouth led to escalating commitments and a success syndrome, whereas worse than expected early results at US West led to de-escalating commitments and a failure syndrome. Wender (1968: 313–314) discusses the acquisition of a sense of competence through the "success-breeds-success syndrome" (or, at the opposite end, of a sense of failure through the "failure cycle") – which impacts the willingness to persist or not at difficult tasks (such as new business creation) which have potential negative consequences.

Burgelman (1988: 82–83) describes escalating commitment to successful courses of action, as in his Medical Equipment case, but he also found escalating commitment to failing courses of action (what some would call the "Vietnam syndrome"), as in his Environmental Systems case – and he hypothesizes that escalating commitment may be easier to contain in unsuccessful cases than in initially successful ones.

16. McCarthy, Schoorman, and Cooper (1993) observed that entrepreneurs who expressed substantial overconfidence were significantly more likely to decide to expand (escalate commitment). These authors recommend entrepreneurs seek objective outside opinions from advisors and board members to overcome bias.

17. The perception of *choice* builds commitment (Salancik, 1977).

18. Van de Ven *et al.* (1989) indicate that excess resources often mask underlying problems and delay subjecting product innovations to the acid test of market. Also see Nohria and Gulati (1996).

19. This is consistent with the view of strategy as a portfolio of real options (Amram and Kulatilaka, 1999; Luehrman, 1998; McGrath and MacMillan, 2000).

20. This is analogous to the boundary systems as defined by Simons (1995), such as formally stated rules and proscriptions tied to sanctions, to allow individual creativity within defined limits of freedom.

Bibliography

Abell, D. F. 1993. *Managing with dual strategies*. New York: The Free Press.

Abernathy, W. J. 1978. *The productivity dilemma: roadblock to innovation in the automobile industry*. Baltimore: Johns Hopkins University Press.

Abernathy, W. J. and Clark, K. 1985. Innovation: mapping the winds of creative destruction. *Research Policy*, 14: 3–22.

Acs, Z. and Audretsch, D. 1987. Innovation, market structure, and firm size. *Review of Economics and Statistics*, 71: 567–574.

Ahuja, G. and Lampert, C. M. 2001. Entrepreneurship in the large corporation: a longitudinal study of how established firms create breakthrough inventions. *Strategic Management Journal*, June–July Special Issue 22: 521–543.

Alderson, S. 1993. Reframing management competence: focusing on the top management team. *Personnel Review*, 22(6): 53–62.

Aldrich, H. E. 1979. *Organizations and environments*. Englewood Cliffs, NJ: Prentice-Hall.

Amabile, T. M. 1988. A model of creativity in organizations. *Research in Organizational Behavior*, 10: 123–168.

1998. How to kill creativity. *Harvard Business Review*, 76(5): 76–87.

Amburgey, T. L. and Miner, A. S. 1992. Strategic momentum: the effects of repetitive, positional, and contextual momentum on merger activity. *Strategic Management Journal*, 13: 335–348.

Amram, M. and Kulatilaka, N. 1999. *Real options: managing strategic investment in an uncertain world*. Boston: Harvard Business School Press.

Arend, R. J. 1999. Emergence of entrepreneurs following exogenous technological change. *Strategic Management Journal*, 20: 31–47.

Aronson, E. 1976. *The social animal*. San Francisco: W. H. Freeman.

Arrow, K. J. 1980. Organizational structure and entrepreneurial activities. *The entrepreneur's role in today's society*. New York: Price Institute of Entrepreneurial Studies.

Baden-Fuller, C. and Stopford, J. M. 1994. *Rejuvenating the mature business: the competitive challenge*. Boston: Harvard Business School Press.

Bandura, A. 1986. *The social foundations of thought and action*. Englewood Cliffs, NJ: Prentice-Hall.

Barnevik, P. 1994. Preface. In *Global strategies: insights from the world's leading thinkers*. Boston: Harvard Business Review, pp. xi–xix.

Barney, J. 1992. Integrating organizational behavior and strategy formulation research. In P. Shrivastava, A. Huff, and J. Dutton (eds.), *Advances in strategic management*. Greenwich, CT: JAI Press, pp. 39–62.

Barringer, B. R. and Bluedorn, A. C. 1999. The relationship between corporate entrepreneurship and strategic management. *Strategic Management Journal*, 20: 421–444.

Baum, J. R., Locke, E. A., and Smith, K. G. 2001. A multidimensional model of venture growth. *Academy of Management Journal*, 44: 292–303.

Baumol, W. J. 1986. Entrepreneurship and a century of growth. *Journal of Business Venturing*, 1: 141–145.

1990. Entrepreneurship: productive, unproductive, and destructive. *Journal of Business Venturing*, 11: 3–22.

1993. *Entrepreneurship, management, and the structure of payoffs*. Cambridge, MA: MIT Press.

Biggadike, R. 1979. The risky business of diversification. *Harvard Business Review*, 57(3): 103–111.

Binks, M. and Vale, P. 1990. *Entrepreneurship and economic change*. New York: McGraw-Hill.

Bird, B. 1988. Implementing entrepreneurial ideas: the case for intention. *Academy of Management Review*, 13: 442–453.

Bird, B. and Jelinek, M. 1988. The operation of entrepreneurial intentions. *Entrepreneurship Theory and Practice*, 13(2): 21–29.

Birkinshaw, J. 1997. Entrepreneurship in multinational corporations: the characteristics of subsidiary initiatives. *Strategic Management Journal*, 18: 207–229.

Block, Z. 1982. Can corporate venturing succeed? *Journal of Business Strategy*, 3: 21–33.

Block, Z. and MacMillan, I. C. 1985. Milestones for successful venture planning. *Harvard Business Review*, 63(5): 184–196.

1993. *Corporate venturing: creating new businesses within the firm*. Boston: Harvard Business School Press.

Block, Z. and Ornati, O. 1987. Compensating corporate venture managers. *Journal of Business Venturing*, 2: 41–52.

Bower, J. L. 1970. *Managing the resource allocation process*. Boston: Graduate School of Business Administration, Harvard University.

Bower, J. L. and Christensen, C. M. 1995. Disruptive technologies: catching the wave. *Harvard Business Review*, 73(1): 43–53.

Bowman, C. 1999. Why we need entrepreneurs, not managers. *General Management Review*, 1(1): 15–23.

Brockhaus, R. H. 1980. Risk taking propensity of entrepreneurs. *Academy of Management Journal*, 23: 509–520.

Burgelman, R. A. 1983a. A process model of internal corporate venturing in the diversified major firm. *Administrative Science Quarterly*, 28: 223–244.

1983b. A model of interaction of strategic behavior, corporate context, and the concept of strategy. *Academy of Management Review*, 8: 61–70.

1983c. Corporate entrepreneurship and strategic management: insights from a process study. *Management Science*, 29: 1349–1364.

1984a. Managing the internal corporate venturing process. *Sloan Management Review*, 25(2): 33–48.

1984b. Designs for corporate entrepreneurship in established firms. *California Management Review*, 26(3): 154–166.

1985. Managing the new venture division: research findings and implications for strategic management. *Strategic Management Journal*, 6: 39–54.

1988. Strategy making as a social learning process: the case of internal corporate venturing. *Interfaces*, 18(3): 74–85.

1994. Fading memories: a process theory of strategic business exit in dynamic environments. *Administrative Science Quarterly*, 39: 24–56.

1996. A process model of strategic business exit: implications for an evolutionary perspective on strategy. *Strategic Management Journal*, Summer Special Issue 17: 193–214.

2002. *Strategy is destiny: how strategy-making shapes a company's future.* New York: The Free Press.

Burgelman, R. A. and Doz, Y. L. 2001. The power of strategic integration. *MIT Sloan Management Review*, 42(3): 28–38.

Burgelman, R. A. and Grove, A. S. 1996. Strategic dissonance. *California Management Review*, 38(2): 8–28.

Burgelman, R. A. and Sayles, L. 1986. *Inside corporate innovation: strategy, structure and management skills.* New York: The Free Press.

Burns, T. and Stalker, G. M. 1961. *The management of innovation.* London: Tavistock Publications.

Busenitz, L. W. 1999. Entrepreneurial risk and strategic decision making: it's a matter of perspective. *Journal of Applied Behavioral Science*, 35(3): 325–340.

Buzzell, R. D. and Gale, B. T. 1987. *The PIMS Principles: linking strategy to performance.* New York: The Free Press.

Cameron, K. S. 1986. Effectiveness as paradox: consensus and conflict in conceptions of organizational effectiveness. *Management Science*, 32: 539–553.

Capon, N., Farley, J. U., Lehmann, D. R., and Hulbert, J. M. 1992. Profiles of product innovators among large US manufacturers. *Management Science*, 38: 157–169.

Carroll, G. and Mosakowski, E. 1987. The career dynamics of self-employment. *Administrative Science Quarterly*, 32: 570–589.

Charan, R. and Tichy, N. M. 1998. *Every business is a growth business: how your company can prosper year after year.* New York: Times Business.

Chattopadhyay, P., Glick, W. H., Miller, C. C., and Huber, G. P. 1999. Determinants of executive beliefs: comparison of functional conditioning and social influence. *Strategic Management Journal*, 20: 763–789.

Cheng, Y. and Van de Ven, A. H. 1996. Learning the innovation journey: order out of chaos? *Organization Science*, 7: 593–614.

Chesbrough, H. 2000. Designing corporate ventures in the shadow of private venture capital. *California Management Review*, 42(3): 31–49.

Child, J. 1972. Organizational structure, environment, and performance: the role of strategic choice. *Sociology*, 6: 1–22.

1977. *Organization.* New York: Harper and Row.

Christensen, C. M. 1997. *The innovator's dilemma: when technologies cause great firms to fail.* Boston: Harvard Business School Press.

Clark, K. B. and Fujimoto, T. 1991a. *Product development performance: strategy, organization, and management in the world auto industry.* Boston: Harvard Business School Press.

1991b. Heavyweight product managers. *The McKinsey Quarterly*, Number 1: 42–60.

Cohen, W. and Levin, R. 1989. Empirical studies of innovation and market structure. In R. Schmalensee and R. Willig (eds.), *Handbook of industrial organization.* New York: Elsevier, Vol. II, pp. 1060–1107.

Cooper, A. C. and Schendel, D. 1976. Strategic responses to technological threats. *Business Horizons*, 19(1): 61–69.

Cooper, A. C. and Smith, C. G. 1992. How established firms respond to threatening technologies. *Academy of Management Executive*, 6(2): 55–70.

Cooper, A. C., Folta, T. B., and Woo, C. 1995. Entrepreneurial information search. *Journal of Business Venturing*, 10: 107–120.

Cooper, A. C., Woo, C. Y., and Dunkelberg, W. C. 1988. Entrepreneurs' perceived chances for success. *Journal of Business Venturing*, 3: 97–108.

1989. Entrepreneurship and the initial size of firms. *Journal of Business Venturing*, 4: 317–332.

Covin, J. G. and Morgan, M. P. 1999. Corporate entrepreneurship and the pursuit of competitive advantage. *Entrepreneurship Theory and Practice*, 23(3): 47–63.

Covin, J. G. and Slevin, D. P. 1991. A conceptual model of entrepreneurship as firm behavior. *Entrepreneurship Theory and Practice*, 16(1): 7–25.

Csikszentmihalyi, M. 1996. *Creativity: flow and the psychology of discovery and invention.* New York: HarperCollins.

Cyert, R. M. and March, J. G. 1963. *A behavioral theory of the firm.* Englewood Cliffs, NJ: Prentice-Hall.

D'Aveni, R. A. 1994. *Hypercompetition.* New York: The Free Press.

David, B. L. 1994. How internal venture groups innovate. *Research Technology Management*, 37(2): 38–43.

Day, D. L. 1994. Raising radicals: different processes for championing innovative corporate ventures. *Organizational Science*, 5: 148–172.

Day, G. S. and Schoemaker, P. J. H. 2000. Avoiding the pitfalls of emerging technologies. *California Management Review*, 42(2): 8–33.

de Charms, R. 1968. *Personal causation.* New York: Academic Press.

Deal, T. E. and Kennedy, A. A. 1982. *Corporate cultures: the rites and rituals of corporate life.* Reading, MA: Addison-Wesley.

Deeds, D. L. and Hill, C. W. L. 1996. Strategic alliances and rate of new product development: an empirical study of entrepreneurial biotechnology firms. *Journal of Business Venturing*, 11: 41–55.

Denison, D. R., Dutton, J. E., Kahn, J. A., and Hart, S. L. 1996. Organizational context and the interpretation of strategic issues: a note on CEOs' interpretation of foreign investment. *Journal of Management Studies*, 33: 453–474.

Deutschman, A. 1994a. How H-P continues to grow and grow. *Fortune*, May 2: 90–92.

1994b. The managing wisdom of high-tech superstars. *Fortune*, October 17: 197–206.

Donaldson, G. and Lorsch, J. W. 1983. *Decision making at the top: the shaping of strategic direction.* New York: Basic Books.

Dooley, R. S. and Fryxell, G. E. 1999. Attaining decision quality and commitment from dissent: the moderating effects of loyalty and competence in strategic decision-making teams. *Academy of Management Journal*, 42: 389–402.

Dougherty, D. 1990. Understanding new markets for new products. *Strategic Management Journal*, 11: 59–78.

1992a. Interpretive barriers to successful product innovation in large firms. *Organization Science*, 3: 179–202.

1992b. A practice-centered model of organizational renewal through product innovation. *Strategic Management Journal*, 13: 77–92.

1995. Managing your core incompetencies for corporate venturing. *Entrepreneurship Theory and Practice*, 19(3): 113–135.

Dougherty, D. and Bowman, E. H. 1995. The effects of organizational downsizing on product innovation. *California Management Review*, 37(4): 28–44.

Dougherty, D. and Hardy, C. 1996. Sustained product innovation in large, mature organizations: overcoming innovation-to-organization problems. *Academy of Management Journal*, 39: 1120–1153.

Dougherty, D. and Heller, T. 1994. The illegitimacy of successful product innovation in established firms. *Organizational Science*, 5: 200–218.

Drazin, R. and Schoonhoven, C. B. 1996. Community, population, and organization effects on innovation: a multilevel perspective. *Academy of Management Review*, 39: 1065–1083.

Drucker, P. F. 1954. *The practice of management.* New York: Harper and Row.

1985a. *Innovation and entrepreneurship: principles and practice.* New York: Harper and Row.

1985b. The discipline of innovation. *Harvard Business Review*, 63(3): 67–72.

Dutton, J. E. and Duncan, R. B. 1987. The creation of momentum for change through the process of strategic issue diagnosis. *Strategic Management Journal*, 8: 279–295.

Dutton, J. E., and Jackson, S. E. 1987. Categorizing strategic issues: links to organizational action. *Academy of Management Review*, 12(1): 76–90.

Eisenhardt, K. M. 1989. Building theories from case study research. *Academy of Management Review*, 14(4): 532–550.

Eisenhardt, K. M. and Brown, S. L. 1998. Time pacing: competing in markets that won't stand still. *Harvard Business Review*, 76(2): 59–69.

Eisenhardt, K. M., and Martin, J. A. 2000. Dynamic capabilities: what are they? *Strategic Management Journal*, October–November Special Issue 21: 1105–1121.

Eisenhardt, K. M., Kahwajy, J. L., and Bourgois, L. J. III. 1997. How management teams can have a good fight. *Harvard Business Review*, 74(4): 77–85.

Elder, T. 1989. New venture lessons from Xerox and IBM. *Harvard Business Review*, 67(4): 146–154.

Ellsworth, R. R. 2002. *Leading with purpose.* Stanford, CA: Stanford University Press.

Fast, N. 1979. The future of industrial new venture departments. *Industrial Marketing Management*, 8: 264–279.

Finkelstein, S. and Hambrick, D. C. 1990. Top-management-team tenure and organizational outcomes: the moderating role of managerial discretion. *Administrative Science Quarterly*, 35: 484–503.

1996. *Strategic leadership: top executives and their effects on organizations.* Minneapolis–St. Paul: West Publishing.

Fiol, C. M. 1996. Squeezing harder doesn't always work: continuing the search for consistency in innovation research. *Academy of Management Review*, 21: 1012–1021.

Floyd, S. W. and Woolridge, B. 1999. Knowledge creation and social networks in corporate entrepreneurship: the renewal of organizational capability. *Entrepreneurship Theory and Practice*, 23(3): 123–143.

Foster, R. N. 1986. *Innovation: the attacker's advantage.* New York: Summit Books.

Foster, R. N. and Kaplan, S. 2001. *Creative destruction: why companies that are built to last underperform the market – and how to successfully transform them.* New York: Currency.

Fukuyama, F. 1995. *Trust: the social virtues and the creation of prosperity.* New York: The Free Press.

Galbraith, J. R. 1982. Designing the innovating organization. *Organizational Dynamics*, Winter: 5–25.

Galunic, D. C. and Rodan, S. 1998. Resource recombinations in the firm: knowledge structures and the potential for Schumpeterian innovation. *Strategic Management Journal*, 19: 1193–1201.

Garud, R. and Van de Ven, A. H. 1992. An empirical evaluation of the internal corporate venturing process. *Strategic Management Journal*, 13: 93–109.

Genadier, S. R. and Weiss, A. M. 1997. Investment in technological innovations: an option pricing approach. *Journal of Financial Economics*, 44: 397–416.

Gersick, C. J. G. 1994. Pacing strategic change: the case of a new venture. *Academy of Management Journal*, 37: 9–45.

Ghemawat, P. and Ricart I Costa, J. E. 1993. The organizational tension between static and dynamic efficiency. *Strategic Management Journal*, Winter Special Issue 14: 59–73.

Ghiselli, E. E. 1966. *The validity of occupational aptitude tests.* New York: John Wiley.

Gilbert, X. and Strebel, P. 1988. Developing competitive advantage. In J. B. Quinn, H. Mintzberg, and R. M. James (eds.), *The strategy process: concepts, contexts, and cases.* Englewood Cliffs, NJ: Prentice-Hall, pp. 70–79.

Glaser, B. G. and Strauss, A. L. 1967. *The discovery of grounded theory: strategies for qualitative research.* Chicago: Aldine.

Goold, M., Campbell, A., and Alexander, M. 1994. *Corporate level strategy: creating value in multibusiness companies.* New York: John Wiley.

Grant, R. M. and Jammine, A. P. 1988. Performance differences between Wrigley/Rumelt strategic categories. *Strategic Management Journal*, 9: 333–346.

Greene, P., Brush, C., and Hart, M. 1999. The corporate venture champion: a resource-based approach to role and process. *Entrepreneurship Theory and Practice*, 23(3): 103–122.

Greenfield, S. M., Strickon, A., Aubey, R. T., and Rothstein, M. 1979. Studies in entrepreneurial behavior: a review and an introduction. In S. M. Greenfield, A. Strickon, and R. T. Aubey (eds.), *Entrepreneurs in cultural context.* Albuquerque: University of New Mexico Press, pp. 3–18.

Guth, W. D. and Ginsberg, A. 1990. Guest editors' introduction: corporate entrepreneurship. *Strategic Management Journal*, 11: 5–15.

Guth, W. D. and MacMillan, I. C. 1986. Strategy implementation versus middle management self-interest. *Strategic Management Journal*, 7: 313–327.

Hambrick, D. C. 1987. The top management team: key to strategic success. *California Management Review*, 30(1): 88–108.

   1995. Fragmentation and other problems CEOs have with their top management teams. *California Management Review*, 37(3): 110–127.

Hambrick, D. C. and Abrahamson, E. 1995. Assessing managerial discretion across industries: a multimethod approach. *Academy of Management Journal*, 38(5): 1427–1441.

Hambrick, D. C. and MacMillan, I. C. 1985. Efficiency of product R&D in business units: the role of strategic context. *Academy of Management Journal*, 28: 527–547.

Hambrick, D. C. and Mason, P. A. 1984. Upper echelons: the organization as a reflection of its top managers. *Academy of Management Review*, 9: 193–206.

Hambrick, D. C., Cho, T. S., and Chen, M. 1996. The influence of top management team heterogeneity on firms' competitive moves. *Administrative Science Quarterly*, 41(4): 659–684.

Hamel, G. 1999. Bringing Silicon Valley inside. *Harvard Business Review*, 77(5): 70–86.

Hamel, G. and Prahalad, C. K. 1994. *Competing for the future*. Boston: Harvard Business School Press.

Hammersley, M. and Atkinson, P. 1983. *Ethnography: principles in practice*. New York: Routledge.

Hanan, M. 1976a. *New venture management*. New York: McGraw-Hill.

   1976b. Venturing corporations – think small to stay strong. *Harvard Business Review*, 54(3): 139–148.

Hansen, M. T. and von Oetinger, B. 2001. Introducing T-shaped managers: knowledge management's next generation. *Harvard Business Review*, 79(3): 106–116.

Harrigan, K. R. 1983. Research methodologies for contingency approaches to business strategy. *Academy of Management Review*, 8: 398–405.

Henderson, R. M. 1994. Managing innovation in the information age. *Harvard Business Review*, 72(1): 100–105

Henderson, R. M. and Clark, K. B. 1990. Architectural innovation: the reconfiguration of existing product technologies and the failure of established firms. *Administrative Science Quarterly*, 35: 9–30.

Hisrich, R. D. and Peters, M. P. 1986. Establishing a new business unit within a firm. *Journal of Business Venturing*, 1: 307–322.

Hitt, M. A., Hoskisson, R. E., Johnson, R. A., and Moesel, D. D. 1996. The market for corporate control and firm innovation. *Academy of Management Journal*, 39: 1084–1119.

Hitt, M. A., Ireland, D. R., Camp, M. S., and Sexton, D. L. 2001. Guest editors' introduction to the special issue on "Strategic entrepreneurship: entrepreneurial strategies for wealth creation." *Strategic Management Journal*, June–July Special Issue 22: 479–491.

Hitt, M. A., Nixon, R., Hoskisson, R., and Kochhar, R. 1999. Corporate entrepreneurship and cross-functional fertilization. *Entrepreneurship Theory and Practice*, 23(3): 145–167.

Hof, R. D. 1993. Hewlett-Packard digs deep for a digital future. *Business Week*, October 18: 72–75.

Hofstede, G. 1980. *Culture's consequences: international differences in work-related values*, Beverly Hills, CA: Sage.

Hoopes, D. G. and Postrel, S. 1999. Shared knowledge, "glitches," and product development performance. *Strategic Management Journal*, 20: 837–865.

Hornsby, J. S., Naffziger, D. W., Kuratko, D. F., and Montagno, R. V. 1993. An interactive model of the corporate entrepreneurship process. *Entrepreneurship Theory and Practice*, 17(2): 29–37.

Hoskisson, R. E. and Hitt, M. A. 1988. Strategic control systems and relative R&D investment in large multiproduct firms. *Strategic Management Journal*, 9: 605–621.

Howard, R. 1992. The CEO as organizational architect: an interview with Xerox's Paul Allaire. *Harvard Business Review*, 70(5): 107–121.

Ireland, R. D., Hitt, M. A., Bettis, R. A., and De Porras, D. A. 1987. Strategy formulation process: differences in perceptions of strength and weaknesses indicators and environmental uncertainty by managerial level. *Strategic Management Journal*, 8: 469–485.

Ireland, R. D., Hitt, M. A., Camp, S. M., and Sexton, D. L. 2001. Integrating entrepreneurship and strategic management actions to create firm wealth. *Academy of Management Executive*, 15(1): 49–67.

Jackson, S. E. and Dutton, J. E. 1988. Discerning threats and opportunities. *Administrative Science Quarterly*, 33: 370–387.

Jarillo, C. J. 1989. Entrepreneurship and growth: the strategic use of external resources. *Journal of Business Venturing*, 4: 133–147.

Jassawalla, A. R. and Sashittal, H. C. 2000. Strategies of effective new product team leaders. *California Management Review*, 42(2): 33–51.

Jelinek, M. 1979. *Institutionalizing innovation: a study of organizational learning systems*. New York: Praeger.

Jelinek, M. and Schoonhoven, C. B. 1990. *The innovation marathon: lessons from high technology firms*. Cambridge, MA: Basil Blackwell.

Judge, W. Q., Fryxell, G. E., and Dooley, R. S. 1997. The new task of R&D management: creating goal-directed communities for innovation. *California Management Review*, 39(3): 72–85.

Kahn, R. L., Wolfe, D. M., Quinn, R. P., and Snoek, J. D. 1964. *Organizational stress: studies in role conflict and ambiguity*. New York: John Wiley.

Kanter, R. M. 1982. The middle manager as innovator. *Harvard Business Review*, 60(4): 95–105.

1983. *The change masters*. New York: Simon and Schuster.

Kantrow, A. M. 1980. The strategy–technology connection. *Harvard Business Review*, 58(4): 6–21.

Kaplan, R. 1987. Entrepreneurship reconsidered: the antimanagement bias. *Harvard Business Review*, 65(3): 84–89.

Katzenbach, J. R. 1997. The myth of the top management team. *Harvard Business Review*, 75(6): 82–91.

1998. *Teams at the top: unleashing the potential of both teams and individual leaders.* Boston: Harvard Business School Press.

Katzenbach, J. R. and Smith, D. K. 1993. The discipline of teams. *Harvard Business Review*, 71(2): 111–120.

Kent, C. A., Sexton, D. L., and Vesper, K. H. 1982 (eds.). *Encyclopedia of entrepreneurship.* Englewood Cliffs, NJ: Prentice-Hall.

Kets de Vries, M. F. R. 1985. The dark side of entrepreneurship. *Harvard Business Review*, 63(6): 160–167.

Khurana, Rakesh. 2002. *Searching for a corporate savior: the irrational quest for charismatic CEOs.* Princeton, NJ: Princeton University Press.

Kirton, M. 1980. Adapters and innovators in organizations. *Human Relations*, 33(4): 213–224.

Kirzner, I. M. 1979. *Perception, opportunity and profit: studies in the theory of entrepreneurship.* Chicago: University of Chicago Press.

1997. Entrepreneurial discovery and the competitive market process: an Austrian approach. *Journal of Economic Literature*, 35: 60–85.

Klein, K. J., and Sorra, J. S. 1996. The challenge of innovation implementation. *Academy of Management Review*, 21: 1055–1080.

Knight, D., Pearce, C. L., Smith, K. G., Olian, J. D., Sims, H. P., Smith, K. A., and Flood, P. 1999. Top management team diversity, group process, and strategic consensus. *Strategic Management Journal*, 20: 445–465.

Knight, K. E. 1967. A descriptive model of the intra-firm innovation process. *Journal of Business*, 40(4): 478–496.

Kogut, B. and Zander, U. 1992. Knowledge of the firm, combinative capabilities, and the replication of technology. *Organization Science*, 3: 383–397.

Kotter, J. P. 1982. *The general managers.* New York: The Free Press.

Krueger, N. F. Jr. and Brazeal, D. V. 1994. Entrepreneurial potential and potential entrepreneurs. *Entrepreneurship Theory and Practice*, 18(3): 91–104.

Kuratko, D. F., Montagno, R. V., and Hornsby, J. S. 1990. Developing an intrapreneurial assessment instrument for an effective corporate entrepreneurial environment. *Strategic Management Journal*, 11: 49–58.

Lant, T. and Mezias, S. 1990. Managing discontinuous change: a simulation study of organizational learning and entrepreneurship. *Strategic Management Journal*, Summer Special Issue 11: 147–179.

Lawrence, P. R. and Lorsch, J. W. 1967. Organization and environment: managing differentiation and integration. Division of Research, Harvard Business School.

Leavitt, H. J. and Lipman-Blumen, J. 1995. Hot groups. *Harvard Business Review*, 73(4): 109–116.

Leifer, R., McDermott, C. M., O'Connor, G. C., Peters, L. S., Rice, M., and Veryzer, R. W. 2000. *Radical innovation: how mature companies can outsmart upstarts.* Boston: Harvard Business School Press.

Leonard-Barton, D. 1995. *Wellsprings of knowledge: building and sustaining the sources of innovation.* Boston: Harvard Business School Press.

Levinthal, D. A. and March, J. G. 1993. The myopia of learning. *Strategic Management Journal*, Winter Special Issue 14: 95–112.

Levitt, B. and March, J. G. 1988. Organizational learning. *Annual Review of Sociology*, 14: 319–340.

Lipin, S. 1997. Corporation's dreams converge on one idea: it's time to do a deal. *Wall Street Journal*, February 26: A1

Lorange, P. 1999. The internal entrepreneur as a driver of growth. *General Management Review*, 1(1): 8–14.

Lounsbury, M. and Glynn, M. A. 2001. Cultural entrepreneurship: stories, legitimacy, and the acquisition of resources. *Strategic Management Journal*, June–July Special Issue 22: 545–564.

Luehrman, T. A. 1998. Strategy as a portfolio of real options. *Harvard Business Review*, 76(5): 89–99.

Lumpkin, G. T. and Dess, G. G. 1996. Clarifying the entrepreneurial orientation construct and linking it to performance. *Academy of Management Review*, 21: 135–172.

Lynn, G. S. 1998. New product team learning: developing and profiting from your knowledge capital. *California Management Review*, 40(4): 74–93.

McCarthy, A. M., Schoorman, F. D., and Cooper, A. C. 1993. Reinvestment decisions by entrepreneurs: rational decision-making or escalation of commitment? *Journal of Business Venturing*, 8: 9–24.

McGrath, R. G. 1999. Falling forward: real options reasoning and entrepreneurial failure. *Academy of Management Review*, 24: 13–30.

McGrath, R. G. and MacMillan, I. 2000. *The entrepreneurial mindset: strategies for continuously creating opportunity in an age of uncertainty*. Boston: Harvard Business School Press.

McGregor, D. 1960. *The human side of enterprise*. New York: McGraw-Hill.

MacMillan, I. C. 1987. New business development: a challenge for transformational leadership. *Human Resource Management*, 26(4): 439–454.

MacMillan, I. C., Block, Z., and Narasimha, P. N. S. 1986. Corporate venturing: alternatives, obstacles encountered, and experience effects. *Journal of Business Venturing*, 1: 177–191.

McNulty, J. E. 1962. Organized decision-making: a proposal for studying the influence of entrepreneurial aversiveness to risk-taking on bureaucratic structure. In W. W. Cooper, H. J. Leavitt, and M. W. Shelly II (eds.), *New perspectives in organization research*. New York: John Wiley, pp. 305–313.

McTaggart, J. M., Kontes, P. W., and Mankins, M. C. 1994. *The value imperative: managing for superior shareholder returns*. New York: The Free Press.

Maidique, M. A. 1980. Entrepreneurs, champions and technological innovation. *Sloan Management Review*, 21(2): 59–76.

March, J. G. 1991. Exploration and exploitation in organizational learning. *Organization Science*, 2: 71–87.

Maritan, C. A. 2001. Capital investment as investing in organizational capabilities: an empirically grounded process model. *Academy of Management Journal*, 44: 513–531.

Markides, C. 1998. Strategic innovation in established companies. *Sloan Management Review*, 39(3): 31–42.

2000. *All the right moves: a guide to crafting breakthrough strategy*. Boston: Harvard Business School Press.

Martin, J. 1992. *Cultures in organizations: three perspectives*. New York: Oxford University Press.

Meyer, G. D. and Heppard, K. A. 2000 (eds.). *Entrepreneurship as strategy: competing on the entrepreneurial edge.* Thousand Oaks, CA: Sage.

Michael, S. C. 2001. Book review of *Entrepreneurship as strategy: competing on the entrepreneurial edge* by G. D. Meyer and K. A. Heppard (eds.). *Academy of Management Review*, 26: 133–135.

Miles, M. B. and Huberman, A. M. 1994. *Qualitative data analysis.* Thousand Oaks, CA: Sage.

Miller, D. 1983. The correlates of entrepreneurship in three types of firms. *Management Science*, 29: 770–791.

1990. *The Icarus paradox: how exceptional companies bring about their own downfall.* New York: Harper Business.

Miller, D. and Friesen, P. H. 1983. Strategy-making and environment: the third link. *Strategic Management Journal*, 4: 221–235.

Miller, D. and Shamsie, J. 2001. Learning across the life cycle: experimentation and performance among the Hollywood studio heads. *Strategic Management Journal*, 22: 725–745.

Miller, D. T. and Ross, M. 1975. Self-serving biases in the attribution of causality. *Psychological Bulletin*, 82: 213–225.

Mintzberg, H. 1994. *The rise and fall of strategic planning.* New York: The Free Press.

Mone, M. A., McKinley, W., and Barker, V. L. III. 1998. Organizational decline and innovation: a contingency framework. *Academy of Management Review*, 23: 115–132.

Morgan, G. 1983. Action learning: a holographic metaphor for guiding social change. *Human Relations*, 37(1): 1–28.

Mueller, R. K. 1971. *The innovation ethic.* New York: American Management Association.

Myers, I. B. 1976. *Introduction to type.* Palo Alto, CA: Consulting Psychologists Press, Inc.

Nadler, D. A., Spencer, J. L., and Associates. 1998. *Executive teams.* San Francisco: Jossey-Bass.

Naman, J. L. and Slevin, D. P. 1993. Entrepreneurship and the concept of fit: a model and empirical tests. *Strategic Management Journal*, 14: 137–153.

Nemeth, C. J. 1997. Managing innovation: when less is more. *California Management Review*, 40(1): 59–74.

Noda, T. and Bower, J. L. 1996. Strategy making as iterated process of resource allocation. *Strategic Management Journal*, 17: 159–192.

Nohria, N. and Gulati, R. 1996. Is slack good or bad for innovation? *Academy of Management Journal*, 39: 1245–1264.

Nonaka, I. and Takeuchi, H. 1995. *The knowledge creating company: how Japanese companies create the dynamics of innovation.* New York: Oxford University Press.

Nonaka, I. and Yamanouchi, T. 1989. Managing innovation as a self-renewing process. *Journal of Business Venturing*, 4: 299–315.

Normann, R. 1971. Organizational innovativeness: product variation and reorientation. *Administrative Science Quarterly*, 16: 203–215.

Nystrom, H. 1979. *Creativity and innovation.* New York: John Wiley.

O'Connor, G. C. and Rice, M. P. 2001. Opportunity recognition and break-through innovation in large established firms. *California Management Review*, 43(2): 95–116.

O'Hara-Devereaux, M. and Johansen, R. 1994. *Global work: bridging distance, culture and time*. San Francisco: Jossey-Bass.

Oster, S. M. 1994. *Modern competitive analysis*, 2nd edn. New York: Oxford University Press.

Palmer, M. 1971. The application of psychological testing to entrepreneurial potential. *California Management Review*, 13(3): 32–38.

Pascale, R. T. 1984. Perspectives on strategy: the real story behind Honda's success. *California Management Review*, 26(3): 47–72.

Pearce, J. A., II, Kramer, T. R., and Robbins, D. K. 1997. Effects of managers' entrepreneurial behavior on subordinates. *Journal of Business Venturing*, 12: 147–160.

Pearson, G. J. 1989. Promoting entrepreneurship in large companies. *Long Range Planning*, 22(3): 87–97.

Peters, T. J. and Waterman, R. H. 1982. *In search of excellence: lessons from America's best-run companies*. New York: Harper and Row.

Peterson, R. A. 1981. Entrepreneurship and organization. In P. Nystrom and W. Starbuck (eds.), *Handbook of organization design*. New York: Oxford University Press, pp. 65–83.

Peterson, R. W. 1967. New venture management in a large company. *Harvard Business Review*, 45(3): 68–76.

Pfeffer, J. and Sutton, R. I. 1999. The smart-talk trap. *Harvard Business Review*, 77(3): 134–142.

    2000. *The knowing–doing gap: how smart companies turn knowledge into action*. Boston: Harvard Business School Press.

Pinchot, G., III. 1985. *Intrapreneuring: why you don't have to leave the corporation to become an entrepreneur*. New York: Harper and Row.

Polley, D. and Van de Ven, A. H. 1996. Learning by discovery during innovation development. *International Journal of Technology Management*, 11: 871–882.

Poole, M. S. and Van de Ven, A. H. 1989. Using paradox to build management and organization theories. *Academy of Management Review*, 14: 562–678.

Porter, M. E. 1980. *Competitive strategy: techniques for analyzing industries and competitors*. New York: The Free Press.

    1987. From competitive advantage to corporate strategy. *Harvard Business Review*, 65(3): 43–59.

    1990. *The competitive advantage of nations*. New York: The Free Press.

    1996. What is strategy? *Harvard Business Review*, 74(6): 61–78.

Quinn, D. P. and Rivoli, P. 1991. The effects of American- and Japanese-style employment and compensation practices on innovation. *Organizational Science*, 2: 323–341.

Quinn, J. B. 1980. *Strategies for change: logical incrementalism*. Homewood, IL: Irwin.

    2000. Outsourcing innovation: the new engine of growth. *Sloan Management Review*, 41(4): 13–28.

Ramamurthy, R. 1986. Public entrepreneurs: who they are and how they operate. *California Management Review*, 28(3): 142–158.

Raynor, M. E. and Bower, J. L. 2001. Lead from the center: how to manage divisions dynamically. *Harvard Business Review*, 79(5): 92–100.

Reich, R. B. 1987. Entrepreneurship reconsidered: the team as hero. *Harvard Business Review*, 65(3): 77–83.

Reinertsen, D. G. 1983. Whodunnit? The search for new product killers. *Electronic Business*, July: 62–66.

Repenning, N. P., Goncalves, P., and Black, L. J. 2001. Past the tipping point: the persistence of firefighting in product development. *California Management Review*, 43(4): 44–63.

Robello, K. 1994. Newton: will what fell down go up? *Business Week*, July 11: 41.

Roberts, E. B. 1980. New ventures for corporate growth. *Harvard Business Review*, 58(4): 134–142.

Roberts, P. W. 1999. Product innovation, product-market competition and persistent profitability in the US pharmaceutical industry. *Strategic Management Journal*, 20: 655–670.

Ronen, J. 1983. Some insights into the entrepreneurial process. In J. Ronen (ed.), *Entrepreneurship*. Lexington, MA: Lexington Books, pp. 137–169.

Ronstadt, R. 1982. *Entrepreneurship: a selected bibliography*. Dover, MA: Lord Publishing.

Rosner, M. M. 1968. Administrative controls and innovation. *Behavioral Science*, 13: 36–43.

Rothaermel, F. T. 2001. Incumbent's advantage through exploiting complementary assets via interfirm cooperation. *Strategic Management Journal*, 22: 687–699.

Rotter, J. B. 1966. Generalized expectancies for internal versus external control of reinforcement. *Psychological Monographs*, 80 (Whole No. 609).

Rumelt, R. P. 1974. *Strategy, structure, and economic performance*. Cambridge, MA: Harvard University Press.

Salancik, G. R. 1977. Commitment is too easy. *Organizational Dynamics*, Summer: 62–80.

Sandberg, W. R. 1992. Strategic management's potential contributions to a theory of entrepreneurship. *Entrepreneurship Theory and Practice*, 15(3): 73–90.

Sapienza, A. 1984. Believing is seeing. D.B.A. dissertation, Harvard Business School.

Sarasvathy, D., Simon, H., and Lave, L. 1998. Perceiving and managing business risks: differences between entrepreneurs and bankers. *Journal of Economic Behavior and Organization*, 33: 207–225.

Sathe, V. 1982. *Controller involvement in management*. Englewood Cliffs, NJ: Prentice-Hall.

   1985a. *Culture and related corporate realities*. Homewood, IL: Irwin.

   1985b. Managing an entrepreneurial dilemma: nurturing entrepreneurship and control in a large corporation. In B. A. Kirchhoff, W. A. Long, W. E. McMullan, K. H. Vesper, and W. E. Wetzel, Jr. (eds.), *Frontiers of entrepreneurship research*. Wellesley, MA: Babson College, pp. 636–657.

   1988a. From surface to deep corporate entrepreneurship. *Human Resource Management*, 27: 389–411

1988b. A model of large-firm entrepreneurship. In H. Leibenstein and D. Ray (eds.), *Entrepreneurship and economic development*. New York: United Nations Publications, pp. 37–52.

1989. Fostering entrepreneurship in the large, diversified firm. *Organizational Dynamics*, Winter: 20–32.

2000. Creating change in mindset and behavior. *Ivey Business Journal*, May/June: 84–89.

Sathe, V. and Davidson, E. J. 2000. Toward a new conceptualization of culture change. In N. Ashkanasy, C. P. M. Wilderom, and M. F. Peterson (eds.), *Handbook of organizational culture and climate*. Thousand Oaks, CA: Sage, pp. 279–296.

Schein, E. H. 1969. *Process consultation: its role in organization development*. Reading, MA: Addison-Wesley.

1978. *Career dynamics*. Reading, MA: Addison-Wesley.

1985. *Organizational culture and leadership*. San Francisco: Jossey-Bass.

1993. How can organizations learn faster? The challenge of entering the green room. *Sloan Management Review*, 34(2): 85–92.

Schollhammer, H. 1982. Internal corporate entrepreneurship. In C. A. Kent, D. L. Sexton, and K. H. Vesper (eds.), *The encyclopedia of entrepreneurship*. Englewood Cliffs, NJ: Prentice-Hall, pp. 209–229.

Schon, D. A. 1963. Champions of radical new inventions. *Harvard Business Review*, 41(2): 77–86.

1971. *Beyond the stable state: public and private learning in a changing society*. London: Temple Smith.

Schoonhoven, C. B. and Romanelli, E. 2001 (eds.). *The entrepreneurship dynamic: origins of entrepreneurship and the evolution of industries*. Stanford, CA: Stanford University Press.

Schrage, M. 2000. *Serious play: how the world's best companies simulate to innovate*. Boston: Harvard Business School Press.

Schuler, R. S. 1986. Fostering and facilitating entrepreneurship in organizations: implications for organization structure and human resource management practices. *Human Resource Management*, 25: 607–629.

Schumpeter, J. A. 1942. *Capitalism, socialism, and democracy*. Cambridge, MA: Harvard University Press.

Schwartz, J. J. 1973. The decision to innovate. D.B.A. dissertation, Harvard Business School.

Shane, S. A. 1994a. Are champions different from non-champions? *Journal of Business Venturing*, 9: 397–421.

1994b. Why do rates of entrepreneurship vary over time? *Academy of Management Best Paper Proceedings*: 90–94.

1995. Uncertainty avoidance and the preference for innovation championing roles. *Journal of International Business Studies*, 26(1): 47–68.

Shane, S. A. and Venkataraman, S. 2000. The promise of entrepreneurship as a field of research. *Academy of Management Review*, 25: 217–226.

Shane, S. A., Venkataraman, S., and MacMillan, I. C. 1995. Cultural differences in innovation championing strategies. *Journal of Management*, 21(5): 931–952.

Shapero, A. and Sokol, L. 1982. The social dimensions of entrepreneurship. In C. A. Kent, D. L. Sexton, and K. H. Vesper (eds.), *The encyclopedia of entrepreneurship*. Englewood Cliffs, NJ: Prentice-Hall, pp. 72–90.

Sharma, A. 1999. Central dilemmas of managing innovation in large firms. *California Management Review*, 41(3): 146–164.

Shelton, L. M. 1988. Strategic business fits and corporate acquisition: empirical evidence. *Strategic Management Journal*, 9: 279–287.

Shils, E. B. and Zucker, W. 1979. Developing a model for internal corporate entrepreneurship. *Social Science*, 54(4): 195–203.

Siegel, R., Siegel, E. and MacMillan, I. C. 1988. Corporate venture capitalists: autonomy, obstacles, and performance. *Journal of Business Venturing*, 3: 233–247.

Silverman, D. 1993. *Interpreting qualitative data: methods for analyzing talk, text and interaction*. Thousand Oaks, CA: Sage.

Simon, H. A. 1986. How managers express their creativity. *Across the Board*, March: 11–16.

Simons, R. 1995. *Levers of control: how managers use innovative control systems to drive strategic renewal*. Boston: Harvard Business School Press.

Singh, J. V. 1986. Performance, slack, and risk taking in organizational decision making. *Academy of Management Journal*, 29: 562–585.

Sirower, M. L. 1997. *The synergy trap: how companies lose the acquisition game*. New York: The Free Press.

Sitkin, S. B. 1992. Learning through failure: the strategy of small losses. In B. M. Staw and L. L. Cummings (eds.), *Research in Organizational Behavior*, 14. Greenwich, CT: JAI Press, pp. 231–266.

Slevin, D. P. and Covin, J. G. 1990. Juggling entrepreneurial style and organizational structure – how to get your act together. *Sloan Management Review*, 31(2): 43–53.

Smircich, L. 1983. Concepts of culture and organizational analysis. *Administrative Science Quarterly*, 28: 339–358.

Smith, C. G. and Cooper, A. C. 1988. Established companies diversifying into new industries. *Strategic Management Journal*, 9: 111–121.

Smith, D. K. and Alexander, R. C. 1988. *Fumbling the future: how Xerox invented, then ignored, the first personal computer*. New York: William Morrow.

Steele, L. W. 1983. Managers' misconceptions about technology. *Harvard Business Review*, 61(6): 133–140.

Stevenson, H. H. and Gumpert, D. E. 1985. The heart of entrepreneurship. *Harvard Business Review*, 63(2): 85–94.

Stevenson, H. H. and Jarillo, J. C. 1990. A paradigm for entrepreneurship: entrepreneurial management. *Strategic Management Journal*, 11: 17–27.

Stopford, J. M. and Baden-Fuller, C. W. F. 1994. Creating corporate entrepreneurship. *Strategic Management Journal*, 15: 521–536.

Strauss, A. L. 1987. *Qualitative analysis for social scientists*. Cambridge: Cambridge University Press.

Strauss, A. L. and Corbin, J. 1990. *Basics of qualitative research: grounded theory procedures and techniques*. Newbury Park, CA: Sage.

Strebel, P. 1987. Organizing for innovation over an industry cycle. *Strategic Management Journal*, 8: 117–124.

Stringer, R. 2000. How to manage radical innovation. *California Management Review*, 42(4): 70–88.

Subramaniam, M. and Venkatraman, N. 1999. The influence of leveraging tacit overseas knowledge for global new product development capability: an empirical examination. In M. A. Hitt, P. G. Clifford, R. D. Nixon, and K. P. Coyne (eds.), *Dynamic Resources*. Chichester: John Wiley, pp. 373–401.

Subramanian, R. 1998. The strategic influence of newly hired executives. *Academy of Management Executive*, 12(3): 82–83.

Sykes, H. B. 1985. The anatomy of a corporate venturing program: factors influencing success. *Journal of Business Venturing*, 1: 275–293.

    1986. Lessons from a new ventures program. *Harvard Business Review*, 64(3): 69–74.

Sykes, H. B. and Block, Z. 1989. Corporate venturing obstacles: sources and solutions. *Journal of Business Venturing*, 4: 159–167.

Taylor, W. 1990. The business of innovation: an interview with Paul Cook. *Harvard Business Review*, 90(2): 97–106.

Teece, D. J. 1987. Profiting from technological innovation: implications for integration, collaboration, licensing, and public policy. In D. J. Teece (ed.), *The competitive challenge: strategies for industrial innovation and renewal*. Cambridge, MA: Ballinger, pp. 185–219.

Thomke, S. 2001. Enlightened experimentation: the new imperative for innovation. *Harvard Business Review*, 79(2): 67–75.

Timmons, J. A. 1994. *New venture creation*, rev. 4th edn. Chicago: Irwin.

Tushman, M. L. and O'Reilly, C. A. 1997. *Winning through innovation: a practice guide to leading organizational change and renewal*. Boston: Harvard Business School Press.

Utterback, J. M. 1994. *Mastering the dynamics of innovation*. Boston: Harvard Business School Press.

Van de Ven, A. H. 1986. Central problems in the management of innovation. *Management Science*, 32: 590–607.

Van de Ven, A. H. and Polley, D. 1992. Learning while innovating. *Organizational Science*, 3: 92–116.

Van de Ven, A. H., Venkataraman, H. S., Polley, D., and Garud, R. 1989. Processes of new business creation in different organizational settings. In A. H. Van de Ven, H. Angle, and M. S. Poole (eds.), *Research on the management of innovation*. New York: Ballinger Press, pp. 221–297.

Vancil, R. F. 1979. *Decentralization: managerial ambiguity by design*. Homewood, IL: Dow-Jones Irwin.

von Hipple, E. 1978. Successful industrial products from customer ideas. *Journal of Marketing*, 42(1): 39–49.

    1988. *The sources of innovation*. New York: Oxford University Press.

von Hipple, E., Thomke, S. and Sonnack, M. 1999. Creating breakthroughs at 3M. *Harvard Business Review*, 77(5): 47–57.

Walton, R. E. 1987. *Innovating to compete*. San Francisco: Jossey-Bass.

Ware, J. P. and Barnes, L. B. 1983. Managing interpersonal conflict. In L. A. Schlesinger, R. G. Eccles, and J. J. Gabarro (eds.), *Managing behavior in*

organizations: text, cases and readings. New York: McGraw-Hill, pp. 196–
209.

Wender, P. H. 1968. Vicious and virtuous circles: the role of deviation amplifying
feedback in the origin and perpetuation of behavior. *Psychiatry*, 31: 309–324.

West, G. P., III and Meyer, G. D. 1998. To agree or not to agree? Consensus and
performance in new ventures. *Journal of Business Venturing*, 13: 395–422.

Williams, M. L., Tsai, M., and Day, D. L. 1991. Intangible assets, entry strategies,
and venture success in industrial markets. *Journal of Business Venturing*, 6:
315–333.

Williamson, O. E. 1975. *Markets and hierarchies*. New York: The Free Press.

Winters, T. E. and Murfin, D. L. 1988. Venture capital investing for corporate
development objectives. *Journal of Business Venturing*, 3: 207–222.

Woo, C. Y., Daellenbach, U., and Nicholls-Nixon, C. 1994. Theory building in
the presence of 'randomness': the case of venture creation and performance.
Journal of Management Studies, 31: 507–523.

Woodman, R. W. and Schoenfeldt, L. F. 1990. An interactionist model of creative
behavior. *Journal of Creative Behavior*, 24(4): 279–290.

Woodman, R. W., Sawyer, J. E., and Griffin, R. W. 1993. Toward a theory of
organizational creativity. *Academy of Management Review*, 18: 293–321.

Young, G. J., Charns, M. P., and Shortell, S. M. 2001. Top manager and network
effects on the adoption of innovative management practices: a study of TQM
in a public hospital system. *Strategic Management Journal*, 22: 935–951.

Zahra, S. A. 1991. Predictors and financial outcomes of corporate entrepreneurship. *Journal of Business Venturing*, 6: 259–285.

Zahra, S. A. and Covin, J. G. 1995. Contextual influences on the corporate
entrepreneurship–performance relationship: a longitudinal analysis. *Journal
of Business Venturing*, 10: 43–58.

Zahra, S. A. and Dess, G. G. 2001. Entrepreneurship as a field of research:
encouraging dialog and debate. *Academy of Management Review*, 26: 8–10.

Zahra, S. A., Ireland, R. D., and Hitt, M. A. 2000. International expansion by new
venture firms: international diversity, mode of market entry, technological
learning, and performance. *Academy of Management Journal*, 43: 925–950.

Zahra, S. A., Kuratko, D. F., and Jennings, D. F. 1999. Guest editorial:
entrepreneurship and the acquisition of dynamic organizational capabilities.
Entrepreneurship Theory and Practice, 23(3): 5–10.

Zajak, E. J., Golden, B. R., and Shortell, S. M. 1991. New organizational forms
for enhancing innovation: the case of internal corporate joint ventures. *Management Science*, 37: 170–184.

Zaltman, G., Duncan, R., and Holbek, J. 1973. *Innovation and organizations*. New
York: John Wiley.

Index